THIS·HUT·IS·PRESENTED
TO THE SCOTTISH
MOUNTAINEERING · CLUB
BY
D͏ᴿ·AND M͏ᴿˢ·INGLIS·CLARK
IN LOVING MEMORY OF THEIR·SON
1ˢᵀ·APRIL·1929

THE SCOTTISH
MOUNTAINEERING
CLUB JOURNAL

| Vol. XL | 2009 | No. 200 |

THE CIC HUT – A CUSTODIAN'S TALE

By Gerry Peet

MY FIRST VISIT to the CIC was in January or February of 1961, as a member of the Glasgow JMCS. It was a Friday night walk up in very deep snow via the Distillery. We arrived about midnight, quite knackered, to find the eight bunks occupied by FRCC members, who had decided to stay on beyond their booking.

Fortunately, we had Jimmy Simpson of the SMC with us and he raised merry hell, and we got our beds. So, my first visit alerted me to one of the existing problems – anarchy!

The other main problem was that the hut was built in the more leisurely and mannerly days of 1929. By the 1950s, with the growth of winter climbing standards and numbers, eight individual bunks were too few, and not good use of space compared to many continental huts.

A year or two after my first visit I proposed a scheme to increase the bed capacity, and, at about the same time, J.R. Marshall proposed another scheme. Both schemes were a little too complex and eventually, the custodian (Ian Clough), along with another joiner friend, ripped out the old bunks and installed two-tiered sleeping shelves, and doubled the capacity at reasonable cost.

The installation of Calor Gas a year or two earlier had created a much improved environment. In place of a coal stove, Tilley lamps and Primus stoves, we now had gas lighting, gas cooking and a gas fire. The old pot-bellied cast-iron coal stove was (allegedly) retrieved from outside the hut and installed in Jacksonville by the Creagh Dhu.

In 1967 at a CIC work party, Donald Bennet, the Hut's Convener, asked me if I would take over the custodianship from Ian Clough. Without any hesitation, I agreed and began a 13-year crusade to do two things. The first was to remove the anarchy and bloody-minded behaviour of the so-called hard men and others. The second objective was to gradually upgrade the facilities and standards in the hut.

The main tool in the first task was to become more bloody-minded and outrageous than the offenders i.e. fight fire with fire. At that time, I

A young Charlie Inglis Clark climbing 'The Arête' on Salisbury Crags, Edinburgh. He married in October 1916, became a father in 1917, but was killed in the Great War (March 1918) 'somewhere north of Bagdad'. The CIC Hut on Ben Nevis was built in his memory in 1929. Photo: SMC Archives

could take random days off work so, a few times each winter, I would visit the hut midweek. There was always work to do and I did catch quite a few either directly or indirectly. On one occasion I walked up in poor weather, and as I approached the hut, three figures set off up the hill. In the hut, I met with one of the booked parties and asked who the three were. They did not know, but they were gatecrashers. I asked which was their gear. Stuffing three sleeping bags in my sack, I left a message that they could be collected from Fort William Police Station.

On another occasion, a booked party leaving on the Friday stopped at my house the next day to drop off the key, and reported that a large party had gatecrashed the hut. I had heard on the radio that three people were missing on the Ben. I phoned the Fort William Police to see if they were still looking for the three. They had been found, and I asked if they still had any men at the hut. They had, so I asked them to go into the hut and identify the members of two clubs, and throw the rest out.

By these and other means, I gradually removed the anarchy, and members began to return to the hut from a low 5 per cent of bed nights, to a high 23 per cent.

I learnt that my tactics were better known than I realised when I stayed in the Glenbrittle Hut and found a home-made board game of snakes and ladders. It had been modified for climbers, and there on one square was 'Caught at CIC Hut without a permit by Gerry Peet – miss two turns'.

The four winter meets, December, January, February, and March, were very successful, particularly the one a few days before Christmas. At one meet, Malcolm Slesser was heard to ask if the club was training 'another wee bastard' to replace me when I retired. I took this as a compliment.

Next came the upgrading of the hut, which was gradual and long-term. The washing facilities (for dishes and people) were extremely primitive. Two buckets for water and a plastic basin on a very scruffy worktop meant that the kitchen floor area was always wet and disgusting, and cutlery was constantly thrown out with the dishwater. A stainless steel sink with drainer and a plumbed-in drain improved things out of all proportion to cost and effort.

Bill Young, who was always very good on ideas, came up with the suggestion of two watering cans with cranked spouts, and it was now possible to fill a glass without spillage.

The only way to dry clothes was to hang them up above and around the fire, which was not very effective. However, since the change to gas, there was no longer a 40-gallon drum of paraffin in a cradle in the vestibule/porch, and a cupboard at the back seemed to have no purpose. I removed the cupboard, fitted doors where the 40-gallon drum had been, put a lum through the roof, made a fixed window in the wall into the hut, piped in gas to a boiling ring, and lo! We had a drying room. The thinking behind the window was that if anything went on fire it would be visible. This was in the days before regulations required the services of a qualified CORGI engineer for all gas installations. Nevertheless, we never had anything go wrong, and it functioned very well until the first extension was built.

Next thought to improve things was to try for piped water into the hut. In winter in the 1970s, it was not uncommon to have to dig down two metres or more to reach water in the Allt a' Mhuilinn. First try was to put sixty metres of plastic pipe among a pile of boulders in the Allt a' Mhuilinn, and lead it to a standpipe at the rear of the hut to see if it would flow throughout the winter. However a flash flood dumped the lot below the hut like a bundle of spaghetti. I was also told that an even bigger flood had also washed a large boulder out of the bed of the burn and trundled past the hut, clipping the south-east corner on its way past.

The next try was in the opposite direction towards Coire na Ciste. From a good spring, I piped water to a standpipe opposite the old doorway. My theory was that, as long as the spring flowed from underground, even if it was as cold as 2°C, it would have enough latent heat to flow through a black pipe uninsulated. For a year or two, I appeared to be right, and the ground below the pipe was often a sheet of thick ice. Then, one year it did freeze and David Whitham came up with a probable cause – Boundary Layer Flow, which is an aerodynamic phenomenon, which would also apply to hydrodynamics. Namely, air flowing across a surface has a very shallow layer flowing slower than the mainstream. In water this boundary layer would freeze and a new boundary layer would form and freeze and so on. I think David was right.

Not long into my stint I had to refuel the hut and contacted the previous contractor. The whole operation proved to be very slow and inefficient. He required me to guide him to the hut. He used a snowcat tracked vehicle towing a sled with a dozen gas cylinders. This took two days to accomplish, and he left them half a mile from the hut. It was not cheap and created a lot of dodging on the part of the hut user to avoid carrying a cylinder.

This made me consider using a helicopter. It sounded very expensive with the cost of flying from base to the dam and return, plus the actual lifting. One company which did a lot of work for the Forestry Commission said there would be no positioning charge if I could go at 24 hours' notice when they were passing by en route north or south. I agreed and asked Macrae & Dick in Fort William to drop off two dozen cylinders at the dam. A day or two later I had a call from the pilot saying that tomorrow was the day.

I now had to get four people including me, and failed. I asked the Huts Convener (Sandy Cousins) and he also failed. In desperation, I phoned

Hamish MacInnes (Hon. Member) who agreed at once. Hamish and I met at the dam, and shortly afterwards the chopper arrived – a small Hiller as in M*A*S*H. Out stepped the pilot, Dave Clem, in wellies and roll-neck sweater, and no lifting gear. Hamish dug around his car boot and produced some slings and krabs. Hamish took one set in the chopper up to the hut, while I stood four cylinders upright and threaded a sling through the lifting handles and waited with the krab held up. Within minutes the chopper was hovering about two feet above my head. I placed the krab on the hook and off he went. Hamish was doing the same with four empties. Four up and four down took about eight minutes, and it was quite hectic.

All went well – too well, and near the end a sling broke and dropped a 'stick' of four 200lb 'bombs'. Fortunately, nobody was on the track, and Hamish and Dave retrieved three, but the fourth was a long way away and was not found for 18 months. It had struck a rock, and had a badly dented base.

This whole operation showed me how cost effective helicopters were and subsequent lifts with the correct lifting gear were usually uneventful. Dave Clem flew the wind turbine up many years later.

In 1973, Bill Young as Convener, George Wilkinson as our building expert and I got together and drew up plans to build an extension. This would give more room for storage, a better and safer drying room and space for people to get out of their wet gear.

I suggested that if the Committee agreed to our plans, we should do it without planning permission, as it was almost certain that the building would not be on any local authority radar. This was agreed, and Jim Donaldson, the Treasurer provided the funds.

Work commenced on Sat 22 June 1974 (Bill Young and I started on the previous day (see *SMCJ*, 2004, 38, 691). This was a weekend of incredibly good weather and there was a large turnout of members who were all regular CIC users. The helicopter flew for eight hours, transporting about 25 tons of materials. One squad was occupied at the dam weighing and loading bags of sand, cement and gravel, breeze blocks, timber, corrugated iron, and gas cylinders. Another squad at the hut was busy offloading and storing materials, returning empty cylinders etc. A third squad was busy digging out the foundations.

This third group had a very hard job, as the ground at the rear was boulder clay, which is very like concrete and contained a very large boulder. When this boulder was finally removed, it revealed a spring, which had to be diverted. The boulder required five people to remove.

The conditions that weekend were probably the best all summer for the routes on Carn Dearg Buttress and many envious looks were cast at non-SMC climbers as they passed by. Among the foundation party were two future presidents, Colin Stead and Ken Crocket. Not being used to manual labour of such intensity, they finished the day with fingers set like claws.

Next day we shuttered the foundations, mixed and laid the concrete and achieved our targets. The esprit displayed at this work party was superb with everyone being motivated because they used and valued the hut. The next work party of similar calibre was at the wind turbine installation in 1999.

A stone mason and two assistants followed and built the shell, and another three or four smaller work parties completed the work. The cost was £1,700. The extension gave us a better (and safer) drying room and more space. However, I have to admit that the technical specification was not high enough, although it lasted nearly 34 years.

The first break-in to the extension was not by the usual culprits but 45 Commandos on Arctic training. They claimed to have been caught in a November blizzard and, with two hypothermic members, they used a gas cylinder to smash in the door. Bob Richardson, the Huts Convener, wrote to their CO pointing out that if they could not survive on the Ben, they would not be much use in the Arctic.

I also wrote to the same gentleman outlining two solutions to the damage done by his men. Option 1 would be a brand new door, but this would have the same problem as all new doors in Lochaber – they absorb moisture and expand, requiring continued planing. Option 2 would be to repair the existing door and reinforce it with a full-size 3mm thick stainless steel panel.

Option 1 would still leave the door vulnerable, so I intended using Option 2. After I had drilled the panel for the keyhole and fixing bolts, I would leave it at Fort William Police Station and his men could take it up to the hut and leave it for me to fit. However, they cheated by using a chopper.

This gave us a very strong door and things were OK for a while, until late on a summer evening Malcolm Slesser arrived with a party including wives and children to find that some vandal had found an old woodscrew lying around and hammered it into the lock. So, in went the door again (rightly so).

This time, as a final solution, I made a lock cover 13mm thick pivoted on a fixed bolt at the top and locked at the bottom by an Allen screw. So now, the usual Chubb key was backed up with an Allen key and this worked until the present system.

A typical day's work for a custodian at CIC was a two-hour drive, followed by a two-hour walk to the hut with materials, time on the job and anything else needing done. A one-and-a-half hour walk down and a two-hour drive home. My two successors have to do likewise.

So, going back to Malcolm Slesser's earlier question, I can only point members to who followed me.

GRAHAM MACPHEE

By Ken Smith

A CLIMBING HOLIDAY was never planned but, on the morning of 23 February 1963, Graham Macphee, then in his veteran years, joined a guided walk up Mount Teide, on the island of Tenerife. Macphee was taking a break with his wife, who was recovering from illness. He had not brought his boots, yet the urge to climb the highest point on the island must have overcome his caution, as he set off in plimsolls, no doubt, thinking he could control the odds by his experience. Teide is generally considered an easy mountain but at the time was covered by an unusual amount of ice and snow. Once at the top, perhaps bored with the slow pace and the tourist chatter, he offered his thanks to the leader, left the group, and descended on his own – it was the last time he was seen alive.

When he had not returned to his hotel that evening his wife reported him missing. A rescue party, which included Lady Hunt, wife of Sir John Hunt of Everest fame, was organised and a search was mounted the following morning. A fresh fall of snow had covered his tracks and it was two days before his body was discovered at the bottom of a small crevasse, near the 13,000ft summit. Medical evidence given at the autopsy concluded that he probably died instantly as the result of his fall. His camera was lying open nearby and it is thought that he slipped backwards whilst taking a photograph – he was sixty-five years of age.

George Graham Macphee was one of the dominant figures in British mountaineering in a remarkable career that spanned almost fifty years. Many of his peers remember him as a great motivator and one of the toughest seconds around, who pushed the likes of Colin Kirkus, and A.T. (Albert) Hargreaves[1] to outstanding efforts. Although Macphee was not up there among the recognised band of top rock climbers, he was certainly no one's caddie and was regarded as a fine, all-round

---

[1] A.T. Hargreaves, who first made his name on gritstone, was considered the leading Lakeland climber in the early thirties. As a representative for Nestles he had a company car when few climbers owned vehicles. In 1937 he became the first warden of Brackenclose, FRCC's Club Hut, situated in Wasdale, and wrote FRCC's 1936 Climbing Guide to Scafell. In partnership with Syd Cross he opened the Old Dungeon Ghyll Hotel in Langdale which they ran for many years. In partnership with Macphee he led many quality routes, both in the Lakes and a few on the Ben, although Macphee was not there in 1933, when he pioneered *Rubicon Wall* on Observatory Buttress. This 400ft climb, graded Severe, was once considered the hardest climb on the mountain. He was killed in 1952 by an avalanche whilst skiing in the mountains near Obergurgl in Austria. A.T.H. was no relation to A.B. (Alan) Hargreaves who was active about the same time.

mountaineer in his own right, with an affinity for and knowledge of Ben Nevis that few could match.

His first visit to the Ben was on 25 June 1906, accompanied by his father. It was one of those rarified spring days where the panoramic views, from a dazzling, snow-bound summit, stretching as far as Ireland, left a lasting impression on the eight year old. Later he was to confide that from that day onwards one of his ambitions was a 'week in June' at Fort William. It was the beginning of a love affair that was to exert a powerful motivating force throughout his life.

Macphee was born in 1898, the son of a Glasgow doctor. During the Great War, at the age of seventeen, he joined the Highland Light Infantry and received a commission. Later, he transferred to the Royal Flying Corps and trained as a pilot but was taken prisoner when he was shot down. His Spartan toughness and strength of character could well have stemmed from the horrors of the trenches and his nine months as a POW – this stoic resilience is perhaps illustrated by a nasty ankle injury sustained when he fell from Cromford Black Rocks, and which was to plague him for the rest of his life, yet few ever heard him complain.

At the end of the war Macphee graduated in both medicine and dental surgery, settling in Liverpool in 1928 where he set up a lucrative practice as a dentist. It is said he was the most expensive dentist in the North of England and one of the wealthiest. Apart from his work as a consultant to several Liverpool hospitals he become a part-time lecturer at Liverpool University. He founded the Liverpool University Climbing Club and was a hands-on President for some thirty years and, despite their feckless organisation, which infuriated him, he took an active part in their activities, often providing transport in his cavernous Humber estate car that had been used as a First World War ambulance. On another occasion, his paternal responsibility kicked in when he hired a pony to transport the students' heavy camping equipment en route to the Ben – it was a side to him that he did not advertise!

As a firm believer in the fellowship of mountaineering Macphee became a member of the Fell & Rock, the Rucksack Club, the Wayfarers Club, and the Scottish Mountaineering Club, which he served as President from 1952 to 1954. There was also a three year stint as President of the British Mountaineering Council, and he was elected Vice-President of the Alpine Club. His contribution to the Mountain Rescue Committee and his efforts to promote mountaineering in Scotland were outstanding.

Macphee could never be described as nondescript; he was a tall, immaculate individual of military bearing emphasised with a neatly clipped moustache. Many found him difficult, his caustic humour, superior manner and Kelvinside accent could cause offence – some took this, rightly or wrongly, as arrogance. As in any sport there is sometimes a clash of personalities and the pre-war climbing fraternity was no exception. There was mutual and intense dislike between him and the diminutive, and often prickly, A.B. (Alan) Hargreaves – even in his twilight years A.B.H. did not have a kind word to say about him. There was also more than an element of friction between him and the Scottish mountaineer and SMC Journal Editor, Dr Jim Bell. Their animosity may have stemmed from an incident during an Alpine climb when Macphee's partner lost his ice axe and Macphee left it to Bell to safeguard him down. Bell thought this deplorable – the incident was not one of Macphee's finest moments.

It could also be said that part of Macphee's unpopularity, allied with his penetrating sarcasm, was his tendency to harbour a grudge. On the other hand, you knew how you stood with him and such were his self-esteem and powers of conviction he did have the capacity to inspire. Tom Price, who served his mountaineering apprenticeship with the LUMC and one of the few mountaineers still around who climbed with Macphee, recalls him with affection: 'My association with him began in 1938 and lasted until his death...he was not universally liked and had a long standing feud with Graham Brown. But the longer I knew him the better I liked him, although he was not, by nature, very forgiving.'

As an example of his zero tolerance, Tom Price recalls Macphee describing an incident on Scafell when A.B. Reynolds[2] fell from the crux whilst leading *Tower Buttress* in the rain. His second, George Basterfield, managed to field him but, in the process, the thin alpine line severed his thumb at the centre joint. Incredibly the friction from the rope-burn fused the skin and, apart from a light dressing, probably applied by Macphee, the damaged digit required no further treatment. Tom Price again: 'The leader was so pleased with himself for having escaped unharmed, and so indifferent, it seemed, to his second's injury, that Macphee never forgave him.' Incidentally, the missing digit was never found.

Now settled in the north-west, within striking distance of the Lakes, he soon made his mark with the first recorded descent of Scafell's Moss Ghyll Grooves in 1928 and during the same period was involved in several first ascents on Gimmer Crag of which *The Crack,* regarded for a number of years, as the hardest route in Langdale, took centre stage. In

---

[2] Arthur Basil Reynolds was among the few 'Very Severe' leaders operating in the Lakes during the late twenties. He made an early ascent of Central Buttress and a second ascent of Deer Bield Buttress. It would appear he sometimes enjoyed climbing barefoot and followed G. Bower up CB minus footwear. He climbed with Macphee whom he led up the first ascent of Gimmer Crack. Despite being a Quaker and a pacifist he felt compelled to fight in the Great War. He moved to South Wales and died of a brain haemorrhage in December 1960, aged 57.

September of the same year whilst Macphee and team mates were engaged on a second ascent a group of undergraduates turned up, on their way back to university, from a climbing holiday in Skye. Unaware of the route's reputation, Charles Warren[3], who was one of the students, shouted across to Macphee asking if the climb was worth doing. Instead of advising what they were up to and probably thinking here was a chance to teach these upstarts a lesson, Macphee, usually critical of the cavalier attitude of most young climbers merely said, 'Yes!' Match fit and raring to go, they took him at his word and shot up the climb, dislodging a chockstone on the way much to the obvious annoyance of Macphee.

Towards the end of the twenties he began to explore the smaller outcrops in the Lakes and in 1927 opened up Green Gable Crag, and a year later he made several visits to Castle Rock, Triermain, usually in the company of Mabel Barker. They could make no impression on the main face but climbed four new middle-grade routes on the south face. Despite the crag's close proximity to the road these were the first recorded climbs here. Later he introduced A.T. Hargreaves to the crag where he led the excellent *Direct Route* (VS).

On 16 February 1930 he seconded A.T. Hargreaves up the formidable *Deer Bield Crack*, considered by many as one of the hardest routes of the era. (This climb has now collapsed.) It may be difficult to believe, especially for anyone who managed to struggle up the desperate crux chimney (HVS 5b), but the climb was at first only graded Severe by them. Considering the time of year and given the antiquated protection of the period, it was a remarkable effort.

Now in his early thirties and at his peak as a mountaineer, these were halcyon years for Macphee, and as his professional fees increased so did his choice of cars – he initially drove a Sunbeam, then a Riley, before he invested in a Bentley. Not many climbers of the day owned a car and he was able to range far and wide. There were trips to Wales with Colin Kirkus, whom he took under his wing, and together they pioneered the *Great Slab* on Clogwyn Du'r Arddu, regarded at the time as a major breakthrough on the cliff.

His horizons and experience were extended in the Alps and he made several first ascents including one in 1933 on the South Face of Aiguille Noire de Peuterey. On that occasion he set out from the hut at 3 a.m. with his partner Menlove Edwards, but Menlove was tired and going very slowly. They had an argument over what to do. In the end Edwards

---

[3] Charles Warren developed into a skilled mountaineer and made three attempts to climb Everest including the 1935 push led by Eric Shipton. He continued to climb throughout his life and was on the Cuillin Ridge when he was seventy-two and made his last rock climb in the Lakes on his 80th birthday. He died at the age of ninety-two.

turned back and Macphee continued on alone. Shortly after this Edwards declared that he'd had enough hard climbing and headed off down the glacier, on his way back home, attache case in hand. Macphee stayed on and teamed up with an assortment of other climbers and did further routes including the Brenva. The two rarely spoke afterwards.

Macphee made a successful bid to join the elite French Groupe de Haute Montagne, quite an achievement for someone from outside of mainland Europe, as membership required a constant high level of alpine climbing with a points scoring system in place – the severity of the route determined the amount of points awarded. Over the years it became a constant battle for Macphee to keep his tally up to scratch.

But his infatuation with the Ben still lingered, and in 1931 he accepted the task of editing the SMC Climbing Guide to Ben Nevis. This entailed the daunting drive, albeit in his Bentley, from Liverpool to Fort William, weekend after weekend – a round trip of around 640 miles. It was a pilgrimage that has now passed into SMC folklore. It was his personal campaign over the next few years that introduced a standard of climbing on Ben Nevis which, although not a tidal shift in terms of difficulty, at least gave an indication of what was possible on Scotland's premier mountain, especially in winter conditions. It was a long overdue wake-up call to young Scottish climbers.

At this point, it should be emphasised that the impetus of Scottish mountaineering between the wars had generally been in stagnation with little concerted effort to carry on Raeburn's splendid pre-war traditions. Many of the important routes of the day were snatched by English interlopers – they included the likes of Piggot, Bower, Wilding and A.T. Hargreaves, who all brought their gritstone skills to Scottish crags. The reason for this inertia, among local talent, is difficult to understand. Even as far back as 1889, Collie's ascent of *Tower Ridge* in winter conditions brought forth this revealing comment from Naismith, 'the Sassenachs have indeed taken the wind out of our sails maist notoriously, I wull say that...those beggars were more wide-awake than we.' Yet, despite this rallying call, it would take another thirty years before the thrust of pioneering began to shift towards home-grown climbers and it would be Graham Macphee who led the charge.

Another decisive factor in the Renaissance of Scottish Mountaineering was the construction, in 1929, of the Charles Inglis Clark Memorial Hut in the upper reaches of the Allt a' Mhuilinn Glen. Here the logistics of the mountain were transformed during the short winter days, when snow and ice conditions were at their best, enabling Macphee to bring his extensive Alpine experience to bear on the Ben's unclimbed ice gullies and cliffs, now only a short walk away. The hut became almost a second home to him and twenty-five years later he celebrated spending one hundred nights there.

But it was in 1935 that he probably came of age as a pioneering leader, with eleven new routes, five of them in the winter. The pinnacle of his achievements came on 17 March of that year, with the first true winter ascent of Tower Gap West Chimney (*Glover's Chimney*). The day began with an uncharacteristically late start and the three man team did not reach the foot of the climb until after midday. I wonder if Macphee had any inkling of the epic that was about to unfold, as his two companions, George Williams and Drummond Henderson, tied on to the 200ft alpine line. Perhaps there was that heady mix of excitement, nervous energy and uncertainty as Macphee began his stamina-sapping, step-cutting up the vertical 120ft icefall, which was overhanging in places. Two hours later, after descending for a rest, he found a stance and brought up the other two. Macphee then discovered he had brought the hut's fire-lighters in place of sandwiches – although hunger was perhaps the last thing on their minds. Despite overcoming the crux pitch it would be another five-and-a-half hours of unrelenting step-cutting and the hazardous navigation of ice-coated slabs, and deep snow on ice, before the party finally topped out.

It is worthy of mention that Macphee needed to drop a looped rope before his two colleagues could follow him on the upper section of the final chimney. Williams later wrote a graphic description of Macphee, running out 100ft of line, seeing the sparks fly as his axe penetrated the ice and struck bare rock, then emerging from the gloom of the gully before being silhouetted against a darkening sky as he neared Tower Gap, followed by an uncharacteristic bellow of triumph announcing his safe arrival. Such were Macphee's values the excursion could not be considered complete until he'd visited the summit to round off the day. All that remained was a descent of *Number Three Gully* and they arrived back at the hut at midnight – it had been a 14-hour sortie and the twenty-word entry in the Hut Log, by Macphee, usually the least demonstrative of men, said it all:

> 'Under the existing conditions, this magnificent climb was one of the most arduous & exacting expeditions the present leader has ever accomplished.'

In terms of commitment it was a remarkable example of courage, determination and will-power, made even more impressive as the climb was led entirely in nailed boots. It was probably the high point of his climbing career and, although Macphee continued to pioneer routes on the Ben, never again was he able to match the overall intensity of *Glover's Chimney*.

The following summer while prospecting an ascent of *The Castle*, for the new guide, he found Maurice Linnell's ice axe and Kirkus's broken shaft, which had lain there since the fatal accident to Linnell the previous winter – it must have been a sombre moment of reflection as he knew both men well.

He had set himself the task of repeating all the climbs on Ben Nevis for the guide. It became clear, however, that this was a losing battle, especially with Bell and others snapping at his heels and pioneering new climbs. He was eventually forced to admit defeat, and the guide was finally published in 1936.

As he eased past middle-age his energy appeared boundless. From his youth he saw the benefits of regular fitness training and used the gym and swimming pool at the Adelphi Hotel in Liverpool. His fitness regime continued from his weekend caravan, by the side of Brotherswater. He usually started the day with exercises and an early morning dip, often encouraging his wife to join him. In 1953 he compleated the Munros – only the twentieth person to do so – and two years later he added all the Tops. He was probably the first person to climb, unsupported, all three summits of Snowdon, Scafell Pike and Ben Nevis in under twenty-four hours. In his late fifties he was still able to ascend at a rate of two thousand feet an hour, and in the process chalked up one hundred ascents of the Ben.

Brian Kellett would have been the obvious person to write the next edition of the SMC Climbers' Guide to Ben Nevis, but with his untimely death on Ben Nevis the burden of responsibility once again fell upon Macphee. His career overlapped several generations and during the war years, with many climbers away in the forces, he teamed up with a young Bill Peascod[4], a young Cumberland miner. They first climbed together on Grey Crag, Buttermere and produced *Spider Wall* (MVS), *Rib & Wall* (D) and *Long Tom* (VS). Macphee, who was now fully engaged on the new Ben Nevis guide, introduced Peascod to Scotland, and en-route to Fort William, they climbed *Clachaig Gully* in Glen Coe. The 1700ft curving chasm cleaving the southern flanks of Sgorr nam Fiannaidh was first climbed in 1938 by Bill Murray and party and seven years later it was still a major undertaking. Macphee's team climbed the route in four-and-a-half hours – knocking three hours off the accepted time.

Looking back on his first visit to the Ben Peascod was astonished by the lack of detail in the existing 1936 Guide. Compared to his homely Buttermere crags, the sudden impact of these huge sweeping faces must have jolted his confidence. In complete contrast to the Fell & Rock climbing guides that tended to give almost a hold-by-hold description – it was, in his own words, 'a shock to the system.' But with the weather holding fair Peascod pulled himself together as they climbed *Rubicon*

---

[4] Peascod became a college lecturer and a well-known painter. He died in 1986 after suffering a massive heart attack at the start of *Great Slab* on Clogwyn Du'r Arddu.

Wall without any problems, at the time the hardest route on the cliff. However it was on *The Long Climb* where the 'rules of engagement' snapped sharply into focus. They climbed on Macphee's 200ft alpine 7mm rope, used double, until the long runouts forced them to give way to a single line. After several rope-lengths of climbing and an alarming absence of belay points Peascod found a tiny spike of rock of doubtful security, took a stance and called down to his partner of his concerns. Macphee soon joined him and wanted to know where was this poor belay? Peascod later described how Macphee then grabbed the belay rope and proceeded to hang on it with his full weight, hundreds of feet above the ground, before announcing: 'That's all right.' Peascod was horrified and if we are to judge by what he later wrote about the affair, perhaps wondered if he had packed clean underpants. It was an extraordinary show of bravado and totally alien to Macphee's usual wide level of safety. The pair reached the top after eight hours and without further incident.

The mountain beckoned again in August 1950 and, at Macphee's invitation, Peascod and his climbing partner Brian Dodson hitched up to Fort William, probably to help him with the new Ben Nevis guide. Once established in the CIC Hut Macphee set out the house rules. To save time there would be no heating water to wash dishes. At the end of the meal plates and cutlery would be cleaned with a half slice of bread. It was certainly a world apart from his gentlemen's club, the exclusive, Liverpool-based 'Athenaeum', where he was President.

It was during this visit that Macphee was involved in his last pioneering climb on the mountain. Along with C. Peckett and J. Renwick he followed Peascod and Dodson up *Gargoyle Wall* on Number Three Gully Buttress. The next day he was forced to retreat whilst attempting a first ascent of *Minus Two Gully*, after sustaining a nasty head injury from a falling rock. Typically, he insisted on making his own way down. His concerned companions watched him stagger towards the hut, at the same time trying to stem the flow of blood with a handkerchief. Peascod and Dodson went on to finish the route which was then given a grade of Very Severe. The new Ben Nevis guide eventually appeared in 1954, some eighteen years after the previous edition.

In 1957, at the age of fifty-nine, he moved to Heversham within sight of the Langdale Pikes, his zest for life undiminished. Harry Griffin recalls a telephone call from Macphee late one evening asking why he was going to bed on such a wonderful moonlit night. With typical directness he told Griffin to get his boots on – they were going to Helvellyn. Once on Striding Edge Macphee insisted that all the towers must be climbed en route. In the shelter they dozed in their sleeping bags until the dawn burst upon them. 'It came precisely at ten minutes to five,' reflects Griffin, 'we watched the whole golden rim swell into a great ball of fire lighting up the whole of Lakeland. The views were remarkable, mountain and sea stretching well into the lowlands of Scotland. We finished off with coffee and rolled up our sleeping bags and rattled down Swirral Edge...we were home before breakfast...and somehow we had stolen an extra day.' During the jaunt, Griffin was intrigued by Macphee's ingenious raincoat, which he was able to convert by a clever system of hems and cords into an anorak, and was able to drop the skirt after climbing to keep out the rain – this was before they became commonplace in mountaineering fashion.

In 1958, five years before his death, he made his last visit to the Alps at the age of sixty. During the holiday he climbed eleven peaks over 4000m and afterwards attended the Alpine Club centenary meet at Zermatt. In his after-dinner speech the President of the Alpine Club described him as a 'remarkable elderly gentleman.' Macphee was not pleased and said this remark was uncalled for as he was neither old nor remarkable!

Macphee died, as he lived, meeting life head on refusing to acknowledge the fragility of advancing years. Perhaps another time, another place he would have been rewarded in the New Year's Honours List, for his services to mountaineering – this would surely have met with his approval – and when his time came he might have been laid to rest in the small cemetery in Glen Nevis, within sight of Ben Nevis. But it is rarely an ideal world and it was cruel irony that Graham Macphee was buried in the British Cemetery at Puerto de la Cruz, Tenerife, far from the British mountains to which he gave so much. It was a sad and rather ignominious end for this powerful and restless mountaineer.

References
Some of the publications referred to include:
SMC, F&RCC, and Rucksack Club Journals.
Ben Nevis: Britain's Highest Mountain – Ken Crocket, SMT, 1986.
Journey After Dawn – Bill Peascod, Cicerone Press, 1985.
Liverpool Echo.
Liverpool Daily Post.

I would particularly like to thank Matt Shaw, Macphee's grandson, for his help with this article. He was able to confirm various details by referring to his grandfather's 'meticulous, very factual diaries'.

*

First ascents on Ben Nevis in which Graham Macphee was involved
17 June 1931   *Route 1*, Carn Dearg Buttress, Severe.   A.T. Hargreaves, Macphee, H.V. Hughes.

19 June 1931   *Observatory Buttress Direct*, VDiff. A.T. Hargreaves, Macphee, H.V. Hughes.

20 June 1931   *Raeburn's Arête variation*, Severe. A.T. Hargreaves, Macphee, H.V. Hughes.

24 June 1931   *Macphee's Climb*, North Wall of Carn Dearg, VDiff. Macphee, H.V. Hughes.

8 Oct 1933   *East Ridge*, Garadh na Ciste, Mod. Macphee, G.C. Williams, P. Ghiglione.

24 June 1934   *1934 Route*, South Trident Buttress, Severe. Macphee, G.C. Williams.

17 Mar 1935   *Glover's Chimney,* VDiff. Macphee, G.C. Williams, D. Henderson.

The Very Difficult grade covered both a winter and summer ascent. A surprising choice considering the extreme conditions experienced during the original winter ascent.

[April 1935   *Cousins' Buttress.* Macphee, G.F. Todd.]

Climbed in thaw conditions and left unrecorded at the time.

1 May 1935   *Direct Start variation*, North Trident Buttress, VDiff. Macphee, J. Jackson Murray, D.J.S. Harvey.

5 May 1935   *Jubilee Climb,* VDiff. Macphee, G.C. Williams, D. Henderson.

15 June 1935   *Ruddy Rocks Route*, VDiff. Macphee, G.C. Williams.

22 June 1935   *Eastern Climb*, North-East Buttress, Severe. Macphee, G.C. Williams.

5 Aug 1935   *Gardyloo Gully*, VS. Macphee, R.C. Frost.

1 Sep 1935   *Macphee's Route*, The Great Tower, VDiff. Macphee, G.R. Speaker.

28 Sept 1935   *The Great Chimney*, Severe. Macphee, A.G. Murray.

29 Sept 1935   *Left Wall variation*, South Castle Gully, VDiff. Macphee, A.G. Murray.

29 Sept 1935   *North Gully*, Creag Coire na Ciste, VDiff. Macphee, A.G. Murray.

30 Sept 1935   *Bayonet Route*, Severe. Macphee, A.G. Murray.

10 Apr 1936   *South Gully*, Creag Coire na Ciste, Mod. Macphee.

14 Apr 1938   *Intermediate Gully*, VDiff. Macphee, R. Ashley, C.H. Oates.

7 Apr 1939   *Good Friday Climb*, VDiff. Macphee, R.W. Lovel, H.R. Shepherd, D. Edwards.

28 Aug 1950   *Gargoyle Wall*, Number Three Gully Buttress, Severe. W. Peascod, B.L. Dodson, C. Peckett, J. Renwick, Macphee.

The details of these routes are taken from the 1954 SMC Climbers' Guide to Ben Nevis by Graham Macphee and the grades of the climbs may be different from the present day.

A SCOTSMAN'S DUTY!

By Gordon Smith

Part 1: A Promise Not Quite Broken

IN MY DAY walking up the Allt a' Mhuilinn to the CIC Hut from the distillery was a horrid, mucky business. Bog-trotting was what we called it and often we wore wellies to keep our climbing boots, our socks, and our enthusiasms dry. There was this one time that I was bog-trotting up the hill I came across one of those Englishmen. He said his name was Terry King; Terry to his pals but he was Kingy to me from that day on. He was wandering down in the late afternoon with his mate looking fed up after a day of mucking about doing nothing much at all. I was on my own which, being a teenaged climbing vagrant, I often was. I had a vague plan to do some soloing the next day but Kingy straight away made me, an utter stranger, promise to stay an extra day or two after and do some climbing with him when he came back up the hill. And so I did. I promised.

Now, I didn't have a tent and being a vagrant had no rights or expectations of staying in that luxurious den of the Scots Climbing Aristocracy and their well-appointed guests, the CIC Hut. But never mind I had my orange polythene bivouac bag with me together with a foolish intention to bivouac under the stars. Stars indeed. In Scotland. In the winter. I kipped that night outside the CIC but inside my poly bag, having dined sparingly upon cold stovies[1], boiled up a day or two previously in my mother's kitchen in Blairgowrie and carried in a poke[2]. The stovies were chased down with a handful of damp peanuts from a family-sized bag spirited out of my mother's cupboard. Cold water was supplied by the burn on the other side of the CIC, dug up out of its covering of snow. There were no stars. The wind howled. Powder snow drifted over the poly bag with me damp inside. I didn't sleep very much. Then in the morning, there being no incentive to stay long in my bed, I was up early and out at the crack of dawn.

Just as I was gathering my meagre belongings from out of the drifted snow Sudsie and Spike from Nevisport went thundering past, full steam ahead. So I jumped up and followed them like a little lap dog towards *Point Five Gully*. They busied themselves at the foot of that the most famous gully in all the world while I wandered up *Hadrian's Wall Direct* in order to try out my new Terrordactyls. It didn't take very long and so, it being still too early to clock off for lunch, I ran down Number Four and up *Green Gully*. It is an interesting point to note that a year or two later, once I had acquired some experience of real climbing, that is to say climbing in the Alps, *Green Gully* became the standard of

Top: Eighty years on, the CIC Hut gets a major new extension. This photograph, taken in June 2009, shows the Mark I porch. Photo: Noel Williams
Bottom: The interior of the new extension at the CIC Hut. Photo: Andrew James

difficulty against which I compared everything ice-climbing in the Alps. A bulge of green ice in some snowy alpine couloir; a dizzily vertical goulotte plastered in ice and cleaving a silver line up an alpine face; a precipitous field of ice clinging precariously to an alpine North Wall; all were compared with *Green Gully* on Ben Nevis. But on that particular morning all this comparisons stuff was future nonsense. I ran up *Green Gully* and, finding myself on the plateau with it still being too early to clock off for lunch, I ran back down Number Four and set off up the *Comb Gully*. *Green Gully* and *Comb Gully* are a natural pair of twins. I had done the one and so I had to do the other also, no question about it. I ran, therefore, up that one too and finding myself on the plateau with it still being too early to clock off for lunch, ran back down Number Four again and right back up the *Comb Gully Buttress* for a bit of fun.

At about this time I was starting to flag a little, but thinking that Sudsie and Spike might be finishing up on Point Five I ran back down Number Four, around the Douglas Boulder and up the lower part of Observatory Gully to the base of that the most famous gully in all the world. There was a party, not Sudsie and Spike, at the top of the first pitch footering about and getting ready to do the next, when I arrived at the stance. Of a sudden I hit the wall. Oh I was that hungry. So much rabid exercise after forgetting to eat my breakfast, cold stovies from that poke together with more of those damp peanuts. I had to eat. Straight away. And thus back down again I climbed. To eat. My lunch.

Being fed up with cold stovies and those damp peanuts I gathered together my poly bag and bits of stuff from their snowdrift outside the CIC and snuck off down the Allt a' Mhuilinn towards the fleshpots of Fort William clutching my shilling, or whatever it was in those days, and dreaming deliriously of the delectable delights at the closest chippy. Unfortunately, and almost within spitting distance of the distillery and the road, I met Kingy coming the other way. He sternly rebuked me and reminded me of my duty to keep my promises. He dragged me, my belly still empty and whimpering, back up to the CIC and another cold, windy, and snowy night tucked up in a wet poly bag. And fed, sparingly, on cold stovies from my poke chased down with more of those damp peanuts. And a cup of icy cold water. Kingy had brought his own poly bag and his own provisions, including a stove for his regular cups of hot tea, which only goes to show that even then he was a clever chap, not relying on Scotch accommodations and Scotch food.

The next morning, there being again little incentive to linger long in my bed under the drifted snow, I was up early and dragging Kingy out from his frosted burrow. After Kingy's cup of tea, we climbed the length of Observatory Gully towards the higher flank of Observatory Buttress. Tut Braithwaite, one of those famous English mountaineers who later

Top Left: Graham Macphee, second from left, shows his profile at Inverarnan. Photo: Tom Weir.
Top Right: Matt Shaw in the chimney of Route 1 (first climbed by his grandfather). Photo Andy Tibbs
Bottom: Mount Teide, Tenerife. Photo: Peter Nijenhuis

went on to climb on Everest and other very big mountains, had told me the previous day, before my attempted escape from Kingy's clutches, that he and Jeff Lowe, an American climber with an enormous reputation, had just done some wonderfully fine new route up on the Indicator Wall. He also told me that the crag was dripping with them, new routes to do, like ripe raspberries just waiting to be plucked. As soon as I had told this story to Kingy his eyes lit up and he insisted that we should go up there straight away and start plucking. And so we did. To a degree at any rate.

I ambled up the hill at a gentle pace, Kingy lagging far behind for he was a desperate addict of the leaf in those days and therefore huffing and puffing and snorting like a steam engine due for retirement on some scrap heap. When at last Kingy rejoined me perched in a little bucket hole in the snow at the foot of the wall, just to the right of the central rocky section, and after he had rested awhile and satisfied his abominable cravings, we decided upon a certain steep slab, thickly iced, as a good line that would go. We were, of course, hoping that Tut and Jeff had chosen some other good line as their new route. I don't remember now, after more than thirty years, the details of the climb. Some glimpses, some disjoint flashes, reveal that well-iced slab, at the top of which was a great bank of ice on the left, and beyond that another slab with delicate and gripping tip-toe-tapping over thin, eggshell ice. There was a rock corner bounding a little rock buttress fringed with ice above and on the right. To the left of the corner there was a steep frieze of ice that strenuously dripped large icicles. A steep swing out of the corner onto that icicle fresco led, via a ramp of snow above and left of the little rock buttress, finally to the summit cornice. The plateau again. And when we got there I was hungry. So very hungry. A Spartan diet, I must say, has not much to be said for it. We retired, therefore, a lazy pair of rogues with just the one raspberry plucked from that wall generously dripping with the fruit, to our bivouac site and more hard rations for the night.

After another cold, windy, damp night drifted over in our poly bags we were back up the hill at the crack of dawn for more climbing. I'd read Murray's account of climbing the long rock climb *Slav Route*, on the Orion Face, in the wet. It was that account where MacKenzie, standing in his stockinged soles on a slab streaming with water, calls for a piton like Richard the Third calling for a horse at Boswell. A winter ascent of the *Slav Route* boded a fine expedition, almost of alpine proportions and a fit entertainment for young vagabonds out to make names for themselves. Unfortunately I'd heard vague rumours that Messrs Quinn and Lang, a pair of elderly gents from Dundee, had already done the first winter ascent of the route the previous year. Hacking steps, no less. Well, what the heck maybe it wasn't true. We reached the foot of *Zero Gully* with Ed Grindley and Alan Petit hard on our heels. They were bound for Zero, we for Slav.

Kingy had the first pitch, a shallow rocky groove thinly coated with ice and frosting and just below and to the left of the first pitch of Zero. Having flowed up that icy gutter like dear Mr Murray's friend MacAlpine progressing towards a milk saucer, in the manner that is to say of a Persian cat[3], Kingy belayed below a large overlap. A single, slender icicle drooped languorously, rather like a Chinese moustachio (the sort of moustachio that would have belonged to a very ancient Chinese Sage, of course, being silvery-white), down from the lip of the overlap to merge with the iced slab to Kingy's right. I had graciously permitted Kingy to lead the first pitch so that, in the natural order of things, the icicle would fall to my lot. While I grunted and grappled with that icicle, a mere boy engaged in a man's work so to speak, Grindley, directly below and choosing to ignore the twenty downward points of my crampons and the Damoclean icicle to which I was pinioned and, of course, the important factor that all were aimed straight at him, hurled abuse from the first pitch of Zero for all the snow and ice I was dropping on his head.

'Cut it out, you bloody wee Jock', he cried at me in his exasperation, 'you keep your rubbish to yourself or I'll throw you into Loch Linnhe.' Finally he called out, very loudly, 'Bloody Scots!' clearly forgetting that a Scotsman, Petit, was safeguarding his own rope.

Fortunately for him I managed to finish struggling over my icicle with it still standing. Thus Englishman Ed survived unscathed and the other Englishman, Kingy, still had something to climb in his turn. Kingy, as he approached the foothold in the ice that was serving as a belay stance, gave me that sideways look of his, with lowered brows. 'Very nice, very nice indeed youth. Now, when does the hard bit start?'

Och these English with their games. 'When does the hard bit start', indeed. When, indeed, will the Scottish National Party rid us of the pests?

Many, many long and bare white run-outs have collapsed together among my memories from thirty years ago and more, except for the vast volumes of crusted windslab in the grooves and runnels high up on the wall breaking up under my feet and deluging down on that unlucky pair in *Zero Gully*. And for the shocking clatter and roar of a hapless climber falling the lengths of Tower and Observatory Gullies, all the way to the bottom, late in the afternoon. Ed and Alan were done and gone when we reached the plateau and so we wandered down Number Four by ourselves in the twilight. It was time to give up the hard living, pick up our poly bags and get on down through the night to Fort William, with its chip shops and the warmth of the rented caravan where Kingy was living. And plans for a summer's climbing in the Alps.

Part 2: North Face Novices

THE VERY FIRST alpine expedition that Kingy and I undertook together was planned in the warmth of Kingy's caravan in Fort William after several nights of sleeping rough, curled up in the snow on Ben Nevis like husky dogs. It should, I must say, be remembered that it is very easy, sitting in the warmth of a caravan and lingering over a poke of fish and chips and with several days of doughty deeds in the snow behind one, to imagine that great, stark North Walls, wrapped up in ice and darkly threatening, are places where it is desirable to be. The first alpine route, therefore, at which Kingy and I pointed our noses was a North Wall; the *Merkl-Welzenbach Route* on the North Face of the Grands Charmoz. The Merkl-Welzenbach was graded Difficile Sup at that time, according to an Alpine Club guidebook on the shelves at Nevisport, which we felt made it an appropriate north face upon which north face novices, Ben Nevis trained, could cut their teeth. But the way it all turned out things were a lot tougher and much more uncomfortable than we had imagined. And in the end it was only because we had the gods, or fate, or beginner's luck, or whatever you please, with us that we survived the rigours we had invited down upon our own heads like foolish virgins. We did, however, eventually and after a number of false starts, achieve our first great victory, our first North Wall.

The original team for the ascent included Kingy and me, of course, and Dirty Alex and Bushman Rhodes, a couple of the grubby English ragamuffins hanging about the muddy campsite in the Biolay woods and looking for something to do. We thoroughly cemented our team esprit by going out as four of the numerous co-conspirators upon a famous and highly successful raid on a Chamonix Building Site led by Colin Somebody-or-Other, also known as 'Our Man from the Petits Charmoz' on account of his frequent solo attempts to climb that mountain. The purpose of the expedition was simply to pinch some polythene for our campsite kitchens. But we had returned to the Biolay, in the middle of the night, with an enormous roll of booty, thirty feet long and a yard at least in diameter, on our heads and looking rather like the sort of giant centipede that the late, rather peculiar, Mr Kafka might have enjoyed describing in grotesque and intimate detail had he but known. Burdened by our ill-gotten gains and giggling foolishly from time to time, like a squadron of silly school girls, we sauntered casually through the centre of Chamonix, past the hordes of tourists enjoying late night revelry in les bar-restaurants and past, even, the police station. That roll, as it happened, was destined to provide the Biolay Campers with kitchenettes for several seasons to come.

We hooligans learned very quickly that the walk up to Montenvers is best avoided by lazy buggers, other economies being always preferable.

On our first attempt at the North Face of the Grands Charmoz, therefore, we four left Montenvers after an expensive train ride for the trudge towards the great wall of the Grands Charmoz that frowns over the Mer de Glace. We barged importantly through the crowd of tourists milling around the station like alpine sheep and we pounded the path for an hour or so until we arrived at a large boulder in a copse of stunted trees. This was declared a fine spot for a bivouac. Very early the next morning we set off up the north face of our mountain, scrambling over hideously loose and dangerous ground in the dark, rocks and boulders raining down over those behind from those in front; and we slithered incontinently upon our crampon points and waved our ice axes about ineffectually while struggling up simple slopes of soggy snow in pools of anaemic torchlight. Until, at dawn, we reached the top.

We had reached the summit, but unfortunately it was not the summit of the Grands Charmoz. Indeed we looked down the other side of a very minor ridge, entirely divorced from the North Face of the Grands Charmoz, to the foot of our intended route a couple of hundred feet below us. A very fat alpine marmot surveyed us from a nearby boulder with evident disdain before slowly turning around and waddling off. Turning around ourselves, as if on command and without a word, we scrambled and walked back down to Montenvers. We continued walking down the track to the Biolay campsite because other economies could not be justified against such abject failure. Oh we were such fine budding alpinists, Ben Nevis trained though we were.

The second attempt was marginally more successful in that we four arrived properly at the foot of the correct face in good order and in good weather and prepared to bivouac on the snow. But it stormed that afternoon, as often it does in the Alps, and after a wet bivouac we retreated like whipped curs, in lovely sunshine, to the fleshpots of Chamonix and to our Biolay campsite once more. Those, it must be said, were our failures and we were four.

Now, three is a much luckier number and so for our third attempt we went without Bushman, who was far more interested in sneaking off to climb something else, and with someone else, than waste any more time and energy on that clutch of fumbling fools, Kingy, Dirty Alex, and me. And this time we reached the foot of the face in good order and bivouacked without getting drenched in an afternoon downpour and everything seemed set for the climb on the morrow. On the morrow the weather was indeed fine and we set off as a string of three, not four, and not too early; Kingy, followed by me, and with Dirty Alex tagging along at the back end of the string.

Being a gentleman I do hesitate to point the finger at anyone in particular as having been the flat-footed bringer of bad luck to our earlier attempts, the vile churchman, as it were, on our wandering barque. Indeed, we Scotch not being at all superstitious, I regard this very idea of someone being a jinx to be an utter and complete nonsense. The astute reader, however, might note that as soon as Bushman resigned his position on the team's roster the team's fortunes did seem to improve. This may, of course, have been due simply to three, rather than four, being the lucky number. Or it may have been that unlucky Bushman…but I digress. Enough beating about the bush and on with the story.

The opening pitches of the climb involved hard mixed climbing, the kind of mixed climbing which you would have expected in the seventies on Ben Nevis and much harder than we had expected on an alpine route first climbed in the early thirties. Kingy led the first section up a rocky chimney and grooves with an occasional ice bulge, and I led the second section up snowy grooves with rocky bits and icy bulges to a long, shallow trough leading to the bottom left-hand side of the central ice field. Dirty Alex, meanwhile, tagged along at the back end of the string.

By the time we reached the central ice field we were all quite tired. By the unaccustomed effects of altitude, I should point out, rather than by exertion for we were young and should, theoretically at least, have been fit. Altitude is, of course, not something that you have to bother much about on an ascent of *Green Gully* or even *Point Five Gully* on Ben Nevis even though those climbs do lead directly to the summit plateau of the Ben, the highest mountain in all of Britain. But now, being at altitude and with miles and miles, or so it seemed, of plodding up a sheet of ice before us the effects shortly made themselves felt. In addition it was terribly easy climbing up that ice, and very quickly we dispensed with the idea of climbing for ever and ever from wobbly ice screw belay to wobbly ice screw belay and just moved together, a little caterpillar of three, puffing up the slope. I led, Kingy followed and Dirty Alex, meanwhile, tagged along at the back end of the string. We did have to be careful, as even we novices realised, for the ice, higher up the slope and in the lower reaches of the summit couloir, was covered in snow, fresh powder snow, and in imminent danger of sliding off the face. And us, a trio of huffing, puffing and gormless little vermicelli, with it.

We arrived, in due course and with great care, at a steepening of the summit couloir. Here there was a great bulging of the snow in a constriction. Looking at the face from below, and in our ignorance, we had assumed that all the white bits were just easy angled snow and that we would run up them no bother at all because we had climbed in Scotland in the winter and this was just the Alps and in the summer. The opening pitches of the climb, however, had made us wonder. And the upper couloir was to provide two of the hardest pitches of pure snow climbing that I have ever undertaken. Even Kingy, My Famous Kingy who had led Stony Middleton's *Our Father* without so much as a prayer, who had battled through the jaws of Wen's *Tyrannosaurus Rex* on the sharp end of the rope and won through, and who had winked up Gogarth Upper Tier's *Winking Crack* in the blink of an eye, turned down the offer of a lead on the second rope-length in the bulging constipation of the upper couloir! It was that hard and very, very scary.

Having been handed the short straw, being the Scotsman, I led off up the first steep pitch of the upper couloir. It didn't seem so hard…just steepish snow. But the steepish snow got steeper and steeper, and remained snow and very powdery. And it didn't turn out to have reassuringly solid bulges of good ice poking out from underneath. I had a Terrordactyl axe, with its lovely broad adze, that worked so wonderfully well in this kind of thing; and I had a Terrordactyl hammer that didn't work worth shit in this kind of thing. I could have asked Kingy for a loan of his Terrordactyl axe, so that then I would have had two axes, but pride would not let me admit that I was having difficulty on this simple snow slope. And, as we all know, pride comes before a fall! But I didn't fall off, although it was a close run thing indeed. Instead I patted out big footholds in the snow and tried to make them firm enough to support me by pressing down on them. And I tried digging a deep trench up the snow, with my wonderful Terrordactyl axe in lieu of a shovel, in an attempt to make the angle of the snow seem less than vertical. I ended up, therefore, looking like a little pile of snow slowly moving straight up the middle of the couloir and leaving a shallow groove behind to mark my progress. How much I succeeded in reducing the angle of the slope with my trench I don't know, but it was enough. I didn't fall off. In spite of my pride.

Meanwhile the afternoon storm began and today, unlike yesterday, thunder and lightning did their noisy and noisome thing above us. And snow began to fall, quantities of powder snow and a furious gale with it, and constant spindrift avalanches that plastered up my face behind my spectacles and built upon my eyelashes little piles of snow, so very like piles of heavy sand. I climbed with my spectacles jammed into my mouth so that I could see where I was going. And I climbed with my eyes wedged shut by those little piles of what felt like heavy sand so that I couldn't see at all what I was doing. And, perhaps that was just as well, for Kingy and Dirty Alex down on the stance were getting impatient with the slow progress of the 'Scottish Master of Ice Climbing' on this simple snow slope, and fidgeting and mucking around and playing the fool to keep warm. With the ropes full out I was able to find a rock spike deep under the snow to loop a sling over, and I sagged down on the rope clipped through the sling and wept over my frozen hands in my frozen Dachstein mitts and stuffed under my armpits. After an age of weeping I tied on properly, realising as I did so that I had been staring Auld Nick straight in the face and me without a single runner between myself and my friends playing about in the cold one-hundred-and-fifty feet below like naughty schoolboys.

Kingy followed, floundering wildly up my groove and looking more and more desperate as he realised that there was nothing in the bottomless powder to get a hold of and that there was a serious risk that the snow was all going to fall down with him balled up inside like the jam centre in a roly-poly pudding, or the chewy caramel inside the yummiest of Roses Chocolates. Dirty Alex, when Kingy finally had arrived at the stance and had wept over his burning hands, was brusquely told by Kingy to wait. And then Kingy backed off the next lead – the only time I ever saw him do that.

'No, no, you just carry on. You're doing fine. Besides, it's much more your kind of thing. It is snow, after all, and you're the Scotsman. This is what you're here for!'

I had to lead on first before Kingy could bring Dirty Alex up to our little bucket in the snow. And I led on up more of the same. Patting down big footholds in the bottomless powder and attempting to dig another deep trench through the falling snow and hissing spindrift avalanches. By this time, however, the spindrift had become even worse than before and as fast as I dug my Sisyphean trench it filled the bloody thing up. And it topped up those little piles on top of my eyelashes that felt so very like little piles of heavy sand. And it coated me in layers of frosted snow so that I looked very much like a large snowball rolling upwards in defiance of all the laws of gravity, real and imagined. And that flood of spindrift, it tried and tried to push me off. Blind, frozen, numb with terror I ploughed my very slow and lonely furrow up that vertical wall of snow that seemed to be moving down as fast as I was moving up until Kingy called out 'Stop!'

And I stopped straight away, grubbing around under the snow to find myself another rock spike. The little one that I found was the only protection of the pitch and I lashed myself to it, shuddering. Then I wept and wept over my frozen hands in my frozen Dachstein mitts and stuffed under my armpits as I hung there, a sad little bundle of frozen, weeping snow.

I had a fair bit of time to recover, for Kingy still had to bring Dirty Alex up to the stance below, and Dirty Alex, after his long wait in the blizzard, was frozen almost into a statue. Dirty Alex, having cracked off his statuary of ice, climbed up to Kingy, Kingy climbed up to me, and Dirty Alex climbed up to us. Then, when we were all together again, both said simply, not knowing the full story and in unison like the opera chorus after a particularly riveting aria: 'Good lead Smithy.'

Kingy led us on up a mixed face through the falling snow that was being whipped up by the wind, and I resumed the helm and steered us into a narrow passage, and Kingy continued along the narrow passage that led him to a col on the summit ridge between two pinnacles. I followed Kingy up that last pitch, and Dirty Alex, meanwhile, tagged along at the back end of the string and finished the climb.

As darkness was falling rapidly we got out our orange polythene bivouac bags, a tiny crew of miserable, dripping ne'er-do-wells who lacked the fortitude even to get out the stove and brew up something warm to drink. I carried a large bag for Kingy and myself to pass the night in, while Dirty Alex, travelling, as it were, supernumerary, had his own little one. Like fools we took off our boots, in order to be more comfortable, sitting in our poly bags. This was extremely silly for they froze very hard in the night, being heavy leather things in those days and soaking wet. In the morning, therefore, we had a heck of a job to get them bent enough to fit onto our feet, without socks even. We sat wretched through that long night without brewing up (even Kingy went without his cup of tea); without eating even the tiniest nibble; and without a moment's kip. For the afternoon storm went on into the middle of the night. Then, when the stars came out at last, it got very, very cold and perched on our little ledge between the pinnacles, stuffed into the sopping insides of our poly bags which froze solid into crackling crisp pokes of ice, we could do little but sit and wriggle and squirm.

In the morning we hobbled slowly down a ridge, making long abseils because we had no idea where we were going, and we hobbled slowly down a baby glacier with our noses pointed towards the wooded meadows of the Plan des Aiguilles, and thence we hobbled slowly down the long path through the trees to Chamonix and to our campsite in the mud of the Biolay woods. I had a blistered toe and a black toenail after that little outing that hurt like hell whenever I went climbing, causing me to forswear Alpine climbing forever after each successful ascent of the summer. The toenail eventually fell off and the blister turned black and then all the skin fell off. It wasn't until a couple of years later, after I had been badly frostbitten on the Grandes Jorasses, that I realised what that black and blistered toe had meant. I had been suffering quite badly from frostbite. But at the time I was just an alpine novice and too ignorant to know. And what the head doesn't know the heart doesn't grieve over. Which is what they say, anyway.

Funnily enough it just so happened that sitting here thirty years later, and declined, so to say, into the dismal vale of years, I started thinking back over the remarkably difficult and frightening Difficile Sup with which we had opened our Alpine partnership, Kingy and me and with Dirty Alex tagging along at the back end of the string. Looking at a topo photograph of the North Face of the Grands Charmoz generously provided by that most famous of Alpine Databases, known to us all as Luca Signorelli, however, it soon became apparent that instead of doing the *Merkl-Welzenbach* Difficile Sup as we had supposed, a route which wanders off onto reasonably easy rocks on the left of the summit couloir, we had done, in fact, an approximation of the *Heckmair-Kroner North Face Direct*, straight up the central couloir itself, a climb graded Tres Difficile Sup or, in modern parlance, V4+M. Whatever such a grade actually means, and I should be remiss if I were not to admit that I do not in the least understand the meaning of modern grading systems, our little excursion up the north face of the Grands Charmoz certainly provided a deep enough bowl of adventure for a daft trio of fresh-faced North Face Novices to sup their fill. For their first alpine route together, at any rate.

For our next North Faces Kingy and I, bursting with ambition, went on to make the first British ascent of *The Shroud*, again towing Dirty Alex along with us. We followed the line of Desmaison's notorious Walker Spur route for nearly a thousand feet of difficult rock climbing entirely free in order to avoid the large rocks falling down the lower runnels of *The Shroud*, before dribbling over onto *The Shroud* ice field itself and running up that in a couple of hours under a hail of shot and shrapnel from higher up. Kingy and I followed *The Shroud* with a rather athletic race up the *Cornau-Davaille Route* on the north face of Les Droites against a pair of cheating Americans (they pipped us at the post, trailing us out of the rimaye and for much of the face, having a single 300ft rope which they stretched out into 300ft pitches while we were stuck, seething, with our 150ft pitches). Dirty Alex had, by the way, been divested to a competing rope which came in a very poor third. A few days later we continued our efforts with the first British ascent of the *Dru Couloir*. Both the *'Davaille* and the *Dru Couloir* were, in those days, graded Extremement Difficile and therefore significant objectives. It has to be admitted however that those two cheating Americans, being American and therefore far less indolent than we, having pipped us on the *'Davaille* managed to turn around and get to the *Dru Couloir* the day before us, thereby robbing us of the bronze medal for that particular climb. Damn their eyes!

That same season Kingy and I also wandered up the *Cassin Route* on the Walker Spur, free-climbing Cassin's original line right from the bottom of the pillar (just because we were too lazy to go around the corner to the easier French start) to the top of the mountain, except that Kingy dragged me kicking and squealing over Whillans' free-climbing traverse instead of doing the usual abseil pitch. I must say that when Kingy goes absolutely silent for a long time and the rope doesn't move you know it's going to be tough; and Kingy was silent and unmoving on that traverse for a very long time. He says, even now, that it was hard. Finally, before the end of the summer and at Kingy's interminable and bleating insistence, we travelled all the way to Grindelwald and did the notorious *Heckmair Route* on the north face of the Eiger. The whole dark, frosted-up pile of limestone interspersed with a kilometre or two of plodding up sheets of ice and powder snow (we were far too frightened to be bored, but we still huffed and puffed our way up together, as a little caterpillar of two, rather than climbing for ever and ever from wobbly ice screw belay to wobbly ice screw belay). We climbed in crampons every foot of the way; and without the whiff of a single falling stone! I wept with relief on that summit. Secretly.

In spite of the awful reputations held by all these other great North Walls for difficulty and danger I must confess that I have always felt for our first great North Wall, the North Face of the Grands Charmoz, a great affection. I feel, even now, that it was the equal in many ways of those other, greater, North Walls. I have never again, for example, felt quite as heroically frightened as I did in that upper couloir when Kingy pointed out to me that, as a Scotsman, it was up to me to dig those trenches in the snow for my English companions to follow. Indeed *'A Scotsman's Duty'* was what he called it. Pah! These English! 'A Scotsman's Duty'! Digging trenches in the snow 'for my English companions to follow', like any old Irish navvy[4]! When indeed will those Scottish Nationalists rid us of the pests?

The End

Footnotes (for our English friends, who may not know):

[1] Stovies: A delicious and cheap Scotch dish of potatoes and onions boiled up with beef dripping. It goes excellently well with cold ox tongue, or tolerably in a sandwich made with thick slices of Mother's Pride bread lathered in Blue Bonnet margarine. Unfortunately I had neither the cold ox tongue nor a loaf of Mother's Pride with me on Ben Nevis.

[2] Poke: a bag. On this occasion a little polythene poke, as from a supermarket, as opposed to the big orange polythene pokes that we kipped in.

[3] According to Mr Murray '…MacAlpine flowed up the icy gutter like a Persian cat to a milk saucer.' W.H. Murray, *Mountaineering In Scotland*. Murray et al. were not, it should be noted, climbing Slav Route at that time; it must have been an icy gutter somewhere else.

[4] Irish navvy: This may seem, it must be admitted, a dreadful and very racist slur on the Irish. But 'Irish navvy' was, in those days, simply the standard illustration for referring to one who worked hard at manual labour. The English, as is generally recognised, never worked hard at anything, preferring that the Scots and the Irish should do their hard work for them. The Scots, naturally, reserve themselves for hard work of the pecuniary kind, while the Irish have always been reserved for more manual labours even though they do seem to be unaccountably good with words (when, of course, the words can be understood).

BACK WHERE WE CAME FROM

By Iain Smart

Okay, so this is not mountaineering but it is the origin of our climbing skills and is thus of some antiquarian interest even to modern climbers. Tree climbing can be regarded as a refresher course in what life was like in the good old days before the trendy smart Alecs (who are always with us) started to walk about on the ground. As if that wasn't enough they evolved bigger brains and we, their descendants, became more and more sophisticated and forgetful of our origins.

The trees are still there and we have retained a lot of the original adaptations still lodged dormant in our deep programming. We can still climb trees quite well. If I had anything to do with it, it would be a condition of Club membership for applicants to have climbed at least one tree of an acceptable standard in the year prior to their application to show their versatility and sense of historical continuity. Alas, if I ever brought up such a proposal at the AGM everyone would think I'd lost my marbles. Be all that as it may, I have had some interesting experiences among the branches of our arboreal homeland; here are a few of them.

Avenue of Beeches

THE DRIVE UP to the Big Hoose has ten copper beech trees along its north side. They are very special beeches in that they have produced a profusion of branches radiating from a short central trunk. Not for them the conventional straight pillar and huge canopy of the majestic classic giants; these eccentrics have explored the format of a giant bush.

My favourite in the row is the second one. Struggle through the first branches then you lose sight of the ground and become a denizen of the tree.

In the spring of the year the leaves are soft and bright green and the tree's interior is filled with a green glow. It is a bit like the Mallorm trees that Tolkien describes in the land of the Elves. A climb of maybe thirty feet of Moderate standard takes you to the crown. It is an agreeable experience to emerge from the summit of its canopy of whispering leaves into the blue dome of heaven.

In summer when the leaves turn copper the mood is different. The mature leaves are paper hard and flutter rather than whisper in the wind and the contrast between the dark copper-green shades of the inner tree and the heaven above is even more dramatic.

Best of all is to climb it on a starry winter's night after the leaves have been blown away in the autumn gales. At such a time the wild wind sings in her bare branches and her dark tresses are full of diamonds. It's quite an experience...

Swinging Birches
Robert Frost has a poem that begins:

> *'When I see birches bend to left and right*
> *Across the lines of straighter, darker trees*
> *I like to think some boy's been swinging them.'*

Until I read this poem I had never thought of swinging a birch tree. One day on a visit from my friend Stewart McGavin, a fellow Frost aficionado, we decided to do some research on the topic. As explained in the poem the technique is to select a sapling with a single trunk sturdy enough to bear your weight almost to the top. When it starts to bend maybe twenty feet above the ground, you grip the narrow stem with both hands and launch yourself into space. After a moment of free flight, the good birch tree lowers you gently to the ground and on release springs back up again. At the time of this research project there were a number of suitable saplings near our house. We spent a happy morning swinging from heaven to earth from a couple of dozen youthful birches. We found this experience in practical poetry exhilarating and very satisfying. It didn't seem to do the supple birches any harm. Fifty years on they are still straight and graceful whereas Stewart and I are bent and painfully stiff.

In and out the Dusky Bluebells
According to Katherine Briggs in her *Dictionary of Fairies* you have to be careful travelling through woods at night. Oak and willow woods are particularly dangerous. Oaks, as befits their ancient, god-like status, bitterly resent being cut, and an oak coppice springing from the roots of a felled oak wood is malevolent and dangerous to travel through at night, 'more especially if it is a blue-bell wood.'

I have never traversed a coppiced oak wood in the dark but I have walked through an un-coppiced wood carpeted with bluebells in the dusk; there is one quite near us.

I have a form of colour vision deficiency in which, in poor light, I lose the low-energy radiations of the greens and reds so that in the gloaming only the high-energy blue radiations trigger the cones in my retina. In fading daylight blues continue to glow in the gathering dusk; it is quite an eerie effect. People with normal vision retain greens and reds for longer and have a more balanced rendering of colour even in poor light. They must miss the spooky effect of blue lamps glowing in the dusk.

D.H. Lawrence probably had a similarly diminished ability to transduce the lower-energy light waves to judge from his poem *Bavarian Gentians*. In this well-known poem he goes on about gentians being:

'torch-flower of the blue-smoking darkness, Pluto's dark-blue haze,
black lamps from the halls of Dis, burning dark blue,
giving off darkness, blue darkness...'

He was obviously highly strung and blue gentians in the dusk must
have spooked him mightily. At the end of the poem he wanders off with
one in his hand down the path into Pluto's dark kingdom in search of
Persephone, a metaphor for his lost youth and innocence.

In the wood I am talking about, however, the mood was soft and
gentle, under the benediction of subtle Aphrodite, goddess of immanent
beauty, rather than Pluto, king of the dread dungeons of lost time.

Creepy Willows Muttering in the Darkness
Willows, according to Katherine Briggs, are even more sinister. These
trees, it is said, have a habit of uprooting themselves on a dark night and
following a solitary traveller, muttering. The fact that they 'mutter'
gives the story a hint of authenticity – who would invent the idea of a
willow tree following behind you 'muttering' unless they had actually
heard one do it?

I once encountered a willow wood in the deep dusk when we were late
off the hill and lost the path. There was indeed a lot of malevolent
muttering following behind me and the noise of something that could
have been roots being withdrawn from mud. It was of course, my
companion whose progress was impeded by bog and wilfully
obstructive willow scrub. The trees didn't have to bother doing
anything, except get in the way.

Lonesome Larch in the Moonlight
About a mile from our house high on a bare hillside there is an isolated
larch tree. It is a lucky tree to have survived on a heathery hill patrolled
by sheep cattle, deer, rabbits and sundry small rodents – or else it enjoys
some sort of protection. It must have been a sapling when the great gale
that demolished the Tay Bridge felled the rest of Persey Wood. It is not
one of those straight up and down things, that have grown up
imprisoned in a plantation, nor is it a bush, like the beeches lower down
near the house. It is a free tree that has made it on its own, surviving for
more than a hundred years, full half a mile from its nearest neighbour. It
is now about fifty feet tall and has many branches, supporting a
spreading canopy; its sturdy roots grip the solid bedrock of its homeland
– a sound survival strategy for both man and tree.

To get onto its lowest branch is a Severe move. From there on the
route is Moderate; its branches toughened by many winter storms are
robust enough to take you to the very top and give you a panoramic view
from the Cairnwell at the top of Glenshee to the Sidlaws on the other

side of fair Strathmore. I have climbed it in all seasons of the year and times of day. Most memorably I was up there one midnight, under the light of a Hunter's Moon, shining high in a clear sky. The air was still and frost crystals were a-twinkle in the silence. Scarves of mist wound among the dark evergreens surrounding the hidden loch a hundred feet below. Then, three swans glided in from the north like ghosts and disappeared among the trees, presumably to land on the loch.

It is possible that I was the only person in all the broad lands of the fair Kingdom of Scotland who was thirty feet up a tree on that particular night appreciating a very 'Private Viewing' – not in an over-sophisticated Art Gallery but at a True Showing of the Real Thing. Any attempt to record it in pigment or pixels would have caused the equivalent of a collapse of the wave function: it would have changed from direct sensual magic to Gothic bathos.

The Anatomy of Brachiation

After all that it would be best to end up on a practical note of some relevance to modern climbing to which this Journal is dedicated. Tree climbing offers all the usual rock climbing moves of traverse, mantelshelf and overhang. In some trees you can actually brachiate. I don't know if you have ever looked at the anatomy of the shoulder girdle but if you raise your arm above your head and observe the muscular configuration in a mirror you will see your muscles converge around your oxter as a hollow half cone with its base attached to your trunk and its apex around the shoulder joint. The original function of our upper limb in this position was to provide a dynamic pendulum for swinging from branch to branch. It's a very efficient means of locomotion as you use the momentum of the gravity-assisted downward swing to propel you on the upswing.

It is only a few million years since we were really good at brachiating. We have almost lost the knack after so many generations spent running along the ground. Were it not so our corridors would have bars along the ceiling and we would swing along with a fraction of the effort of walking; even better if we had retained a prehensile tail. Nevertheless, the ancestral memories are still there somewhere in our deep programming.

Modern gymnasts have retrieved these old routines and by constant practice have taken them to fantoush lengths of ballet-like precision. An intellectual ape would be astonished at the extraordinary routines performed at the Olympics, but would be dismayed by the pointlessness of their predictability and the amount of repetitive practice required for their perfection. Conversely gymnasts wouldn't be much good at traversing the variability of the holds on offer in the jungle.

Principles and Practice of Brachiation in Rock Climbing
Brachiation hasn't much of a role in rock climbing, since to brachiate successfully the next hold must be visible and sufficient to provide a fulcrum for the next swing and, once embarked on, the move cannot be cancelled. Also you are more or less compelled to swing with your body facing the rock and your head turned to identify the hold you are hoping to grip in the very near future. I am sure I remember doing a manoeuvre like that once or twice somewhere or other.

A special application of the brachiation principle is the pendulum at the end of a rope, like the famous King Swing on *The Nose* of El Cap in Yosemite. In this case you build up momentum gradually by adding velocity as you run up and down the increasing segment of a circle whose radius is the length of the rope. With persistence you reach a hold high on the far side of a smooth slab. The trick is to reverse quickly at the end of each run when your momentum is momentarily zero. At this crucial point it is necessary to keep tension on the rope and start running back down to build up momentum again; otherwise you will enter free fall and be struck like a match against sand paper.

There is a possibility of transferring this technique to tree climbing à la Tarzan. Lianas, as used by our hero, are not features of Scottish woodlands but could be replaced by a doubled rope looped over a branch sticking out towards the next tree, near enough to reach it when you swing. It's unlikely to catch on if you will forgive the pun. But no doubt if it does, the first tree crossing of Scotland without touching the ground will be a notable achievement.

Keeping in the Swing
There is a tree near our house where you can do simple brachiation relatively safely because the suitable branches are near the ground. Starting high up you can jump for a lower branch and swing onwards to catch another at the same height and swing onwards to do it once again. In this case it is easy because the elastic recoil of each branch helps you on your way and gives you a moment of free floating 'air time' and a brief sensation of what life was like in the good old days.

On one occasion when I was sure no one was looking or within earshot I beat my chest and gave a Tarzan call before swinging on my way. But all that was long ago when I was emotionally immature and as elastic as the branches. Even then I couldn't have gone on for very long. The arms get tired of living in the past.

Quickstep V,5, Ben Nevis. Climber: Mark 'Ed' Edwards
Photo: Tony Stone

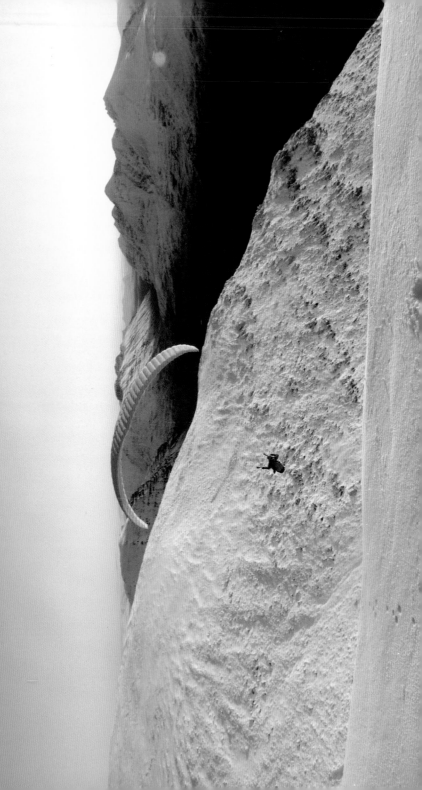

A DIFFERENT PERSPECTIVE

In 1991 I first saw a paraglider in the air. Huddled on a small stance part way up the Bonatti Pillar and desperately thirsty after being chased away from our intended water stop in the approach couloir by a sky full of falling rocks, I saw a brightly-coloured paraglider wafting past. Almost close enough to touch. We spent a few moments contemplating the pilot setting down his wing in a Chamonix field and strolling into the nearest bar for a glass of nicely-chilled beer before returning to the job in hand. Tongues stuck to the roofs of our parched mouths.

We eventually returned to our Argentière campsite a couple of days later, successful, happy and severely dehydrated. The remainder of the trip passed in a blur of summer sun, blue sky and snowy mountains. And in between routes we spent our days lounging around on the campsite, watching as more 'parapentes' drifted down from the Midi.

I don't ever remember making a conscious decision to learn to fly after that visit to the Alps, but sure enough, fast-forward 20 years and here I am, still plodding up mountains. Only now, often as not, instead of a rack and rope, my sack contains a paraglider.

The following story is an account of one such day out with fellow Highland pilots Andy McGregor and Ed Delves. Written by Andy and originally published in *Skywings*, the magazine of the British Hang Gliding and Paragliding Association, in May 2008, it is republished here with Andy's kind permission.

Mark Robson

By Andy McGregor

BRRRI... I WAS awake seconds before the alarm went off and switched it off before it had a chance to ring properly. One of those mornings when you're keyed up and your body knows you just have to be up on time. I staggered downstairs and the phone went just as the kettle was boiling – Ed Delves calling to make sure I was awake and to let me know he was up and about.

He picked me up 20 minutes later – 3.00 a.m. on a frozen January morning in Inverness – what a ridiculous time to be going flying. Outside the air was still, the roads and pavements, all rimmed with ice, glistened under the street lights.

We met up with Mark Robson in a deserted Forestry Commission lay-by and loaded all the kit into his car – gliders, boots, crampons, ice axes, food.

This was all his idea. The three of us had moved to the Inverness area roughly around the same time and had started flying together, slowly trying to work out the best options from the many hills and mountains surrounding us. The previous year we'd talked about a walk up one of

Mark Robson takes off from Tom na Gruagaich, Beinn Alligin.
Photo: Andy McGregor

the local hills to bivvy out overnight with a dawn flight down. Some time around the longest day had been suggested, but a washout summer had meant that we'd never got our act together and actually done it.

Now in deepest winter, Scotland had been hit by a good cold snap and the hills were covered in snow. The ski resorts would be having a bumper weekend for a change. North-West Scotland was lying in a col between two lows and all the weather forecasts were saying that Saturday would be a clear, light-wind day, although they couldn't agree on quite which direction any wind would come from, with somewhere between south and west looking most likely.

We decided this was a prime opportunity for a wee flying adventure and picked a trip to the mountains of Torridon on the west coast. With a good cover of snow and ice, ice axes and crampons were a necessity and, having never before used these, I'd hired a set from a local outdoor shop. New technical toys to play with all added to the excitement and part of the previous night had been spent trying to work out just how to fit them into my harness for the flight without running the risk of impaling myself on a point in the event of a dodgy landing.

On the way over to Torridon, Mark glugged on Red Bull to keep awake, while Ed and I took the chance for some sneaky shut-eye. The only things we passed on the road were the gritter out on its early rounds and a few deer, sheltering close by the road for warmth. What chat there was was all about which direction the wind would be coming from and which would be the best hill to tackle. We wanted a few options for different wind directions and a halfway decent take-off site too. In the end, we decided that Beinn Alligin would be our target, since it had a broad westerly-facing slope that looked from the map as though it would make a good launch.

It took us about an hour to reach the car park at the foot of the hill. Loading up in the frozen darkness, by the car lights, putting on woolly hats and duvet jackets, this seemed a long way from the pictures of sky gods cranking it up high over the Alps in summer that generally feature in the paragliding magazines.

The lower slopes of the hills were clear of snow, but still icy and the rocks were treacherous in places. We spent the first hour or so trudging up the path lit only by our head torches. There was a very faint glow to the southern skyline and Venus could be seen shining out brightly above the village of Shieldaig.

The advantage of the Torridon hills being by the sea is that you've got all that height to play with before landing back by the lochside: the disadvantage of course is that you've got to carry your kit up every one of those three thousand feet. The plod up gave me plenty of time to mentally weigh every piece of my kit and to start dreaming of lightweight mountain gliders and ultralight reserve parachutes.

We didn't hit the snowline until we reached the foot of Coir' nan Laogh. We'd now climbed about 1500ft which meant that we were about halfway to the top. The southern skies were just starting to turn orange and there was purplish glow to the snow. So now I could use the camera as a good excuse for the occasional rest stop. So far there had been no hint of any wind, but we could just make out some cloud forming around some of the slopes in the distance. Beinn Alligin was still clear though and I had my fingers crossed that it would stay that way. It would be gutting to get to the top, find it unflyable and have to carry our gear back down again.

Now the going got quite a bit steeper and we were lucky that someone else had been up here the previous day leaving a nice set of footsteps to follow. The snow was still pretty soft so there was no need for crampons, but as the side wall of the corrie got steeper I had the ice axe out. A fall here and, weighed down by a sack full of paraglider, you'd have a good chance of taking the Gore-tex-assisted downhill speed record. The very last 100ft were hand-and-knees stuff and I was concentrating very hard on not slipping.

Eventually I topped out at just under 3000ft, completely knackered. The others had been there 10 minutes before me and had already got their breath back and were champing at the bit to get into the air.

The views were spectacular and the skies all around were suffused with a rosy pink glow as the sun was just about to rise. Now it was time to switch on our piloting heads and assess the conditions. The wind was coming from the north-east, only the complete opposite to what we'd expected! But the good news was that it was light enough to be flyable and the summit was clear of cloud. The wind direction meant a pretty committing launch right over the wall of the corrie we'd just climbed up. We debated for bit whether there would be any rotor from the far wall of the corrie but decided that it would be safe enough if we kept to the right immediately after take-off.

Just as we agreed this was the place to launch, the sun finally made it above the distant hills, and we were rewarded with fabulous views as the snow glowed and turned from purple, through pink and then orange.

We didn't spend much time enjoying the hard-earned view. Previous experience has shown that if you're on the top of a Scottish hill and it looks flyable – then get in the air. If you wait around for conditions to improve it's more than likely the wind will pick up, cloud will move in, it will start to rain/snow, or all three will happen at once. There was just time for a few photos and to gulp down a Mars bar before laying out our gear. Although my ice axe had fitted perfectly in my harness the previous night, now I struggled to get it in and had to leave the point sticking up, covered with a spare glove.

As ever, Mark was first to get ready. He pulled his glider up and stormed off the hill. The yell he let out just as his feet left the ground showed that the launch over the edge of the corrie would get the heart going. He headed right and made it out of the corrie without any problems.

Not wanting to be left last and alone on the hill, I finished up in double-quick time. Time for a last check that all was well and then pull the wing up. There was just enough breeze to make this a straightforward reverse launch. I slithered in under the glider as it came up overhead, checked it, turned and ran awkwardly in my muckle boots. Whoa, what a rush as the steep snowy cliff edge dropped away under me, hang a right and breathe a sigh of relief as I made it out of the corrie.

Now I could relax and enjoy the flight. To minimise weight we hadn't brought any flight instruments along and this made for a very chilled flight – no beeping nuisance, no radio chatter, no expectation of climbs and so no need to concentrate where the lift was. In fact the air was very smooth and quite floaty. I was hands off most of the time, taking in the view, and hanging back upside down in my harness trying to get shots of Ed as he took off behind me.

The flight down only took about 10 minutes. The sky overhead was clear and blue, the snow-capped peaks contrasting with the russet-brown glow of the lower slopes and the loch completely dark and still. The only signs of life were the jet contrails overhead and the post van that had stopped on the road to watch these three nutters float to earth.

There was plenty of room to land on the heather by the edge of Loch Torridon, although next time I should think more carefully about which side of the deer fence to touch down on – it's not the easiest thing in the world to get over a six foot fence with a glider on your back.

Afterwards, sitting by the lochside drinking tea and taking in the view, it felt strange to have had a full day out by 10 a.m. on a Saturday morning. Although there was plenty of time in the day to try to fly somewhere else, we were well content. Despite finding no lift and making no cross-country distance this was still one of my most memorable flights. What a super start to the 2008 season.

***

If there are any other pilots lurking out there in the SMC, do get in touch. The Highland Hang Gliding and Paragliding Club website is at:
   http://www.highlandhgpgclub.co.uk/

There's also a Google group set up at:
   http://groups.google.com/group/parahighlands

It would be great to hear from you!

LAST ON THE LIST

By Phil Gribbon

OLD FIRBEAG dragged himself towards this moment of ultimate achievement.

He felt that this hill had to be climbed even if it was the last hill he ever managed to do. Another failure to reach his last Corbett was unthinkable.

He sensed something was looming out of the driving mist swirling across the ridge. A shadowy figure was tottering slowly towards him as it wove between the rock blades cutting into the gloom. Was this his lost companion who he had not seen for hours?

Once the phantom figure of the Fearmor had trailed the famous mountaineer Professor Norman Collie across the high slopes of Ben Macdui in the Cairngorms. Was this a supernatural encounter with another Old Grey Man risen from the depths of the sea below? Could this strange encounter be avoided by turning down the steep sides of the ridge?

Old Firbeag shut down his brain and cautiously went on. He knew that misty lonely places can produce illusions when the shrouded surrounding world becomes an uncertain reality. Living with delusion was preferable to extinction.

The figure was growing ever more solid and substantial. It was his companion retracing the ridge to bring word that he had found a minute heap of small stones at a high point. Was that the summit?

A few minutes before, Old Firbeag had dropped abruptly from the cairn at the junction of the three ridges of Buidhe Bheinn. It was an unknown descent towards an unseen objective but all was consistent with his character because he often travelled alone without a map or compass, mobile phone or GPS. This induced a primitive response that heightened every one of his senses. He was working on a memorised map and navigating with the help of the wind direction. Every decision needed care to be both rational and safe.

There were scant traces of footsteps along the ridge. The far end of a remote double Corbett hadn't yet attracted the hordes of those who tick off the appropriate mountain summits listed in the guidebook. Some scuffed step marks or a fresh sliver of schist that had slid off a ledge told of the infrequent passage of some who had trodden this high walkway. Red deer might be able to wander along but they wouldn't be so stupid, would they? These beasts knew instinctively that there were better places down in the glen where the grass was lush and tasty. A fox? Well, it goes where it will, defining its boundary and leaving wee twisted scat lumps stuck on green hummocks. Humans? Yes, they alone have the eroding feet that clump along while their owners search for the glory of attaining of the summit.

They went on together. The highest point was close and only a few steps ahead beyond the bedrock tines forking the mist. They stepped along little sheltered mossy ramps and passed dwarf bilberry plants, skirting round moist slabs of rock. A ledge often ended at the blankness of space. They were moving with the cloud clamped hard against the lee slope so that any sense of the depth towards the valley was obliterated. Over their heads the soft mists of summertime drifted by unconcernedly. It just had to be the finale of Old Firbeag's mountain days.

Yes, this was the last hill needed to complete his list of Corbett ascents.

For years there had been just two hills outstanding but he had refused to rush for them. However underneath his nonchalance there was a nagging feeling that his capability was fading and time was running out. If he was not willing to attempt a final hill as soon as possible then his target would lapse beyond redemption. That would mean that his life would be blighted by an unthinkable failure. This compleation endeavour was a serious business.

It had turned out that his penultimate or one-before-this-last Corbett was Beinn Dearg Bheag in the Fisherfield Forest, but when the moment came Old Firbeag really didn't feel he was up to it. The whole rigmarole of a Corbett collection looked about to collapse unceremoniously.

He took a risk and gambled with his sanity. This time some companionship was good for safe reassurance. She strode without a care, while he staggered through the deep deer grass growing luxuriantly on the marshy ground. He toiled on with frequent halts, resting to recall winter days spent in the innermost recess of corries on An Teallach. Twisting snow gullies spiralling up and crampons crunching footsteps biting old névé. His mind drifted into the past.

What relief when the moorland path canted downwards to Shenavall bothy. A night's rest might restore some strength and breed some competence.

Next morning after fording the stream to the track along the southern shore of Loch na Sealga, they began slanting upwards. Her speed and fitness were a marvel, but why did he find the hillside so steep, the heather so deep? Where was his energy output? Why could he not keep her in sight? Frequent halts for view admiration became mandatory. Climbing up Everest must be like this.

The ridge angle fell back. Calm and peace got into his body. She had waited for him. His mind was so receptive to tiny details. He was aware the tundra was telling him he was crushing out the dry lichens that were crackling beneath his boots. In front a pair of sandy-headed gullies were eroding back into the ridge, one from the left, one from the right, and he felt he was living in geological time with erosion speeding up, there and then, with every second. Suddenly he felt as ancient as Methuselah. Late post-glacial timescales were not inappropriate. He felt his age was grasping at every cell in every one of his sinews. What could happen next?

Oh! The top, at last. Stop. Sink. Soporific sun. Old Firbeag had collapsed on the ground and drifted into semi-consciousness. Was she talking to someone? Does all the world reach a top at the same time? What was going wrong inside his body? He was quiet, saying nothing. His problem would pass, of course. There was little could be done so many miles from anywhere. He spun out his rest as long as possible. Off and down. At the bealach between the two Deargs he paused and wistfully looked to the west. There was the great rounded hump of Beinn a' Chaisgein Mor. That was the only one left, it was to be his last Corbett!

Time passed and then his body went on strike. Let's call it low level pulmonary oedema when deep bubbling water begins sloshing inside the lungs. This happened in deepest England and at nearly sea level. Essential NHS intensive care service was to hand with injections, pills, tubes, and wires working away.

All thoughts of the Corbett compleation were banished, and even the ascent of a minor bump seemed ruled out. Perhaps it had been tempting fate to have glanced at that Corbett. After all Beinn a' Chaisgein Mor means the *big forbidden hill*. Were the fates trying to tell him something?

Was Old Firbeag finished?

Not yet, and not finally.

Gradually his daily dose of pills controlled his problems and he convinced himself that an attempt on that Last One in the List might be feasible. It was time for a lone expedition into the last great wilderness. Allow a week, spin it out, *n'allez pas trop vite*. Move lightly, wear spare clothes, bivouac out, no stove or pan, eat with mug and spoon, survive on cheese, oatcakes, dried fruit and muesli. Take a mobile phone, but first learn how to use it. Who knows if it would work out in the back of beyond. It would pacify her, she was very sensible, he was trying to emulate her.

The long solstice days of summer arrived. A forecast promised stable fine weather. The car was left at Poolewe, and he unslung his ancient bike from the rack and pedalled slowly up the road that led towards Kernsary farm. Overhanging birch trees wafted the fresh tang of their new leaves across the road. Down the bank the river draining from Loch Maree ran swiftly to the sea. He started to walk and knew it had to be one foot in front of the other until he reached the bothy at Carnmore. The track split at some Scots pines when two walkers appeared. They brought tales of genuine beds waiting to welcome wandering stravaigers at the distant bothy. This was a far cry from its earlier incarnation as a cowshed where once he had slept on a floor littered with dry bracken while the corrugated iron roof resounded to the spatter of falling rain. It had functioned as an adequate refuge with primitive comforts, a base for the routes on the rocks.

As he walked on, the scenery shifted and niggling thoughts plagued his mind. Ranked ribs like drooping teeth scarred Beinn Lair. Had he cheated on that route? Was he justified when a massive chockstone blocked his way up a grime-filled gully. His only way to surmount the obstacle had been to whirl overhead a big Moac nut on a sling until it jammed in a side crack and so provided a hanging looped handhold on which to pull up and over into a bunch of yellow globeflowers growing in the detritus above the chockstone.

With light rain sweeping round the valley sides he skirted under the pale Ghost Slabs and crossed the causeway that separated the lochs of Fionn and Dubh and turned towards the bothy. A curlew with its haunting call lurked in the rush sward of an abandoned field. Two bedraggled cows looked resignedly at the visitor. From the keeper's house came a black barking dog to sniff at Old Firbeag, while the idle fisher folk peered out of their accommodation and waved dismissively. Wet cloud curtains were pushing down the top pitches of Fionn Buttress but he had long accepted that this was a route he would never climb save in his imagination.

Pushing open the door he entered a spacious wasteland. Translucent roof sheets filtered gloomy light onto a rusty row of scrawny iron bedsteads underlain with scuffed plastic sheets covered with deep dunes of dust. His imagination had conjured up a beneficent landowner who provided polished wooden bunks in little dormitories. It had been just a pleasant dream that he had created to while away the long walk in. This reality with the risk of dust asphyxiation would do all right, he thought munching cheese and oatcakes, and prepared for a uncertain night. By morning he expected to be imprinted with the diamond-shaped array of bare bed springs.

The great day of the Last on the List went without fuss or incident. He ambled up a scenic path below the crags, tottered along parallel to the river, and at the high point paused on a soft lichen bed to feed on dried banana. All that remained was a gentle rise towards the summit. Was Beinn a' Chaisgein Mor really superstitiously forbidden? Mountain azalea, white rather than pink, growing underfoot seemed a better omen. Deer unconcernedly grazed nearby, and although his ascent threaded through them his presence was ignored. Slowly he approached the highest point, a cluster of shattered gneiss blocks, and then into view came the magical western coast, its indented sea arms, its ragged peninsulas, so many talons spread like claws across the sea towards the Outer Isles. Ancient basal gneiss pocked with blue lochans fanned to the coast. Perfect conclusion.

His instructions, ring her up: her expectations, answer the phone. I'm on the top, it's the last on my list. Was he pleased, delighted, euphoric? He didn't really know. He had never been here before. How should he feel? Sing a Gloria, leap through heaven, float and dance on sprung turf. No, I've got some tasty sardines, I'll celebrate and eat them.

What now? Why not spend a night with 'the maiden'? Let's do it and consummate delight in the embrace of A' Mhaighdean. Off across the valley and follow the old stalking path below Ruadh Stac Mor to seek out the lost howff nestling at the bealach between the two mountains. Squeezed in a sandwich between big boulders and gaps walled with blocks and turf he found a dark hole into a sunken pit. Old Firbeag dropped his pack within and still a-tingle with his out-of-this-world sensation he wafted up to the top of the Maiden. Golden glowed the fading sunset of the day, far off she dipped towards the lands of Tír na nÓg.

While sitting at home on a winter's evening his achievement began to pall and unravel. For years he had used some tattered photocopied pages with sketch maps of the Corbetts where he conscientiously entered up each successful foray. Later he acquired the Scottish Mountaineering Trust guidebook but he refused to read the relevant account beforehand. Knowing what hill he was about to do would have spoiled the uniqueness of its ascent. He began to transfer all the past ascent details into the guidebook. He read at the descriptions as he wrote and was dumbfounded when on page 177 in the Second Edition, he read:

> 'These two hills have been given the same height by the Ordnance Survey. As the drop between them is only 122m, they cannot both be Corbetts so have to be regarded as Siamese twins or part of a double summited Corbett and are given a unique joint status as one Corbett. Both summits should be visited by a prudent hillwalker to claim the Corbett…'

Gosh, and shock horror! Was he prudent? Did he deign to be a hillwalker? Was he being forced to add on this unwanted bump to his list? Buidhe Bheinn had never featured when years before he had skipped in disintegrating gym shoes over the originally listed summit of Sgurr a' Bhac Chaolais on the South Cluanie Ridge. He had collected with the strict principle that every one of the currently-accredited Corbetts recorded in the book had to be ticked. No cheating, no jacking, no falsifying, and never any doubt whether a top had been honestly attained. The prize was personal satisfaction. Memory would store the many days leading to the successful compleation. Be thankful for the days gone by and ignore the anticlimax when all those days are over.

Old Firbeag slowly realized that he had no option but to attempt to get up Buidhe Bheinn. Firstly he needed a companion for health and safety reasons, even if he was loath to abandon his solo outings. He put the idea to one side and waited for inspiration. Word of his discomfort began to circulate and his grandson made the offer Old Firbeag couldn't refuse. Being young, bold and into cars the lad would just love to roar his pride-and-joy over hill and dale to the head of Loch Hourn. Close to the speed of sound it all happened and Old Firbeag stumbled shakily out of the car and breathed deeply to blow away his nausea and starvation. Up there lost in the cloud awaited that Buidhe Bheinn thing.

It should be no problem to tidy up his personal list. It would work like a charm. He had read the book, studied the map, thought about it, and knew his plan. He failed to know he could fail, and he was about to do so ignominiously. Blame his cockiness and concentration, and the baleful influence of modern technology!

Thus he toiled up the winding path and eventually gained the ridge that led to the top. His grandson was out of contact somewhere up in the clouds. Old Firbeag knew in his brain that the true summit was along another subsidiary ridge that ran northwards to the Cluanie Ridge. A gap in the mist gave a quick glimpse of this marginally higher tooth on the north ridge. Suddenly there was the more concrete form of his grandson perched by a substantial cairn that marked the apex of the three ridges of the mountain.

What was he doing now? Glibly chatting on the phone that now had made contact with the rest of the universe. The conversation concerned the price, specifications, condition and value of a third-rate Astra going cheap in Angus. Old Firbeag was overwhelmed and cleansed of all his senses. The existence of the nearby required Corbett summit escaped from his mind. With the car talk concluded the lad announced he had just time to dash downhill, then drive frantically across Scotland and collect his girlfriend from work. Off downhill they tore and hours later snug in the car Old Firbeag realized the full measure of his incompetence. How could he have been so distracted by trivial dealings and longings conducted from mountain tops by mobile phone?

The secret of his failure soon seeped out, and murmurings of his need to have a final fling were rampant. One of his friends suggested but not in so many words that if the time came when Old Firbeag could summon up his strength then they together could make sure of the tantalising Buidhe Bheinn summit.

They parked the car, crossed the burn flowing into Loch Hourn, and sneaking behind the big house zigzagged up through the eucalyptus grove on to open ground. Old Firbeag made his own pace and toiled slithering on the gravel up the steep path to the bealach. where the electricity pylons marched on towards the Isle of Skye. The cables hummed overhead and talked in whispered megawatts as the power flowed westwards.

The left path was the right path, but all the surface underfoot seemed unused, and if his companion had come this way he had left no trace. Little streams burbled at his side and stretches of soggy flushes alternated with thyme banks. He gained height with the stalkers' path swinging up in gentle curves until it died beside a water-filled pond. Here the garrons must have waited patiently for the stags shot by the big hoose sportsmen. Now he was alone with visibility poor and damp mist penetrating his worn garments. Staggering slightly he threaded a route amidst greasy stones and grassy hummocks. The cairn appeared but offered no relief or sense of achievement. Onward, and alone, as needs be.

Old Firbeag was unaware that somewhere ahead was his companion returning from the topmost point. He went on, continuing into the mist that cloaked everything.

The looming figure clinched the inevitability of imminent success. They met, they turned, they went on.

There was the most insubstantial heap of tiny stones. Here was the climax of the years. They shook hands and raised a faint hurrah in subdued exaltation and then stood in silence, lost in thought.

Mountain-top banality took over.

'You're sure this is it? There is no sign of anyone being here.' Old Firbeag still had some doubts about the validity of calling this the summit.

'Yes, I've looked further on. Nothing feels higher. We've done about the right distance in about the right time.' His companion who had paraded back and forth on the ridge knew what he was talking about.

'Facts, man. It's facts not feelings that win the day.' He was being awkward, but inside he trembled and knew his pilgrimage was over.

'C'mon, what more can you expect of an extended Corbett. It will do. Convince yourself that it's the top. Let's go home, and call it a day.'

'Okay, I'm cold and damp, and I've done it. Yes, DONE IT. Let's go.'

Was this really and truly the end for the Last on the List? Who knows?

FRIENDS IN HIGH PLACES

By Roger Webster and Gareth Williams

PYTHAGORAS was born c. 580BC on the Aegean island of Samos. After years spent travelling, he settled in southern Italy, where he founded a secret brotherhood that believed natural numbers held the key to the universe. This led to number mysticism in which numbers were ascribed special meanings. Thus, one stood for reason, two for opinion, three for harmony, four for justice, five for marriage and six for creation. Today the Lottery and TV shows like 'Deal or No Deal' feed on a culture of lucky numbers.

This fanciful number mysticism led the Pythagoreans to take the first steps in developing number theory, the abstract study of integers, with their early recognition of even, odd, prime, and other types of numbers. An undoubted highlight of their mathematics was the discovery of the pair of numbers **220** and **284**, each of which is the sum of the proper divisors of the other:

$$220 = 1 + 2 + 4 + 71 + 142$$
$$284 = 1 + 2 + 4 + 5 + 10 + 11 + 20 + 22 + 44 + 55 + 110.$$

Such a pair is called **amicable** or friendly. As the number mystics saw it, the numbers 220 and 284, each being composed of the parts of the other, symbolized perfect friendship. Superstition held that two talismans bearing them would seal friendship between their wearers. Indeed, Pythagoras described a friend as *another I such as are 220 and 284*.

The numbers came to take on a mystical aura, playing a role in magic, astrology, sorcery and horoscopes. Even so, commentators failed to find a high profile appearance of this friendliest pair of numbers. All the literature offers is two low profile appearances: Jacob's gift of 220 goats to Esau (Genesis 32:14), seen by some as a secret way of securing friendship, and the testing of their erotic effects by tenth century Arab El Madschriti, who baked confections in the shapes of the two numbers, with a friend eating the smaller number, while he ate the larger, the outcome going unrecorded!

The Munros originated as a list of Scottish mountains over 3000ft first drawn up by Sir Hugh Munro. The first Sassenach to conquer all the Munros (and Tops), John Rooke Corbett†, subsequently drew up a list of Scottish hills between 2500ft and 3000ft which are now known as the Corbetts. Although not acquainted personally, these climbers were

---

† Whilst attending St John's College, Cambridge University, from 1895 to 1898, Corbett walked from Manchester to Cambridge at the beginning of each term, and back again at the end.

kindred spirits in a common quest, who may be poetically described as *friends in high places*, a friendship sealed in Pythagorean lore, for there are 220 Corbetts and 284 Munros.

*

[Now I'm sure there will be some readers who, in the light of recent measurements, will quibble with these figures. But it would be a shame to spoil a good story with an inconvenient fact. In any case, as there seem to be at present 220 Corbetts (with an obligation to include an additional summit as well – see page 307) and 283 Munros, these figures could be regarded as oscillating around amicability!

It was many centuries after Pythagoras before further pairs of amicable numbers were discovered. The Swiss mathematician Leonhard Euler found several dozen pairs of amicable numbers in the eighteenth century, but the second smallest amicable pair (1184 and 1210) was not discovered until 1866 – by a 16-year-old schoolboy, Nicolo Paganini. How many Marilyns are there in Scotland...?   Hon Ed.]

Suilven – John Mitchell

SNAKES AND LADDERS

By Ian Sykes

YOSEMITE TAKES a bit of getting used to. I thought Tuolumne Meadows were in the same valley until we got there to find them a forty-mile drive away, ten as the crow flies – the park's a big place.

We didn't fancy Camp 4 much; it was full of healthy-looking Spanish types with earrings and huge haul sacks, not much in common with us Bus Pass holders. The grub in Curry village was great though, self-service as much as you can eat and a discount for old age pensioners. $16 for the two of us and sadly nobody asked for proof.

Anyway, we stocked up and went to Tuolumne first and climbed on the most immaculate rock – just like the Etive Slabs but bigger, with distant bolts and no greasy bits, and wall-to-wall sunshine.

Brian has a bit of a problem on slabs, his foot and ankle keep dislocating, they go back in okay but the screams at 50ft intervals can be rather disconcerting so I do the slabby pitches and he does the steep stuff. It adds to the excitement!

We had an interesting day on Cathedral Peak. Having failed to find the obvious path through the giant Redwoods, we bushwhacked (American term for rummaging about) our way up through scrub and over slabs, and arrived late at the foot of our climb to discover it was Saturday and the entire population of San Francisco awaiting their turn. We joined the back of the queue and happily followed two nubile Californian girls in tights. Everybody was very friendly though, especially when we told them we were from Scotland. I failed to say I was a Yorkshire man, not wishing to be too boastful. We reached the summit at 6 p.m. and abseiled down into darkness.

'Have you got a torch?' Brian asked.

'No, I thought you had.'

This was all very silly, if we couldn't find the path in broad daylight, how on earth would we manage in pitch darkness? This was going to be exciting. We were still struggling down at around midnight when our luck changed and a bunch of incredulous backpackers with headlights discovered us grubbing about in the woods and in less than five minutes we were dispatched onto the road. We packed our torches after that!

After one or two escapades on the Drug Dome (named after the 1960s culture), we headed back to Yosemite Valley, the plan to climb *Snake Dike*, a classic route on Half Dome. Our intent was to plod up to Little Yosemite and bivvy to save the six-mile, 3000ft walk to the foot of the route. Apparently to do this you needed a Wilderness Permit, very rightly so, the rangers are pretty frugal with these and I spent the next two mornings at 7 a.m. queuing outside their office. At least this got us up early and we filled in the days climbing glorious sun-baked slabs on Glacier Point.

One spends a lot of time sorting food into Bear Boxes in the Valley. Apparently these local inhabitants have an easy way of entering a car; they simply smash the window and tear off the door. Last year that happened to over a thousand cars. We found bear pad marks on our car window and I got very manic about this although I have the suspicion that perhaps one of the Spanish types did this to take the piss!

Having at last found our parking spot and emptied everything into our Bear Box we set out up the valley totally missing the John Muir Trail, the world's largest and most well-signposted footpath, and bushwhacked for a couple of hours before realising that something was wrong and returning to our starting point. I sheepishly asked a couple of tourists the way. After that it was easy, we just followed thousands of backpackers up a tarmacadam trail the same way we had been going but a hundred feet above. The slog up to Little Yosemite was spectacular, following the Merced River, passing under Liberty Cap and the 600ft high Nevada falls. We camped in an idyllic spot under giant Redwoods on the riverbank. During the night something big came snuffling around, I kept my head down, it peed contemptibly against the tent and then shuffled off.

We started early and bushwhacked up to the south face of Half Dome and scrambled up slabs to the foot of the climb. To our surprise a Swiss guide and his client were already there having bivvied at Lost lake. They rapidly vanished into the air never to be seen again. We watched the sun rise and then started up.

Snake Dike is graded US 5.7 R (i.e. about Mild VS). Protection is very poor with long run-outs. There is not much point in taking a lot of gear; you just can't get it in. The original pioneers must have been very bold as some of the pitches have very little protection. After the first two delicate slab pitches traversing around some overlaps you finally get on to the Snake Dike itself. This is a continuous quartz rib running the whole length of the south face. It's rather like the vein on a bald head, you climb up this raised about a foot above the smooth slabs. The holds are adequate but protection is pathetic. Pitch four has a full 165ft run-out with a single bolt at 35ft. A fall here would be spectacular to say the least. There are no ledges, just a couple of belay bolts at long intervals. The view below is what the Americans call 'awesome' with Yosemite Valley some 5000 ft below punctuated on one side with the great wall of El Capitan and facing you Glacier Point with its apron of glorious slabs above a green carpet of giant Redwood trees.

Of course, we got our rope into a tangle at the top of pitch four and lost a good half-hour sorting out the knitting. Meanwhile a host of Californians were racing up the dike behind us. There was nowhere here for overtaking and we were anxious to get a move on. We did pull away in the end and for the next four or five pitches didn't need a guidebook. We just followed the snake as it soared up into the distance. Imperceptibly the angle eased and you begin to wonder if you dare take off the rope. The guide says 'follow the slabs for ever' and that is exactly what happens. On and on you go, slab padding for a knackering thousand feet or so, still following the dike when suddenly the rock dips over and to our amazement we were in a crowd of hundreds of people milling about on the summit.

We lay around for an hour or so basking in the view and wall-to-wall sunshine, chatting to two climbers who had followed us. Strangely the rest had backed off. But the biggest surprise was yet to come; the descent was to prove truly astonishing. A wire ladder dipped over the edge of Half Dome, with wooden slats against the near vertical slabs. A tumult of walkers and backpackers were fighting their way on to this and meeting a similar number coming up. The two meeting masses were struggling past each other at times four to a rung with the brave ones (Japanese?) working up the outside cable. It was far more terrifying than *Snake Dike*. The ladder was about 400ft long and a fall from here would be very serious. I followed a large German gentleman in lederhosen down, frantically hanging on to the cable and hoping if anything happened I would land on him.

I asked one of the Rangers, later that evening, if there were many accidents and he told me cheerfully: 'This has been a good year, we've only lost three so far!'

One has to admire the American spirit, the vast number of people here were inexperienced tourists, and many were seriously overweight and had walked the nine miles and 5000ft of the John Muir Trail to the ladder, nothing was going to stop them climbing the last 400ft to the summit.

Brian and I joined this merry throng and, feeling somewhat self-conscious festooned with ropes and hardware among this cheerful crowd dressed in shorts and cameras, we hobbled our way down to the valley. It had been an unforgettable day, a game in reverse. Up the Snake and down the Ladder.

Top: 'The Snake.' Snake Dyke, 5.7 R. Climber: Ian Sykes. Photo: Ian Sykes Collection
Bottom: 'The Ladder.' The descent off Half Dome. Photo: Ian Sykes Collection

A DAY ON SCUIR-NA-GILLEAN

By Gilbert Thomson

The following article originally appeared in *The Essayist*, a handwritten magazine produced by the Pollokshields Free Church Literary Institute (No.2, 1883–4, 23–32). It describes an ascent of Sgurr nan Gillean on Skye made by Gilbert Thomson, D.O. Croal and local guide John Mackenzie on 27 July 1883. I thank Stuart Pedlar for unearthing this delightful account. **Hon Ed**.

***

Yon northern mountain's pathless brow,
And yonder peak of dread,
That to the evening sun uplifts
The griesly gulfs and slaty rifts,
Which seam its shiver'd head?

Scott

LAST SUMMER the writer & a friend, after much concern to get holidays to suit, set off in the end of July for a trip among the western islands. The plan adopted was to take return tickets for Stornaway by Messrs Macbrayne's steamers, and after enjoying the sail to Stornaway, to drop off at Portree on the homeward passage & see as much of Skye as possible in the five days we had to wait for the next boat.

Loch Coruisk & the Quiraing are the great sights in Skye, & both of these can be seen with only ordinary exertion, but for those who can appreciate stiff work, a climb up Scuir-na-Gillean is an irresistible attraction. This peak is the highest of the Coolin range [now known to be the third highest after Sgurr Alasdair and the Inaccessible Pinnacle], & though only 3220 feet high [overestimated by almost 60ft], its rugged & precipitous sides make it one of the most difficult & even dangerous in Britain. In fact it was thought to be inaccessible till the famous mountaineer Professor Forbes reached the top some fifty years since.

The ascent is made from Sligachan, which we reached on Thursday forenoon. The remainder of that day was devoted to Coruisk, & Friday was fixed for the climb. At first we had an ambitious notion of going without a guide, but everybody advised us to take one, & the result fully proved that we were wise to follow that advice. Skye weather is proverbially uncertain, & when we looked out in the morning, & saw that the mountain was hidden in mist, our fears were not quite removed by the assurances of the natives that we would have a grand day for all that. Breakfast was over about nine, & very soon after we were trudging across the moor, straight for the peak, under the guidance of a sturdy

On Pinnacle Ridge, Sgurr nan Gillean, Skye. Looking back to the Third Pinnacle from Knight's Peak.
Photo: Roger Robb.

Highlander [John Mackenzie]. Each was provided with a stout stick, a field-glass & a pocketful of sandwiches, & it would be difficult to say which of these was most important. For a mile or more we kept to the low ground, scrambling across one or two burns, & splashing through some swamps. Then we began to rise, gradually at first, & with no worse footing than rough grass. The slope soon got steeper, & at the top of it we made our first halt, beside a spring the sight of which in the distance had been urging us on. Here we looked round, & saw Glen Sligachan stretching along beneath us, with the huge bulk of Marscow towering above us on the other side, & the inn & Loch Sligachan at the foot of the glen. But we had no time to stop. A hint from the guide was sufficient to set us off, not over grass now, but over loose shingle, or in scientific language, 'glacial debris'. Of all the substances one may have to climb on, this is about the worst. In the middle of a step the foothold gives way, & down you come. The legs & the patience are equally tried, & the firm rock which follows is an agreeable relief. One gully up which we scrambled reminded us of old Edinburgh days, when we used to climb Arthur's Seat by the 'Gutted Haddie'. Others were filled with large loose stones, beneath which we heard water gurgling down, quite out of reach & only serving to make us feel more thirsty.

Again we stopped & looked round. Marscow was facing us still, but it now seemed an insignificant hill, entirely below us. Evidently we were well up, though we could not yet distinguish the top. 'Now' the guide remarks, 'we'll leave our sticks here'. We had already found them an encumbrance in rock-climbing, & the remaining few hundred feet was all precipitous rock. After some climbing with both hands & feet we stepped on to a peak, but only to see the real summit, a few feet higher, some fifty feet away. To reach it a narrow ridge had to be crossed, & this was done by creeping along in a fashion hardly dignified, but tolerably safe. Then there was a final climb up a rock face 10 or 12 feet high, & at last we were on the top. But the glorious view we expected was gone. We seemed to be in the midst of a hollow sphere of mist. We looked round & saw it curling about the neighbouring peaks; we looked down, & saw it embracing that on which we stood, gleaming with rainbow colours, & concealing the depth of the precipice. The scene was majestic, & afterwards, when the mist cleared away, we felt that we had been specially favoured in seeing this scene of lonely grandeur. We were in no hurry to return, & while waiting, the thought struck us to try the depth of the precipices by dropping stones. On one side of the ridge we had crossed, the depth was about 300 feet, & on the other about 700 feet, to the place where the stones struck first. We left our names in a bottle which lies hidden in the cairn, & which already contained several cards. The guide told us of a party who had reached the lower peak, & dared not cross the ridge, but they sent him over for the bottle, put in their names & then sent him back. We heard that ladies had sometimes reached the top, & though at first we could hardly see how this was possible, a remark from the guide threw some light on it. He had once been up with ladies, he said, & could hardly walk for a week after. 'There should always be two guides for each lady.' It turned out that they were carried over the difficult parts. We both agreed that this would be a splendid honeymoon trip – for the other.

As we sat thus, talking & demolishing our provisions, the mist began to move. It broke for a moment, & we saw the dismal Lotta Corrie – nothing but bare rock & desolation. It closed in, but again it broke, this time toward Glen Sligachan, & gradually it rolled back, giving us a wider & wider sweep, till, except to the west, the horizon was clear. Before, the dismal solitude had been majestic, now the scene was milder, though not less grand. Southwest & south we saw the sea gleaming in the sunlight, broken by the Scuir of Eigg, with the companion islands of Rum and Muich, & by the rocky point of Ardnamurchan. Eastward the Grampians were visible almost to Inverness, while close beneath was the bleak glen, 'compared with which Glencoe is Arcadia'. To the northeast, Portree & the Old Man of Storr were conspicuous. Eagerly our glasses swept round the horizon, & eagerly they were directed westward where MacLeod's Maidens were still hidden. Our patience was rewarded. 'There are the Maidens' cried the guide, & through a momentary rift, 'the Maidens with their breasts of snow' appeared among the waters, – a picture set in a delicate framing of mist. Another moment & it was gone. Again & again we looked round, & feasted our eyes on the grandeur of the scene, & at last we reluctantly commenced the descent. Cautiously we let ourselves down the rocky face to the ridge below, & having crossed this, we thought that the only serious danger was over. We soon had an example of another, while scrambling down a steep gully, with loose stones & precarious footing. The guide was last, the two of us being in advance, one a few yards below the other. 'Look out.' A stone had rolled from the feet of the second, straight for the leader. There was no room to dodge, the stone was too heavy to catch, all that could be done was to punt it aside as it came within reach. This just succeeded & no more, the only damage being a bruised finger nail. Our sticks were soon picked up, and gradually Marscow began to tower above us again, as we got lower & lower. A long halt was made beside a stream of icy water, & about three o'clock we got to the inn.

A dip in Loch Sligachan, then dinner & a quiet stroll in the evening, filled up the day, & before long, instead of the mountain breezes, we were breathing the smoky atmosphere of Glasgow, but looking forward to the time in some future year, when we hope again to stand on the top of Scuir-na-Gillean.

THE GREATER TRAVERSE – REMEMBERING THE IMMORTALS

By Helen Forde

ON THE 11 June 1939 two young men completed the first Greater Traverse of the Skye Cuillin. It is now seventy years after that well planned and executed event in mountaineering history, which led Ben Humble to declaim that they were now among the immortals in the climbing world. One of these men was Ian Charleson PP SMC and the other, Woodhurst Edward Forde SMC, was my father.

I have only childhood memories of my father and would like to have known him better but this was not to be. Events which touched millions and overturned the lives of so many families occurred on 3 September 1939 when World War II was declared. Two days later on 5 September the supremely fit, twenty-eight year old conqueror of the Cuillin, W.E. Forde joined up to serve with the Royal Engineers. As thousands of families of that era found out, the man who left was not the man who returned. I would like to celebrate the 70th anniversary of the first completion by attempting to recreate the spirit of my father's life before, during and after those hours on the Scottish Alps which must have been, for him, a defining personal achievement.

George Square, Edinburgh, in 1918 was an interesting place for a boy to grow up: vast rooms, other children to play with in the central gardens and the comprehensive Carnegie Library nearby. As an avid reader, especially on the topics of exploration, climbing and adventure, he used all the family library tickets and carried the books back in an old Gladstone bag. *Scott of the Antarctic* was a great favourite. Encouraged by reading Whymper's *Scrambles in the Alps* led to trying out a mantel-shelf problem.

To achieve success in this daring venture required that the conditions should be perfect – no onlookers, a good foothold, a clear mantelshelf and a slight physique. He was certainly small, his preparations were comprehensive, but the objective still loomed above him cold and massive. He launched his body upwards, feet scrabbling searching for toeholds. Now the problem he had read about presented itself – a knee on to the shelf which was fortunately wide and thick and finally he stood upright. Standing on top of a marble Adam mantelpiece, Woodhurst Edward Forde, aged seven, had successfully completed his first rock climb.

An annual Sports Day was held on the track that ran around the George Square gardens and Teddy took part. One year he was mortified at being beaten by a girl so he started training. The track was used by

University students, one of whom regularly overtook my father but slowed down to give him encouragement giving gave him the opportunity to say, in later years, that he had trained with Eric Liddell. Dreams of climbing in the Alps or the Himalaya led to literally saving up pennies. The University used live mice for research and would pay a penny for each specimen. The Georgian houses were rich in mice and Teddy's mother would pay him a penny for each dead animal. Using ingenuity, my father started breeding them in the huge empty attics and the savings grew – much as the mouse population did, one surmises.

New interests arose, such as Scouts, and my father became the youngest Cub Scout leader in Scotland and also OTC at school meant a wider world beckoned, especially the great outdoors. With long cycling trips and wild camping, the pull of the hills was strong. Every New Year was always celebrated by expeditions, one of the more memorable being a cycle from Edinburgh to Brig o' Turk youth hostel 'Craig Dhu', with a snowy climb up Ben Venue the following day then returning for a meal at night. Busy with pots and pans, the jovial crowd was aware of an unidentified strong smell and opened all the lids to find its source; then someone opened the oven and a vast cloud of stinking smoke belched into the room. When it cleared, the oven door fell off to reveal about a dozen pairs of boots and shoes and as many socks glowing redly in the depths. A poker was used to identify the remains; there was horrified silence then laughter broke the tension. Next morning was wet and people set off for home in slippers and sandals, no doubt the story passing into hostelling lore.

My father joined the Edinburgh JMCS and his mountaineering exploits are well described in the 2002 Journal in *The Boys from Edinburgh* – a group photograph shows Ted Forde at one end and Ian Charleson at the other. I have archive material of an impressive 50 Munro ascent 3–13 June 1934, and postcards from my mother written home to Edinburgh that prove she too was very much involved in the strenuous days which spanned the Aonach Eagach, An Teallach, Beinn Eighe, Beinn Alligin, Liathach and finally Skye.

But the big expedition to Skye was years in the planning, involving secrecy, strategy and strength. In 1938 when Humble was climbing in Zermatt with Ian Charleson, training for the Matterhorn traverse, the talk turned to the Cuillin – as it always will do, even in the great Alps; Ian pointing out that the ridge plus Blaven and Clach Glas had never been done and, although nothing was said openly, Humble was not too surprised when a postcard arrived from Sligachan the following June announcing their triumph. In one way the record by Charleson and Forde will never be beaten for they carried with them a full-size alarm clock and set it whenever they sat down to rest in case they fell asleep. To beat that record a party would have to do the Greater Traverse carrying with them a grandfather clock. I wonder if W.H. Murray ever considered that, when he made his attempt in August 1939?

Ian Charleson described their outing in that November's SMC Journal (*SMCJ*, XXII, 127-32), and my father wrote the following account which appeared in two parts in the *Weekly Scotsman* on 12 and 19 August 1939.

The Black Cuillin
Record climb of 14,000 feet in a Day
By Woodhurst E Forde

The Black Cuillin of Skye are unique amongst Scottish hill masses both in their geological structure and in the close relationship between each peak and its neighbours. They consist roughly of a long serrated and sharply defined ridge of some eighteen major peaks and numerous outlying ridges often terminating in or consisting of subsidiary peaks which form a series of corries, unsurpassed in their black grandeur and in the steepness of their bounding walls.

There are two types of what might be called 'hill enjoyment' in which the enthusiastic climber may indulge – firstly scrambling of every degree of severity over the finest and soundest rock in the world, in gullies and chimneys, on faces and buttresses that provide a variety of problems to suit every taste and technique; secondly, ridge-walking, which in fine weather will raise the climber's soul to the immortals and give him for ever pictures of enchanted isles floating 'twixt sea and sky and will lead him too when the mists come swirling over the ridges and the wind whistles amongst the corries to a sympathetic understanding of the Isleman's belief in water-kelpies and the little folk.

Many years ago, two prominent Scottish mountaineers hit on the brilliant idea of making a complete traverse of the whole long ridge in one day and setting out very, very early one June morning in 1911, duly completed their expedition. They penned such a glorious description of this 'tour de force' that as the years rolled by, other climbers followed in their wake until the traverse became the culminating point of the Cuillin ridge-walker's career.

A bold venture

A friend and I, after several seasons' climbing on these hills, felt that our knowledge, experience, and fitness might allow us to join that select band which, starting with Shadbolt and Maclaren, contains such 'well-kent' names as Somervell, Bell, and Smythe. In our minds there was a germ of an idea planted by the Scottish Mountaineering Club Guide Book and fostered by remarks appearing in articles and lectures. The idea was that we should include the kindred peaks of Clach Glas and Blaven in the day's climbing.

These two hills are of the same geological structure as the peaks of the main ridge and have the same characteristic appearance. (They are composed principally of gabbro intersected with basalt dykes which, due to their different rate of 'weathering', form ledges or gullies depending on the angle at which they occur.) This venture, therefore, if successful would mean the ascending of all the Black Cuillin peaks within twenty-four hours, a thing which had never been done before.

We talked it over doubtfully for months always wondering at our own temerity in entertaining the idea of adding well over 3000ft of extra ascent to the already great total of some 10,000ft which the complete ridge climb is reputed to reach. We went on with our plans however (sometimes laughing at ourselves for ambitious fools), took as much exercise as possible to toughen our city-softened frames, and said nothing to anybody.

Our preparations became colossal; we looked with dismay at the growing volume of equipment and food that seemed the minimum necessary to the venture, we shuddered at the thought of what might happen to the little old car which was to carry this immense load over the bumpy Skye roads, we thought of the dismal failure the whole thing might prove to be, but we persisted.

Small tent pitched

We planned to carry out the project from camps and our first step was to pitch a small tent near the mouth of Harta Corrie and almost immediately below the eastern shoulder of Sgurr na h-Uamha. This tent was equipped with sleeping bags, spare clothes, food, primus stove, and cooking utensils. Its purpose was two-fold; it was strategically placed to provide us with a good meal under cover after the descent from Sgurr na h-Uamha and before setting off across the moor to the other hills; it would also be waiting for us after the day's journey was over and would save us the ordeal of marching the many weary miles to the nearest habitation.

Our next step was the dumping of little caches of food and drink in easily-remembered crannies on the ridge. The food was chosen for its energy-giving value and its ease of assimilation; the sites were picked as being the points we hoped to reach for the appropriate meals.

Having increased our fitness by five days scrambling in very mixed weather, which worried us not a little by its unpredictability, we prepared a load which represented another complete set of camping equipment. With this, two smaller rucksacks for the day's climbing and a new 100-foot length of Alpine line forming our loads, we left Glen Brittle shortly after mid-day on Sunday and found a fair camping site near the foot of Gars Bheinn, the most southerly peak of the ridge.

I must confess to a feeling of nervous excitement, which my companion's imperturbability did much to subdue. Yet, instead of sleeping as had been hoped and anticipated, we lay smoking and chatting desultorily while we gazed out over the most glorious view I have ever seen through a tent door. Just across a narrow strait lay the small, low island of Soay, while the further seas were dotted with other isle; Eigg looking almost grotesque with its queer-shaped sgurr; Rhum, that noble prince of the Inner Hebrides, supporting on its sharp and savage mountains the whitest, fluffiest and most peaceful cloud one could possibly imagine; ordinary looking Muck and a host of others that we could not identify, so great were the distances we could see.

Winter clothing

We rose at 12.15am, had a good meal, and secured the tent with heavy stones to prevent it being blown away by the strong and gusty wind. At 1.30 we started climbing, forcing ourselves to the slow pace we intended holding to all day. We ascended steadily and were surprised to find the cushions of moss, usually soft and wet, now crisply frozen. This low temperature, coupled with the strong wind which persisted all day, made us very grateful for the winter clothing which we wore; Balaclava helmets, woollen gloves and Grenfell windbreakers did no more than keep us comfortably warm.

The first few tops provide no real rock work though we had to be very careful to guard against being overbalanced on these narrow edges by the keen and blustery gale. Even thus early in the morning we were enjoying magnificent views; almost all the hills were standing out clearly in silhouette against the light of the northern sky; the islands to the south appeared ghostly and sleeping while ever and anon a distant lighthouse flashed its warning beam. Down below us on our right lay the pale sheen of Loch Coruisk, but on our left the wee lochans in the high corries gloomed blackly.

After traversing three tops we were confronted by the first problem – the crossing of the Thearlaich–Dubh Gap, a cleft in the ridge with vertical rock walls giving two short but interesting climbs, one down into the gap and the other up and out. We roped up and crossed without difficulty. We then scrambled rapidly over the next two peaks, one of which, Sgurr Alasdair, is the highest of the Cuillin, and were astonished to find that snow was not only falling but actually lying, and that many of the rocks were varnished with ice – and this was the sunny month of June.

King's Chimney

The next obstacle to our progress was King's Chimney, which leads from the Thearlaich–Mhic Choinnich col to the summit of Sgurr Mhic Choinnich. We enjoyed this climb for two reasons; it was sheltered from the cold wind and gave us a chance to have a hasty snack at its foot in some comfort, and it is so steep and delightful as to give mental fillip that urges one on with renewed zest. Another hour of up and down work took us to the foot of the 'Inaccessible Pinnacle' which we traversed rapidly and easily during a temporary lull in the wind.

This burst of speed was not unconnected with a sudden realisation that out first cache of food was waiting for us at the foot of the short side of the pinnacle. The mere thought of cheese, dates, 'hard tack' biscuits, chocolate and oranges had acted almost as powerfully as the food itself. The time was 8.30am, the weather still cold and windy, though any mist blowing over the tops was dry and caused us no inconvenience. Our appetites were good, but we would have dearly loved even a quarter of an hour of the sunshine that we could see shining entrancingly and tantalisingly 3000ft below on Loch Brittle, making a dazzling speck of the white motor boat that calls every morning from the Isle of Soay to take Glen Brittle visitors to Rhum, Coruisk, or wherever they please.

But we could not endure the cold long and in 30 minutes' time we were clattering down loose rocks and scree towards Sgurr na Banachdich, where we each endeavoured to take a photograph of our 'snow-man' appearance in the sudden flurry of flakes that was quickly obscuring the nail scratches we were, sheepishly, using as a trail. That day, as often before, we compared our progress over well known and frequently used routes with that of the pioneers to whom every new peak meant a new problem in route finding as well as rock-climbing.

Sgurr Thormaid and Sgurr a' Ghreadaidh were passed quickly, with no stop other than that necessary for the noting down of the times and weather condition, and we were both pleased to reach Sgurr a' Mhadaidh, where we anticipated some good scrambling on the numerous short but steep basalt pitches with which this many-topped hill abounds.

(II) Success Comes as Hands near Midnight

I would point out that one of the charms of the Sgurr a' Mhadaidh ridge traverse lies in the amount of 'climbing down' on moderately difficult rocks which gives it every claim to be considered a first-class mountaineering expedition.

We were grateful that the clouds were off the hills at this juncture, as the ridge, normally fairly consistent in its general trend, twists in such a way, that, in our opinion, the erection of a couple of R.A.C. 'bend' signs is almost a necessity! Our pleasure in the scrambling was becoming rather marred by the rapid wear making itself evident on our clothing; my companion's special climbing breeches, for example, were developing a decidedly hairy appearance due to his liking for a technique often used in negotiating chimneys and sloping slabs, when descending. My almost new woollen gloves were becoming singularly adapted to the type of climbing we were encountering; when walking I could, by shutting my hands, benefit by the heat of the wool, but when climbing, my fingers stuck through the numerous holes and gave me the confidence of flesh to rock contact.

To return from this digression. We duly traversed Sgurr a' Mhadaidh and, after an uneventful descent and ascent, reached the top of Bidein Druim nan Ramh. Our great concentration on the summit of this peak was responsible for the paucity of our mental images of this section. We were once again full of the thought of food, for food and drink in plenty were lying in wait for us in a cleft in the cairn. We hastily pulled away the stones and moss, reached in for the tin and then the bottle, only to discover to our immense chagrin that some previous frost had cracked the over-full bottle and there was not a drop of liquid left. It made us doubly careful of the meagre supply in our 1 litre Alpine flask which had been giving us a refreshing mouthful from time to time; it also turned our slight annoyance at the coldness of the day into a feeling of relief that this was not one of the blistering spells that at times makes the ridge as dry and thirsty a place as one could imagine.

An Casteal

Having satisfied our hunger and discovered a slight but only temporary stiffness through sitting in a humped-up attitude in the lee of the cairn, we pushed on to An Caisteal (the castle) whose gully-seamed faces meet in a narrow, and in places, deeply cleft ridge. A long-legged climber can easily step across the top of these 30-odd-feet deep cracks, but a smaller or less experienced man might prefer to scramble down a bit before crossing.

We had a brief discussion on the next little excrescence (which name is better suited than the word 'peak' for some of the lesser projections on the ridge.) The Gaelic name is Sgurr na Bairnich (hill of the limpets) and our opinions differed as to whether this was based on its very conical shape when seen from below or because of the extraordinarily tenacious grip of the rocks on our aforementioned badly worn clothing. The former we decided to be the more probable, as most of these hills were named long before any recorded ascents had been made.

For many hours past I had been looking forward to reaching Bruach na Frithe – not on account of any good climbing or views, not even for that gross but pleasant reason, food; but because I felt that if we reached that hill in a reasonable fit state we could allow some optimism to colour our hopes. We could feel fairly certain of finishing the main ridge satisfactorily and then – our thoughts unbounded rose – we might (we still said 'might') be able to have a stab at the other hills.

We reached the top in good fettle and pushed on with scarcely a pause towards Sgurr a' Fionn Choire, which summit we treated shamefully, bestowing on the cairn no more than a hasty pat in passing, for finer game was in sight, the Bhasteir Tooth with that delightful tit-bit, Naismith's route, to relieve our jaded appetite – jaded, that is, for rocks.

Boots Off

We climbed singly over the lower easy part and then worked about with our rope for some time on the satisfactorily broad ledge below the final and most difficult section. The leader decided that his rucksack was the best place for his beautiful new boots, more out of consideration for the rock than anything else, so he took them off, left them and his rucksack in his second's care and nimbly skipped up the climb. Then, in encouragement to the overloaded second, he pronounced the verdict 'Easy, nothing to it.' The second, feeling like a Himalayan porter, struggled up, carefully nursing his sacred burden. I had forgotten to mention that among the cameras, food and clothing was a life-size alarm clock, in case we felt in need of a sleep at any time.

Passing rapidly over Am Basteir and proceeding thence to the bealach, we were soon on that thoroughly sporting western ridge of Sgurr nan Gillean, the only two outstanding pitches being a short and interesting chimney and the famous 'Gendarme'. The top itself called for a short halt and a hasty snack before, swinging round and travelling in almost the opposite direction to that taken in the morning, we set off for Sgurr Beag and Sgurr na h-Uamha, which lay conveniently south of Sgurr nan Gillean and therefore more or less in the direction of our second tent. Sgurr Beag we took in our stride, but Sgurr na h-Uamha surprised us by being both steeper and higher than it had appeared from the distance.

On the long easy descent to our tent we had ample time for consideration and reflection. We were able to sum up our condition and the possibilities of completing our task. They did not seem good; we were both tired and we both had sufficient grounding in the code of the mountaineer to realise the folly of attempting the ascent of any hill and particularly a Cuillin peak in misty weather, late in the evening, and in an exhausted state.

Returning Energy

We talked it over and agreed to postpone our decision until we had had a good meal and a rest. We allowed ourselves an hour and a quarter for these important matters and were agreeably surprised at our returning energy and enthusiasm. We fed with gusto and stretched our bodies luxuriously inside our little tent; we concentrated our attention on sweet and fruity stuffs with gratifying results.

We walked right sprightly along the path along the path round the foot of Ruad Stac and kept a steady pace up the grass and heather below Clach Glas. We slowed down a lot on the scree we encountered on the last few hundred feet, and I think that, for the first time, we were able to appreciate to some small degree the amount of will-power and spirit required of the man who goes high on Everest.

Our flagging energies returned in amazing fashion when we reached the rocks and we, in real truth, enjoyed our scrambling to the full. Our hopes rose high as we munched a quick snack of oranges and chocolate by the cairn of Clach Glas, for we suddenly saw through a break in the mist the huge bulk of Blaven; we felt cheered right through. Cautiously we climbed down to the bealach and set off on the last lap. Steadily we worked our way round and up by a peculiar diagonal fault on the eastern face. Soon we were on the final slopes, but there was no quick dash for the summit. We wanted to reach our goal but also to find a safe and easy descent on the north-west face. We knew it was there, but amongst the multitude of gullies the easy, safe one was hard to find in the mist and approaching darkness. Our sense of relief on finding it was immense and we advanced rapidly, bagged the first summit and seven minutes later the second. We had succeeded; the time was 11.12pm. We shook hands.

My thoughts on the descent were concentrated on every form of luscious and indigestible food, on the joys of sleep and seeming everlastingness of the stone shoot we were running down. We drank deep from every burn we passed, no thoughts of training to disturb us now; we sleep-walked along the track; we plumped down in our tent and slept with all our clothes on; we woke and fed at intervals and blethered unimaginable nonsense to each other, but we didn't realise till days later how tired we really were.

It had been a glorious expedition, and we felt deeply thankful at having been able to complete it.

* * *

And afterwards? In 1945, my father, who was by now an acting major, was in France in a scout car which went in front of the so called 'silly tanks' which were especially designed to flail the ground and blow up land mines before the British infantry advanced. His car was blown up but he amazingly survived, unconscious for three weeks in a Belgian hospital, then sent back to Scotland. His injuries healed but he would never climb again. He returned to his family, wife Grace, son Iain and baby Helen, a very different man from the Teddy Forde who sang with sheer joy when ascending the *King's Chimney* on the Cuillin six years before. He did stay in Edinburgh with us for a while and I found that an immortal in the climbing world is rather a hard act to follow especially when you are only four years old and toiling up behind him on your first Munro.

He eventually left to go to New Zealand and took his ice axe with him for no reason other than sentiment. He died in November 1990 and the axe was sent back to me, which I am not ashamed to say caused some tears of regret that we were never able to talk of blue remembered hills, where he went and cannot come again.

BLACK CUILLIN – RED HILLS TRAVERSE

A number of remarkable Cuillin outings have been made over the years since Charleson and Forde pioneered their route in 1939. While the Greater Traverse will never perhaps be regarded as 'an easy day for a lady', some hill runners now include it as part of an even bigger round. After much arm-twisting by the Hon Ed, Mark Shaw jotted down these notes about his solo outing on 21 July 2002.

By Mark Shaw

JANUARY 2002 began very quietly for me with no climbing or running. It was a very wet month and my many working hours were spent on the large roof of a house we were helping to build. There was no forklift on the job and for fear of developing a lopsided physique I swapped shoulders each time I carried slates up the ladder onto the scaffold.

February came and we made some progress on the hill with two new winter climbs on Ben Cruachan, *Thompson's Route* on the Ben, and two more first ascents on Skye. March saw the block work finished on the house, more wheelbarrowing and ladder climbing interspersed with days on *Orion Direct* and *Rubicon Wall*. April arrived with lots of scaffolding and rendering, also *Smith's Route* and a good run over the Etive hills. May and June also brought great hill adventures such as an 8hr traverse of the Reds Hills and Bla Bheinn, a 12hr hilly weekend in the Island Peaks Race, a sub-4hr Jura race, the Lowe Alpine Mountain Marathon in the Trossachs, followed by a sub-4hr Highland Cross.

We had arranged to drive to Skye for the Glamaig hill race on 20 July, but by this time I was beginning to think about attempting a bigger challenge instead. In the week before the race I was concreting and manoeuvring materials into place for another house. I took Friday off for a rest, and headed for the Misty Isle with the intention of only watching the race and taking in Glamaig on the following day as part of a bigger round. I decided on Camasunary bothy as a starting/finishing point for an attempt on the Greater Traverse, and, if going well, I'd try to include Glamaig, the Deargs, Marsco, and Garbh-bheinn as well.

I set off at 3.05 a.m. and took the coastal path via the Bad Step to the Coruisk hut. A climb south-west from Loch na Cuilce took me to the summit of Gars-bheinn by 5.25 a.m. After an hour of progress on the ridge I had reached Sgurr Dubh Mor. Approaching the T-D gap at 6.45 a.m. I realised the rock would be cold and possibly still damp so I decided to bypass it on the Coir' a' Ghrunnda side before continuing up Sgurr Alasdair.

King's Chimney was cold on the fingers but in a few minutes led me onto Sgurr Mhic Choinnich. I passed An Stac and climbed the east ridge of the In Pinn. Climbing it I remembered a previous ridge traverse when

I'd suddenly appeared on top of the pinnacle to an audience of a dozen people sitting below on Sgurr Dearg. One of the group asked 'Why is he climbing down that way?' No one answered as they silently watched me downclimb the short side. As soon as I was down they gave me a round of applause. On this occasion it was 8 o'clock, much earlier in the day than before, and with nobody around I climbed back down the long side.

Another 3hrs of ridge and I was starting to think about the Tooth which could possibly, I thought, be wet. Again remembering a previous traverse, I had been aware of two people coming onto the ridge just west of the Tooth as I was climbing *Naismith's Route* unroped. I overheard one saying to the other 'That guy's got a serious head problem!', which wasn't really very encouraging and I definitely didn't get a round of applause from them. But today I opted for skirting below *Shadbolt's Chimney* (one of our winter ascents in February), and climbing up the east ridge of Am Basteir. I took the west ridge onto Sgurr nan Gillean and descended the south-east ridge.

I now had a lot of work to do getting across to and up Glamaig. Once in Glen Sligachan I headed north until I was close to the road before crossing the river and climbing to a pool in the Allt Daraich for a refreshing orange, a dip, and a short rest.

Then off up Glamaig from where I could see the remaining six hills stretching away to the south of me. The main difficulties ahead lay in the Black Cuillin peaks – the tower of Clach Glas, the exposed descent of the Impostor and the 18m chimney on the way up Bla Bheinn. In 5hrs time I would be making the final descent to the bothy.

Things couldn't have gone much better. Although the weather had been wet on Friday night, Saturday morning had brought fresh northerly winds and sunshine. On the day it stayed dry with dark, high cloud making cool conditions until mid-afternoon. The wind had turned south-west in the morning and was very light. Cloud closed in on the main ridge by 6.00 p.m., but Bla Bheinn remained clear until after the final descent to the bothy – where friends were waiting. Managed to dodge the rain too, but only just. Down it came at 9.30 p.m. as we were reaching the car on the Elgol road after the walk out from Camasunary.

Camasunary	3.05 a.m.	Bruach na Frithe	11.14 a.m.
Gars-bheinn	5.25 a.m.	Am Basteir	11.38 a.m.
Sgurr nan Eag	5.51 a.m.	Sg. nan Gillean	12.08 p.m.
Sgurr Dubh Mor	6.28 a.m.	Glamaig	2.33 p.m.
Sgurr Alasdair	7.06 a.m.	Beinn Dearg Mhor	3.11 p.m.
Sgurr Mhic Ch.	7.32 a.m.	Beinn Dearg Mhead.	3.34 p.m.
In Pinn	8.08 a.m.	Marsco	4.36 p.m.
Sg. na Banachdich	8.45 a.m.	Garbh-bheinn	5.42 p.m.
Sg. a' Ghreadaidh	9.14 a.m.	Clach Glas	6.21 p.m.
Sg. a' Mhadaidh	9.32 a.m.	Bla Bheinn	7.14 p.m.
Bidein D n R.	10.10 a.m.	Camasunary	7.51 p.m.

BURIED TREASURE

By P.J. Biggar

'We must away ere break of day
To seek the pale enchanted gold.'

J.R.R. Tolkien

OUT OF THE darkening corrie below my feet thin wisps of pink vapour like the breath of a sleeping dragon crept ever so slowly up towards us. The summit breezes were starting to blow and there was just a touch of spindrift lifting from the ridge. Since early morning we had toiled in sunlit perfection up icy slopes, down rocky gaps, even over the crest of Knight's Peak, never too exacting but always with the sense that the mountain was saving the hardest bits for last. And the daylight could not be stretched out for ever.

I had failed on this route before. I remembered a jammed rope, soggy snowfields in the mist and tramping back over endless moorland with Phil Gribbon. I had climbed with Phil for thirty years, but Roger Robb and I had never climbed together, unless one counts the indoor wall.

I looked back. Roger was watching attentively, hunched against his boulder, white hair just visible below his helmet, fringing a weather-beaten face with sharp eyes. He had sized me up for several weeks on the climbing wall before suggesting that we might do a route together. Now I knew he was very fit and a good, steady climber. What did he know about me? I didn't want to let him down again, for the last pitch had been a mess: Roger, going well, had tackled the rocky crest direct; the only trouble was that his runner had come out meaning that if I slipped I would take a swing. I had tried to follow by climbing a snow-choked runnel below the ridge but the snow was rotten and, of course, the rope snagged on rocks. I was hot and bothered when I got to Roger, but he had been nice about it and we had swapped food and considered our position calmly.

'Slowly, slowly,' he said. 'We'll get there. This is the face of Gillean itself. We're not so far away.'

The notch I was trying to climb out of was steep and slabby. Above me Sgurr nan Gillean towered into the sunset. Away to my right were the jagged rocks of the West Ridge with tendrils of dragon breath wreathing round them. My crampons made horrible noises on the rock as I tried to edge my way to the right and my picks found only a smear of frozen snow.

'No good this way, I'll have to go left.'

Now that I looked more closely to the left, there was a sort of shallow scoop in the rock with a bollard near its base. Perhaps I could wangle a sling round it? Standing on awkward footholds I struggled and struggled with a piece of tape. It went down about an inch below the rear surface of the bollard. I grunted to myself. Roger made no sound; he just let me concentrate on the move.

I weighted the insecure tape with superfluous metal-ware and took some deep breaths. If only I could get a foot onto the bollard I might have a chance. I looked behind me at the plunge to the snowfields below and I didn't look again. My first attempt was no good. Failure loomed large.

'Come on, come on!' I even encouraged myself out loud. Still Roger said nothing while the hillside was darkening and the breeze finding chinks in our armour.

When I stood on the bollard at last I almost wished I hadn't, but the thinnest of thin ledges snaked out towards the left. Trying to move with the precision of a cat, claws tucked behind tiny nodules of ice-crust I edged along, one paw at a time, over the creaking surface. Would the little snowfield beyond the slabs be a snare or a saviour? Either way there was no going back. Then my left axe bit deep into snow-ice ('Thank the Lord!') and several moves followed in quick succession.

'Are you on better material now?' Roger called, the prosaic question perhaps disguising his anxiety at my slowness. I reassured him.

Utterly spent, I collapsed in a cave-like recess under steep walls at the top of the snowfield. The belay was excellent. I couldn't see what lay ahead and I didn't care very much either. It was Roger's problem.

My day had begun at 4.30 in Kessock, creeping about the sleeping house. I had followed Roger's directions easily and picked him up in Dingwall at 6. By 8.30 we were crunching off over the frozen moor by Sligachan, relishing the stillness of the air and the silence, a skin of ice across the lochans and the Cuillin white and jagged above us. We met a lone photographer coming back down the path after capturing the sunrise. He wore old-fashioned tweeds and seemed to belong to a different age.

'Is the pace all right for you?' Roger said. 'I could go faster,' he added, 'but I'm certainly not going to.' I could see he liked to be in front and that suited me fine; it left my mind free to wander.

The rope came in slowly, slowly. For quite a long time it stopped and nothing much happened and then it came in again, even slower. I felt pleased. My backside was getting cold sitting in my little cave, but inwardly I was smiling. My thoughts went back to earlier in the day.

We had left the sun for the cold shade at the foot of the ridge and traversed round to the gully between the first and second pinnacles. The snow was good and we had climbed back into the sunlight. It was a feature of our day that the hard climbing was mainly done in cold shade. We had roped up for the steep pitch near the top of the third pinnacle. Roger led it fast. I could see he was good.

Abseiling off the third pinnacle in winter is intimidating because of the situation. We were climbing on a single 9mm rope to reduce weight and this just gave us enough to reach the middle of the lower chimney. I watched anxiously as Roger descended into the shadows on the northern side, his crampons scratching and slipping on the rock.

Phil and I had failed at the abseil, but this time, with one little tug, the rope slid down to us. Perhaps the magic doors were opening?

A dark figure appeared below me on the snowfield and climbed steadily up.

'That was a good lead,' he said. 'It was quite awkward wasn't it?' he added.

'It was, a bit,' I said, glowing inside but trying not to show it.

'Where does it go now?'

'I think it's round the corner.'

'Did you see the eagle?'

'No, was there an eagle?'

'Aye, it came right across the ridge just as you were on that slab. Its feathers looked really gold.'

He seized some gear and vanished upwards. There wasn't much daylight left. Another long wait began.

Skye, for me, has always had a special kind of smell. I become conscious of it as soon as I get to Kyleakin. I think it has to do with peat smoke, but maybe there are other factors too. Now, looking out over the dark moors below the snowline, I fancied I could catch the peat reek. I thought of my mother sitting in her house at Torvaig in her last years, looking out over the sound of Raasay. That room, full of old books and ancient furniture, had the same scent, but magnified.

'And have you been doing much climbing?' she would ask. 'Your father was always off to the hill. It runs in the family like wooden legs.' And she would smile.

The rope was going out, but not fast. I could hear faint clinks and clanks from above. Some grim struggle was going on. Perhaps the dragon was stirring? Its breath was icy. I was starting to shiver.

I thought I had led the crux, and maybe it was a crux of sorts for me, but as I followed the distant shout round the rock wall and into a narrowing gully, I became all too aware that there was no cause yet for celebration. The chimney which followed bristled with cunningly-placed dwarfish gear. As he pressed upwards, Roger discovered that the steepest way was the way to avoid benightment. His diary gives a flavour of it:

'...following a trace of steps to the foot of a rising stepped corner [I] placed a runner at the start of what would be the hardest pitch of the climb. On steepening ground [I] climbed another corner on fortunately good snow-ice, getting good axe placements to get over the difficulties.

Further steep snow-ice led to the foot of another corner with a good runner position. Awkward moves out of the corner led onto further steep snow-ice [I found] a belay with only 5 or 10 feet of rope left. Quite a pitch.'

One move sticks out in my mind: I had to enter a slender vertical fissure. There was no material at its back. My placements were wobbling. I glanced beseechingly upwards.

'I think,' said Roger, 'I wedged a boot right across that.' He smiled as if instructing some callow apprentice on the oil rigs. 'Can you hold it there a moment while I take a photo?'

A few more tense strenuous moves and I gained a position where success was assured. Relief flooded through me.

'Great lead!' I roared. 'That was good IV!'

'Did you think so?' He looked mildly surprised, but I think he was pleased.

I grabbed some slings and hurried on up easier snow slopes which were turning pink towards a little rocky gap like a missing dorsal spine in Gillean's West Ridge.

'That's a good belay,' said Roger passing the rope round the summit cairn, 'I'll just use the last of the light to take a few photographs.' Our delight was considerable. We even spared a thought for our regular partners: 'Peter MacDonald will be spitting nails!' Roger chuckled.

'Barry's face will be a picture!'

The scene was worth recording: a darkening sky with strange bright blue patches; silver light behind savage ridges and pink vapour rising in fantastical patterns from deep cauldrons, all the drama of the old serpent twisting its way from Gars Bheinn to Gillean. We felt so privileged just to be there at that moment. But the dragon was stirring in his sleep and dreaming of human eyes feasting on his treasure. His snorting breath drove stinging particles into our faces.

'Are you getting cold?' said Roger. We had worn only light fleeces all day, now it was time to rummage in frosty sacks for something better.

Virgil says the way down is easy, but he means morally. Night was upon us and clouds were stealing up the hillsides. Roger set off first down the South-East Ridge and I stumbled along in the rear bringing the rope up taut at every difficulty. He guided us with ease on ground he knew better than me.

'Are you all right?…Are you all right?' echoed cheerfully up from the hunched figure below.

'Are *you* all right?' I responded eventually.

'Sorry,' he grinned, 'was I fussing too much?'

Slithery slabs were slid down, fearful drops avoided – mercifully obscured by the dark – and the last steep wall negotiated. Looking back we could see that a thick cloud had descended on the summit. A strong breeze had sprung up, it was very cold. We threw down our sacks and felt about for food and drink. Our world contracted into pools of torchlight on the snow.

'I could eat a scabby horse between two dirty mattresses!' said Roger, but I discovered that he never ate cheese or dark chocolate. You find out all sorts of interesting things about the people you climb with. As we made our way over the many boulders which litter the corrie and then down the glassy paths back to Sligachan, I learned why Roger always puts a stone on top of every peak he comes to. He even told me where his ashes are to be scattered. I'm sure he found out things about me.

The moon was starting to peep over the Red Hills to add to the glimmer of our torches and by the time we reached the lower moorland it was so bright that they were redundant. Not a breeze stirred a movement in the grasses, the cold intense, the silence eerie. Nothing moved but a heron, which, unnerved by our footfalls on the hard path, took to the wing with an angry squawk.

Down on the road my old van was covered with a film of ice and the engine only just started. We had seen no one all day but the solitary photographer, and, but for the footprints he had left in the snow, he might have been the ghost of Norman Collie.

SGURR THUILM

By Hamish Brown

I MET BONNIE Prince Charlie on top of Sgurr Thuilm. He blinked at my appearance and fingered my Gore-tex jacket with interest. I only let him do so as I – then – thought he was some weirdo who might react violently to any hint of aggression on my part. After all, he was an unprepossessing sight and, in the afternoon's westerly breeze, didn't smell so good either.

In my pocket I had a tube of Smarties which I'd saved for the summit (my 239th Munro) so I offered them. A grubby hand was held out and the gaudy sweets were studied carefully. When I popped some into my mouth there was a gasp. Two or three other disreputable characters had come up unnoticed and they grabbed the tube from me. Both ends popped out so Smarties scattered over the schisty rocks and they were all down, snatching and popping the sweets into their mouths. What a lot of savages I thought. They must have escaped from some loony bin. When another ragged character in a dirty kilt came peching up, dropped on his knee before the young one, and said, 'News, your Highness,' I began to wonder just who was going bonkers.

'Macmillan of Glen Pean has managed to get away and will be up betimes to take you northwards: doon tae Glen Pean and over Carn Mór.'

'Corbett' I commented, almost without knowing I'd spoken.

'Corbett?' several voices asked suspiciously.

'Aye, him that listed all the hills over 2500ft. J. Rooke Corbett.'

'A Sassenach?'

'Aye, but you can't hold that against him. He spent all the time possible up in the Highlands. Must have known them as well as anybody – A.E. Robertson, Munro and the rest.'

'Sound like a lot of spies to me,' a shaggy lad sneered.

'Or maybe they'd be useful guides. Are you in touch?'

'Well, yes, but only a photocopy of this area. Section 10. I'm not lugging the two books about all the time. Look.'

I produced my photocopies. They went from hand to hand. I suspect one or two had learning difficulties as they held the damned things upside down. The young lad who seemed in charge could read. He said what sounded like 'Merde' which, I suppose, might have been Gaelic.

'Did you steal these?' he asked.

'No I copied them. The Late Shop has a 5p copier.'

'And you'll guide us?'

My mouth fell open. 'What! Over Carn Mór?'

'Yes.'

'But I've done it. I want Sgurr nan Coireachan now,' and I nodded west. 'I don't want to drag all the way up from Strathan again just for a Munro I can do today.'

There was a bit of muttering in which the name Munro came up once or twice. Someone mentioned a Colonel Munro. 'Effing Munro's regiment…. Cut the Frasers to pieces on Drumossie Moor.' I quickly interjected to point out this was the list of Sir Hugh Munro, Bart. of Lindertis in Angus, a most pacific gentleman only interested in finding his way up all the Highland hills. It was a bit of a speech.

'He spends all his time climbing mountains? Like this one?' The young one sounded incredulous.

'Aye.'

'What for?'

'Fun – I suppose.'

'Fun!' he grimaced. 'The man's mad.'

There were times I rather thought the same about Munro-bagging – but I wasn't going to admit that to this lot of scruffs. I launched into a somewhat long-winded defence of Munros, Corbetts et al., how it gave one good exercise, got one away from life's ordinary pressures, taught self-reliance and gave an unrivalled knowledge of the Highlands.

There were some nods at the last anyway.

'Useful,' the young one smiled. 'My knowledge is growing by the day. This Sgurr Thuilm is a Munro then?'

'Yes.'

'And the next?'

He looked west. 'Sgurr nan Coireachan? Aye it's a Munro.'

Suddenly the young man smiled, which improved his looks somewhat. He suggested. 'Couldn't we walk – and talk – along to it then? Instead of skulking up here all day?'

There was an outcry at this. Movement was too easily seen. They might appear against the skyline. The cordon ran right along Glen Pean to Loch Morar. They'd made arrangements with Macmillan. And much more of the same.

The young man sighed.

'Your pressures may be at home, mine, alas, are always with me. Can I keep these delineations?' He held up my photocopies of Section 10.

I was about to ask for them but I recalled a situation in Primary 3 when the big boys got our football and I asked for it back. This lot might deliver more than a bloody nose. So I took my leave.

'See you.'

'You going along there?' someone demanded.

'Why not? It's not the stalking season.'

'What if he's seen?' the man asked their leader.

He smiled and just waved me away. Condescending sod. As I left I heard the word 'decoy' whispered.

It's a right in-and-out, up-and-down ridge, but I got the second Munro for the day. In peace.

It was in the bothy that night I really began to think about this encounter. Just what had happened. Nobody was busy filming John Prebble or D.K. Broster. Those yobbos were authentically dirty (and smelly) and, besides, I'd been there at tea-break time and nobody had knocked off for a helicopter ride or for refreshment. It was all a bit strange, and it became even stranger as my imagination worked on it over the months, and years, following.

I didn't ever mention my encounter to the boys. Nor the wife. Especially not the wife. She made snide enough comments when I began to read lots of books about the Forty-Five and sat, headphones on, over several nights, listening to the Talking Book of Nigel Tranter's *Prince in Hiding*, the story of his wanderings after Culloden. It was awful, read by an Englishman who could pronounce nothing correctly (Benbecula became Ben Beculiar) but one thing did become clear from my researches eventually. Bonnie Prince Charlie had been on top of Sgurr Thuilm. Several books give details of his route. That made things all very peculiar indeed.

The years passed. The Corbetts were added to my Munros round and plans laid for going Furth of Scotland. I'd almost forgotten Sgurr Thuilm or I tried to convince myself I had. I was heading home early one Sunday (the weather a complete wash-out) and turned off at Perth to get milk and bread at Tesco. I saw there was a car boot sale next door so I had a nosey round it. I usually pick up a few books if nothing else.

I found a cheap copy of one of John Buchan's short story collections, one I'd had from the library and had been fascinated to find in it an account of Dr Johnson having an encounter with the dispirited and debauched Bonnie Prince when they were both wandering on the continent. Then I found a real treasure. It cost me all of 50p, being a hardback. It was Alexander Kirkwood's *True Records of the Rising of 1745 in sundry original documents by persons concerned therein, containing...* containing another twenty lines of just what there was: letters, reports, autobiographical accounts, all in packed small print, for 680 pages. And no index.

I went back into Tesco for a coffee and flicked through my find, reading a bit here, a bit there, till arrested by the name Dr Samuel Johnson leaping out from another wordy section title. This told of his wanderings in France and Switzerland in 1776. I wonder if Buchan used this text as his source? The setting was the same: an inn at Thiers.

The ponderous doctor had made his guess at who the wino next door was and was rather sad. Ever since his wanderings with Boswell round the Highlands and Islands he'd had a sneaking softness for the sorry Jacobite saga. His own unchancy health and ungainly body was no joy but to see the prince who had once set the heather afire reduced to such a state was dismal.

Being who he was however he set his table near the wall and noted down the snatches of talk that came through the thin partition that separated their rooms. (Bugging becomes history it seems as Kirkwood duly included the sage's notes.) Some of the talk did not make much sense, for which the meticulous doctor apologised ('methinks his erratic articulation at times arose from the distress of ancient remembrances') but there was one bit had me gasp. Listen.

'P.C.: I once delighted in physical exertion.

'COMPANION [too soft to note]: ...march to Derby, your Highness.

'P.C.: That was but strolling, sir. It was in the hills I found my best days. Moi fois! But I was like a deer on the hill. [pause] Never like it since. [pause] My only regret is that I climbed but one Munro in that time.

'COMPANION: And what might that be?

'P.C. [with some vigour]: Sgurr Thuilm, sir, Sgurr Thuilm.'

THE CURIOUS CASE OF THE CLANDESTINE CASE

By M. J. Conrad-Doyle

Limit oneself strictly to observing facts (Raymonde de Saussure)

I WAS STANDING at the bay window, listening to Gerry Rafferty's *Baker Street*, and quietly musing. It was bizarre how events had panned out over the years. Who could possibly have ever imagined that the mighty Sherlock Holmes had managed to conceal such a humdinger of a personal secret all his life? I knew about his more open penchant for the seedy opium dens of London, of course, but that this more particular skeleton had remained hidden in his cupboard for so long was just typical of the inscrutability of the man. Even so, why had he never confided in his only true friend, my father, who had always suspected that Holmes's fondness for Miss Adler bordered on the passionate? A man has his sexual needs, obviously, and accidents clearly happen, but nevertheless the eventual outcome was a remarkable and intriguing coincidence.

The hawk-faced dark-haired man sitting in the armchair, gazing in deep contemplation at the priceless Ming vase by the fireplace, raised his eyes, as if suddenly aware that I was scrutinising him. He removed the curved pipe from the corner of his mouth and held me with his disconcerting, penetrating eyes –

'Well, Watson, did you enjoy your sojourn to the Highlands of Scotland?'

'Ahem,' I cleared my throat and thought carefully.

'Come now, man, you must have been invigorated by our escapade on Ben Nevis.'

'Quite frankly...no...no; I don't see the point, after all these years. What's it all for? What good can possibly come of it now?'

'Och!' He had clearly caught a touch of the local dialect. *'Where's your bottle? I thought you liked to get the blood stirring in your veins and a bit of adrenalin is a potent and entirely legal drug. You're getting too stuffy, just like your old man.'*

This barbed comment was too much and I rose to the bait –

'You seem to have caught the Scottish affliction, Holmes?'

He fixed me with a cold stare and it had the most peculiar affect upon me. I felt that I could have been turned to stone as he launched into a withering and entirely unjustified verbal assault –

'You forget, Watson, that I am a master of disguise and that includes the voice. You must learn, as I have instructed you on countless occasions, that things are seldom as they appear. You are too easily duped by even overt deception and it does not become a man of your supposed

intelligence. The key to this case, I suspect, is in the masquerade itself and you would do well to remember my words. By the way, which gentleman's outfitter in Savile Row do you use?'

I turned to hide my embarrassment but I felt his laser-like stare penetrate my very being as my cheeks burned.

'Er, to what case do you refer?'…I stuttered, almost adding… *'Sir.'*

'Not now, man. We must make haste…I have booked two places first-class on tonight's sleeper from Euston. Hoots mon…we have a meeting with Professor Stirling in Auld Reekie first thing tomorrow's morn and then I have some other business to attend to. I see you look confused but all will be explained. Now hurry up and make ready.'

This time I kept my silence.

*

As the express thundered north through the night I contemplated the scene through the rain-spattered window in gloomy mood. Row upon row of orange neon lights were beginning to light up street after identical suburban street, high-gain aerials and satellite dishes. Everywhere, no matter where I looked, I could see vehicles, those false gods that demand our worship, the red corpuscles of modern living rushing around the arterial highways, perversely pumping their toxins into the air. Perhaps he was right, perhaps I was too deliberate, but I could do no more about it than he could change his intellectual sangfroid. We were our father's sons and, consequently, both victims of our genes. No, the phenomenon, if that it be, lay in the most peculiar of improbabilities that had thrown us together in the first place. Somewhat fortuitously, he interrupted my thoughts –

'What are you thinking about, my friend?'

'Oh, nothing much, but please tell me why we are visiting Scotland again so soon?'

'Because we are on the trail of a wicked villain who has blighted the lives of too many innocent victims and it is time for justice to prevail. Shortly after our return from The Ben'…he paused slightly and I could see the hint of a smile at the corners of his mouth… *'I made a call to my recently-retired colleague, Munro Stirling, as a matter of urgency. He may be able to help throw some light upon a mystery which I have already spent some considerable time researching. You will recall that he contributed, some thirty years ago, a learned treatise to the Journal[1] of that august and aged body, the Scottish Mountaineering Club. Unfortunately, the good Professor made a basic omission in his essay,*

---

[1] For readers who do not possess the relevant Journal, the item may be viewed at http://www.psychology.stir.ac.uk/staff/rcampbell/Eyeglasses_002.html

*as my researches in the permanent snowfield in Observatory Gully have
so recently revealed.'*

*'Actually, I have never read any of these journals. Why would I? And
are you referring to the rusty remains that could have been old nails
thrown down the awful chasm known as Marylou, I believe?'*

'I think you mean Gardyloo,' he corrected me with a needless snort,
'and may I request you not to question my interpretation of clues?'

*'I'm sorry, Holmes, but I fail to see the relevance of our excursion or
why we needed to stay in that dismal hovel full of stinking and uncouth
teuchters.'*

*'Goodness me, man! Although I detect a derogatory tone, you have
accidentally chosen an apt description. You were lucky indeed to rub
shoulders with truly tough and courageous mountaineers, testing their
mettle on the mighty northern precipices of snow and ice. And their high
abode, you are surely aware, is not yet a luxury hotel but an old
memorial hut where they take shelter from the elements.'*

*'Well, it is still an unsavoury cruck, peopled by barbarians who
murder hill sheep for the fun of it. I had to sleep right next to one of
them...urgh ...his foul breath hot upon my neck, so please don't try to
dissuade me.'*

'Very well, let us speak no more of it.'

We had a most passable breakfast with porridge and a type of sausage,
known locally as black pudd'n, at a hotel near to Waverley Station.
While the waitress, a young beauty with long silky hair, poured our
coffee, we were joined by a friendly man wearing a tweed jacket who
immediately made himself welcome. I must admit that I paid rather
more attention to the cleavage of the delicious maiden as she leant over
our table, a fact that did not go unnoticed by Holmes –

*'Watson, if you could avert your lecherous eyes for a moment perhaps I
may be permitted to introduce you to Professor Stirling.'*

I was helped in my distraction, for Stirling was also sizing up the
bonny lass, as he referred to her, in a most salacious manner. She smiled
provocatively and departed, wiggling her bottom, knowing that foolish,
middle-aged men were prepared to pay for dreams and were easily
seduced into leaving nice, large tips.

'Ah, a man after my heart,' the Professor proclaimed, regarding me. *'I
see that you, too, appreciate the finer things in life'* and then let out an
uproarious guffaw of laughter that I found most congenial, *'Well,
gentlemen, perhaps we should compare notes about this latest turn of
events.'*

Holmes immediately reached into the inside pocket of his jacket and
carefully unfolded a letter and what looked like a receipt, both of which
had the appearance of great age, and handed them to Stirling. The

Professor fumbled about and, after much searching, said –

'I'm very sorry but I seem to have misplaced my eyeglasses. You'll have to summarise the contents for me.'

'That won't be necessary.' Holmes replied, with a hint of exasperation, and handed over a large magnifying glass, a valuable part of his inheritance, *'For God's sake, man, don't drop it on the floor.'*

While Stirling was carefully examining the papers, I noticed that he also sported tweed breeches, relics of wet days spent trolling the charity shops of Portree, I was informed by Holmes, who then addressed me –

'There is no need for you to remain with us, Watson. You would be better employed in other activities. Firstly, I must ask that you take a bus to the old port of Leith where you will collect some packages from a shop. It is a purveyor of mountaineering equipment and you will be required to pay cash. Do not expect to negotiate a discount. Secondly, you will then proceed to the offices of 'Pacific & Orient' where you will be able to examine copies of shipping mandates and passenger lists for the SS Sardinia in 1921, outward bound for Calcutta. I want names and numbers. Then make your way to George IV Bridge where I will meet you at three o'clock.'

Seeing that I looked a trifle befuddled, he handed me a copy of the bus map for the city and added, as though he were addressing a nincompoop –

'Don't be late.'

*

I stepped off the number 23 double-decked bus at the appointed hour, having been forced to walk much of my return journey with my recently-acquired massive load of exorbitant goods. In some small compensation, however, at least my wallet was empty. Holmes was nowhere to be seen. Exactly where was I supposed to meet him, for the street bustled with life and movement? Suddenly, there was a tap on my shoulder and I turned to see the two men standing behind me, as if out of thin air –

'Oh, you startled me, Holmes. Where did you come from so suddenly?'

'Really, Watson. You must train your mind more productively.'

He gestured to the large building behind him and, somewhat more sympathetically, Stirling added –

'We have been examining the archives of the Scottish Mountaineering Club, the contents of which I happen to have more than a passing familiarity. In fact, we have been studying some case notes that were written by your father and upon which I had based my earlier research. I have to confess that I quite overlooked an important clue but the matter is now clarified.'

At this point Holmes interceded –

'I am sorry but we must proceed at once, otherwise we shall miss our train. I will fill Watson in on the details later. I thank you, Stirling, for your consideration and may your lum aye reek.'

Once again the Professor let out a side-splitting roar of mirth, to the visible discomfort of Holmes and, rather exaggerating his manner of speech, declared–

'Aye, mon, we'll mak a Scotsman of ye, bye and bye. Now remember, dinnae dae onythin' that I widnae and I hope that ye have a good trip. I just wish that I was gangin' tae.'

With that he turned and disappeared into the throng. Holmes and I hurried down the Mound and turned right along Prince's Street. As we went, he said –

'I see from the enormous rucksack on your back that you accomplished your mission. By the way, take no notice of Stirling, I like to humour him but the man is incorrigible. He likes to call a spade a spade but I prefer to ca' canny...' and added for my benefit, as he tapped the side of his nose, *'...softly softly catchee monkey, Watson.'*

I confess that I did not understand the drift of his meaning at all so I changed the subject –

'Were your researches fruitful, Holmes? And to what trip was the honest Professor referring?'

'Yes, yes, very fruitful. The trip? Oh, yes...we're going to the Greater Ranges, Watson' and his voice rose in excited exultation... *'We are going to Tibet...to honour the heights of Himachal, the sacred abode of snow...to be precise, to the bays of Mount Everest, better known to the cognoscenti as CHOMOLUNGMA!'*

I had never seen him so animated and I almost dropped to the ground in my astonishment … and also, I must add, under the weight of my huge cargo. As I staggered, I was aware of the amused glances of some Oriental tourists and the rude comments of a gang of vacuous juveniles. I beseeched my colleague to relieve me of part of my burden but he merely replied that it was good training for the trials and tribulations yet to come. However, he condescended to carry a vicious-looking ice pick and, at that, he marched off, scattering the onlookers to the four winds, while I was left to trail in his wake.

We managed to catch our train by a whisker and, as we settled into our seats, Holmes, who was only slightly out of breath in contrast to my furious panting, started his explanation.

*

'Watson, before I begin, please may I scrutinise the results of your researches?'

I handed over the list of facts and figures that I had so diligently copied from the shipping manifests and Holmes perused them carefully, before letting out an exclamation of success –

'Aha, just as I thought. Look here at this name…Count McGregor. The scoundrel, Watson. Now, let's see…how were the packing cases numbered aboard the ship? Oh yes, what a give-away…brilliant, quite brilliant…and to think that he got away with it for so many years. Now let me give you some background information, Watson.'

In all my days I hope that I never again hear a tale of such unadulterated, cloven-hoofed debauchery as that which Secundus Holmes then related. He told me about a malevolent fiend who practised his black arts under a variety of pseudonyms which, in my horror, all escaped my immediate attention except for one – Count McGregor! This diabolical monster had believed that he was remarkable from the moment of his birth and claimed that he bore on his body the distinguishing marks of a Buddha. Like many such reprobates, he was considered by his followers to be a mighty prophet, magician and mystic and, I was warned, he still had dangerous adherents who worshipped his memory, for the man was now, fortunately, long dead. It sent a cold shiver down my spine, even accustomed as I was to such dreadful stories.

'But what has all this got to do with Ben Nevis?' I queried.

'Simply this; the adventure so admirably described by Professor Stirling hinged upon strange marks in the snow and that one of the protagonists, the great Harold Raeburn, speculated that they may have been made by steigeisen – crampons, Watson, as the Germans call Eckenstein's thorny invention. They wished to interview Eckenstein's close friend, alias McGregor, back at the Alexandra Hotel but the bird had flown; yes, it was no accident, I think, that he departed early from the SMC's Easter Meet of 1896 and thus escaped justice. I can tell you, too, as Stirling has just confirmed to me, that this early recruit of the Club took an instant dislike to Raeburn who, although he was but a mere guest, took it upon himself as the older man by some ten years to assume leadership and issue instructions.'

'Surely not? This is flimsy justification indeed for attempted murder'

'Quite so, Watson, but have a look at these photographs.'

He pulled two pictures out of the capacious pocket of his overcoat, neatly folded on the seat beside him. I examined them carefully before concluding that they were one and the same man. Holmes advised me to look again whereupon I could see some dissimilarity between them; however, the resemblance was remarkable.

'Who are these men, Holmes?'

'The one in your left hand is Harold Raeburn. The other is a man called Bishop, a vicious, cruel bully and uncle of our suspect. The *unfortunate nephew, after the premature death of his father, was sent to live with him and suffered continual beatings before he managed to escape to Cambridge University where he took up mountaineering; hence his presence on Ben Nevis. I believe that his mind, like that of many gifted individuals, was distraught and that he came to regard the two men, Raeburn and Bishop, as one – and hate them both in equal measure.'*

'Well, well. And what happened to the young cad?'

'I'm afraid that he went on to even greater depravity. In 1900, he moved to Boleskine House on the shores of Loch Ness, a remote location where he could continue his practices in magic, and where he is said to have summoned demons, held the black mass and to have indulged in sexual orgies…'

'Oh my word! Do you have any more…um…precise details?'

'NO. I can only tell you that it all got out of hand and there were tales of madness, animal sacrifices, curses and unexplained deaths. He was, to put it bluntly, an evil genius who positively revelled in controversy.'

'Indeed. Did the swine continue his mountaineering?'

'Oh yes, for a while. He even demonstrated the effectiveness of crampons to a colleague of your father, a certain Dr. Tom Longstaff, on an icefall near the Col du Géant in the Alps. And listen to this …' – he pulled a small book called *The Spirit of Solitude* out of his pocket –

'In Mr. Harold Raeburn's book he argues amiably against them. He admits that one can walk up hard snow at easy angles without steps, but fears to do so lest, returning later in the day, he should find the snow soft, and then where would he be without a staircase? He seems to have no idea that the supreme use of claws is on ice and that the harder the ice the surer the hold. Yet Mr. Raeburn pits himself against Everest, where claws would convert the most perilous passages into promenades, and ice slopes whose length and steepness make step-cutting impracticable … the policy of boycotting Eckenstein and his school, of deliberately ignoring the achievements of Continental climbers, to say nothing of my own expeditions, has preserved the privilege and prestige of the English Alpine Club …It is one of the most curious characteristics of the English that they set such store by courage as to esteem a man the more highly the more blindly he blunders into disaster.'

'And then, of the expedition the following year, which ended in death and controversy, he says' –

'In March 1922 I heard of the composition and projects of the Everest expedition. I wrote an article predicting failure and disaster, giving my reasons and showing how to avoid the smash. No one would print it. I was told it was not the thing to 'crab' these gallant gentlemen. No. But should my prophecies come true, then was the time to explain why.

What I had foretold came to pass precisely as I had predicted it. But I was still unable to get a hearing. Why add to the tribulations of these heroes by showing up their stupidity? Besides, England had failed – better not talk about it at all.'

'Actually, that all sounds very enlightened to me.'

'I have to agree with you, Watson. It is quite clear what our man thought, even then, about the celebrity status of the English climbing prima donnas. He also claimed that between them, he and Eckenstein had held all the world's mountaineering records with the sole exception of the greatest height attained by man. Did you know that he applied to join the first ever expedition to Mount Everest in 1921 and was rejected by Collie and the other stuffy old members of the Committee?

'Hardly surprising, I would say. Did he seriously expect to be chosen, especially as his old enemy Raeburn was the mountaineering leader?'

'Fancy you knowing that! Actually, his credentials were first-rate. He had already attempted to climb the second-highest peak in the world, Chogo Ri, in 1902 with Eckenstein. They spent 63 days surviving on the Baltoro Glacier and he claimed to have climbed alone to a height of 22,000 feet, until he was driven back by severe storm. I am only surprised that he didn't claim to have reached the summit! Then, in 1905, he tried his luck on the third-highest mountain, Kanchenjunga, but was thwarted again amidst further controversy and death. Now, why not try for the highest? The only trouble for him was that he was considered to be an iniquitous traitor for writing anti-British propaganda for the Germans during the First World War as well as continuing his other foul practices in Italy with his then-current scarlet woman. So, he had several points...hah...to make, after all.'

At that he pulled out the spiky metal objects that we had found amongst the debris on Ben Nevis and, withdrawing into contemplative mood, muttered to himself –

'Claws...paws and claws...'

*

The following weeks passed in a frantic whirl of activity that quite set my mind in a dizzying pirouette. Were it not for my diary I would not now be able to recall the sequence of events that unfolded at such a frantic pace that I was barely able to think at all. I will not bore you, patient Journal reader, with the details about how Holmes had arranged for us to join, only two days after our return to London, a commercial expedition whose ambition was to trek among the mountains of Tibet. We flew from Heathrow, via Beijing, to Lhasa, from where we were driven south-westwards through the townships of Gyantse and Lhatse.

We travelled through the arid hills of a barren highland plateau towards a skyline of snowy peaks that stretched from horizon to horizon and seemed to hang in the air even though distant by, I was informed, a hundred miles or more. All this time I felt nauseous from the altitude but I had put my medical training to good use by packing special medicines to ameliorate the effects of the reduced oxygen pressure and these I now prescribed for myself. Holmes, as usual in these matters, seemed unaffected. We eventually reached the end of the road at the township of Kharta Shika where the other members of the group set off on foot. After protracted negotiations, however, we were fortunate to procure the use of some mules and their handlers, two guides and an excellent interpreter called Gyalzen, for Holmes wished to explore in a different direction.

For three days we rode and walked up beautiful valleys rich in alpine flowers and over gruelling high passes to reach, eventually, a delightful campsite beside a bubbling stream of clear water in the Kama valley. The view southwards to the awesome amphitheatre of rocky precipices, glaciers and magnificent ice mountains, called Lhotse, Makalu and Chomolonzo, quite took my breath away. I doubt that I will ever again witness such a wonderful spectacle as I glimpsed these mighty peaks through the clouds, at incredible heights above our camp. To the west was Chomolungma itself and its great ridges, only three or four miles away, seemed quite impossible of ascent. Like the foaming wake of a super-tanker, a great plume of snow blew from the highest bastions of the mountain where, in the upper atmosphere, this most implacable of immovable objects met the unstoppable forces of Nature and I shivered to think that men, dressed in a similar manner to Stirling, had vainly added the ingredients of pride, egotism and physical effort – all equally pathetic.

'Are your mountain boots satisfactory, Watson?'

'Oh yes, a perfect fit, as luck would have it. My clothing, too, is very comfortable although I don't think that these garish colours really suit our environs. How did you know what sizes to order for me?' I knew the answer, almost as soon as I had opened my mouth.

'A simple matter ... and it wasn't luck. You gave me the name of your London tailor and a couple of phone calls ...'

'Yes, yes ... you don't need to continue, Holmes.' I said, annoyed with myself.

'Good, so be it. We will need to use Shanks's pony from here on. But we will spend two more days at this lovely spot to acclimatise further to the altitude and prepare ourselves for our forthcoming adventure. We are about to retrace part of the route taken by some of the members of the Everest Reconnaissance Expedition of 1921 and I hope to throw some light upon two of the world's most abiding mysteries, Watson. Here, read this book, it will add to your historical knowledge. I must spend some time interviewing Gyalzen.'

He handed me a battered old hardback. It was the official report about the 1921 expedition and I found a sheltered, sunny spot behind a boulder to begin my reading. I was transported back to the time of our forefathers and I found it difficult to understand, although I looked up at the same immutable mountains as they had done, that I even lived in the same world. Everything now was different and, as if to emphasise the point, an invisible aeroplane scarred the blue heavens with a white vapour trail which moved rapidly sideways across the sky as the jet stream winds tore it to shreds.

*

'What do you know about the Abominable Snowman, Watson?'
  'Nothing to speak of.'
The rarefied atmosphere had done nothing to improve my companion's irritation at my various shortcomings –
*'You astound me, Watson. Your ignorance of rare species of fauna seems to have no bounds. Please allow me to enlighten you. According to some, the hairy creature is a giant ape, the size of the beast confirmed by recordings of its footprints in the snow. It could be **Gigantopithecus blacki**, a primate relic of the Pleistocene epoch, but this genus is of decidedly dubious status, being based on the evidence of no more than three molar teeth recovered from a drugstore in Hong Kong. However, most experts believe that a large bear is a more plausible explanation for the sightings, the obvious candidate being the Himalayan brown bear, **Ursus arctos isabellinus**. I hope all that is clear?'*
  'And what is your definitive opinion upon the matter, Holmes?' I queried innocently.
  'There is no need for petulance, my friend. Perhaps you should take a sniff from your oxygen cylinder. I believe that a simple matter of nature may have become a tangle of deceit and lies, manipulated by the design of man to confuse the innocent.'

We had left our camp early in the morning accompanied by our two guides, both of whom transpired to be excellent mountaineering instructors, and had followed alongside a rocky moraine to reach a glacier. Here we roped up, as it is referred to, and crossed the easy glacier without mishap, eventually to reach the foot of a steep wall of rock which looked decidedly formidable. However, it proved a pleasurable experience to be grasping firm granite and, apart from the excitement of the occasional loose stone, we made excellent progress in the warm sunshine. I was an apt pupil and came to relish the thrill of the moments as, indeed, did my companion, even though he already had Alpine experience to his name.
In next to no time, it seems now, we reached a snowy col known as the

Karpo La and were able to have a long rest. The altitude registered on my companion's multi-function wrist-watch was in excess of an amazing 20,000 feet. Eventually we descended a reasonably gentle slope, although the snow was very soft and powdery, to reach the Kharta Glacier which again, and to our surprise, we crossed without too much difficulty. Although it was only mid-afternoon I felt de-hydrated and overcome by a strange lassitude, so that a strong effort of both mind and body was required to make any progress at all. We had then spent a considerable time seeking a suitable location for our next camp, which we eventually established, at Holmes's insistence, on a stony terrace between two glaciers.

We now lay in our tents, after a night of 18 degrees of frost, as the sun slowly rose and brought a semblance of warmth to the scene. I was aware from my reading that our camp was in close proximity to one of the 1921 Expedition's highest campsites as they had attempted to reach the Chang La, or North Col, from the east. Holmes appeared at my tent door with a mug of steaming tea in his gloved hand and urged me to action as we chatted –

'I'm not sure that it would be very wise for me to go any higher, Holmes. I have a bit of a headache and I don't want to risk cerebral oedema.'

'That's fine, Watson. We have reached our final destination, I believe. Did you realise that this place has a certain poignant significance for it was also the limit of Harold Raeburn's efforts in 1921 although, and not many people realise this, he did make a solitary first ascent of a 21,000 ft summit overlooking the camp, perhaps the unnamed peak you see behind me. However, we must spend some time in the boulder field over there or perhaps exploring those small outcrops, for I am convinced that a vital clue lies concealed somewhere hereabouts. I feel in my bones that a mystery that has baffled humankind for nearly a century is about to be revealed. As soon as you are ready please join me in the search. Just let me know if you spot anything unusual.'

An hour or so later, I joined my companion who was rooting around amongst the huge boulders and gaping holes, and climbing through clefts into icy caverns. We soon became separated as we searched in different directions and I rapidly grew tired of the cold and fruitless hunt. I decided to return to the camp and, as I turned, I glimpsed the most appalling apparition out of the corner of my eye and froze in silent terror, my mouth dry as powdered chalk. About to launch itself upon me with hideous fangs and razor claws was a grizzly bear and, with an evil wink of its eye, it raised its vicious paw – and then pulled off its own head to reveal none other than…Secundus Holmes!!

My knees wobbled and I sank to the ground with delayed shock, and inadvertently uttered several foul oaths at the wretched knavery of my false friend, who just stood there sniggering inanely to himself. After a while, I managed to squeak out –

'It's just as well for you … you bastard, Holmes … that I left my father's service revolver in the tent.'

'Oh come now, I'm sorry, I didn't mean to frighten you unduly. Let's return to the camp and I'll pour you a tot or two of brandy.'

'Yes, let's return and I'll just load up my pistol with a few rounds of ammunition. Then we'll see who's laughing.' I got up and stumbled off.

Back at the tents I rummaged in vain for my weapon but it was nowhere to be found and, after several large refills from the bottle, I began to calm down.

'I think that you owe me a full and honest explanation, Holmes. What exactly have you been playing at?'

'Very well, my trusty comrade, I think I can now explain everything. I discovered this obsolete gorilla suit in yonder cave and thought to try it on for size. It has been lying preserved in the dry mountain air for nearly a hundred years.'

'But how on earth did it get there in the first place?' I enquired.

Once again, I listened in transfixed amazement as Holmes described a story of quite outrageous audacity.

'It's a long tale which starts back in England in 1920. You will recall that McGregor, for all his faults, was a forward-thinking innovator who was ever ready to question accepted wisdom? Well, he had been conducting trials of a breathable fabric for mountaineering based on the principles of hairy animal skins and when I have the chance to examine the material of this suit in more detail I think we will discover that it is a precursor of so-called modern technology and sufficient in itself to keep the wearer warm and dry under any weather conditions. It is also remarkably light and…ah, yes…here is even the maker's label which, as I thought it would, matches the name on the receipt that I showed to Stirling. And see how the bear-like mask would frighten casual investigation, yet is perfect insulation for the face and head. It is a brilliant and visionary concept. When the scoundrel's Everest application was rejected he decided to join in anyway…but anonymously. You will be aware that although the ancient customs of the Tibetan peoples have been undermined, they still have a wonderful tradition of story-telling and in such a manner their cultural heritage is passed on to succeeding generations. Gyalzen has given me the details, as fresh in his mind now as they were to his grandfather, who was hired, as were many others, by the Expedition in Darjeeling. They were a hotchpotch mix of all sorts of different tribesmen and it would have been a piece of cake for a swarthy outsider to pass himself off as one of them

and to keep himself somewhat apart from the Europeans. Gyalzen has confirmed that there was such a renegade, a coolie known as Paramahansa Shivaji. We know this man; WE KNOW HIM, my friend, more infamously as McGregor, or none other than...Aleister Crowley!!'

'The wretched knave. But how did McGregor, or Crowley rather, get there?'

'Simple. He joined the SS Sardinia at Marseilles although his packing case was shipped with the rest of the Expedition's equipment from England, as your research in Leith established. The self-betrayal, typical of the man's arrogance, was the number he had stamped on his case...666, the mark of the Great Beast. He was even able to shadow a dashing mountaineer called George Mallory who was also on the boat but travelling first-class. As they trekked through Sikkim on the approach march, he bided his time, watching and waiting, full of both loathing and envy at Mallory's charisma.'

'Surely not; now your imagination is certainly running away with itself. Remember, Raeburn had met him before and could easily have recognised him.' I said, feeling slightly befuddled by the alcohol.

'Quite so. Crowley wasn't prepared to take that risk and so he hatched a dastardly scheme with Poo, one of the cooks, to poison the two Scotsmen and fellow SMC members, the only people who might have rumbled him. In such a manner he killed Alexander Kellas, and poor Raeburn, at death's door, was forced to leave the Expedition to recuperate. This left the way open for Crowley to await his chance. It is well documented that a mystery thief broke into the Expedition's store-room at Kharta and made off with a yak-dan – a type of leather trunk, Watson – into which he packed the suit. He then took to the hills, as it were, raiding the high camps at night for food. He might even have crept into a tent at night for a bit of human warmth. One of Mallory's diary entries does recall a vivid dream in which he imagines that he is once again sharing his bed with Ruth, his beloved but unusually hirsute wife. What's all that about? Crowley's dastardly plot was nearly revealed when some of the sahibs saw his footprints but, luckily for him, the Tibetan porters just thought that these were the tracks of the mythical Metohkangmi...the wild man of the high snows.'

'How on earth did you discover all this?' I queried.

'You remember the letter that I showed Stirling? It was found amongst some of Eckenstein's papers in the archives of the Alpine Club and confirms the cad's intentions. Circumstantial information found in an Expedition diary confirmed my suspicions.'

'All this is quite unbelievable Holmes. Are you seriously expecting me to believe that Crowley, disguised in this horrible furry monkey-suit with these inbuilt crampon-claws, hoped to be the first man to climb Everest *by stalking these mountaineering pioneers and then pipping them to the post? It's all too ridiculous for words.'*

'So it would seem but, in fact, I will go further; there is every chance that Crowley succeeded in his ambition. If so, the Yeti was the first to reach the summit of Chomolungma. You know well that I follow the precept to firstly eliminate the impossible. Thus, I am left only with this explanation of the facts, highly improbable as the hypothesis might appear.'

'Well, I'm afraid that we'll never know the answer, Holmes.' I should have known better –

'Not so fast, Watson. When we return home, a photographic analysis of the film inside this Kodak camera, which I found in an inside pocket, will confirm my theory I think, just as Crowley intended. However, with the unexpected re-appearance of Harold Raeburn on the scene, he was suddenly forced to abort his plan and make a rapid escape, legging it to Calcutta. He left his high-altitude suit behind, intending to recover it the following year. Unfortunately for him, the approach to the Chang La taken by further expeditions was by way of the northern Rongbuk route and no team has been this way for decades. Crowley made a very basic mistake in under-estimating the strength and determination of his old foe, Harold Raeburn, who had steadfastly managed to recover from his severe gastro-enteritis.'

'I see, I see. Then it's all rather alimentary, isn't it?'
Holmes smiled and added –
'By the way, is this what you have been looking for?'
He held my pistol in his outstretched hand.

*

As we made our slow way down the Kharta glacier we heard a most appalling and heart-rending series of desolate howls echoing around in the thin air of these magnificent mountains and we stopped in our tracks. Even Holmes, for once, seemed slightly shaken and introspective.

'What the hell is that, Holmes?'

'Probably just movement deep in the glacier. I understand that it is a common phenomenon.'

'Really? You know something – and you might mock me for saying it – but I don't believe that life is always ruled by the laws of logic and science. There is ever something that escapes us; something which is unpredictable and often so dangerous that reason has to be abandoned. That noise sounds more…well…sort of human, to me. Don't you think?'

He paused, before quietly conceding –
'Quite possibly. In that case, perhaps you should amend the description to inhuman.'

*

After all the excitement of the preceding few weeks it was something of an anti-climax to return to Holmes's flat in the dreary, litter-strewn metropolis, where awaited a large pile of unopened mail which a friendly neighbour, a Ms Linda Hudson, had retained for him. I watched as Secundus settled in his comfortable armchair and sorted through the correspondence.

'Good God, there's one for you here, Watson! It must have got mixed up with all my stuff. Hmm, the writing looks familiar.'

'Oh, really, this is most unexpected?'

Holmes handed me the letter and I took a seat on the other side of the Victorian fireplace. It was postmarked as having come from Edinburgh and it was with great surprise and delight that I read that Professor Stirling had issued an invitation to me to attend, as his esteemed guest, the forthcoming Annual Dinner of the Scottish Mountaineering Club in the Highlands of that captivating country.

'Well, my dear fellow, this is a most generous offer' I remarked to Holmes as I told him about my invitation and forthcoming re-acquaintance with his old friend.

'Indeed, George' he said, and I even detected tones of umbrage and self-pity in his voice, *'but are you certain that the invitation is not intended for both of us? After all, Stirling and I have been colleagues for years.'*

At this point, perhaps caused by all my recent arduous undertakings, I felt a rising resentment with my colleague's presumption and could not curtail my reply –

'It would appear not. I'm very sorry but it would seem that the letter is addressed to me only. Here, you can examine it if you wish...and then you may stick it in your pipe and smoke it.'

NEW CLIMBS SECTION

With a new publication date for the Journal, the deadline for new routes each year is now 31 July. Winter routes should still be sent at the end of winter.

OUTER ISLES

LEWIS, Butt of Lewis, (Rubha Robhanais):
Immediately behind the lighthouse is a west-facing pillar. Abseil to a narrow ledge from a carefully parked car on the cliff edge (check your handbrake!).

Mondeo Man   20m   HVS 5a. Charlie Henderson, Robert Durran. 9 July 2008. Climb a short steep crack above the left side of the ledge and then finish more easily rightwards.

Trojan Wall (see SMCJ 2005):
Access: abseil down the line of *Trojan Horse* from stakes 20m back (not in situ). It is possible from rocks but not advised as these are poor.
The wall can be easily viewed from the cliff-top on the west side of the geo. The wall is split into four distinct sections, from left to right these are; Seaward Buttress, Three Corner Buttress, The Wall and Right End Wall. Right of this the rock is loose and broken.
   Routes are described from left to right starting at the large chimney in the corner that separates Seaward Buttress from Three Corner Buttress.

Seaward Buttress:
The buttress at the left end of the wall contains *Journey over the Sea* (2004).

Three Corner Buttress:
The buttress that extends rightwards from the large chimney in the corner. *Gneiss Achilles* (2004) climbs the left corner of the chimney.

Apple of Discord   13m   VS 4c. Ross Jones, Andrew Wardle. 6 September 2008. Climb the right corner of the chimney.

Just to the right is a 5m wide wall undercut on its left-hand side.

Hector   15m   HVS 5a **. Andrew Wardle, Ross Jones. 6 September 2008. The arete right of *Helen's Chimney* (2004).

Aphrodite's Promise   15m   E2 5b ***. Ross Jones, Andrew Wardle. 6 September 2008.
The excellent overhanging arete right of *Odysseus* (the middle corner – 2004). Pull out right through the overhang and then left onto the wall right of *Odysseus* to finish.

The Wall:
The following routes take the wall to the right of the corner to the right of Three Corner Buttress.

How Many Husbands...   15m   Hard Severe 4a. Andrew Wardle, Ross Jones.
10 September 2008.
Climb the right-facing corner, stepping right at the overhang to finish as for
Trojan Horse.

Right End Wall:
Patroclus   15m   E1 5b **. Andrew Wardle, Ross Jones. 6 September 2008.
Start by a niche and left of a short pillar. Climb the wall and step left at the
overhang and climb the chimney to an airy finish.

Upper Tier:
The following routes are non-tidal. The first route on the north wall just left of
the arete.

Trojan Work Ethic   25m   E4 6a **. Robert Durran, Charlie Henderson. 9 July
2008.
Climb the crack and get into the groove (all hard work). Continue steadily to the
top.

The remaining climbs are on the west-facing wall.

Hermione's Exit   18m   VS 4c. Andrew Wardle, Ross Jones. 6 September 2008.
Climb the left-facing corner-groove on the left side of the west-facing wall. Step
left and up the next short corner and traverse right under a hanging niche on the
final headwall to finish. Finishing up the niche is 5b, but protection and rock are
poor.

The middle of the main wall is *Trojan Horse. Hidden Agenda* (2004) climbs the
wall 2m right of *Trojan Horse.*

Sinon   12m   HVS 5a. Ross Jones, Andrew Wardle. 10 September 2008.
Pull up the right arete onto the wall left of the arete and up to an overhang
(junction with *Hidden Agenda*). Pull onto the pillar above from the right and
climb this in a fine position.

BEARASAIGH, Upper Hadrian's Wall Area:
Time of No Reply   15m   Severe 4b. Keith Archer, Paul Headland. 14 June 2008.
From the same start as *Finger Ripping Good*, climb 2m then climb the crack in
the wall to the left. Follow it to the top.

The Dancing Tiger   16m   HVS 5a. Paul Headland, Keith Archer. 11 June 2008.
Climb the left-hand side of the hanging prow in the centre of the wall to a ledge
and a short overhang.

Working the Seam   18m   VS 5a. Keith Archer, Paul Headland. 11 June 2008.
Start from the short wall which abuts the left side of the coal face, laybacks and
smears lead to the finishing niche just right of the corner.

Lower Hadrian's Wall Area, St Bees Sector:
Illicit Thursdays   19m   Severe. Keith Archer, Paul Headland. 12 June 2008.

From just right of the descent crack at the centre of the buttress, climb a blocky corner, pull onto the slab above and follow it to the top.

Main Sector:

Dan's Last Day 20m Severe 4b. Paul Headland, Keith Archer. 13 June 2008.
Begin up a short scoop 3m left of the black rock band, (just right of *Birthday Route*), climb direct through two short black spiky walls.

Lick the Tins 24m HVS 5a **. Keith Archer, Paul Headland. 13 June 2008.
Start up a short corner, right of the base of the cleft where the sea cuts through the access platform. Climb to a sloping ledge, then directly up through a short overlap. Cross a rib to gain a corner and follow this to finish.

Grass with Everything 26m VS 4c. Keith Archer, Paul Headland. 14 June 2008.
Start 3m left of the base of the cleft. Climb a short corner to a sloping ledge, traverse diagonally right and climb the left arete of the cleft for 3m, then step left to go up a short slabby wall to gain the base of the long expanse of overhanging wall. Finish up the twin cracks on its left.

The Villain 28m VS 5a. Paul Headland, Keith Archer. 14 June 2008.
Start 1 metre left of the previous route. Climb blocky ledges trending slightly left to a short steep slab. Climb this and follow the right-slanting ledge for 8m until below a large crack splitting the overhang above. Climb this direct.

2nd Birthday Route 30m HVS 5a **. Paul Headland, Keith Archer. 15 June 2008.
Start 5m left of *Birthday Route* where the platform narrows and steepens. Follow the left-trending dark band of rock to reach the lower right corner of the prominent central wall. Climb the crack that splits its right side on excellent jugs and continue up the right-hand of two cracks that split the right side of the overhanging wall above.

Acairsaid Slabs:
The south-facing, easy-angled slabs at the northern end of Geodhachan Ruadha. Access to the routes is initially as for Hadrian's/Pictland, but once down the short corner turn east and walk to, and then along, the north-eastern ridge to its highest point. Abseil from here down a broad gully to a large non-tidal ledge.

...And the Nut was Good 22m Very Difficult. Paul Headland, Keith Archer. 12 June 2008.
Traverse left and step onto the main slab; continue up its centre to reach the abseil point.

Alexandra Elene Maclean Denny 23m Very Difficult. Keith Archer, Paul Headland. 12 June 2008.
From the same start, step left onto the slab and follow the flaky undercut edge leftwards. Go up to finish left of the abseil point.

I shot a Rhino in Reno   24m   Very Difficult. Paul Headland, Keith Archer. 12 June 2008.
Start as for the previous routes. Leave the flaky undercut edge and traverse left again to follow the edge of the slab to the top.

The following route starts at the far left end of the slabs where they abut the big broken back wall, possibly one of the earliest routes in the Hebrides, used as a way up in 2008 but would be committing at the time of its first ascent, given a name retrospectively for the first ascensionists. For the full effect try it barefoot.

Hard Times   30m.   Moderate. Neil McLeod & party. 1613.
From the boulder beach take the easiest way up the cracked slab, keeping close to the corner near the top.

Weatherman's Geodha:
The Whole of the Moon   26m   E1 5a **. Keith Archer, Paul Headland. 15 June 2008.
The compelling big corner at the left end of the huge back wall. Abseil down just to one side of the route. Start from a big pedestal just above the base of the corner. Step left into the corner and follow it directly until the crack finishes. Move left onto the slab to finish.

Dental Area:
The big north-facing buttresses on the southern side of Weatherman's Geodha. Access by walking down (eastwards) the grassy ridge which forms the top of the area to reach a black gully. Descend this until possible to drop (northwards) down a second gully to arrive at ledges, non-tidal at first but becoming tidal, which give access to both areas.
   The area is divided into two distinct sectors by a huge central gully. On the left (eastern side) is the NHS Sector, on first inspection rather scruffy and down at heel but will look after you! On the right of the big central gully is The Private Sector, immediately appealing and more attractive, but it may rip you off! The routes are described left to right, starting at the NHS Sector just to the right of the descent.

NHS Sector:
Los Dientes   23m   Hard Severe 4b. Paul Headland, Keith Archer. 9 June 2008.
Start at the left of the sector to the left of the pyramidal monolith. Go up a short narrow gully to gain a crack in the back wall. Climb this to a niche, exit up and leftwards onto a slab to finish by the descent gully.

Milk Tooth   20m   VS 5a. Paul Headland, Keith Archer. 10 June 2008.
Start as for *Los Dientes*. Go up the gully to a niche behind the monolith. Follow the slab and cracked wall above to a belay next to the descent path.

Root Canal   24m   VS 4c **. Keith Archer, Paul Headland. 9 June 2008.
Start 5m right, to the right of the pyramidal monolith. Climb to a niche, then exit through the cracked overhang to finish 3m right of the previous route.

Amoxicillin 22m E1 5b **. Paul Headland, Keith Archer. 9 June 2008.
Start 6m right of *Root Canal* at a short corner. Climb the corner and cracks to enter a niche. Follow a right-trending ramp to a footledge below flakes. Use these to gain a cracked wall above; follow the left-hand crack. Powerful stuff!

Flossing 35m HVS 5a. Paul Headland, Keith Archer. 13 June 2008.
Start 4m right of *Amoxicillin*. Climb the black slab on the right of the gully for 15m, step round a promontory to gain the upper wall and climb this (as for *The Tooth*) to finish.

The Tooth 37m HVS 5a *. Keith Archer, Paul Headland. 10 June 2008.
Start 8m right of *Amoxicillin* at an area of shattered rock a few metres left of a square block below a V-shaped feature. Take the right-hand exit of the V feature to gain a right-trending ramp. Follow this around an arete, then climb a slabby wall (by a niche) to a pedestal. Climb the cracked wall above via a mantelshelf to gain a slab; finish behind the tooth. Good sustained climbing.

Abscess 34m VS 4c. Paul Headland, Keith Archer. 8 June 2008.
From the non-tidal ledge start just right of a prominent square block below parallel twin cracks at 10m. Climb to these but bypass them on the right to a ramp. Follow this around a short arete, then up a short wall to a lichenous slab. Climb up and diagonally right to finish up a short corner right of the prominent tooth.

Phil McCavity BDS 36m HVS 5a, *. Keith Archer, Paul Headland. 8 June 2008.
From the platform named above, start just left of the prominent square block. Climb direct to a triangular niche and step right to another short wall. Go up this to climb a crack in the slab direct to the finish of the previous route.

Private Sector:
Extraction 34m HVS 5b. Keith Archer, Paul Headland. 8 June 2008.
Start from the far right of the sector, on a large ledge a few metres up at the base of a right-facing corner with a compelling crack-line. Climb the corner to a ledge, then layaway up the crack and mantel onto a ledge to the left. Continue up a short corner to gain the crack above, then move left to gain a left-facing slab. Go up this to a corner just left of the triangular top of the central wall.

Tottering Chloroform 40m VS. Keith Archer, Paul Headland (alt). 12 June 2008.
1. 18m 4b From the start of *Extraction* climb the corner of the slab on the right to a stance below a short wall.
2. 22m 4b Climb the short wall just left of the stacked blocks to gain a left-trending ramp. Follow this to finish up a short cracked corner at the apex of the buttress.

Nae Bother Buttress:
Situated on the south-eastern corner of the island just north of a small stack and

separated from offshore rocks by a wild channel. Access by abseil to a ledge just above a prominent block with a small inverted pyramidal pool.

Nae Bother   22m   VS 4c. Keith Archer, Paul Headland. 10 June 2008.
From the ledge climb blocky rock to a right-facing corner. Follow this for 4m then step left to a flaky wall. Go up this to a ledge beneath the final 'chest of drawers' finish.

The Boatman   20m   VS 4b **. Paul Headland, Keith Archer. 11 June 2008.
From the ledge traverse 2m left and climb a short slab to a jammed block. Step on to this and climb the slabby wall above direct.

Creel Boat   24m   Very Difficult. Keith Archer, Paul Headland. 11 June 2008.
From the ledge climb a slabby ramp rightwards. When the ramp fades continue in the same direction to finish through a notch on the right side of the buttress.

Captain Peter Love   22m   Severe 4b. Paul Headland, Keith Archer. 15 June 2008.
From the stance, follow the right-trending V-groove until possible to climb the left arete of the slab.

The Morning Ferry   24m   Very Difficult. Keith Archer, Paul Headland. 15 June 2008.
Abseil to a pedestal below a corner, 8m left of the start of the previous routes. Climb the corner for 3m then follow a right-trending ramp for 5m until possible to climb cracks in the slabby wall above. Finish up the line of the abseil.

Air Mor Mangurstadh, Buaile Chuide, Screaming Geo, North West Face:
The next two routes finish in the arete of the prominent corner in the top section of the north-west face (to the left of Shonkey). Access by abseil down the corner and right of the large spike under the ledge above the overhung lower wall and left-facing corner/flake system.

Life on the Asteroid Belt   50m   E2 5b *. Ross Jones, Andrew Wardle. 8 September 2008.
1. 35m 5b Climb the steep right-slanting ramp for 4m to a small overhang. Traverse left and up to a ledge (bold). Climb a right-slanting cracked groove to the left-facing overhung corner. Pull through right onto the arete and step back over the corner into another corner. Pull through an overhang and easy ground right of a large spike to the bottom of the corner.
2. 15m 4c The fine corner-crack.

Asteroid Direct   15m   E1 5b *. Ross Jones, Andrew Wardle. 8 September 2008.
Five metres right of the corner is a right-facing overhung corner that borders the right of the wall. Climb this to the top.

Roinn a' Roidh:
(NB 507 658) Non-tidal North-west facing
The routes are in a geo just north of a cairn which has a stone serpent at its base and is 20mins walk from the lighthouse. The base of the climbs can be made by

a traverse of the opposite wall of the geo and stepping over a gap onto the wall. Stakes (not in situ) are needed to belay and are best used for abseil.

Knucker 25m E1 5b. Andrew Wardle, Ross Jones. 6 September 2008.
Climb the slanting crack-line on the left of the wall and right of the niche to the overhang. Traverse left around the overhang and pull right onto the wall above to finish.

Nagini 25m E2 5b ***. Ross Jones, Andrew Wardle. 6 September 2008.
Start from a ledge under the overhang on the right side of the wall and climb up leftwards to the wall just left of the right-facing hanging corner. Climb the wall and shallow capped groove-crack above to pull out left and then rightwards to a ledge and niche above to finish. Fine climbing.

Rubha na Beirghe:
Twenty metres right of *Internal Exam Crack* are some large boulders on the cliff-top. An abseil from the most north-easterly boulders through a V-groove just left (as you look at the cliff from the sea) of the edge of the overhanging cliff-top gives access to the following route.

Soaked by a Wave 25m VS 4c *. Ross Jones, Andrew Wardle. 9 September 2008.
Belay on a small ledge left of overhangs and 8m above the sea. Climb the steep crack-line up the wall to a ledge system beneath the overhanging cliff-top. Climb the wall and V-groove on the left to finish.

Above the Swell 20m Severe. Andrew Wardle, Ross Jones. 9 September 2008.
From the most north-westerly cairn follow a fault-line direct to the cliff edge. Abseil to a hanging belay on a very small ledge above the overhang. Climb cracks up the steep wall to the top.

AIRD UIG, Geodha Gunna (NB 033 363):
The big south-facing cliff holds the 1997 routes, *Rabid Wanderings* and *Lucid Visions* (SMCJ 189 p565). The western seaward side of Geodh Gunna has a retaining wall which takes the form of a lovely clean slab, facing east. 'Brilliant little black slab and corner' says p102 of the guidebook.

Little Gem 30m Severe ***. Mick Tighe, Bill Newton & co. 1980s.
Approach by abseil. Take the left-facing corner where the slab butts against the north wall. A small Friend in the right crack protects the initial tricky moves up the immaculate slab, after which the corner is followed to the top on improving holds and protection.

Gun Run 30m Hard Severe *. Mick Tighe, Angela Gillespie, Tracy McLachlan. 29 May 2000.
Approach by abseil. Start 10m left of *Little Gem* below a broken black groove. Climb the groove for 8–10m before making a difficult move out right onto the slab, which is followed direct to the top.

Around the corner from *Gun Run* is a broken wall with broken ledges just on the high tide line. Two routes were done here on 29 May 2000 by Mick Tighe, James Armour, Roger & Tracy McLachlan. A few metres around the corner from *Gun Run* a hanging crack/chimney line gave *Pop Gun* 20m HVS, exiting on the slab part way up *Gun Run*. Left again is a fine crack/open groove which proves rather gymnastic – *Gun Crack* 30m HVS 5b.

The Legend of Finlay MacIver 25m E1 5b ***. Mick & Kathy Tighe. 29 May 2008.
At the north-west corner of Geodha Gunna, where the south-facing and west-facing walls meet, is a wee recess from which springs a fabulous crack-corner curving gently rightwards to the top of the crag. Wonderful climbing with excellent protection on perfect rock. Approach by abseil or traverse in from the north under an interesting looking wall.

Rubha Talanish (SMCJ 2005):
Notes: *Doctor MacDonald's...* is the same route as *Blackhouse Arete* but gained by a traverse pitch from boulders at base of crag rather than abseil to a sloping ledge at base of arete.
    Stormy Slab is to left of *Blackhouse Arete* (not right). All other routes are to the left.

Tigh na Geal 25m E3 6a. Iain Small, Susan Jensen. 20 May 2007.
Abseil to the same ledge as *Tigh Dubh*. Climb an awkward crack to gain the hanging corner left of *Tents Away*. Follow this, then take the fine crack in the left wall. Pass a bulge and finish up the widening crack.

Gael Force 30m E4 6a. Iain Small, Susan Jensen. 20 May 2007.
The right edge of Thatch Top buttress. Start just left of *Beached Whale* from the large boulders. Delicately gain a diagonal crack left of an overhung recess; follow it to a flake-crevasse and ledges. Tackle the wall above from a recess below an overlap making bold moves out right to gain a crack leading to a sloping ledge on the arete. Surmount the overhang above on the right and follow the pocketed wall.

NORTH HARRIS, SRON ULLADALE:
Wee Eck 95m E5 6b. Iain Small, Pat Nolan. 28 June 2009.
1. 25m 5c As for pitch 1 of *Big Luigi*.
2. 25m 6b Follow *Big Luigi* into the quartzy groove, then swing out onto the right arete to gain a good footledge. Hard moves right lead to a corner which is followed by good square-cut ledge.
3. 25m 6a Step right off the ledge, climb a white groove to an overlap, then follow the break out right around the arete to a footledge. Take the bulges above on the right to a long thin ledge.
4. 20m Take an easy corner on the right to easier ground.

SRON A' SGAOTH:
(NB 14616 03962) Alt 304m
Sron a' Sgaoth is the western top of Sgaoth Iosal. Park opposite the quarry off the A859, 10mins drive north from Tarbert. The crags can be reached in 30mins.

Descents for all the routes lie down a gully up left (north-west) of the routes, where a grass shelf near the base leads back left to the foot of the routes. The crags lie on the west and south-west prow of the hill. Steep slabs with a prominent brown water-worn streak lie on the right, facing south-west whilst a steeper nose lies above and left, facing west. The rock is good quality gneiss, mostly very clean.

Aon 30m VS 4b/c *. John Mackenzie, Eve Austin. 5 July 2009.
The nose is split by two corners with a tier of rock below. The climb takes the right-hand corner which has an overhang at the top. A very nice climb on excellent holds which is reached by scrambling up a broken gully just right of the nose.
1. 13m Climb the lowest rocks above blocks and move up right to below the right-hand corner.
2. 17m Climb the corner, stepping left under the overhang and pull over this to the top.

The slabs are the lowest crags on the face with a steep lower wall on the left with a grass shelf above and the brown water streak to the right and less continuous slabs right again. Though the lines are aesthetically contrived, they give the best climbing.

Da 60m VS 4c *. John Mackenzie, Eve Austin. 5 July 2009.
1. 25m 4c The lower wall has a little curving crack leading to a wall and bulge at the top. Climb the crack and wall to near the bulge, move left to twin thin cracks at a rust-coloured section (obviously much easier if the route is started to the left but not so good) then up a short wall moving right (avoiding the grass shelf) to belays in a little corner above a ledge.
2. 35m 4b Step right and climb just right of a bulge (4 Friend hole) and climb to a little ledge and corner on the right. Climb the good corner and up short walls to belay at a 'thin-sling' spike.
40m of scrambling leads to the top.

Tri 60m VS 4b *. John Mackenzie, Eve Austin. 5 July 2009.
This climbs the brown water worn streak 6m to the right of *Da*. Start at a gravel patch.
1. 30m 4b Climb letter-box holds up and right over shelves, including a mantelshelf, then straight up to belay by the good corner of *Da*.
2. 30m 4a Move left and climb the diagonal shelf left of the overhang to enter an arched niche and wide crack to the left of grass. Climb the wide crack to the same belay as on Da. Scrambling to finish.

AN CLISEAM, Coire Dubh Slabs:
(NB 14724 07288) Alt 433m
Park at the east end of Loch na Ciste off the A859 at a slip road lay-by. Follow slopes by the burn to the bealach then contour round the southern spur of An Cliseam descending to a bright green grass patch within Coire Dubh where a short ascent leads to the lowest point of the slabs; 1hr 15mins.
The Coire Dubh slabs are composed of the finest-quality clean grey gneiss

giving friction climbing. There are numerous possibilities of easier but grassy lines which are often very wet. The quickest-drying (less than 24hrs) lines are the balder slabs and the line chosen takes the most continuous rock, often straightforward, left of the straight grassy gully mentioned on p65 of the guide. The slabs are sub-divided into three by two left-slanting rakes, the first above the lowest spur of slabs and the second, starting from the gully, separating the main slabs from the upper. The main slabs are characterised by a clean line of slabs well left of the gully and the upper by a square-cut recess and three curving overlapped corners to its left.

The Original Route, mentioned in the guide, appears to take the defined rib that borders the grassy gully, avoids the upper slabs then re-enters higher to finish up broken ground.

The Harris Jig 250m HVS 5a **. John Mackenzie, Eve Austin. 10 July 2009. A very pleasant outing that can be combined with a round of the tops; pitches 2 and 4 are particularly good. Start 12m left of the base of the rocks at a left-facing corner.
1. 50m 4a Go easily up the corner to overlaps which are taken centrally to easier ground and a belay on the rake directly below a small pointed block that is left of a much bigger one.
2. 50m 5a Climb the smoother slabs below the smaller pointed block, past a short corner beneath a bigger balder slab which is bounded by a grassy (wet!) corner on the right. The slab has a partially cleaned thin crack for quite good gear nearer the corner. Climb the slab left of the cleaned crack direct to an overlap, all on lovely friction. Move right and break leftwards through the overlap to belay at the 'small' pointed block.
3. 50m Move left and up a coarsely crystalline rock to the second rake at a black wet patch of slab, taking an overlap above this to arrive below the square-cut recess.
4. 35m 5a The recess encloses a smooth friction slab, entirely without cracks. To its left the recess has a wet corner leading to a double overlap that runs across the top of the slab. Wet streaks often run beneath this overlap. Climb up the slab moving into the corner at about halfway up, depending on confidence. The alcove at the top of the corner beneath the overlaps is well protected but was very wet. Move right to a dry flange and mantel onto the slab between the overlaps then traverse back left to the alcove and up this to belays in a recess on the left.
5. 40m Step left and up a red feldspar slab easily followed by scrambling to belays beneath a nice slab on the right.
6. 25m Climb the pleasant slab.
Scrambling remains to the top. An escape rightwards into the top of the grass gully should be possible after pitch 4.

TEALASDALE SLABS:
These are slow to dry after the winter as they were seeping in a very dry spell in May.
Islivig Direct has a helpful cairn at the start of the route.

Top: John Lyall on Pitch 1 of Grand Slam (V,7), Beinn Eighe, during the first ascent.
Bottom: Andy Nisbet enjoying the sunshine, also on the first ascent of Grand Slam (V,7).
Both photos: Pete MacPherson

CAITIOSBHA:
(NB 403 171)   Alt 100m   South-West facing
These roadside crags are of good quality gneiss but unfortunately not very steep. From the road walk uphill to arrive at the slab in one minute.

Left-Hand Slab:
Far Left   28m   Moderate *.
There are two lines on the slab. Climb the left one.

Yellow Patches   28m   Moderate *.
The right route on the slab.

Upper Cracks   18m   Very Difficult *.
Up and right of the slab is a crack in a short wall, climb this to a grassy ledge then move left and climb another crack.

Right-Hand Slab:
One   20m   Moderate.
The far left-hand route.

Two   22m   Moderate **.
The fine left-hand easy-angled crack.

Three   24m   Moderate **.
Walk up the right-hand crack.

Juniper Buttress:
This is right of the slabs and slightly steeper.

Ceilidh Minogue   40m   Very Difficult **. Colin Moody, Cynthia Grindley. 12 May 2008.
Fine climbing up the longest bit of rock. Start at the toe of the buttress left of a spike. Climb up then move right above a large juniper bush and climb the rib.

Black Blobs   25m   VS 4b *. Cynthia Grindley, Colin Moody. 12 May 2008.
Right of *Ceilidh Minogue* is a grassy corner then a rib, start at this. Climb up on black blobs then continue up the rounded rib above.

Vitamin T   25m   Severe *. Cynthia Grindley, Colin Moody. 12 May 2008.
Just right of *Black Blobs* is a right-slanting corner with heather patches. Climb up just right of these.

The Jimmy Shandrix Experience   15m   Difficult *. Colin Moody, Cynthia Grindley. 12 May 2008.
Right of the previous route is a vegetated corner. Climb the fine scoop to the right.

The Battersea Boys   15m   Difficult *. Colin Moody. 12 May 2008.
Start 2m right of *The Jimmy Shandrix Experience* and climb another scoop past a clump of heather at 4m.

Tess Fryer on Sugar Cane Country (E4 6a), Pabbay, Hebrides.
Photo: Neil Carnegie.

Brown Scoop   15m   Difficult *. Colin Moody. 12 May 2008.
Start 5m right at quartz crystals; climb pleasantly up.

SOUTH UIST, Maol na h-Ordaig, Corner Crag (NF 839 151):
A crag formed by an open-book corner with an undercut left wall.
Slob Trout   10m   Hard Severe 4b. Graham Stein, Ian Hall, Claire Stein. 10 June 2008.
Start on a boulder below the main crack in the left wall. Follow the crack, mostly on its left, exiting left at the top.

Loch Aineort, Creag Mor Sea Cliffs (NF 821 272):
A west-facing crag bounded on the left by a steep grassy gully with a huge chockstone at its top. The upper half of the crag is dominated by impressive overhangs. Beneath the overhangs runs a marked left-rising discontinuous break finishing above the chockstone in the grassy gully. The approach on the FA was from the sea, but abseil from the west (left side of cliff looking from bottom) should be possible, to reach rocks at sea-level. The crag is visible from a promontory at the west side of the green gully.

Captain Zim's Drascombe Longboat   55m   E1. Graham Stein, Ian Hall, Claire Stein. 12 June 2008.
1. 25m 5b Climb an obvious crack-line immediately left of the black and white streaked section of wall for 20m until it is possible to pull right onto a small ledge (steep, well-protected). Move more easily up and left to a small ledge.
2. 15m 4b Follow the left-rising line of weakness, pulling up awkwardly behind a detached flake to a good ledge with a white-streaked wall at its right end.
3. 15m 4c Continue up the line of weakness by climbing a wide crack (teetering pile of loose rocks on left) followed by a hand-traverse to gain a grassy terrace. Belay from large blocks just above the large chockstone, from where the top of the grassy gully may be reached by an easy scramble.

BARRA:
Many routes have been climbed here by Kevin Howett, Colin Moody, Pete Whillance, Steve Crowe and others. With confusion about who was first, details will have to await the new guide.

MINGULAY, Guarsay Beag, Shag's Point:
Artificial Shag   35m   VS 4c. James Thacker, Mark Edmonds. 1 June 2008.
From the same abseil ascend the groove, as for *Easy Day for a Shag*, to pull through the overlap at its widest point. Step left to climb the arete in a pleasant situation.

First in Line   45m   VS **. Mark Edmonds, James Thacker. 1 June 2008.
1. 25m 4b From the base of *Easy Day for a Shag*, make a rising traverse to a bird-filled cave-niche. Belay on the left-hand side at an obvious pink thread.
2. 25m 4c Step left to follow the left edge of the pink overhang, pulling through on excellent black juggy rock, finishing up a faint groove system.

Note: John Sanders made the first ascent of *Condemned to Happiness* in 1998 and the current route description of the first pitch is inaccurate. It should read: Belay beneath a cave. Bridge up the right side of the cave until established in the crack.

The grade should be 4b, and not 4c; the second pitch is 5a.

C2H2 40m Hard Severe **. John Sanders, Alison Sanders. 2 June 2008.
1. 20m 4b Climb the first pitch of *Condemned to Happiness*.
2. 20m 4b From the belay, move left to the open-book corner; climb this and then move awkwardly onto the right wall of the hanging pillar (crux). Climb this direct to the top.

Choctaw Bingo 40m Severe 4b. John Sanders, Alison Sanders. 2 June 2008.
Belay in a small chimney approx. 4m left of the stance for *With a view to a Shag*. Move up and left in a rising traverse to where the crag changes aspect, to be beneath a small overlap split by a mossy crack. Breach the overlap using the crack (crux) and climb direct to the top.

The Ultimate Fascinator 40m Hard Severe 4b ***. John Sanders, Alison Sanders. 5 June 2008.
From the same belay as *Choctaw Bingo*, climb straight up the short chimney and the wall above on excellent holds to a corner (poorly protected – No. 3 Camalot required for the letterbox). From the corner move right, around the overlap, to climb the delicate wall above, and then jugs to the top – superb and sustained throughout.

Guarsay Mor:
Guanomala City 60m VS. John Dale, Mike Coleman. 3 August 2000.
Takes a line between *No Puke Here* and *Grey Rib*. Start as for *No Puke Here*.
1. 40m 4c Climb rightwards via a groove and awkward scoop to a right-trending flake-groove. Follow this for a few metres, then step left and climb directly up the right side of the rounded rib to narrow ledges above a bulge.
2. 20m 4a Climb directly to the top on large holds, passing through the centre of the bulge above.

Dun Mingulay:
Storm Warning Direct Finish 45m VS 4b. Mark Edmonds, Graham Stein, James Thacker. 3 June 2008.
The following variation forms a true finish from the top of pitch 2 (the 5c crux). Follow a direct line, trending rightwards through steep but steady terrain to the top. The original finish scuttles off left to join *15 Fathoms*.

Sula Direct Start 30m E3 5c. James Thacker, Graham Stein. June 2004.
Start 5m to the left of *The Silkie* directly below the left end of the crescent-shaped roof. Climb up towards the bottom of an open groove at approximately half-height, move out right and climb directly to enter a shallow scoop. Move up under the crescent-shaped roof (good runners) before moving right and up to the first stance on *Sula*.

Dun Mingulay, Sron an Duin:
The Swell 210m   E4. D. O'Sullivan, Ross Cowie, Tim Marsh. 5 June 2008.
A right to left girdle of Sron An Duin. For the most part it follows an obvious fault-line. Amazing climbing. At least half of the ground covered is new.
1. 40m 5c Start up *Dun Moaning* and follow this till level with the roof of *Rory Rum*. Traverse left around the arete and gain *Rory Rum* which is followed left under the roof to belay at a slot just beyond where *Big Ken* breaches the roof.
2. 30m 6a Follow the fault strenuously left to the arete and then easily for another 20m.
3. 30m 4c Cruise the juggy fault-line to belay above the plinth of *The Silkie.*
4. 40m 5b Continue easily left for 20m and then descend a few metres to a lower break. This leads left past an orange shield to a comfortable belay on the edge of the huge arch. (This is the *Ray of Light* belay below the 'tusk'.)
5. 40m 5c Now take a diagonal line up and left to gain the break under the huge roof. Traverse easily left for 7m and belay on *Perfect Monsters.*
6. 30m 5c An exposed traverse left on the lip of the roof gains a small ledge. Finish direct.

Searching in the Sun   E4 6a. D. O'Sullivan, Ross Cowie, Tim Marsh. 6 June 2008.
An intimidating line which breaches the lower central area of the huge arch at the north end of the cliff. Belay on ledges at the bottom right-hand side of the huge arch below the wet off-width chimney (left of *Les Voyageurs*).
1. 40m Traverse easily up and left to the bottom of a short black left-facing corner. Climb this and then traverse horizontally left along the the lip of the overhang for 5m. Now launch up the bulging arete to a good rest. Continue up and left to belay among the birds at the prominent horizontal break.
2. Traverse left to gain the upper section of *Ray of Light* pitch 1. Follow this to belay at the big roof.
3. Finish as for *Ray of Light.*

Note from Steve Crowe: On Dun Mingulay we climbed the crack just left of the start of *Perfectly Normal Paranoia* to give an independent (E4 6a) start to *Call of the Sea*, named *Last Call.*
We climbed *Voyage of Faith* into *Perfect Monsters*. We call this *Voyage of Faith* with the *Ocean of Air finish*. E4 6a ****. Phenomenal exposure. Unbelievable territory at the grade. Competent second essential.

The Geirum Walls, Hidden Wall Area:
Sunnyside Up   25m   VS 5a **. Claire Stein, Alison Sanders, Ian Hall. 6 June 2008.
The corner to the right of *Whipsplash*, gained by an abseil descent as for *The Gull Who Shagged Me* to the elevated ledge. Start at the big hole beneath the obvious right-facing corner. Climb up the hole either on its right or by bridging to gain the bottom of the main corner-crack and twin crack on the right. Climb the strenuous corner and mantelshelf onto a square ledge. Follow the series of short continuation corners to gain the right end of a guillemot ledge under a roof. Step right and reach top by an easy rightwards traverse on a ledge and continue to belay on the Platform Wall platform.

Over Easy 25m Very Difficult. Claire Stein, Alison Sanders, Ian Hall. 6 June 2008.
The vague arete to the right of *Sunnyside Up*. Start at the right end of the elevated ledge (facing in). Follow a groove to a ledge on the arete and climb a series of short walls and ledges to belay as for *Sunnyside Up*.

Geirum Walls:
The following routes are east of the Geirum Walls, at the southern end of the island.
Right of Skipisdale Wall is an attractive tidal buttress, Skipisdale Buttress? The first route climbs the left arete. Low tide required.

My Gull's Mad At Me 15m VS 4c. John Dale, Pippa Curtis. 30 May 2001.
Climb the arete, pulling leftward through the bulges, and finish direct.

Happy Landings 15m HVS 5a. John Dale, Nigel Murphy. 30 May 2001.
Start immediately right of *My Gull...* Bridge up the groove for a few moves, then swing right into a shallow scoop. Climb directly up the front face of the buttress, finishing in a short corner. Not overly well protected.

PABBAY:
Note: John Grieve, Will Thompson and Hamish MacInnes were thought to have climbed on Pabbay about 1972.

Hoofer's Headland (The Box):
Tick-tack 20m VS 4c. Paul Drew, Ian Lewis. 9 August 1999.
Start at the foot of the obvious corner. Climb the corner to the top.

Another Tick 20m HVS 5a. Ian Lewis, Paul Drew. 9 August 1999.
Climb the middle of the wall to the right of *Tick-tack*.

Double Tick 20m E1 5c. Ian Lewis, Paul Drew. 9 August 1999.
Start just around the arete forming the right end of the recess. Climb the steep wall with an overhanging start.

Hoofer's Geo:
Wee Bill 15m Severe. Steve Thompson, Paul Drew. 3 July 2007.
Left of the descent. Start on ledges 15m above the sea. Climb the obvious corner with a step start.

More Whine and Whiskey 25m Hard Severe. Paul Drew, Steve Thompson. 3 July 2007.
Wall and pillar to the left of the easy corner-crack. Starts on a good ledge to the left of the deep chimney bounded on the right by the beak-like overhang taken by *Harry Hoofer*.

Tick, Tack, Toe 28m VS 4c *. Paul Drew, Steve Thompson. 3 July 2007.
Takes the wall and arete left of the deep chimney to a fine finish up a crack overlooking the chimney/gash. Start as for *More Whine and Whiskey*.

Palm Tree Wall:
The first cliff reached on the Allanish Peninsula, located about 50m south of Allanish Wall and visible from the approach path to the Arch Cliff. Scramble down ledges on the left (facing out) until a sea-level platform can be reached (not tidal).

One Armed Bandit   15m   VS 5a. John Dale, Yvonne Sell. 4 July 2007.
Start at the extreme left end of the wall. Climb up and rightwards to gain the obvious crack leading to the top.

The Missing Arm   10m   VS 4c. David Barlow, Richard Spillett. 5 July 2007.
Follows the first crack-line. Effectively a direct start to *One Armed Bandit*.

Afternoon Showers   10m   E1 5b *. Des Chadderton, Hugh Merritt. 5 July 2007.
Follow the second crack-line.

Thirty Metre Cheese Course   10m   HVS 5a *. Richard Spillett, David Barlow. 5 July 2007.
Follow the third crack-line.

Barra Crack   15m   VS 5a. John Dale, S.Thompson, Yvonne Sell. 4 July 2007.
Follow the fourth crack-line.
Note: The route was repeated with a more direct finish (not going into the big corner) by Alasdair Fulton & Malcolm Airey on 25 June 2008 (*Frailty of Life* 18m E2 5c **).

Ta Mo Chridhe   25m   Severe. Steve Thompson, John Dale, Yvonne Sell. 4 July 2007.
The corner-crack followed directly.

Black Guillemot   20m   VS 4b *. John Dale, Steve Thompson, Yvonne Sell. 4 July 2007.
Good climbing up the slab to the right of the corner. Following the right-trending crack to the top.

Mr Dressup   20m   Severe 4a. Yvonne Sell, John Dale. 4 July 2007.
Around the corner from the Black Guillemot slab. The route follows two short walls split by a large ledge.

The Galley, East Wall:
The Engine Room   15m   VS 4c. Richard Spillett, David Barlow. 3 July 2007.
Climbs the wall on the opposite side of the geo from *The Galley*, further down from *Wiggly Wall*. Starts from sea-level ledges. Climb a vertical crack which then slants rightwards towards the top of the wall.

Banded Wall:
Parting Shot   50m   E5 6a **. Steve Crowe, Karen Magog. 2008.
A finish to the uncompleted line right of *Geomancer*. Climb the corner left of *Geomancer* to the large sloping ledge. Continue up the wall above to eventually

join *Geomancer* at the sling runner below the final bulge. Sprint up the headwall as for *Geomancer*.

Banded Wall, South Face, Platform Buttress:

Platform buttress is the lower south-west-facing 10m crag, accessed by abseiling from the left end (looking in) of the platform used to access the Banded Wall South Face routes. Very quick drying, no seepage.

Raindance 15m E1 5b *. Alasdair Fulton, Malcolm Airey. 22 June 2008.
Start at the left end of the ledge, beside a deep man-sized chimney on the left. Climb a small shallow, right-facing groove/crack, over a slight bulge on small but positive holds. Continue up and slightly left on easier ground, then up the steep juggy headwall above to finish on the VDiff spur of *Bald Eagle*.

Beast it Like a Kipper 10m VS 5a *. Malcolm Airey, Alasdair Fulton. 22 June 2008.
Start 4m right of the chimney. Climb a steep wide left-slanting crack to where the crack becomes horizontal. Trend right on good holds up the wall above.

Pink Wall:

Aukward Eascape 45m E4 6a **. Jon Morgan, Martin Cooper, Stan Halstead. 13 June 2009.
Follows a flake-line a few metres left of *Where Seagulls Dare* and finishes at the top of the second pitch of *Tickled Pink*. From the left-hand end of the main Pink Wall platform cross a gully, then up a right-facing corner and traverse left the ledge beneath the obvious flakes of *Where Seagulls Dare* (possible belay) to another line of flakes. Climb these, and where the flakes run out pull up and leftwards onto a pink slab with two useful finger pockets. Pull up left into a smaller flake system and follow it with increasing difficulty until you can step left into the top of the chimney of *Tickled Pink*, and block belay as for that route.

The following route was approached by a mistaken abseil. Instead of abseiling east from the large flat block, an abseil was made from the west end of the ledge, 85m to a ledge 20m above the sea. The rock is quite sandy. Picture provided.

What the Eagle? 90m E3 5b/c **. David Toon, Richard Toon. 30 May 2008.
A steep and character-building climb!
1. 40m 5b Climb a grey groove above the stance to where a traverse right gains a black corner. Climb this to a yellow wall with a down-pointing flake. Climb this on its left to a red firebrick ledge. Belay below the left end of the big long roof.
2. 30m 5b/5c Step left back in to a crack and follow this to an overhang. Surmount this (crux). Continue up until a move left brings another crack. Finish steeply up this and belay on the ledge.
3. 20m 4b Climb over broken ledges to finish.

Bay Area:

Every Cormorant is a Potential Shag E7 6b. Dave Birkett (unsec). 8 June 2008.
Start 10m right of *The Herbrudean* at the left-hand side of the big cave beneath the obvious stepped right-facing corner. Make a boulder problem start into the

first hanging corner. Traverse right to good holds and back left to the V-groove. Move up and rightwards into a shallow groove (good holds and gear on the left). Gain the big break under the roof (big Friends). Traverse left for 3m using a shattered handrail, then pull through the roof into a shallow corner. Finish up and right.

Big Bloc Sloc:
Two routes at the seaward tip of the wedge. From the large wedged block climb down above the left side of the wall until the top of an obvious corner is reached; abseil from here to a small tidal ledge.

Wee Bairns   20m   VS 4c. Matt Kingsley, John Dale. 6 July 2007.
Climb the left side of the wall and continue by lichenous rock to the top.

Two Skulls in the Sunset   20m   VS 4c *. John Dale, Matt Kingsley. 6 July 2007.
Climbs an obvious corner to a triangular roof. Pull through to a flake and follow this to the top.

Rosinish Wall:
Lottie   10m   HVS 5b. Richard Spillett, David Barlow. 3 July 2007.
Just to the left of the fetid pool is a deceptively steep series of cracks up a wall, just to the right of an arete. Climb the cracks, trending rightwards.

More Training Required   20m   E1 5b. Richard Spillett, David Barlow. 7 July 2007.
The groove to the left of the *The Ethics Police* arete, moving onto the arete to avoid the loose yellow exit.

Thuggy Crystal   20m   HVS 5a. David Barlow, Richard Spillett. 3 July 2007.
About 6m right of *Rising Damp* is a black slab, bounded on its right by a V-groove. Climb the groove and the continuation crack to the capping crystal overhang. Pull and hop over it to finish more easily.

No More Ticks   15m   HVS 4c. Paul Drew, Yvonne Sell. 7 July 2007.
On the right of the overhang (see *The Whoop of The Aviator*) is a left-facing corner. Pull into this and reach up awkwardly to a flat hold. Pull up and continue more easily to the top of the crag.

Rosinish Wall:
Squeak   E2 5c. David Toon. 31 May 2008.
The wall right of *Rising Damp*. The move left is the crux.

There is a small 10m wall to the right (looking out) from the Rosinish Wall; it has three cracks.
Wing n' Prayer   10m   E2 5c. David Toon. 31 May 2008.
Climb the right-hand of the three cracks, stepping left at the top.

Lengeigh Point:
This is the most northerly point on Pabbay opposite the small island of Lengeigh. Its west wall forms a series of small buttresses up to 15m high. Go to

the northern seaward end of Lengeigh Point and scramble down ledges on the west side until the first rock step into a deep gully is reached.

Seal Wall 15m Very Difficult. Paul Drew, Matt Kingsley. 5 July 2007.
Climbs the wall left of a deep gully.

Too Hard for the SMC 15m Severe. Paul Drew, Matt Kingsley. 5 July 2007.
Climbs wall right of deep gully.

RUM, Stac nam Faoileann:
(NM 407 932) Tidal South and North-facing
There are two stacks here, about 1.5 km from Dibidil on the path to Kinloch. The first has a broad flat top, the second (at Stoatir Point, and lies a little to the south) is more shapely. Stac nam Faoileann is the broad squat stack connected to the land by a collapsed arch leading to a groove taken by *Faoileann Corner* (1967).

Faoileann Arete 8m Very Difficult. Brian Davison. 30 June 2009.
The arete at the western landward end of the stack. Originally climbed at high tide, this involved swimming to the stack and gaining a ledge above an overhang before following easier ground to the top. This can probably be reached by boulder hopping at low tide.

Faoileann Chimney 10m Moderate. Brian Davison. 30 June 2009.
From the west end of the stack traverse around on ledges to the seaward side to a broad chimney or stepped dyke system which is followed easily to the top.

RUM, Dibidil Bay, Dibidil East Headland:
(NM 395 927) Partially Tidal South-facing
Approach: From the bothy to the east side of the bay avoiding the large geo which cuts back inland just before the headland starts to gain height. Once round the geo scramble down to a large platform. The first routes facing west are on a small wall with a tapering black streak down the middle, taken by *Black Streak* and a smoother shield of rock up to its right. Further right, beyond an undercut arete, the wall offers three groove systems in its top third.

Black Streak 10m Hard Severe 4b. Brian Davison. 29 June 2009.
Climb the centre of the black streak.

Dibidil Wall 10m VS 4c. Brian Davison. 29 June 2009.
Start 2m right at an undercut start and climb the wall to a small overlap to gain the shield of rock. Climb this to the top.

Easy Wall 10m Difficult. Brian Davison. 29 June 2009.
Right of the shield the wall leans back and offers plenty of holds.

Easy Edge 10m Very Difficult. Brian Davison. 29 June 2009.
The right edge before the cliff turns the corner; an undercut start is the crux.

The next three routes are found around the arete and have obvious grooves in their top third; the first starts right of an overhanging recess.

Rum   15m   VS 4c. Brian Davison. 29 June 2009.
Start right of the overhanging recess and climb a wall to a ledge. Finish up the
left-hand groove.

Sodomy   15m   VS 5a. Brian Davison. 29 June 2009.
Start up the steep wall directly below the less well-defined middle groove. From
the ledge finish up the middle groove.

Lash   15m   VS 4c. Brian Davison. 29 June 2009.
The right-hand groove is steeper near the top but starts up easier-angled rock
below.

Dibidil Pinnacle:
(NM 394 925)   Tidal
At the west side of the bay is a 10m stack with a smaller stumpier stack or
boulder to its west. The stack can be reached at low tide by stepping across. The
west face contains some hairy lichen and *Wilderness Experience* (10m VS 4c)
goes up the wall and a faint V-depression near the top at the right-hand side of
the face. The seaward side of the stack offers an easy scrambling descent. The
black east face offers *Deep Water Solo* (10m VS 4c) up the more broken features
of the face immediately left of a blank and compact section of wall. There is
some loose rock at the top.

RUM, Guirdil Bay:
(NG 317 014)   Tidal   North-West facing
The western headland of the bay has an archway clearly seen from the descent
into the bay. The arch and the small bay beyond may be reached at low tide
either by traversing along the landward wall on a shelf above the water, or by
paddling westward into the smaller bay. The seaward leg of the arch may be
reached by wading to chest height.

Underneath the Arches   25m   Severe. Brian Davison. 30 June 2009.
From the sea gain a ledge on the west side of the arch. The remainder of the arch
is easy with care being required with loose rock near the top.

Guirdil Pinnacle   20m   Severe. Brian Davison. 30 June 2009.
The small bay to the west of Guirdil Bay accessed under the arch contains a
small stack accessible at low tide.
   Climb a corner or wall to a steep move onto a shoulder on the seaward side of
the stack. Continue up the seaward side to the summit. A descent was made by
climbing down the landward side for a few metres to a sloping ledge which
allowed access back to the seaward face to downclimb the ascent route.

COLONSAY, Arch Crag:
Toberoran   10m   Very Difficult. Phil Latham, Jane Latham. 28 May 2008.
As you descend into the shingle cove towards the arch there is a long slab wall
on the right running for about 40m. About three-quarters of the way down the
wall there is a very obvious large boulder. The climb starts immediately in front

of this boulder. The route climbs up trending gradually right just under a obvious band of overlaps.

ORONSAY:
Stranded 8m Difficult. Gwilym Lynn. 6 August 2008.
In the small bay behind Eilean Fhionnlaidh beside the track across The Strand is an obvious cave and chimney (NR 363 895). Climb the left rib of the cave and continuing chimney.

Beinn Oronsay:
Columba's Ramp 30m Moderate. Gwilym Lynn. 6 August 2008
About 50m left of *Priory Slab* is a right-trending ramp. Climb the ramp, vegetated near the base.

MULL, Scoor, Urchin Slab (NM 413 182):
The easier routes have been soloed before by Colin Moody but not yet written up. Approach: The tidal sea-stack is clearly visible to the east of Scoor bay, approached along the boulders beyond The Slab. On reaching the stack, pass the 'hanging garden-like' taller stack on the left and round a further lower block to find the clean west-facing wall with a prominent brown smear.
Descent: The north-west side of the wall holds a surprise in the form of a staircase descent down a narrow passageway that takes you straight out to the base of the routes.

Quartz Vein Crack 9m Severe. Stuart Macfarlane, Jeannie Northover. 11 May 2009.
The left-hand of the two narrow cracks in the centre of the wall. Start with a step containing a quartz vein.

Andrea 9m Very Difficult. Jeannie Northover, Stuart Macfarlane. 11 May 2009.
The obvious larger crack to the left of *Quartz Vein Crack*.

Urchin Crack 9m Severe. Stuart Macfarlane, Jeannie Northover. 11 May 2009.
The right-hand of two narrow cracks in the centre of the wall.

Mull Childhood 9m Difficult. Jeannie Northover, Stuart Macfarlane. 11 May 2009.
The obvious larger crack to the right of *Urchin Crack*.

Rushing For The Ferry 9m Difficult. Jeannie Northover, Stuart Macfarlane. 11 May 2009.
The arete at the right end of the slab.

Tioran, Burg Peninsula, Creag Ghillean:
(NM 455 274) Alt 50m South-facing
A steep sound basalt escarpment approx. 400m long. The routes are on good sound rock, with cracks, corners and steep faces. It dries quickly but does have seepage; three days of good dry weather will see crag climbable. Belays are found on pine trees 10–30m behind the lip of the crag, a rigging rope useful.

Colin Moody and Laurie Skoudas climbed here in 1981 but did not record their routes.

Approach: Park at the National Trust car park at Tioran. Follow an estate track. The crag lies off the track down towards the sea, 5mins walk downhill by following old fence line and down over short rock step. Abseil in centrally or walk around from right end facing out to sea.

1. *Thron* 10m (Grade?) ***. Not led.
Follow the excellent fingery moves to a slopey niche and undercut to side pulls in obvious small niches above. Powerful and interesting climbing.

2. *Indecision Cracks* 10m Hard Severe **. Andy Spink, Unai Laronte, Crystal Lanageveld. 14 July 2008.
Steep narrow chimney and crack-line, follows bulgy cracks direct to the top.

3. *Starting Again!* 10m VS 4b ***. Andy Spink, Liam Irvin. March 2008.
Steep bridging up a thin corner-crack, leading to a direct finish on good holds.

4. *It's Starting to Stop* 12m HVS 5a ***. Ryan Glass, Andy Spink. 6 July 2008.
Bridging leads to a large undercut flake. Pull over this to finish.

5. *The Now and Then* Hard Severe 4a. Andy Spink, Sam Harrison, 30 June 2008.
An easy rib is followed to short steep headwall and flat top.

6. *Little Ben* 8m Hard Severe *. Andy Spink. 13 July 2008.
A thin open groove and crack followed direct to the top.

Knockvologan Area:

Cracks in a hanging slab at NM 315 184 gave Andy Spink (1991) *The Early Days* (7m Mild VS).

Two crack-lines parallel to each other can be seen high above small beach and bay at NM 309 188.

Chris 10m Mild VS. Follows a crack-line on the right.

Camilla 10m HVS. Follows a crack-line on the left.

Torr Mor a' Choriarst, School Crag (NM 312 186):

A fine 15m crag with amazing views of the coastline and to Jura. It has been climbed on for many years but routes not recorded. Right to left as viewed.

Red Kite Difficult. Climbs wrinkly rock easily to top. (Andy Spink. 1990.)

Red Coats Hard Severe. Follow slab to finger jams in crack-line, moving back left at top. (Andy Spink, Dick Carter. 1999.)

Red Fox XS. Thin slab climb up centre to obvious small pocket, then niche and so to top.

Kidnapped Severe. Easy groove is followed to nice finishing cracks. (Andy Spink, Dick Carter. 1999.)

Ross of Mull, Torr Mor Crag (NM 30443 24312):

Situated north of Fionnphort, take the minor road to Bruach Mhor shortly before reaching the village and park by the gate. Walk past the Torr Mor quarry and down steps and a track before heading north before the last house on the right. The crags are over the brow of the hill in front in a defile, 20–25mins. A typically perfect pair of granite crags facing north and south but with the problem of grassy cracks in the bigger north-facing crag of 12m. An unknown hero has left a nut near the top of the grassiest crack on the right of the crag. The central area is now clean including the crest giving excellent varied and sustained climbing for its length. The shorter south-facing crag opposite has a variety of overhanging cracks. There is also good bouldering to the left of the south crag and behind it.

North Crag:
Toffs 12m E1 5b ***. John Mackenzie. 20 July 2008.
Climbs the right-hand leg of the obvious central A-shaped crack. Start at a horizontal pod-like break to the right of the crack and climb the wall past breaks to reach the crack and the crux at the top.

South Crag:
Left of the overhanging cracks is a gentle slab with an overlap.
Almost a Stroll 10m Hard Difficult. John Mackenzie. 13 July 2008.
Climb the slab centrally.

Wave Buttress (NM 411 186):
Ripple 10m HVS 5a. Brian Davison, N. Mullinger. 21 May 2008.
The thin crack up the rib between *Tern* and *Wavey Crack* passing rightwards under a bulge at the top. The central section of crack contains loose flakes.
Note: Colin Moody had previously top-roped the route and the flakes appeared to be keyed in. He thought it was harder than *Wavey Crack* which is graded HVS.

ERRAID, Pink Wall:
Five Naked Women 7m HVS 4c *. Colin Moody, Cynthia Grindley. 5 October 2008.
Left of *Panther* is a steep crack which gives the climb.
Note: Left of *Five Naked Women* is a recess. Two corner-cracks in the recess are both Severe.

Mink Wall:
Tower Crack 8m Hard Severe *. Colin Moody, Cynthia Grindley. 18 May 2008.
At the left end of Mink Wall (and slightly higher) is a small buttress with a prominent south-facing crack. Scramble up to the crack and climb it.

Aspen Grove 22m HVS 5a *. Colin Moody, Cynthia Grindley. 14 June 2008.
Start at the right side of the left pool. Climb a short flake-crack, then move left on the large ledge. Follow twin cracks then a jam crack to a grass ledge. Continue up flake-cracks to another grass ledge with small aspen trees.

Guantanimo 13m Hard Severe *. Colin Moody, Cynthia Grindley. 14 June 2008.
Start just right of *Aspen Grove* and left of *Pond Filler*. Climb the cracks above to a ledge then move right and climb a short wide crack to another ledge and easy escape.

Fussing 8m E1 5b *. Colin Moody, Cynthia Grindley. 18 May 2008.
Right of *Red* is a shallow right-facing corner. Climb the corner and continuation crack.

Another Access Route 8m   Severe *. Colin Moody, Cynthia Grindley. 18 May 2008.
The arete right of *Access Route*. Start on the left side and make an awkward move to get started, then climb easily up and right.

Thrutchless Chimneys 10m   Very Difficult. Colin Moody, Cynthia Grindley. 18 May 2008.
Climb the short chimney at the left side of Mink to a big ledge, then climb the short chimney above.

The Sair Finger HVS 5a *. Cynthia Grindley, Colin Moody. 14 June 2008.
The right-facing corner-crack at the right side of the crag (left of *The Mink*). Move right before reaching the roof, pull over the bulge and continue as for *The Mink*.

Asteroid Chasm:
Venus 10m   E1 5a *. Cynthia Grindley, Colin Moody. 15 August 2008.
Climb the slightly overhanging cracks left of *Infinitesimal*.

IONA, Dun Lathraichean:
(NM 262 218) Alt 30m   South-West facing
Approach: As for the other crags to Loch Staonaig, then follow the path round the east side of the loch down to Columba's Bay. The crags are on the hill right (west) of the bay. 45mins from the ferry.
   There are two short crags on the south side of the small hill to the west of Columba's Bay. Climbs have been done on the right-hand crag by Cynthia Grindley and Colin Moody in 2008.

Buckets 6m   Very Difficult *.
Climb the short wall at the left end of the crag.

Matthew 10m   HVS 5a *.
The crack at the left side of the crag.

Mark 10m   E1 5a *.
The shallow corner just to the right, then step left at the bulge. Strenuous with adequate protection.

Luke 8m   VS 4c *.
Climb the right-slanting crack at the right side of the crag.

John 6m   E2 5b *.
Climb the wall at the right side of the crag.

SKYE

In the expectation that the new Skye guidebook will be out soon, and has many routes which have never appeared in an SMC Journal, no routes are recorded here this year.

NORTHERN HIGHLANDS NORTH

BEINN DEARG, Glensquaib Cliffs:

Waiting for Nemo 170m II/III. Martin Holland, Pamela Millar. 3 December 2008.

1.. 40m Start at a 2m wide slot forming a gully/groove 100m right of *WhatawaytospendEaster* and climb it via ice and turf to below a steep icicled wall on the right.

2. 30m Descend a few metres from the stance and make a left-rising traverse to a groove on the left of a small rectangular nose. Follow this to easy ground and a stance near a small pinnacle.

3. and 4. 100m A variety of easy finishes are now possible to the ridge, the easiest being a rightwards rising line finishing through an icy funnel-shaped gully.

Storming Stormont 220m III. John Mackenzie, Andy Nisbet, Neil Wilson. 10 March 2009.

A slightly indirect but still enjoyable line up the buttress to the left of *Rev Ian Paisley Memorial Gully*. Start to the left of the buttress and follow an easy narrow gully to a blockage where the route starts.

1. 45m Follow a right-trending ramp line to where it straightens. Continue up to a narrows then move hard left along a ledge to below a slab.

2. 50m Climb the slab, then move up and left and climb over two short chimneys.

3. 25m Climb a groove to a steep wall, then move horizontally right along a ledge, past a block.

4. 50m Climb up and left to a terrace and up this to the base of the headwall near a right then left-trending ramp.

5. 50m Follow the ramp, moving up and left to the top.

No Falls Road 280m IV,5 **. John Mackenzie, Neil Wilson. 31 December 2008.

An excellent line taking the curving corner in the centre of the buttress between *Emerald Edge* and *Red Handed*. Start in a snow bay below a steep groove left of an overhang and right of an icefall.

1. 45m Climb the groove to the icefall and follow this to belays on the left.

2. 45m Move right back to the corner and climb the icefall to belays on the right below a slabby section. A prominent pinnacle lies above.

3. 35m Climb the thin corner then move left then back right to a steep exit up the corner; move up right into a hidden chimney and up this to a ledge.

4. 45m Continue up the chimney, then follow the ice to a turfy section on the left leading to a small ledge below a steep wall. Climb the tricky wall, crux, to a cave on the right.

5. 45m The easier chimney leads to more broken ground and follow this to the barrier headwall.

6. 35m Move right round a small buttress to a hidden gully/groove which curves round to the left. Climb this to arrive below a steep chimney.

7. 30m Climb the awkward chimney, moving onto its right edge once past an overhang. The rib leads to a short, thin slab and the top.

Note: *Finlay's Buttress* (SMCJ 2007) should have been described as the arete between *Fenian Gully* and *Centre Party*.

West Buttress:
Toffs on the Rocks   250m   III. John Mackenzie. 27 December 2008.
A pleasant route, which comes rapidly into condition after a freeze, on the buttress between *Inverlael Gully* and *Gastronomes' Gully*. A turf or snow runnel lies in the upper central section of the buttress which leads to the arete overlooking *Gastronomes' Gully*. Start to left of *Inverlael Gully* before the gully narrows at a left-slanting diagonal line between two rock masses. Follow the diagonal over turfy steps quite steeply to an easing, moving up and left to reach the steeper runnel which provides some interest before easier ground leading to the arete overlooking *Gastronomes' Gully*. Follow this edge to the top (not included in length).

Snowseekers' Allowance   350m   II. John Mackenzie, Andy Nisbet; Sonya Drummond, Matt Griffin. 2 January 2009.
Takes the rib to the left of *Gastronomes' Gully*. Start in a recessed gully-groove directly below the gully and right of the Direct Start icefall. Climb a turf or ice ramp out left and move up and left to reach the rib. Follow the crest directly, some optional difficulties, to finish up a fine snow arete.

BEINN DEARG, Silver Slabs (NH 2568 7920, Alt 560m):
These are the rectangle of slabs on the south-east face of Creag a' Choire Ghranda (point 885) overlooking Gleann Mucarnaich. Park at the west end of Loch Droma and follow the track north from Lochdrum house over the col between Meallan Mhurchaidh and Meall Feith Dhiongaig and down to Gleann Mucarnaich, crossing the Allt Mhucarnaich. The slabs are on the left side of the hill in front. Allow 1hr 30mins.

The slabs are of silver-coloured massive schist with numerous black areas of water-worn smooth rock. Numerous overlaps cross the slabs with prominent ones at the base and the top. Much of the padding is easy with harder areas very much depending on the line chosen. The rock is mostly clean and sound with some loose flakes in places but almost devoid of cracks save at the overlaps. Friends are particularly useful. The climbing is more interesting than initial appearances suggest and quite varied, though the second pitches are open to variation. The top overlaps are in three sections moving from left to right; the 'tower of blocks' on the left which is separated from the steepest section (usually wet), the overlaps below and above a triangular niche with a white spot, the brown middle overlaps right again, and, just right of a wet corner, the blockier square-cut overlaps that are bordered by black wet walls.
Descent: the safest way is to contour left (looking up), then descend towards the waterslide of the burn before contouring above the scree back to the slabs.

Lost in Translation   160m   VS 4c **. Rick Weld, John Mackenzie. 8 August 2008.
The best route on the slabs taking the top overlaps in an unlikely position for the grade.
1. 45m Start below the jutting block (see *Boom Time*) and climb up to and over

Pete MacPherson on Blood, Sweat and Frozen Tears (VIII,8), Beinn Eighe.
Photo: Mark 'Ed' Edwards.

flakes by its left side to reach clean slabs. Climb these to the long overlap traversed under by *Boom Time* and belay below it on its left side.

2. 45m 4b Step left around the overlap and move slightly rightward to reach and climb a superb smooth slab to belays on a small ledge.

3. 35m 4b Head up the slabs for a triangular niche with a white spot on the left that lies just right of the steepest section of overlaps. Climb the initial overlap just right of the niche then step left into it.

4. 35m 4c Climb the large flake edge to an overlap, step left (crux), then move up to a crack with a downward-pointing spike. Pull over and head up slabs trending left to the top.

Boom Time   125m   Hard Severe 4b *. John Mackenzie, Eve Austin. 6 July 2008.

Takes the centre-left side of the slabs. Start below a jutting block in the centre of the large overlap at the base of the slabs. Some interesting and not-too-arduous climbing but very little protection.

1. 50m 4b Climb slabs direct to the block and into its right-hand corner, then mantel onto the block and onto the slabs. Easily at first then up a blanker black smooth slab on the right to reach a corner with grass at its top on the left and up this to a large overlap. Traverse right directly under it, then over it before a loose-looking flake and up slabs to a cracked block directly above.

2. 50m Climb the smaller overlap above the belay and up to a line of weakness on the right moving gradually left to reach the grass ledge below the top black overlaps. Harder variations left of the line of weakness should be better, such as part of the second pitch of *Lost in Translation*. Traverse left to a niche and small flake left of the black overlaps (which are often wet) and directly below a 'tower of flakes' which forms on the left of the black overlaps.

3. 25m 4a Climb the right edge above to a short wall and juniper. Move left on the glacis and up the booming but massive flakes by a series of cracks and edges in a good position to reach a juniper ledge at the top.

Slideshow   135m   E1 5a *. Rick Weld, John Mackenzie. 8 August 2008.

An excellent and bold first pitch and a good third pitch.

1. 40m 5a Start as for *Misty Mountain Hop* but climb straight up to a right-trending ramp, vital No. 1 Friend in a pocket up left. Continue boldly direct to the big overlap (good Friend runners), step left and climb the nose of the overlap by stepping right with faith. Continue up the slabs to belay as for *Misty Mountain Hop* at the parallel crack.

2. 40m Continue up left towards the middle set of overlaps to belays under an overlap.

3. 35m 4b Continue up slabs leftwards to the middle overlaps and climb the first overlap at a notch, then move up right to a prominent crack.

4. 35m Continue up to and around the overlap above, then step right and climb a short corner. Move right above to reach the thread of *Misty Mountain Hop* but then step left and climb to the top.

Misty Mountain Hop   125m   VS 4c **. John Mackenzie, Eve Austin. 23 July 2008.

Climbs the right-hand side of the slabs taking the most continuous area of rock.

Top: Eddie Barbour on Zebedee (E4 6a), The Burren, County Clare, Ireland. Photo: Ian Taylor.
Bottom: Unclimbed cliff on the Aran Islands, Ireland. There are 9km of cliffs like these!

A fine climb with lots of variety, more protection (save on pitch 1) and opportunities for more direct lines if completely dry (rare!). Start at a pair of right-curving overlaps, aiming for the left end of a heather ledge above.

1. 45m 4b Climb to an overlap and move right under it to step over to reach the ledge. Move left and step on to the upper slab, then climb directly to a hollow block and parallel crack.

2. 35m 4b. Climb the slab right of the stance and move up and slightly left aiming for the large overlaps right of centre but left of the wet black walls.

3. 35m 4c Climb to the overlaps and take the lower of the two big ones just right of a wet area (black rock if dry), then move right to a well protected crack in the top one. The wet corner to the left of the upper overlap would be easier but not so good.

4. 10m Rather than risk sloping heather to the left, continue easily up shelves above to safer ground.

Note: The diamond-shaped slab up and right of the main slabs was investigated on the 23 July by the same party and gave an awful route of about VS 4b in five shortish pitches.

CORRIESHALLOCH AREA:

Arnisdale Falls V,5. Guy Roberston, Tony Stone. 3 January 2009.
The rarely-in-condition icefall at about NH 186 780 climbed in two pitches. Looks steeper than it is. Ten minutes from the A832, crossing the ageing footbridge at NH 186 778 over the Abhainn Cuileig. Worth a couple of stars for esoterica!

Strone Nea:

The crag is called Mac'us Mathair on the 1:25,000 map. There are two approaches:

1. The steep way; leave the A835 at a whin-lined track, NH 185 845, parking in a large clearing. Old tyres on the right lead through 15m of whin, small cairn. Follow the emerging track on the left and follow this to larch trees just left of the main scree slopes and follow to the crag. Move right to the main West Gully which serves as an approach to *The Shaft* and *Summit Slabs*.

2. The long way, leave the A835 at the new car park at the foot of Gleann na Squaib and after the second gate turn right at the Scottish Water hut and follow the clearing via tracks to the crag. Both ways about 30–40mins.

The rock is a juggy schist, mostly solid on the routes but numerous loose blocks on easy ground and ledges, a little traffic would improve matters hugely.

Shafted 105m HVS 5a *. John Mackenzie, Eve Austin. 21 June 2009.
A more direct ascent of The Shaft which follows less satisfactory ground and is probably Severe rather than VDiff. Shafted follows steep walls and commodious ledges. Good belays and well protected in general save the initial pitch. Some good exposed moves on excellent holds. Approach via the main West Gully, an easy scramble to the Memorial Cairn at the foot of the ridge on the left.

1. 20m Climb a slabby rib above the cairn to a good stance on the left side of the ridge.

2. 15m 4a Climb the side wall via a juggy crack to another ledge.

3. 35m 4b Climb a steep wall just right of the edge, move left along a crack to the edge and follow this more easily to a ledge. Continue on the right over blocky ledges and two short walls to a ledge. Climb easily left of the arete to a sloping glacis on the right of the edge to below a short overhanging crack.

4. 10m 5a Climb the excellent slanting crack to below the final rocks.

5. 25m Climb the nose and then along the horizontal arete to a block.

Descend to the neck at the top of the West Gully and East Gully. Abseil or scramble down West Gully to the foot via numerous trees.

OYKEL BRIDGE:
Broken Tooth Gully 70m III,4. Dave Allan, Dave Cumming. 22 December 2007.
A frozen waterfall beside the River Oykell (NH 396 999).

SEANA BHRAIGH:
Pelican Buttress 150m III. Billy Burnside, Mike Dunn. 24 January 2009.
A direct line close to *Pelican Gully* was taken (with scope for a longer approach up the easier-angled crest close to *Diamond Diedre*). Scrambling led to a steepening very close to the gully. Two long pitches of 50m and 60m led to a rock belay just below a large problematic cornice which was outflanked by a long traverse to the right across the top of *Pelican Gully*.

RHUE SEA-CLIFFS, Main Cliff:
Fat Monkey 25m E4 6a **. Tess Fryer, Ian Taylor. 6 July 2008.
A line up the left wall of the giant prow. Climb *Rhue Rhapsody* to a ledge at 8m. Go left 3m, then up to gain the rightmost hanging flake and follow this until below a narrow roof. Traverse right below the roof in an exposed position to a hanging ledge and an easier finish.

Gem Walls:
Welly Direct 8m Severe. G.J. Lynn. 7 July 2008.
Climb directly up the wall to the left of *Wellyboot Route* to join this route at its top.

ARDMAIR note:
Martin Holland notes that *Peace at Last* on the Fish Farm Walls has a large dangerous block on pitch 3. Also pitch 2 was thought hard 5c rather than 5b.

CAMUS MOR:
Ram Raider 25m E4 6a. Iain Small, Susan Jensen. 6 July 2008.
Start at the heathery ledge below *Hit and Run*. Step off the far right end of the ledge using breaks to gain a crack, then a flake to reach a break. Climb a diagonal crack and pocketed wall to better holds and the left end of a rounded ramp. Continue left along the break, then take the wall above on rounded breaks.

CAIRN CONMHEALL, Crucifix Buttress:
Dragon Rider 30m E1 5b. Andy Tibbs, Andrew Fraser. 24 June 2007.
Start 5m left of the buttress nose (about 4m left of *Anarchist Crack*). The route climbs a steep slabby feature bounded by diverging cracks. Climb up to the

diverging cracks and follow the right crack which is actually a shallow corner to flop right onto a pedestal. Finish by cracks on the left.

Note: The route is thought to be just left of *Class War*.

CAIRN CONMHEALL, Middle Crag (above Crucifix Buttress):

Am Fuhran 10m E2 5c. Andy Tibbs, Andrew Fraser. 24 June 2007.
At the extreme right of the crag is a clean corner with a crack in its right wall. Climb it.

COIGACH, Beinn an Eoin:

Sgorr Deas Chimney 120m IV,4 *. Davy Moy, Dave Allan. 3 March 2004.
The obvious chimney at the north end of the west face of Sgorr Deas. Best approached from the east end of Loch Lurgainn past the lochan between the two peaks of Beinn an Eoin. Climb the chimney direct, passing the halfway chockstone on the left side. Descend by traversing left, then head to the south end of the lochan.

SGURR AN FHIDHLEIR:

Castro 280m VII,7. Iain Small, Simon Richardson. 8 February 2009.
A winter ascent of the summer line resulted in a magnificent and sustained eight-pitch expedition. The 4c summer corner (pitch 3) was the crux.

CUL MOR, Coire Gorm:

Steeplejacks' Climb 200m IV,5 *. Dave Allan, Davy Moy. 21 January 2004.
Start about 10m up and left of *Three Chimneys Route*.
1. 40m Traverse rightwards up an easy ramp, then cross the *Three Chimneys* ice pitch to continue up a turf rib. Traverse up left about 15m, bypassing the short continuation chimney and a further blocky break in the wall above. Where the ground steepens, step up on to the wall beneath a small semi-detached block and swing right. Continue up awkward turf steps (crux).
2. 50m Follow easier ground to beneath two obvious chimneys.
3. 45m Traverse right beneath both chimneys and climb a fine open turfy groove.
4. 50m Follow an easy gully above.
5. 15m Climb up to the start of the summit slopes.

CUL BEAG note:

Cul of the Wild is to the right of *Lurgainn Edge*, not right of *Kveldro Ridge* as stated in the Northern Highlands North guide.

STAC POLLAIDH, Pinnacle Basin, Virgin and Child Pinnacle:

Madonna 45m E1 5b *. John Mackenzie, Andy Nisbet. 26 May 2008.
Climbs the south (long or Loch Lurgainn) side of the pinnacle. A fine sustained and varied route on the mountain's most spectacular pinnacle. It has potential quality, given a little traffic.
1. 15m 5b Climb the front of the lower buttress over a cracked bulge to step left and up to a stance.
2. 15m 5b Climb a thin crack on the right to move right to the col.
3. 15m 5b Return left and climb over a bulge via twin cracks to a ledge. Climb

a classic layback and jam crack to thread a keyhole between the twin summits. Abseil descent down the short side.

Vlad the Impaler, Continuation Arete   40m   Severe. John Mackenzie, Eve Austin. 12 June 2009.
From the top of the normal route, either continue up and over the pinnacled arete to arrive at a col overlooking a gully or scramble up the back to arrive at the same place.
1. 30m Climb the arete overlooking the gully via short corners to move right into a little gully and belays near the top.
2. 10m 4c On the left is a short sharp crack which is climbed to reach the secondary top of Stac Pollaidh.

Carragh Dearg:
This prominent north-west-facing crag lies at the east end of Loch Bad a' Ghaill, 2km west of Stac Pollaidh (NC 091 093). Park at a bend in the road, at the bouldering area known as Reiff-in-the-Woods. Zigzag down some steep slopes, then go across some rough ground to the crag. Not as far as it looks, 5mins.

Ossuary   10m   E4/5 6a **. Ian Taylor, Tess Fryer. 15 May 2008.
Takes the front face of the towering crag. Climb up to a ledge on the left, then shuffle right along the break (which contains some mysterious bones!) until able to make a long move to the next break. Continue straight up, pull onto the wall above and finish up shallow cracks.

ALTANDHU BOULDERING: See the topo and photo opposite page 443.

REIFF, Stone Pig Cliffs:
Man and Buoy   25m   E1 5b. James Edwards, Martin Hind. 13 June 2009.
This is on the left side of the smooth black concave wall some 5m from the left end. Climb a line of discontinuous cracks with a hard move to gain a rest on the arete. Step left and go up to finish.

Pigeon Pants   15m   HVS 5a. Ian Taylor, Tess Fryer. August 2008.
The dank chimney left of *Die Another Day*, climbed via flake-cracks on the right wall. Not recommended, but it seemed like a good idea at the time.

Cloud Appreciation Society   18m   Hard Severe 4b *. John Bull. 25 June 2009.
Climb the arete between *Automaton* and *Nalaxone*, trending right in the slabby corners above.

Pinnacle Area:
Droga Artura (Arthur's Route)   15m   E2 5c. Mariusz 'Gienek' Rogus, Grzesiek Bargiel. 29 September 2007.
Starts left of *Tongue 'n' Groove* (Second Geo). Climb the inverted triangular slab. Surmount the overhang to the platform. Finish straight up.

Pool Wall   8m   HVS 5b. Ian Taylor, Murdoch Jamieson. 9 July 2009.
The steepening wall right of *Chimney Corner*.

The Point:
F Crack   8m   Difficult *.
The flake-crack right of *OH Crack*.

Lapwing   6m   VS 5a.
The wall just left of *Rampline*.

Minch Wall:
The Mover   10m   VS 5a.
The arete right of *Slip Jig*. A slightly worrying rocking flake wouldn't budge on abseil.

Bay of Pigs:
Nefertiti   20m   E5 6a. Iain Small, Es Tressider. 7 October 2007.
Takes the overhanging wall between *The Thistle* and *Walks Like....* Start just left of *The Thistle* and follow the flake-ramp to its top. Make a long reach to the big break then traverse it to the right arete and make committing moves up the left side of the arete to give a spectacular finish.

Piglet Wall:
Swinelet   4m   4c.
The wall and sharp arete left of *Jackie in the Box*.

Leaning Block Cliffs:
Adventures on the High Seas   20m   VS 4c *. Michael Barnard. 28 April 2009.
The obvious diagonal fault-line on the back wall of the descent gully (right of *Pirates of Coigach*). Start from the same overhung ledge as for *Pirates of Coigach* and climb the corner-crack in three steps all the way to the top. Escapable but good sustained climbing.

Sixteen Men on a Dead Man's Chest   15m   HVS 5b ***. Michael Barnard, Jonnie Williams. 31 May 2008.
The fine arete left of *Harold*. From the smaller ledge at the base of the corner, hand-traverse left to gain the edge, which is climbed all the way to the top.

Gilt Edge   20m   E4 6a **. Ian Taylor, Tess Fryer. 5 July 2008.
The arete left of *Hydraulic Dogs* gives some excellent climbing. Start just left of the arete at the steep unclimbed corner. Go up the corner for a few metres until able to hand-traverse right onto a ledge on the arete, then follow the arete to the top.

Veedon Fleece   20m   E1 5b **. Michael Barnard, Alex Clarke-Williams. 6 June 2008.
Lies halfway between *Waigwa* and *Golden Fleece*. Climb directly up the twin-cracked wall left of Waigwa, starting up a short corner and finishing as for that route.

Crossfire   15m   E2 5c **. Michael Barnard (unsec). 6 June 2008.
Lies just east of the leaning block (between *Crossover* and *Bow Wave*). The

north-facing wall immediately left of the block is split in its upper half by an impressive short prow with two obvious breaks. Start as for the above, then zigzag up easy ground to below the breaks. Trend left up these (good cams), before breaking out right on small holds to slap for the top.

The Bonus 12m E5 6a **. Ian Taylor, Tess Fryer. April 2009.
The wall right of Losgaidh. Start as for *The Gift* to the cave, then blast straight up the wall above with long reaches between breaks.

Root on the Rampage 10m Very Difficult *. Alex Clarke-Williams, Michael Barnard. 6 June 2008.
Located just left of *Blotto*. Good climbing up the next corner to the left, unfortunately with no belay at the top!

Amphitheatre Bay:
Hyper Oceanic 30m E6 6b. Iain Small, Gary Latter. 4 August 2007.
Takes the prominent roof-capped groove left of the big square-cut corner with a large raised platform at its base. Bold and scary gaining the main corner. From behind a large boulder climb a wide easy crack to the right end of the first roof. Difficult moves out left lead to a large incut hold (sling over this), then pull over on breaks before delicate moves left into the groove and gear. Climb leftwards up the wall then make further difficult moves over the next two roofs to good holds. Continue to a capping block, then hand-traverse left to good finishing holds.
Note: Grade confirmed by Niall McNair.

Lost at Sea 25m E4 6a. Iain Small, Gary Latter. 4 August 2007.
The obvious groove starting just right of the large raised platform. Climb the groove and right-trending line leading to a roof. Traverse left then up with difficulty to better holds, finishing more easily up a crack in the headwall.

Note: A line up the left wall of the square-cut corner, finishing up the fine cracked headwall, was also climbed and thought E5 6b. A Glasgow team had been on it earlier in summer and it was assumed they made the first ascent.

Jig-Saw Wall Point:
The following two routes lie on the tidal east face. Low- to mid-tide access is possible by traversing in from the boulder beach to the left of the wall. At high tide, abseil to small ledges at the base. The wall has a slabby lower section then steepens markedly near the top.

Creative Juices 15m E1 5a *. Ian Taylor, Tess Fryer. 16 June 2009.
This climbs a bold line a metre or so left of the right arete.

Crossword Puzzle 15m E2 6a *. Ian Taylor, Tess Fryer. 16 June 2009.
The central line of disjointed cracks. Start from a niche and climb the cracks until a steep hard move gains a ledge and an awkward top-out.

Rubha Ploytach:
Red Nose Day 12m Hard Severe 4b. Jonathan Preston. 19 April 2009.
The rib between *Fancy Free* and *Labrador Chimney*. Start just left of *Labrador*

Chimney beneath the undercut prow. Make committing moves up the right side of the prow to the crest. Finish more easily up the deep groove above.

Lone Ranger   8m   VS 4b. Jonathan Preston. 19 April 2009.
The crack left of *Celtic Horizons* (escapable).

Beach Life   15m   E3 5c. Iain Small, Susan Jensen. 6 October 2007.
The right-facing corner to left of *Making Waves*. Climb the corner to a break. Pull out left, then back right to a thin crack.

Note from Ian Taylor: Right of the descent to *Marie Celeste* (facing in) is an obvious corner. This is *RP Corner* (6m Severe). The wall left of the corner is *Rehab* (6m Hard Severe 4c). The arete right of the corner is *Smart Arete* (6m VS 5a *).

Silver Foil   10m   VS 5b *
The wall right of *Trefoil*.

LOCHINVER CRAGS, Strone Crag:
Party Pooper   25m   Very Difficult. Jonathan & Diana Preston. 30 May 2008.
A route at the far left end of the crag, beyond a big heather ledge that runs across the slab. Start 8m down and left of *Whitewash*, just left of a rowan sapling. Climb steeply on good holds to a V-groove. Go up this to a ledge. Climb the slab above with the crux just below the top.
Note: The same party climbed on a gneiss crag just inland from Split Rock at NC 041 269. The clean slab on the left side of the crag gave a pleasant Difficult; the rest of the crag is a bit broken (31 May 2008).

OLD MAN OF STOER Notes:
Andy Innes and Neil McGeachy linked pitch 1 of *Diamond Face Route* with pitch 3 of *North-West Corner* by climbing diagonally right across *Original Route* at a sandy E1 5a (17 April 2008).
The note in SMCJ 2008 should have had the names Dave Cronshaw and John Ryden.

POINT OF STOER, Clashnessie Bay Crag:
Joachim's Spuds   8m   Very Difficult. Tim Bourne, Gethin Jenkins. 6 June 2008.
This route is reached by scrambing down the east side of the headland from the top, and then turning left and scrambling towards the seaward point of the headland until a platform is reached beyond which there is a foot traverse continuing round. The route takes the traverse for 2–3m until one can climb up a V-shaped corner. Somewhat tidal.

QUINAG, Bucket Buttress:
The Great Gig in the Sky   45m   VII,7 ***. Pete MacPherson, John Lyall. 2 December 2008.
1. 30m Climb cracks and a groove up the arete right of *The Touchline*, to a ledge on the right.
2. 15m Follow cracks above to the top.

QUINAG, Western Cliffs:

Popgun 150m II/III. Ed Edwards, John Lyall, Andy Nisbet. 12 February 2009.
A gully which separates *Tenement Ridge* and *Drumbeg Tower*. All easy except
for a short chimney section at mid-height. This will vary in difficulty according
to the build-up.

Assynt of Man 150m VI,6. Ed Edwards, John Lyall, Andy Nisbet. 12 February
2009.
The gully right of *The Pillar of Assynt*. Climb steep turf to the base of its
impressive chimney. Follow this over several bulges to easy ground (45m).

Jack the Lad 150m III,5. Sonya Drummond, Andy Nisbet. 13 February 2009.
The gully left of *The Pillar of Assynt*. A steep initial section was climbed just
right of thin ice. This led to a long easy section. The main gully jinks left up a
short wall, climbed on the left. Again the ice was too thin, so a subsequent steep
section was climbed by a well protected short corner on the right, returning to
the gully to finish on snow.

Ricketty Ridge 150m V,7. John Lyall, Andy Nisbet. 11 February 2009.
The winter route followed a corner line just right of the crest. Start up a broad
scoop right of the summer line and follow this, then go left to the base of the
corner line (80m). Follow the corner to where there is a prominent crack in its
right wall (25m). Climb the crack and return to the corner which leads to the
upper crest (25m). Follow this past the left side of a short wall to the easy upper
slopes (15m).

The Am Fasgadh Alternative 120m IV,4. Ian Taylor, Tess Fryer. 8 February
2009.
The first ridge right of the second col gully. Starting from a corner at the toe of
the ridge, follow the crest of the ridge with occasional deviations to the left. The
ridge ends at a small col with some pinnacles. Either descend easily leftwards or
continue up Grade I/II ground for a long way to the main ridge.

QUINAG AREA, Accessible Pinnacle (NC 241 295):

This is a spire-like quartzite pinnacle a few minutes from the road. A lay-by
exists by the bridge. Slightly wobbly but sound in principal and gives a good
exposed climb with the loose bits adding to the atmosphere. To descend, either
abseil or downclimb the East Arete.

East Arete 10m Difficult. John Mackenzie, Eve Austin. 18 April 2008.
The short side reached by scrambling up the narrow scree gully. An easy level
section followed by a short exposed wall to the top (three joined 8ft slings will
encircle the summit).

Birthday Party Arete (West Arete) 20m VS 4b *. John Mackenzie, Bob
Brown, Andy Nisbet, Eve Austin, Colin Tarbat, Charles White. 15 June 2008.
The long side! A narrow and exciting route up the west arete on square-cut
holds. Some good gear but go gently with the rock though most is quite sound.
Traffic will rapidly either improve the stability or demolish the pinnacle.

BEINN AN FHURAIN:
Reign Fall   250m   IV,4 *. Dave Allan, Simon Nadin. 22 January 2008.
Start approx. 200m right of Fhuaran Fall at a big icefall in a bay. Climb the
icefall to easy snow (60m). Climb the next quartzite tier diagonally leftwards,
starting just left of a rockfall scar (60m). Continue up the buttress and easy snow
heading for a prominent ice chimney (60m). Climb the chimney (55m).

GLAS BHEINN:
Eas a' Chual Allan   75m   IV,4. Dave Allan, Davy Moy. 2 March 2004.
Unlike its illustrious neighbour and near namesake, this is one of the shorter
waterfalls in Britain. The icefall is visible from the road (NC 248 281) and
20mins approach. A near vertical 15m start leads to a belay at 25m, 4m left of
the ice. Continue to the top.

TARBET SEA-CLIFFS, Raven's Crag:
The following two routes lie on the impressive sweep of wall right of *Black
Ross*.

Raving   25m   E4 6a **. Ian Taylor, Tess Fryer. 18 August 2008.
Follow *Black Ross* to the ledge and a possible belay. On the wall above the ledge
is a narrow black ramp. From the start of the ramp go up to a hand ledge, then
traverse right until able to gain the ramp at a worrying flake. Make a move right,
then climb up to a crack which leads into a groove and the top. Climbing the
ramp directly would be possible but would be very bold.

Losing the Plot   45m   E4 **. Ian Taylor, Tess Fryer. 18 August 2008.
Start at sea-level ledges just left of the central leaning corner and below a large
round hole.
1. 25m 6a Climb up to the hole, step down and left to a thin crack and go up
with difficulty to flat holds below a big roof. Traverse left via a horizontal flake
to gain a big ledge. Belay below a right-trending crack in black biotite.
2. 20m 5c Steep moves up the crack and its vertical continuation lead to a
steepening with some poor rock. Make an energetic move out right to finish up
easier ground.

Balmy Slabs, White Slab:
The highest point above White Slab is at NC 1590 4978.

Camouflage   20m   HVS 5b **. Andy Nisbet, Jonathan Preston. 28 April 2009.
A clean and very well protected (small wires) route. Start at a right-facing corner
5m right of *Writer's Cramp*. Climb the corner and a left-slanting thin crack to
reach a 2m narrow sloping ledge. Make a move up a shallow corner, then move
right to a final slab.

The Balmy Boys   20m   HVS 5a *. Jonathan Preston, Andy Nisbet. 28 April 2009.
A slab between *Camouflage* and *Writer's Cramp*. Start 1m left of the corner of
Unnamed. Climb straight up to a left-trending overlap. Follow this to the narrow
sloping ledge. Climb the corner of *Camouflage* but continue left under the
subsequent overlap to finish near *Writer's Cramp*.

Western Sector:

Round the Horn 20m E1 5b **. Jonathan Preston, Andy Nisbet. 28 April 2009.
Cornucopia requires middle to low tide and was thought only worth two stars.
This route climbs the wall to its right. Start from the barnacled ledge from which
Cornucopia steps left. Pull up into a short right-facing corner, then move up left
under a bulge into a left-facing corner. Go up this, then step right across the
corner on to a hanging slab and a small ledge. Move back left into a crack and
finish up this.

The following three routes lie on the far west side of the western sector. The wall
can be viewed by scrambling down at the far end to the foot of *Black Tidings*.
Continue round left (looking out) to the edge of a rocky promontory. Looking
back from here is a fine area of steep but well-featured rock. Just visible on the
right is a huge cleft cutting into the lower half of the cliff; this is the line of *A
Bridge Too Far*. The routes can be accessed at low tide by scrambling round on
ledges, while at low–mid tide they can be gained by abseil. For the latter, locate
the top of *Black Tidings* (the obvious fault splitting the end of the headland).
Abseil to ledges from cracks in the vicinity of the smaller of two pools of water.

Barmy Slab 15m VS 5a **. James Duthie, Michael Barnard. 25 July 2009.
Belay on ledges 4m right of the huge cleft. Start up a crack in the initial steep
wall; where this gets difficult a move right gains the slab above. Step back left
on the edge of the slab to finish up the crack immediately left of the large open
corner.

A Bridge Too Far 20m HVS 5a ***. James Duthie, Michael Barnard. 25 July
2009.
An excellent and contrasting route giving memorable positions. Start at the foot
of the huge cleft. Back and foot up this to gain the slab on the left, step left under
the overlap above and climb straight up to finish.

Variation: Direct Finish E1 5c **. Michael Barnard, James Duthie. 25 July 2009.
From the slab follow the crack straight through the overlap.

Fantabulous Flake 20m E1 5c ***. Michael Barnard, James Duthie. 25 July
2009.
The superb diagonal flake-crack left of the huge cleft. Climb this to its top,
before finishing directly up the headwall above.

Dolphin Crag:

Split Decision 20m VS 4c *. Bob Hamilton, Steve Kennedy. 5 May 2008.
On the seaward-facing wall left of *Misty Arete* is an obvious right-facing corner
with a dark right wall. Climb the corner directly.

Dementia 20m Very Difficult. Steve Kennedy, Bob Hamilton. 5 May 2008.
Climb the blunt edge about 5m right of *Split Decision* just left of a large flake.
Finish up the wall above.

Tiptoe Slab 20m VS 4c *. Steve Kennedy, Bob Hamilton. 5 May 2008.
Start at the foot of the corner of *Split Decision* and climb the hanging slab on the

left. Move rightwards from the top of the slab and finish up a system of shallow corners.

No Sign of Life 20m Severe 4a *. Bob Hamilton, Steve Kennedy. 5 May 2008.
Climb the initial slab of *Tiptoe Slab*. From the top of the slab move left for 2m then finish up a prominent corner.

FAR NORTH-WEST CRAGS, Ridgeway View Crag:
Lurking Wolf 20m E2 5b *. John Mackenzie, Eve Austin. 24 May 2008.
Right of the cracked slab of *Oars Aft* is a short chimney. Climb this to move left onto a ledge and block. Climb the overhanging wall right of a groove up past a crack and onto the slab nose up which the climb finishes leftwards. Good strenuous pocket pulling.

Creag an Fhithich:
Pap, Snackle & Crop 25m E2 5c. Ian Taylor, Tess Fryer. 25 May 2008.
Start right of *Honey Monster* where the shelf reaches ground level. Climb a shallow groove in the right rib of the main wall, trending left to finish up the last few moves of *Honey Monster*.

Note: The abseil descent off the worrying sapling (at the top of *The Swirl*) is not recommended. It is far better to gain the terrace above, then walk to its right end, where there is an in-situ thread, and abseil from here.

Sandwood Bay, Crag 2:
Mustard Pickle 15m Hard Severe 4b. Andy Moles. 26 May 2009.
Climb the obvious right-trending crack to the left of *Sandal Wood* to finish just next to that route. A good obvious line.

Sea Rocket 40m HVS 5a *. Bob Hamilton, Steve Kennedy. 27 September 2008.
A line between *Marram* and *Sea Campion*. The thin crack of *Sea Campion* is about 2m left of *Marram*. Left again is a stepped crack leading slightly leftwards up the slab (directly below the prominent flake). Climb the crack and the slab above to reach the flake (*S.C.* reaches the flake from the corner on the right). Finish up the right edge of the flake (as for *S.C.*).

SHEIGRA, First Geo, South Side Inner Wall:
Hanuman for a Day 25m E5 6a **. Ian Taylor, Tess Fryer. 25 May 2008.
Start just left of *Monkey Man*. Go up to some hanging flakes, then follow a thin crack slightly left to easier ground (junction with *Blind Faith*). Step right and climb a hard thin crack in the leaning headwall. Low in the grade.

First Geo, Outer Walls:
Flotsam 20m E6 6b **. Ian Taylor, Tess Fryer. 18 May 2009.
Start just left of *Sound of the Surf* and climb more or less directly to a crack at a steepening. Hard but well protected moves lead to better holds and a sloping ledge. Sidle left along the ledge to better holds, then go steeply up via large holds and ledges to the top.

Note: Second Geo – *The Black Edge* is the same route as *Lucifer's Link*, which also originally climbed to the Black Pedestal from the belay at the base of *Shark Crack*.

WHITEN HEAD, The Maiden:
The Gaelic name for these stacks is Stacan Bàna (White Stacks). The western stack is 46m and the eastern stack 56m.

Western Stack:
Waterfront Wall Direct 45m VS 4b **. Ross Jones, Neil Wilson. 10 May 2008.
This direct route appears to cover better ground than the original route.
1. 25m 4a As for *Waterfront Wall*.
2. 20m 4b Climb up for 4m and rightwards to a broken crack-line. Climb this, then the crack-line on the left on the vertical wall and easy ground to the top.

Eastern Stack:
The west face was climbed by Ross Jones & Neil Wilson by the obvious line of weakness through the first and second overhangs and combined pitches of *March's Route* (1970) and *Ode* (1988). The first overhang is common to both routes. *March's Route* then uses the hanging crack through the second overhang and is 5b not 5a (*Ode* goes off right and joins the route again at the belay). The second pitch is the same as *Ode* and the big block does feel dangerous and loose! (*March's Route* heads off leftwards).

NEAVE ISLAND, Rubha Dubh:
(NC 664 647)   Non-tidal   Various aspects
This is the sea arch on the most northerly point of the island and was home to St Columba's missionaries in the seventh and eighth centuries. Approach either by a scramble to the top of the arch and abseil, or by boat direct to the base.

West Face:
Arch Arete 35m   Severe. Neil Wilson, Simon Nadin. 2 August 2008.
Start just right of a short left-facing ramp and climb the broken west-facing wall and the arete above to finish up easy ground on the north face at the top.

Splash Landing 35m   Severe. Simon Nadin, Neil Wilson. 2 August 2008.
Start 4m to the right. Climb broken corners that split the west and south wall to join the arete and finish up *Arch Arete*.

Monastic Life 35m   E1 5b **. Ross Jones, Clare Bradley. 2 August 2008.
Traverse right 4m along ledges on the south face to the furthest overhang. Pull through this with a hanging pull-up and then the next overhang, stepping right into the corner. When the corner meets the arete, step out right onto the hanging west wall and climb this to the top (missing the final headwall reduces the overall grade to HVS 5a).

The next route starts as for *Splash Landing* and crosses *Monastic Life*.

Heathen's Door 35m   E3 6a ***. Simon Nadin, Ross Jones. 2 August 2008.

Start left of overhangs. Climb up 3m and traverse rightwards above overhangs for 5m to an overhang. Pull through this and traverse under the corner and the hanging roof of the arch. Climb the hanging crack to an alcove beneath another overhang. Pull out left onto the hanging crack and climb this to the top. A superb finish.

East Wall:
The Warrior Saint 25m   Hard Severe 4b *. Ross Jones, Clare Bradley. 2 August 2008.
The broken/striated wall right of the arch to a ledge at 15m. Finish up the corner-groove above.

St Finian's Apostle 25m   Severe. Ross Jones, Clare Bradley. 2 August 2008.
The corner to the right to the ledge. Finish as for the route above.

Note:
The grid refs for the two routes mentioned in the guide (p336) are *Bonxie* (NC 659 646) and *Northern Exposure* (NC 663 646).

BEN LOYAL, Sgor a' Bhatain:
Hazard 35m   E6 6b. Simon Nadin (unsec). May 2009.
Start to the right of *Loyal Flush* behind a prominent finger of rock. Climb easily to the first bulge where an awkward move leads to the start of the crack system. Follow this to where the wall steepens considerably. Difficult moves are made to gain a good but very steep jamming crack and then a ledge above. Step off the right of the ledge into a flared crack leading with tricky moves to the roof/bulge. Launch through this via open cracks to gain a standing position on the headwall. Finish airily rightwards up this. Well protected. Either scramble leftwards down the rake or finish up the next route.

The Rigging Finish 20m   E5 6c. Simon Nadin (unsec) June 2009.
This follows the overhung flared crack splitting the prow of the crag. Access is by scrambling up the diagonal rake from the left side of the crag until the belay of *Hazard* is reached, from where it is sensible to rope across the exposed ledge to a belay below the crack (just before the ledge peters out). The crack is climbed first on poor hand jams, then fist before finally resorting to head or body jams or anything else that aids progress.

SKERRAY SEA-CLIFFS:
Sidestep 20m   E1 5b. Simon Nadin, Neil Wilson. June 2009.
Abseil to a small platform to the left of the start of *Arch*, and climb a steep crack marking the boundary between pink and grey rock to join *Arch* at half-height.

CULFERN CRAG:
See Northern Highlands North p345. This should have a separate heading in the guide, as it is not part of Indian Chiefs. Culfern Crag is situated about 6km south of Melvich, at the northern end of Strath Halladale (NC 901 587). This collection of gneiss outcrops is located above Culfern Farm on the east side of the Strath, and can be easily seen on the hillside to the left of the A897 when

travelling south. The rock is solid gneiss, varying from very steep clean walls to more lichenous slabs. The compact nature of the rock means that protection is often scarce, with some marked exceptions. Predominantly facing south and west, the crag is a sun-trap in the afternoon and evening. The crag is split into three sectors, which form a line from south to north.

Southern Sector (Creag an Daimh) NC 900 585:
The most disparate sector of Culfern is easily approached from the gated farm track a few hundred metres south of the farm, weaving past a small wall before passing under an obvious 10m slab (seen from the road when coming from the south).

Easy Slab 10m Difficult.
Assumed to have been climbed previously. The obvious unprotected slab above the track.

Run for Cover 10m HVS 5a *. Gareth Marshall, Chris Edwards. 28 September 2008.
Fifty metres left of *Easy Slab* is a prominent blunt slabby arete. Initially bold, but protection improves once the crack to the right is reached. An obvious and rewarding line.

Turtle Head Ridge 8m Very Difficult. Chris Edwards, Gareth Marshall. 28 September 2008.
A slabby ridge protrudes from the rocky slope another 30m left, and is broken by a left-trending flake leading to an arete. The flake leads to a tiny spike at the foot of the arete, which is taken direct, or via the crack to the right.

Central Sector (NC 901 587):
The obvious wall is the most continuous area of rock at Culfern, but also the steepest and blankest! One route has been climbed, skirting the steepest section.

Eka Be 12m E1 5c **. Gareth Marshall, Chris Edwards. 27 September 2008.
Toward the right end of the wall twin vertical cracks lead to a small hanging corner on the left. Hard moves from a ledge at 2m gain the cracks, which are followed to the top. An excellent route, sustained and well protected.

Northern Sector (Creag nan Iolair) NC 904 589:
A hundred metres north of Central Wall, this unassuming looking collection of wooded crags provides a series of slabs and steep walls with up to 10m of clean rock. Cleaning of the slabbier sections would yield several worthwhile lines. From the south, the first routes climb the obvious south-facing slab with a dark lichen stripe down the centre.

Prickly Pear 8m Severe. Chris Edwards, Gareth Marshall. 27 September 2008.
Start from the heather ramp at the right of the slab and climb the vague groove to the right of the dark stripe, finishing directly through the orange band.

Flow Country Scene   10m   HVS 5a *. Gareth Marshall, Chris Edwards. 27 September 2008.
This route climbs to the left of the dark stripe, linking the obvious break at 4m with the thin cracks above. Good, but spaced, protection.

The next route is found further north. Beyond lichenous slabs and a gently leaning 10m wall is a smaller wall with an attractive orange band rising diagonally from right to left. Vertical cracks are found at either ends of the wall.

The Merlin   6m   E1 5c *. Gareth Marshall. 11 September 2008.
The left-hand crack: more of a highball problem than a route, though protection is available. Edges lead to holds in the orange band, from where the crack is gained and climbed direct.

SARCLET, Waterfall Stack (ND 336 414):
Waterfall Stack   25m   HVS 4b. Duncan Tunstall, Francoise Call. 28 May 2009.
Approach the stack by descending easily just to the east of a sea-cove waterfall. At low tide the wee zawn can be by traversed to the south or a 3m swim solves the problem. Climb the west face close to the arete to a ledge after 15m. Climb the left end of the wall above, finishing on the arete. Rock less than perfect. The summit was made of loose blocks with no belay or abseil anchors, so descent was made by down climbing the *East Face* (Moderate). There were signs of previous visitors on the descent in the form of a tissue paper. The stack has two summits and the slightly lower looks like it can be reached more easily by taking the descent scramble up and left.

MID CLYTH, Inset Wall:
The description of Inset Wall as 'non-tidal' is not strictly correct! This is a good route to do when the tide is high.
The Tide is High   10m   E1 5b. Andy Tibbs, Davy Moy. 12 September 2008.
Abseil off a thread from a cliff-top boulder to gain an obvious ledge above the sea (the ledge is on *Adagio* and *Oxter*, and could be reached from below at lower tide). Climb the centre of the wall right of *Adagio* to finish just left of a short smooth corner. Well protected.

ORKNEY, YESNABY, False Stack Area:
Mist, Rain and Sunshine   15m   E1 5b. Ross Jones, Clare Bradley. 5 July 2008.
Climb the starting groove of *Crow's Nest* and the wall above and slightly left.

Ain't No Strange As Folk   18m   E2 5b *. Ross Jones, Iain Miller. 7 July 2008.
From the non-tidal platform at the base of the arete of *Three Wise Idiots*, start 2m left and climb up and leftwards up the side of the first overhang to the roof of the second large overhang. Traverse out right over the first overhang and beneath the second overhang and then straight up to the top of the drawbridge.

Gardyloo Wall:
Dream Weaver   22m   E3 5c **. Tim Rankin, Neil Morrison. 28 July 2008.
The wall and flake-crack just right of *Dream Catcher* gives another fine pitch. Abseil into the small triangular perch just above high tide mark as for *Dream*

Catcher. Make a move up *Dream Catcher* and span right to a horizontal break, follow this right to below the upper crack-line. Climb the wall to below a small roof then gain an obvious jug up and left. Step back right and continue up the crack to the top.

Yesnaby 500   25m   E4 6a ***. Tim Rankin, Neil Morrison. 28 July 2008.
Yet another excellent sustained route; abseil from the concrete strainer post down the back north corner of the inlet to a big tidal ledge (45m rope and swing required or gear to keep in). Traverse left off the ledge and either hand-traverse the low break or step up and use slopers to gain a groove leading to the left end of the roof. Climb the groove and its left arete up over the roof into a shallow groove. Continue over a small roof above and finish up the crack and layback flake. Cleaned on abseil.

Dream Tipper   22m   E3 6a ***. Tim Rankin, Neil Morrison. 8 August 2008.
A superb unlikely-looking route through roofs at the right end of the wall; abseil to the large tidal ledge as for Yesnaby 500. Climb a flake-crack above the left end of the ledge to another ledge below a roof. Step back down and traverse right to a thin crack; climb this to jugs below another roof. Gain a good hold over the lip with interest (crux) and swing left into a groove. Pull over the roof on to a slab and continue up the easier groove above exiting right. Inspected on abseil.

Tower Area:
Superlupo   18m   E7 6c **. Tim Rankin (head pointed). 30 July 2008.
Excellent hard bold climbing direct up the right side of the tower face breaching the seemingly smooth lower wall. Start 2m left of *No Maybes* and climb to the break past a small shallow niche. Climb the smooth wall directly above on tiny crimps to the next break (bold). Move right along the break to a jug and climb the wall above just left of the right-hand of three thin cracks (*Big Swall* climbs between the first two) to another break. Continue more easily up flakes and breaks directly to the top.

Arch Wall:
Überwölfe   22m   E6 6b **. Tim Rankin, Neil Morrison (head pointed). August 2008.
The thin crack and quartz headwall between *Nuckelavee* and *Long Hard Winter*. Climb a crack just left of the start of *Long Hard Winter* to ledges; continue up the left-curving crack and up to a flat break 2m below the roof. A hard move gains a jug under the roof at small jammed blocks. Reach over and pull up left to a good break and protection. Cross the roof with difficulty rightwards and finish straight up on great holds.

Mally the Mallet   22m   E6 6b **. Tim Rankin, Neil Morrison (head pointed). 8 August 2008.
Between *Ronnie the Axe* and *Mack the Knife* a black streak runs the full height of the cliff giving a fine route with excellent technical climbing but with only thin marginal protection on the upper wall. Start off the stepped ledge and climb a thin crack to below the roof and fail-safe protection in a crack over the lip. Use

an undercut pocket in the roof to reach small breaks above, and use these to pull over the roof rightwards to a good break right of the crack. Move up to stand on the ramp of *Ronnie the Axe* and arrange protection (small Friends and RPs), step up again to a quartz sidepull and use this to place crucial RPs in the thin crack on the left. Climb direct up the black streak to a good hold and gain a good ledge out right, continue straight up from this to finish.

The Langer Huddauf Direct Start 7m Severe 4a or S0 4+. John Bull. 20 June 2009.
A DWS start up the little wall of perfect rock left of *Wee Lum*, reversing down *The Langer Huddauf* to escape. Trivial but fun.

Quarry Walls:
There are two main quarries on the headland of Qui Arye Point, both to the north of the superior south-facing sea-cliffs. The most southerly lies a mere 5m north of the sea-cliffs in some places and can easily be descended from the east to gain several sport routes. The following routes climb a fine steep black north-facing slab at the west (seaward end) of the southerly quarry works. Gain the wall from the west by descending easy shelves and ledges.

Iron Stone 8m E2 5c *. Tim Rankin, Neil Morrison (on-sight). July 2008.
Just left of the descent ledges are two small slanting crack-lines. Start below the left-hand crack and climb this to a break with small cams. Step right to the right-hand crack and use a positive ironstone hold to boldly gain the final break. Finish up the central crack in the little headwall.

Secret Pocket 12m E2 5b *. Tim Rankin, Neil Morrison. July 2008.
Five metres left of *Iron Stone* is an obvious left-slanting crack leading to a hanging groove (unclimbed?) and further left a right-facing groove. This fine bold route climbs the blank slab between these two lines. Gain a ledge and good micro-wires, then boldly climb the wall above trending right then back left to a break and good small cams. Continue straight up on small holds to a square pocket and crucial Friend 0.5. Final hard moves on small holds (crux) lead to the top. Inspected on abseil.

ORKNEY, HOY:
An improved description after a repeat in 12hrs, with more direct first and last pitches, combining some smaller pitches, removing the aid point and changing a few of the technical grades.

Testament to the Insane 470m XS 5b. FFA: Ross Jones, Iain Miller. 9 July 2008.
1. 30m To the left of the boulder beach, directly below the arete, climb the short seaward wall of excellent rock and scramble to the only boulder and prominent scar.
2. 35m Scramble easily up the grass to the rock band; belay in cracks at its right-hand end.
3. 40m Continue up the steepening grass to the base of the towering arete; belay at the bottom of the big chimney-groove.

4. 55m 5a Climb the chimney-groove, pull out left at its top to a sloping grassy stance. Climb up steep ledges to another groove and pull out through the roof at its top and follow the short corner to a small stance. Continue up a grassy arete on the right to a superb ledge at the bottom of a right-facing corner.

5. 40m 4a From the right-hand end of the ledge, climb the slabby right-facing corner to easier ground. Ascend this swiftly to a second right-facing corner and climb this to a good stance.

6. 40m 4b Climb up trending left gently to the base of a steep red wall below a huge precarious capping boulder. Traverse right and ascend the steep ramp on better rock to a steep and extremely loose vegetated slope. Climb this delicately to the landward side of another massive perched boulder.

7. 45m 5b Traverse along the grassy ledge to the bottom of the prominent arete, which bounds the right-hand end of the huge slabby upper wall. Pull around the arete on good holds in an exposed position to gain the base of a left-facing corner. Climb the corner steeply to an exposed ledge (several pegs) and belay at the back below a wide groove.

8. 12m 4a Climb up the wide groove and up grass to a good stance.

9. 45m 5a Climb the steep right-trending corner through a wee roof to steep vegetation. Climb this to a recess on the left. Climb the centre of the recess to a huge boulder.

10. 48m Scramble through deep vegetation to the bottom of the headwall. Belay on the high point of vegetation directly below the huge central fault-line.

11. 25m 4b Climb the left-facing corner on the left and up to and into a cave with a huge block on the floor, Climb through the niche in the roof of the cave to the bottom of a big left-facing corner.

12. 20m 5a Climb a hand crack 3m to the left of the vegetated open-book corner to a good triangular niche. At the back of the niche climb the steep hand cracks.

13. 35m 5a Continue up direct in classic chimney fashion to the summit.

Note: Alan Macleay notes that as it says in the Northern Highlands North guide there was unrecorded climbing in Orkney from the late 1960s. In particular Cam Macleay, Ken Martin, Hamish Ross, Cliffy Leonard, Bob Grant and co. climbed there for many years and put up new routes in particular at Yesnaby, Roseness and South Ronaldsay. There must have been at least 50 more decent routes at Roseness than appear in the guidebook.

SHETLAND, ESHANESS:
From the car park head north for 50m. Abseil using large blocks set back from the cliff to a belay ledge 10m above the sea below a series of overhangs. The rock here is generally poor.

Lazy Alien 30m VS 4c. Ross Jones, Paul Whitworth. 15 May 2008.
Climb ledges up and rightwards and a broken crack-line to the right of overhangs, finishing left around a final overhang.

The next three routes are on the groove corners in the north-west wall below the lighthouse. They have a very different character to the other climbs nearby. From the car park head west to a concreted pipeline north-west of the blow hole.

Follow the pipeline to its end, then head directly north to the cliff-top to the top of a corner-groove that forms the exit to the following two routes.

Sting   35m   E2 5c **. Ross Jones, Paul Whitworth. 22 May 2008.
Belay on ledges below the hanging crack-line of *Goblin Cleaver*. Climb twin cracks to a ledge below a hanging crack-line left of *Goblin Cleaver*. Pull through this onto a ledge and the left-facing corner above.

Goblin Cleaver   40m   E2 5c *** (SMCJ 2006)

South of the groove for *Goblin Cleaver* are two more grooves before the wall turns south. The second one is broken and of poor rock. The first provides the following line.

Nenya   35m   E1 5a ****. Ross Jones, Alison Campbell. 17 August 2008.
Start from a small ledge at the base of groove 8m above the sea. Climb the wall on the left to a ledge at 15m. Climb the arete and wall to the top.

Note: *Hanging Arete* (SMCJ 2008) is 30m not 20m.

Narya   35m   E1 5b *. Ross Jones, David (Sid) Rayner. 19 August 2008.
Start as for *Solan* and pull out left onto the wall above the belay niche. Climb the wall just to the right of the arete.

Shetland Girls Are Sturdy   40m   E2 5b *. David (Sid) Rayner, Ross Jones. 19 August 2008.
Start from a hanging belay in the middle of the wall between *Solan* and *Angrist*. Climb up the wall, through a small overhang at 15m and direct up the hanging wall to the top.

Note: *Foy Corner* VS 4c *** (SMCJ 2007) was first climbed by Mick Tighe and party on 20 June 2005.

Vilya   40m   HVS 4c. Ross Jones, Andrew Hunter, David (Sid) Rayner. 24 May 2008.
From the ledge below *Aisha*, climb the groove on the right to overhangs. Pull through the overhangs and climb the groove and wall above.

Note: *Shetland Girls* (SMCJ 2008). The full name for the route is *Shetland Girls Are Easy*.

A Lightness of Heart   35m   HVS 5a. Ross Jones, Paul Whitworth. 21 May 2008.
Start from ledges and climb the hanging arete/rib 5m right of *The Darkness of My Mind*, stepping onto the hanging wall on the left at the top to pull through the hanging crack above.

Stuvva Cave Area:
The cliff right of *Lost Hopes* (2005) then turns southwards into a geo with a blow hole (The Cannon). The rock here is very rough and brittle in places.
Captain Todd   25m   E1 5a. Ross Jones, Carlos Las Heras. 27 May 2008.

From the left end of the wall a ramp rises up rightwards to a hanging crack-line at mid-height. Climb ramp and crack-line.

Last Passage   25m   VS 4c. Carlos Las Heras, Ross Jones. 27 May 2008.
Five metres right of *Cruel Sea* is another steep ramp that leads to a broken groove with poor rock. A further 5m right is another less defined groove/ramp left of a cave. Climb this, traversing rightwards at mid-height for 3m to avoid poor and unprotected ground before finishing up the wall above.

THE FAITHER, Arched Wall:
Look Faither Than This   40m   HVS 4c. Ross Jones, Carlos Las Heras. 30 May 2008.
Belay in a large niche to the right of the arete on the left side of the wall. Climb up into a corner and pull up and out onto the arete. Climb this for 3m and traverse back into a capped niche to the left of the hanging rib. At the top step left and climb direct to the top.

North West Corner:
Non-Tidal   North-West facing
50m north of Hidden Wall is large corner with a hanging crack in the right wall.

The Auspex   35m   Hard Severe 4b. Carlos Las Heras, Ross Jones. 30 May 2008.
The large corner, starting from a large ledge on the left.

North Wall:
Non-tidal   North facing
100m to the north of the Arch Wall is a black north-facing wall. A good alternative when the sun hasn't come around onto the other walls. Abseil down the corner to the right side to the wall to a ledge 10m above the sea.

The Soothsayer   35m   E1 5a. Ross Jones, Carlos Las Heras. 30 May 2008.
From the ledge pull up on to a narrow ledge on the right and traverse with difficulty 5m right into a groove. Climb this to the top.

The Sibyl   35m   E1 5a. Ross Jones, Carlos Las Heras. 30 May 2008.
Traverse 5m left from the ledge. Climb up to a small left-facing corner and then the wall above.

WARIE ARCH WALL:
(HU 239 833)   Non-tidal   West facing
150m north of Warie Gill is a west-facing wall with a cave to the north and arch to the south. A prominent flake-crack runs up the face of poor rock. Access by abseil.

Wary Warie Crack   40m   MXS 5a. Ross Jones, Paul Whitworth. 16 August 2008.
Climb the crack and the wide hanging flake-crack above.

North Head:
(HU 239 839)   Non-tidal   North facing

This is the headland west of the Geo of Ockran. A fine corner of black rock can be seen on the most northerly point of North Head from the cliffs north of the Geo of Ockran. The corner is 100m north of the Hole of Geuda, a deep blow hole. Access by abseil to a ledge below the corner 8m above the sea.

Ockran Corner   30m   VS 4c ***. Paul Whitworth, Ross Jones. 16 August 2008. The corner-crack on excellent rock.

Geuda Wall   30m   E1 5b **. Ross Jones, Paul Whitworth. 16 August 2008. From the corner belay traverse out left and up the centre of the wall to a small shelf below an overhang. Pull out rightwards onto the wall above and climb this direct to the top.

NIBON:
Thule Groove VS 4c was climbed by Al Whitworth and Andrew Hunter and reckoned to be worth two stars.
The following routes are in the geo that contains: *Yogi Braer*, *Puissance* etc. The north side of the geo is a huge arch and the next two routes start from belays on good ledges, well back from the sea, at the back of the arch and immediately under the apex.

Sweetness & Light   45m   HVS 5a **. Mick Tighe, Doug Lee, James Armour, John McClenaghan. 24 June 2005.
Climb cracks and corners in the north-west corner of the geo, trending up and left initially to a small ledge at halfway. A harder direct start leads to the same place. From here climb the corner, a few metres right of the twin cracks of *Yogi Braer*, before breaking out right to finish steeply under a huge boulder.

Black Eyed Biddy   45m   VS 4c *. Mick Tighe, James Armour, Doug Lee. 6 May 2008.
Climbs the fine black diagonal crack-line in the north-east corner of the geo, starting from the same belay as *Sweetness & Light* and finishing up a broken corner where a low stone dyke meets the top of the geo.

NIBON, Cavity Walls:
(HU 2995 7185)   Partly Tidal   West and South facing
50m south of Moo Stack is a small geo bounded on its right by a brown wall. 100m south of this is the wall that includes the route *Cattle Rustler*. A small narrow cave flows under the headland and out through a tidal entrance near Moo Stack. The following routes are on the walls of the small headland between the cave opposite the stack and the central wall of the geo. All routes require abseil to tidal ledges which are accessible at most states of the tide.
   Right of the cave opposite the stack is a black wall.

Amalgam   20m   VS 4c. Andrew Hunter, Al Whitworth. 24 May 2008.
Climb a broken corner on the left of the wall, then trend rightwards at mid-height under a hanging crack-line of poorer rock and up the wall above.

Cavity Crack   18m   E3 5c *. Paul Whitworth, Ross Jones, Andrew Hunter. 24 May 2008.

Climb the steep crack-line up the centre of the wall, pulling left onto easier ground at mid-height.

Right of the wall is a slanting left-facing corner/ramp capped by a roof.

All Gum and No Teeth 12m Hard Severe 4b. Ross Jones, Paul Whitworth, Andy Long. 24 May 2008.
The wall and arete left of the corner.

Capped Root 12m VS 4c. Peter Sawford, Paul Whitworth. April 2005.
The corner finishing out leftwards under the capping roof.

Right of the corner is a left-slanting ramp.

Abscess 12m Hard Severe 4a. Ross Jones. 24 May 2008.
The arete left of the ramp (4b if the lower 5m is also climbed).

Molar Case 12m Severe *. Paul Whitworth, Peter Sawford. April 2005.
The left-slanting ramp.

Right of the ramp is the headwall that splits the seaward wall and the geo.

Ache 12m Severe. Peter Sawford (roped solo). April 2005.
The left side of the wall and arete.

Incisor Information 12m Severe. Paul Whitworth, Peter Sawford. April 2005.
The central crack-line up the headwall.

Pain 12m Severe. Paul Whitworth (roped solo). April 2005.
The right side of the wall and arete.

At the back of the geo and right of a narrow cave entrance is a hanging pillar of rock with a steep hanging right slanting wall/ramp under it.

Local Anaesthetic 20m E2 5b ***. Ross Jones, Paul Whitworth. 24 May 2008.
From a belay on the left side of the pillar climb to a hanging steep ramp. Pull onto this and climb up to hanging cracks above and a ledge. Climb the small right-facing corner and crack to the top. Great route up a compelling line.

AREA OF LANG HEAD (HU 303 704):
A wee lochan drains almost due west. Just south of this there are two sea inlets with a ridge of rock running between. The first two routes are on the south side of this ridge and can be reached by scrambling down seawards and abseiling down to a ledge system at sea-level below a chimney-crack topped by an excellent black open slabby corner.

Come What May 25m Severe *. M. Tighe, D. Lee, J. Armour, N. Kale. 2 May 2008.
Follow the chimney-crack and black corner as described above. A fine outing.

The 'S' Bend   25m   Very Difficult. J. Armour, N. Kale, D. Lee, M. Tighe. 2 May 2008.
Follow the chimney-crack as for *Come What May* and break out right below the black slab/crack to follow a sinuous crack-cum-fault-line to the top.

There is a larger headland just south of here, north of Stivva. It holds a big black north-west facing wall with several unclimbed 25m crack-lines. At the seaward end a lovely pink slab holds the following routes:

May Two Crack   40m   Severe. M. Tighe, N. Kale, J. Armour, D. Lee. 2 May 2008.
The excellent little crack-line just left of centre and broken ground above.

May Two Corner   40m   Mild VS. M. Tighe, N. Kale. 2 May 2008.
A tricky little corner 2m right of *May Two Crack*, and nice easier ground above.

SKELDA NESS:
Two areas have been climbed here on the crags north of West Moulie Geo opposite Moo Stack and at Spoot-hellier the most southerly point. The rock is red granite and provides plenty of variety and some impeccable rock.
Approach: Park at the small lay-by at HU 303 425 by the gate before Scarvister croft and follow the track south to the crags (30mins). Moo Stack is can be easily seen on the approach. Spoot-hellier is south of West Moulie Geo.

West Moulie Geo/Moo Stack:
(HU 298 405)   Mainly non-tidal.   North-West, West and South facing
The walls opposite Moo Stack provide a number of lines. Access for the first two lines is through a slot in the headland opposite the stack that leads to a small terrace with a small steep wall on the left.

Seagull Slayer   15m   VS 4b. Andrew Hunter, Ruairidh Mackenzie. 8 July 2008.
The arete at the southern most edge of the wall.

Three Litre Block   10m   Hard Severe. Andrew Hunter, Ruairidh Mackenzie. 8 July 2008.
From the terrace climb the left-facing corner on the left side of the wall to finish up an exposed block.

Immediately south of geo that contains Moo Stack is a long narrow geo with a large big slab which is accessed from the north.

Jammin Nut   10m   HVS 5c *. Ruairidh Mackenzie, Andrew Hunter. 21 July 2008.
From a hanging belay on a ledge above the sea, make a hard move straight up over a roof section and pull up onto a slab; climb the corner above.

SPOOT-HELLIER:
(HU 299 403)   Non-tidal and partly tidal   East and South facing
Arch Wall Area:
The fine corner of *The Spoot* can be seen easily from the cliff. Access is by a

scramble down a narrow geo to the east and along ledges or by abseil.

Shoostran 25m E3 5c **. Ross Jones, Paul Whitworth. 18 August 2008.
Start from tidal ledges below the corner of *The Spoot*. Climb the wall on the left below the hanging arete and make an airy traverse around the bottom of the arete and pull onto the wall. Climb this to the top. Micro-wires and cams essential.

The Spoot 20m E2 5c ***. Paul Whitworth, Ross Jones, David (Sid) Rayner. 23 August 2008.
Perfect climbing all the way up the wall and corner above.

Right of the corner is a hanging wall which is bordered by another steep wall with creaking flakes. To the right of this is a right-facing stepped corner.

Get Out Clause 20m VS 4c. Andrew Hunter, Ruairidh Mackenzie. 21 July 2008.
The right-facing stepped corner.

Death Tae Da Maet Trowe 20m VS 4c. David (Sid) Rayner, Paul Whitworth. 23 August 2008.
Climb up ledges and the arete to the right of the corner.

Ian & Jen's Route 20m E2 5b *. David (Sid) Rayner, Paul Whitworth. 21 July 2008.
Climb up ledges and a short corner right of the arete to a ledge under a left-slanting hanging corner above. Climb this with difficulty.

Suntoucher 15m VS 4b. Al Whitworth, Andrew Hunter, Anna Pigott. 7 September 2008.
Right of *Ian & Jen's Route* is a deceptively easy-looking corner of cracks and breaks. Well protected but still high in the grade.

Attack of the M&Ms 15m Very Difficult. Andrew Hunter, Anna Pigott, Al Whitworth. 7 September 2008.
Further right still is a stepped corner. Starting on the ledge above the stinking chimney, climb the corner-crack.

Hellier Wall:
To the south-west of Arch Wall is another geo with an arch at the east end that goes straight through to the east side of Spoot-hellier. Hellier Wall is the north wall of the geo. The left-facing corner of *Lambigart* can be easily seen from the south side of the geo. Access by abseil to ledges or at low tide the scramble descent for the Arch Wall area and then traversing around the bottom of fin on seaweed-covered ledges.

Scarface 25m HVS 5a ** Al Whitworth, Anna Pigott, Andrew Hunter. 7 September 2008.
The obvious diagonal break running from the bottom right to the top left of the wall at the left end of the Hellier Wall. Good, exposed and technical climbing. High in the grade.

Tetris   25m   Severe. Ruairidh Mackenzie, Andrew Hunter August 2008
The stepped ledges to the 3m right of *Scarface*.

Prickly Heat   25m   HVS 5a Andrew Hunter, Ruairidh Mackenzie. August
2008.
The small broken left-facing corner right of the ledges and to the left of a steep
flat wall capped at the top by a small overhang. Climb the corner and through
the groove above to the top.

Scarvister Crack   25m   E1 5b *. Ross Jones, Paul Whitworth. 18 August 2008.
Start 10m left of *Lambigart*. Climb ledges and the crack-line to the right of the
wall capped at the top by a small overhang. Continue up the crack as it forms a
small left-facing corner at the overhang and pull through the capping roof above.

Da Maet Trowe   25m   HVS 5a **. Ross Jones, Paul Whitworth. 18 August
2008.
Climb the wall 2m left of *Lambigart* and the excellent hanging flakes above.

Lambigart   25m   VS 4c *. Paul Whitworth, Ross Jones. 18 August 2008.
Stepped ledges and the left-facing corner above.

Hail Da Maet Trowe   25m   E2 5b. David (Sid) Rayner, Ross Jones. 23 August
2008.
The wall right of *Lambigart*. Pull up on to a ledge just right of the arete. Climb
the wall right of the arete. Stepping on to the arete at mid-height, before pulling
back onto the wall and climbing this to the top.

BRESSAY, Muckle Hell:
(HU 527 401)   Party Tidal and Non-Tidal   South and East facing
These are sandstone crags just to the north of Muckle Hell.
Approach: Park at the car park at HU 525 408 and head south-south-east to the
crag. All routes can be accessed by scrambling down nearby except where
stated. Crags are listed from north to south as you approach.

Crocodile Wall:
South facing
Broken by the slanting left-facing black corner system of *Crocodile Corner* in
the middle. Provides a number of low-grade short routes up to E1 along the wall
which descends to sea-level on the right in addition to those listed below:

Unnamed   10m   Severe. Peter Sawford, Julie Maguire. Summer 2007.
The large crack through the broken wall 30m left of the main wall.

Crocodile Corner   9m   Severe. Peter Sawford, Julie Maguire. Summer 2007.
The black left-facing corner.

Unnamed   8m   E1 5b. Peter Sawford, Al Whitworth. Summer 2007.
3m right of the overhang and blunt arete at mid-height. Climb direct pulling
through the overhang.

Main Wall:
South facing
The main wall above a right downwards-sloping shelf into the geo, with a prominent arete in the top section of the central wall and a large right-facing hanging corner on the right.

Pull Through 12m HVS 4c *. Peter Sawford, Ross Jones. 14 May 2008.
Start 4m left of the arete. Climb up into a groove to a ledge and climb the hanging wall above just right of the short blunt arete.

Virdick Flake 10m HVS 4c *. Ross Jones, František Horák. 20 May 2008.
The hanging crack 2m left of the arete to the ledge. Finish as for Route 1.

Unnamed 12m HVS 5a **. Peter Sawford, Julie Maguire. Summer 2007.
Climb the flaked crack below the arete and the groove to the left.

Danté's Traverse 15m Very Difficult. Tommy Robertson. Summer 2007.
Climb the wall under the right side of the arete to mid-height and the right-rising traverse to the top.

Czech Made 12m E1 5b. František Horák, Ross Jones. 20 May 2008.
The wall right of *Danté's Traverse* to a hanging flake and then the short wall above the traverse.

Unnamed 12m Very Difficult. Peter Sawford, Julie Maguire. Summer 2007.
The shallow corner and wall above left of the arete.

Fine Mantel Man 12m Hard Severe 4b *. Peter Sawford, Ross Jones. 14 May 2008.
Start just right of the arete below a right-facing corner at mid-height. Climb grooves to the arete and climb the wall on its left to a fine finishing mantelshelf.

Leirna 12m VS 4c. Ross Jones, Peter Sawford. 14 May 2008.
Start as for *Fine Mantel Man* and climb the right-facing corner.

Pocketful of Faith 12m HVS 5a *. Ross Jones, František Horák. 20 May 2008.
Start just right of *Leirna* and climb to the ledge below the wall. Climb the wall using the perfect central pocket.

Grima 12m HVS 5a *. Ross Jones, Peter Sawford. 14 May 2008.
Climb the wall and small arete to the right and the hanging wall and arete to finish.

Hanging Crack 12m HVS 5a. Ross Jones, František Horák. 20 May 2008.
The slabby wall right of the hanging corner. Traverse in from the right to the hanging thin crack-line. Climb this and the wall above. Good technical climbing.

The bounding wall is Severe and the black wall, just right of the arete of the black wall 10m to the right, has been climbed at Severe (Peter Sawford, Julie Maguire, Summer 2007). Left of the rift that bounds the broken end of the main wall is an undercut wall just under mid-height with thin cracks going through it and a left-facing corner to the right on the mainly broken east-facing wall. Left of this the wall turns south to the next geo with *Black Wall*. On the south-facing wall are two routes:

Unnamed 15m Severe. Peter Sawford, Julie Maguire. Summer 2007.
Climb a shallow left-facing corner from sea-level and the wall above the ledge at half-height.

Unnamed 8m Very Difficult. Peter Sawford, Julie Maguire. Summer 2007.
The wall from the ledge using flakes and cracks on the right.

Black Wall:
East facing
Silent Man 18m E1 5b *. Paul Whitworth, Ross Jones. 16 May 2008.
Abseil to the ledge at the left end of the wall. From the left end of the ledge, climb up and into the left-facing corner and pull through the overhang above.

Dark Noise 18m VS 4c. Ross Jones, Paul Whitworth. 16 May 2008.
Climb the crack from the ledge to the overhang. Pull out rightwards onto the wall and climb the crack-line to the top.

Echos from the Deep 20m E2 5b **. Ross Jones, David (Sid) Rayner. 21 August 2008.
Belay in a niche below a large ledge. Pull out on to the wall and climb wall direct between *Dark Noise* and *Grimsetter Crack*.

Grimsetter Crack 22m E1 5b ***. Ross Jones, František Horák. 20 May 2008.
Belay in a small niche 2m right of and lower than the ledge. Climb the hanging crack to the right and wall direct to the top.

The Brigdi 25m HVS 5a *. Ross Jones, Paul Whitworth. 16 May 2008.
Abseil and belay at the base of the left-slanting crack-line across the face. Climb this.

Unnamed 20m Severe. Peter Sawford, Julie Maguire. Summer 2007.
At the far left end of the black wall is a pale rib that bounds the right side of next wall. Start at the first groove and climb it direct to the top.

ROUND POINT:
(HU 518 373) Mainly Non-tidal South and East Facing
This is one of the headlands to the east of the Sand Vatn Loch. The prominent corner-line of *Shetland Girls* can be seen from the headland of Hamar. Right of the corner is a fine hanging wall with a perfect open corner at the bottom that leads to a ledge at 10m below excellent looking hanging crack-lines (The Main Issue!). To the north of the Round Point is an 80m section of cliff which decreases in height with a right-slanting crack-cum-groove-line in the most northerly corner.
Approach: Abseil from ledges down the most northerly corner and traverse along ledges. Alternatively abseil from stakes (not in situ) or Camalots 5 and 6 can be used in breaks above *Nyuggel*.

Shetland Girls Are Dreamy 40m E1 5b. David (Sid) Rayner, Ross Jones. 21 August 2008.
Climb the steep wall just right of the corner through a small break and up a thin crack to a ledge to the right at 6m. Climb the fine slanting corner-crack above to finish on more broken rock at the top. The section above the ledge is Hard Severe. Climbing the right-hand crack under the ledge at the start may decrease the overall grade.

Right of the corner is an arete to a hanging east-facing wall. Right of the arete is a perfect open corner beneath a ledge. Right of this a 12m east-facing wall split by a groove that leads to the ledge.

Right of the Main Issue 50m E2. Ross Jones, David (Sid) Rayner. 21 August 2008.
1. 15m 5a Climb the hanging groove to the ledge.
2. 35m 5b Climb the large right-slanting corner to a ledge and the hanging wall above to another ledge with a large block. Make an awkward mantelshelf onto another ledge and traverse leftwards and then up the centre of the wall by cracks to a small capping roof of overhangs. Traverse 5m rightwards under the overhangs and finish up the corner.

15–20m right of the hanging wall is a left-slanting corner-crack beneath a large V-groove at the top of the cliff.

Nyuggel 30m HVS 5b. David (Sid) Rayner, Ross Jones. 22 August 2008.
Start from the top of ledges at 10m, beneath an overhang and just right of the corner-crack. Make difficult but protected moves to pull up to the crack. Climb this to the large stepped groove and traverse out right to a mantelshelf. Finish up the arete to avoid loose rock in the corner.

The next route takes the right-slanting crack-cum-groove-line in the most northerly corner of the ledges by the abseil.

Nyif 25m E1 5b *. Ross Jones, David (Sid) Rayner. 22 August 2008.
Awkward moves to get established on a right-slanting crack-cum groove, then a serious of easier V-grooves and crack-line above.

LAMBHOGA HEAD:
Two areas have been climbed here and there is plenty of potential to the south at Vaakel Craigs. The rock is sandstone. Routes are 8–10m.

North Wall:
(HU 409 139) Non-tidal North facing
The rock is sound and fluted with very good gear. The crag overhangs slightly so, although only 10m in height, the routes are surprisingly strenuous. All routes were climbed on 27 August 2007.

Lost Perspective HVS 5a *. Al Whitworth, Peter Sawford.
The crack and then around the bulge at the top to finish

Pringle   VS 4c *. Peter Sawford, Al Whitworth, Julie Maguire.
Up the middle of the least steep wall following the broken cracks

Lambhoga   HVS 5a *. Al Whitworth, Peter Sawford, Julie Maguire.
The first main crack-line 4m in from the right end of the crag

Wailing Wall:
(HU 408 138)   Non-tidal   South facing
On the south side of Lambhoga Head. The featured sandstone is sandy and softer than the North Wall. All routes climbed by Pete Richardson and parties in 1990s and 2000s. Named by the first ascensionists of North Wall.

Entrée   Mild Severe.
Climb the leftmost crack and finish right up the corner.

Headrest   Severe 4a.
Climb the thin crack and finish right up the wide crack.

Slip Sliding   VS 4b *.
The broken cracks straight up the wall.

Off the Mark   HVS 5b *.
Climb the middle of the wall avoiding the cave at mid-height.

Thread the Hole   VS 4c.
Climb above the niche to the large ledge and finish up the wide crack.

NORTHERN HIGHLANDS CENTRAL

BEINN A' MHUINIDH:
The Tallon – Ewan Lyons found it an enjoyable route with modern grade VS 4a, 5a, 4b, 4b **. Pitch 2 only involved one strenuous move (well-protected and short-lived) of 5a pulling over the overhang from the belay. There followed pleasant 4c climbing for the rest of the pitch.

BONAID DHONN:
Route 1   III,6. Roger Webb, James Edwards. 4 December 2008.
Follow the summer line. A route for when all else has failed! Nice views though.

STONE VALLEY CRAGS, Red Wall Area:
The route is left of the Red Wall Area and left of *Bold as Brass* on the other side of the descent path.

Fat Freddy's Drop   10m   HVS 5b. Alex Moran, Martin Moran. 4 May 2008.
The gritstone-like overhanging off-width crack above the descent path. Good but hard to find protection (without a very large cam).

BAOSBHEINN, North-West Face:

Ramblin' On 150m II. Martin Hind. 31 October 2008.
A thin runnel of ice and snow just on the left of *Direct Route*. It should be easier if it fills up later in the winter. Take the right-hand line at each amphitheatre continuing up to the top.

Sgòrr Dubh:
Donald Morris has found this old Gaelic name for Rona Face, which was invented in the absence of anything else. Left of *Merlinswanda*, above its descent route is a scooped face (this faces just west of north and never gets the sun as the left arete of the face completely shades it). There are two obvious chimney lines, one on the left and one on the right.

Left-Hand Route 150m IV,5. James Edwards, Roger Webb. 30 October 2008.
Start as for *Right-Hand Route*, then move leftwards on easy ground. Go up the left gully to a move rightwards to gain an awkward slot. Above this, trend rightwards on easier ground and then up.

Right-Hand Route 130m V,6. James Edwards, Roger Webb. 30 October 2008.
This is the obvious gully on the right side of the face. It is steeper than it looks. Climb the gully to an impasse at half-height which is climbed on good hooks. Continue up to the top of the gully, then move left and climb up to the summit.

AZTEC TOWER:
On the far left of the 'broken NW face left of the main wall'. Left of *Quickstep* is a heather terrace and a gully. Immediately left of this is a small buttress with two routes.

Montezuma's Revenge 10m VS 4c. Jonathan Preston, Hamish Burns. 15 May 2009.
On the right side of the buttress (just left of the heathery gully). A slab, steep wall and another slab lead to a steep finishing crack and heathery finish.

Mexican Wave 10m VS 4c. Jonathan Preston, Hamish Burns. 15 May 2009.
A wide right-facing corner-crack formed by a large block on the left side of the buttress is climbed to a slab and steep finish.

Blank Wall 15m E1 5a. Michael Barnard. 7 June 2009.
An eliminate up the steep wall left of *Astriding Edge*. Start on a flat boulder and climb directly up the wall, reaching for the arete at the point at which it bulges.

RUBHA MOR, Opinan Slabs, Camas Buidhe Eoghainn:
(NG 877 978)   South-East facing   Largely non-tidal
On the east side of the Opinan Slabs headland is a narrow bay filled with huge boulders. The west side of the bay forms a clean wall initially with some pleasant non-tidal micro-routes before a step leads down to a slippery tidal platform where the routes begin. As with the rest of Opinan Slabs the rock is solid and protection is good. The routes described are quick drying.

Flaky Surprise 9m Hard Severe 4b. Andrew James. 20 February 2009.

The main wall is split into three sections by a couple of large dark and often damp cracks. Start up the steep wall just right of the left crack and continue past ledges to follow a thin crack up the enjoyable slab above.

Summer Isle Wall　9m　VS 4c. Conor Brown. 20 February 2009.
Trickier than it appears. A strenuous start up the corner 2m right of *Flaky Surprise* leads past ledges to a delicate move on the slab above.

MEALL MHEINNIDH:
There are many ridges which can each be central according to the viewpoint, so *Glasgow Ridge* was not identified. The first route below is a possibility, but it was longer and better defined than the description of *Glasgow Ridge.*

Weegie Ridge　300m　Very Difficult. Andy Nisbet. 27 May 2008.
The apparently cleanest ridge, starting from a terrace at NG 957 752. The terrace leads right from two gullies which feed the west branch of the stream shown on the 1:50,000 map. The ridge started 100m right of one gully and 50m right of the other. A direct start was made at VDiff but a less direct and more vegetated start might have made the route a poorly protected Diff. The middle section was cleaner and pleasant.

The Meanie　150m　Hard Severe. Andy Nisbet. 27 May 2008.
A steep ridge, almost an arete, at NG 960 745, on a southern extension of the cliff which is shown beyond a gap in the cliff shown on the 1:50,000 map. The gap is a steep ramp which was used for descent. Start just right of an overhanging section of cliff base, where the base takes a curve and rises up left. The right end of the overhanging section forms a narrow chimney. Climb on its right rib and finish up it to a ledge. Gain the main arete on the right and follow it to a bulging section. Pass this on the left where the holds are clean but more sloping (4a but more serious), then return to the crest and follow it to a terrace. The way is blocked by a 5m vertical wall (4b) which leads to an easier crest.

A' MHAIGHDEAN:
White Louse　90m　Very Difficult. Sonya Drummond, Andy Nisbet. 5 August 2008.
A direct but grassier line up the slabs containing *Gladiator*. Start 10m up left from the lowest point of the slabs. Climb direct, crossing *Gladiator* high up, to below a chimney-fault right of the one on *Gladiator* (40m). Go up to the base of the right wall of this chimney-fault, then pull out right. Traverse right under a steep wall and pull round its left end. Go up and return left, then move rightwards again to easier but grassy finishing ground.
Note: The guide describes approaching the climbs by descending the 'nearby big grassy gully (*Trident West Gully*)'. Previous guides also described this. *Trident West Gully* cannot be descended without abseiling. The correct gully to descend is *Pinnacle Gully*, easily identified by Hodge's Pinnacle.

A' MHAIGHDEAN, Stac a' Chaorruinn:
99　180m　Hard Severe. Andy Nisbet, Jonathan & Diana Preston. 24 May 2008.
A second route on the crag, 99 years on from Ling and Glover. Approached from

Corrie Hallie in 4hrs 45mins. The route climbs the slabby section of the north face, starting at the lowest point of the face 50m right of the large gully. Climb a short rib and step left at its top (4b, crux). Go up to a steepening and move right up a fault (30m). Return left and climb rough slabs in four 30m pitches, crossing two diagonal faults. The descent is a grassy ramp about 100m to the west and which slopes down westwards. A final rock step is easy.

Pocket Money   160m   VS 4b. Andy Nisbet. 1 June 2008.
A line up the left side of the slabby face. Start at the left end of an overhanging section of the cliff base. This is about 10m right of the gully. Climb up for 10m to a corner which forms the left end of a red vertical wall. Climb this juggy corner past a clump of vegetation which doesn't affect the climbing and move 5m right to the base of a big scoop in the slabs above. Move up left for 3m, then take a line diagonally right across the scoop on good pockets. One steep move at the end (crux) leads to a red V-groove. Climb the slabs just left of this (or the groove itself) to an easing in angle. Go left across smooth rippling slabs to below a steeper red slab, the main feature of the route. Climb two sections of red slab on positive holds to a ledge below a steep wall. Pass this on the left, then continue slightly leftwards on easier sections of slab overlooking the gully until the slabs become walking angle.

Ling Ylang   110m   Very Difficult. Sonya Drummond, Andy Nisbet. 5 August 2008.
Possibly the line which Ling and Glover attempted, being on the more broken east face. The route is based on a rib which forms the first change from east facing to more north. This is left of a left-facing corner system and has a steep clean wall below it. Walk up right from a lower wall to the steep clean wall, then move up left over a step to its left end.
1. 45m   Pull into a short corner, then climb a ramp rightwards to a terrace. Continue up terraces and short walls to the base of the rib.
2. 40m   Climb the rib to a ledge.
3. 25m   Continue easily up the rib to grassy ground at the top of the buttress.

GRUINARD CRAGS, Car Park Area, Triangular Slab:
Gneiss as Pie   15m   VS 4c. Jo Horne, Nick Horne. May 2005.
Follow the slab between *Gneisser* and *Gneissest* avoiding any of the obvious cracks.

Goat Crag:
The Eightsome Reel   25m   E5 6c **. Ian Taylor. 8 August 2008.
Climbs the thin hanging crack in the upper wall right of *Freakshow*. Start right of *Freakshow* and follow a couple of stepped corners to gain a sloping shelf below and right of the crack. Swing left and follow the crack past a hard section to good holds then continue via sustained climbing to an easing of angle. Move left to the in-situ belay of Freakshow and abseil from here.

The Last of the Grand Old Masters   20m   E4/5 6a *. Ian Taylor, Tess Fryer. 26 May 2008.
Start 15m right of *Freakshow* where a white crack runs up to the left side of

some square-cut roofs. Climb the crack to a good shake-out at the roofs, and then make committing moves rightwards to a rest at the right end of a sloping niche. Go up a groove immediately right of the niche and continue more easily to a fixed abseil point.

Jetty Buttress, First South Wall:
Easy Jet 15m HVS 5a. Charles White, John Mackenzie, Andy Nisbet. 15 June 2008.
Squeezed in between *Limited Stop* and *Bus Stop*. Climb the wall between the two routes, then trend left after touching *Bus Stop* at the top of its corner.
Note: *Dave's Dilemma* and *South-West Arete* were both thought to be HVS 5a. *North-West Arete* doesn't use the crack on the right, although it is useful for a good small runner.

Creag Ghiubhsachain:
Sylvestris 30m Hard Severe 4a. Andy Nisbet. July 2007.
The left and right areas of cliff are separated by a line of weakness. Start off a triangular block at the very left end of this. Climb up 3m, then traverse right for 10m to reach an easier break leading to the top.

Slip Up 25m E2 5c *. Jonathan Preston, Andy Nisbet. 4 June 2008.
A stack of piled blocks lie at the cliff base just left of the overhanging wall which forms most of the right side of the cliff. Start up the right end of these blocks to stand on the rightmost one. Climb a groove slanting slightly left and forming the left end of the overhanging wall. This leads into an easier V-groove.

Lucy Locket 25m E1 5b ***. Andy Nisbet, Jonathan Preston. 4 June 2008.
Climbs the pocketed left edge of the overhanging wall. Start 3m right of the stack of blocks. Climb straight up the left edge of the wall on excellent pockets.

Holy Handrail 25m E1 5b *. Jonathan Preston, Andy Nisbet. 4 June 2008.
Climbs out the left side of the hole and out across the overhanging wall on the left. Climb straight up to the left end of the hole (slow to dry), then swing out left on a handrail and move up into a shallow corner. Finish by a jamming crack.

Mungasdale Crag:
Judgement Day 15m E6 6b. Nick Duboust, Andrew Wilby. 27 July 2009.
Start 3m left of *Officer Jesus* at a shallow left-facing undercut corner. Make hard moves to gain the sloping ledge, then hand-traverse right to the middle of the overhanging wall. Gain big loose flakes and climb straight up the wall. Top-roped, then both led.

AN TEALLACH AREA, The Sidings:
Muice Express 110m VS 4b. Andy Nisbet. 31 May 2008.
Start at a clean tongue of distinctly pocketed slab at a low point of the cliff base 20m right of *The Funnel* and 30m left of *Route 1*. Climb the tongue to its top, then move slightly left and up a thin crack, then slightly left again to cross a prominent right-rising crack. Go up over bulges (crux) towards the left end of a roof, which is clearly seen on the skyline from the start of the route. Take a line

of weakness rightwards under the roof and climb a corner-flake which forms its right end. Finish up mucky slabby ground.

Thomas 140m HVS. Sonya Drummond, Andy Nisbet. 6 August 2008.
A clean band of slabs left of *The Funnel*. This leads into a chimney-corner which *The Funnel* uses to finish. Start below a flake-line at the base of the first slab.
1. 30m 5a Climb to the top of the flake-line, which is below a vertical grass-filled crack. Traverse right into a scoop and go up this to break out left from a corner on to the main slab. Go up to a terrace.
2. 40m 4c Start up a right-slanting ramp, then climb straight up (bold) to a ledge. Climb the next slab just right of a grass-filled crack, then move right on to its crest to reach a hollow flake where *The Funnel* joins.
3. 40m 4a Climb the chimney-corner (as for *The Funnel*).
4. 30m Move left and climb two tiers of clean slabs to the top.

Little Red Train 110m Hard Severe 4a. Andy Nisbet. 14 August 2008.
Towards the left end of the cliff is a more prominent buttress bounded from the main smoother face by right-facing corners. Right of these corners (the left side of the main face) is a vertical band of red rock. The route climbs this, mostly on clean rock, although there is some moss high up (dry conditions recommended). Protection may be limited.

Flying Scotsman 120m E1 **. Andy Nisbet, Duncan Tunstall. 20 August 2008.
Climbs the clean front face of the prominent buttress near the left end of the cliff. Start below a clean white patch of slab.
1. 30m 4c Climb this lower slab to the left end of a ledge below an overlap. There is a large detached block on the ledge to the right.
2. 40m 5b Pull left into a corner, then step right through the overlap to gain an upper slab. Climb this slightly leftwards to a steepening (runners). Step back down and make a short thin traverse right to a crack. Climb this trending slightly left (bold), then back right to a small tree at the right end of an overlap.
3. 50m 5a Layback into a hanging corner, and climb this before stepping left on to a slab. Gain grassy ledges which lead to an upper slab. Climb this to the top.

AN TEALLACH, Ghlas Tholl:
Minor Rib, Flake Chimney Variation 150m V,5. Iain Small, Simon Richardson. 25 January 2009.
The prominent right-facing corner on the right flank of the rib is cut by a steep chimney-flake.
1. 50m Start 15m right of *Minor Rib* directly below the corner. Climb a series of shallow gullies and short walls to belay below a prominent chimney formed by a huge hanging flake on its right side.
2. 50m Climb the corner and belay on a large chockstone below the continuation chimney.
3. 50m Continue up the chimney, passing a large chockstone to reach a girdling ledge. The chimney-line continues above but is blocked by a huge 'impossible' chockstone. Traverse left along the ledge for 20m to reach the tower pitch of *Minor Rib* and follow this to the top.

Right-Hand Chimneys   240m   IV,5. Simon Nadin, Neil Wilson. 1 February 2009.

Start just to the right of *Sixpence* and climb a line of chimneys on the right-hand side of the buttress to reach a small saddle overlooking *Third Prong*. From here finish up a short flared chimney on the left.

Post Hole Prong Phewy!   300m   II *. Will Wilkinson, Davy Moy. 8 February 2009.

A line up the obvious buttress between the *Third* and *Fourth Prong*. Follow a turfy groove up the right side of the buttress. At 150m the buttress splits with a through route up a 3m gully in the centre of the buttress. Climb down and right into this gully and follow it through the gateway and exit right at the top (35m). Continue up the obvious gully to the top (130m).

Note: On the lower buttress, a good option takes a 15m chimney (tech 4).

The Great Dundonnell Slabs:

NH 08135 87143   Alt 432m

These are on the north-west face of Meall Garbh, an outlier of An Teallach. Park in the lay-by 250m west of the hotel and walk up and left to join a track before heading up the hillside, 45mins. The slabs consist of the best quality pink sandstone, water washed and clean, but most of the cracks are grass filled and need cleaning in order to place protection. The Main Slab is on the right of the crags and is split into two tiers separated by a heather ledge, accessible both up and down from the right by a scramble. The climbing is delicate and on excellent friction, often bold but where cracks exist a good range of cams (including No 4), wires, and some larger nuts will be found useful. The lower slab can obviously be used to split routes if required. A bad midge spot in the wrong conditions.

Longer, Steeper, Better   100m   HVS 5a **. John Mackenzie, Eve Austin. 16th and 29 June 2009.

Climbed on two separate days, the lower pitch partially cleaned on abseil, the top two pitches led on sight. Start at the lowest point of the lower slab where a shallow rib lies below the right-hand of two vertical cracks.

1. 55m 5a Climb the rib then the slabby nose to the right of a grassy groove to a good horizontal crack. Move up into a scoop below an overhang bottoming the right-hand crack and traverse right along a shallow break to below discontinuous cracks and climb these to a podded crack. Continue to horizontal holds and move right into a shallow curved corner. Move back left and up to a slanting flake-crack which is followed (Friend 4) to a small overhang near the top. Step left and finish up easier rock to the heather ledge and tree belay. 50m ropes will not reach the tree unless the second moves up 5m.

2. 30m 4b Climb up to the flake-crack above, then move right and climb the good slab to a narrow heather ledge. Climb the lesser-angled but smoother upper slab near a crack above a loose flake. Follow the crack to move right to a little ledge and a narrow horizontal crack.

3. 15m 4c Move back left to the crack and a heather pull over to a block with fixed abseil gear.

Corrieshalloch Area:
Arnisdale Falls 60m V,5. Guy Roberston, Tony Stone. 3rd January 2009.
The rarely in condition icefall at about NH 186 780 in two 30m pitches. 10mins from the A832, crossing the ageing footbridge at NH 186 778 over the Abhainn Cuileig. Approached by abseil. Worth a couple of stars for esoterica!

THE FANNAICHS, Sgurr nan Clach Geala:
Alpha Crest 140m IV,4. Sonya Drummond, Andy Nisbet. 14 December 2008.
Based on the summer line. Protection is limited, but there is some on the hard sections. Climb the lower crest to a terrace at half-height. Continue more steeply up the crest to a corner on the left (belay), from where a grass ledge leads left. Follow this to its end, then make an axe-traverse left across a diminishing slab to gain a steep groove which is followed to easier ground and the summit of the buttress.

STRATHCONON, Creag Ghlas:
Bearded Lady 70m E2. Brian Duthie, Forrest Tempelton. 25 July 2008.
The stepped buttress left of *Hall of Mirrors*. Start at the toe of the lower buttress.
1. 25m 5b Climb up to a horizontal break. Pull over the bulge above and climb steepening cracks as close to the arete as possible. Break out left at the top onto a heather ledge and two small trees.
2. 45m 5b Climb rightwards around the edge directly above and climb the cracks immediately to the right of the edge and left of *Hall of Mirrors*. Break out left onto an easier-angled ramp at the top, a sustained pitch. To finish follow *Hall of Mirrors* to the top or abseil down its main pitch.
Both pitches were climbed on sight and would benefit from cleaning. Good climbing but protection less obvious than *Hall of Mirrors*.

MOY ROCK:
Breakdown 50m E3/4 5b. Robin Thomas, Sheila van Lieshout. June 2009.
This route has been added since the others were bolted. It climbs the obvious flake-crack right of *The Fly*. To reach a decent belay at the top, 60m ropes are required. Climb rightwards along an easy ramp from base of *The Fly* to gain the crack. Follow this steeply and boldly until it eases and fades; from its top traverse rightwards past a tottering block to an easier exit. Take a large rack and don't fall off! Interesting climbing throughout but never harder than 5b (poorly protected in several places, lots of gear but very suspicious rock!). Robin Thomas requests no bolts near this route as they will detract from its exciting nature.

Note: There are more sport routes – see:
http://www.scottishclimbs.com/wiki/Moy_Rock

NORTHERN HIGHLANDS SOUTH

MEALL NA TEANGA:
Left Central Route 200m IV,4. Roger Webb, Simon Richardson. 6 December 2008.

A line of weakness up the steepest part of the face left of *Central Gully*. Start up a wide open gully and follow this for three pitches to below the steep central section defined by a right-facing corner system. Move up right of the corner and climb a stepped groove to a ledge. Climb up and right to a terrace and follow mixed grooves to the top.

GLEOURAICH:
Rusty Rib   120m   II. Roger Webb, Simon Richardson. 23 November 2008.
The easiest line up the broken grooves defining the left flank of the buttress at the head of Coire na Fiar Bhealaich.

DRUIM SHIONNACH, West Face:
Sunny Slab   70m   VS 4b. Andy Nisbet. 28 June 2009.
A clean slab on the right side of the buttress left of *Deceptive Chimney* (*Eurhythmics* takes the left side of the buttress). Scramble up to a ledge below the slab (10m). Climb the centre of the slab, with a section moving right and back left on quartz holds, to reach a groove below a roof. Climb the groove and roof, then continue slightly rightwards before moving back left to a corner. Climb this and easy loose ground (50m). Scramble to the top (10m).

The Gust   90m   IV,4. Donnie Williamson, Hamish Burns. 3 February 2009.
Climbs an icy groove which defines the buttress with *Eurhythmics* on the left. Start below a bay with a short buttress below.
1. 30m Climb a corner in the short buttress to snow in the bay and belay on the left wall.
2. 30m Climb the icy groove and trend left at the top over blocks.
3. 30m Climb easy slopes to the top.

Aye   40m   III,4. Donnie Williamson, Dave Bowden, Mark Francis. January 2009.
The buttress left of *The Gust*. Start up a corner left of two steeper parallel chimneys. Continue up a turfy groove straight up to easier ground.

GLEN ELG, Scallasaig Crag (NG 853 205):
These climbs are on the lowest and rightmost crags in the area. Park in the lay-by heading in to Glenelg just before the cattle pens at Scallasaig. Go through a closed gate and walk up rightwards for a 200m. Good clean rock.

Beolary Craic   15m   VS 4b *. Eachann Hawthorn, Eric Hawthorn. 1 August 2008.
The most obvious crack right of centre on the face has a small sapling at the top. The crack becomes more prominent with height.

Black Ripple   12m   E1 5c ***. Eachann Hawthorn. 1 August 2008.
This climb is on a small crag immediately above the first climb. It goes up the obvious left-slanting crack-line in the centre of the wall. Well protected; steep and strenuous at the top.

BEINN FHADA, Sgùrr a' Choire Ghairbh, North-East Face:

Birthday Ramp 100m I. Neil Wilson. 22 November 2008
Climbs a slanting line immediately to the left of *The Needle*.

Summit Left Buttress 290m III. Simon Nadin, Neil Wilson. 6 December 2008.
Climbs the right edge of the buttress immediately left of *Left-hand Gully* in six pitches, utilising a short chimney slightly to the left on the fourth pitch. The bottom of the route is avoidable, but it improved with height. Generally the turf was semi-frozen, and the rock slabby and unhelpful. The grade assumes better conditions.

BEINN LIATH MHOR, South Face:
Artemis 350m II. Sonya Drummond, Diana Preston. 8 February 2009.
Follow the Coire Lair path and break off the path about 500m before Loch Coire Lair, to go up south-south-west-facing slopes to the cliff. Start at the foot of the third buttress from the left (NG 983 511). Climb directly up rock bands broken by snow slopes until below a steep wall. Avoid the steep wall by a left traverse, up and round to a snow field. Continue directly up the snowfield, then go slightly right and then back left to an awkward slabby corner (crux). Go up the corner to the crest of a rib and climb the rib up to another steepening, before breaking left into a fine gully. Climb the gully to its termination, where it rejoins the rib. Carry on easily up the rib to the top.

Note: Iain Thow notes that the *South-East Rib* is marked wrongly on the diagram in Highland Scrambles North. The description is correct but the line is just off the diagram to the right. Also, the buttress towards the left of the face, as it starts to turn the corner and rise up the hillside, is a good Moderate. There is scope for good two-pitch routes in the middle of the face, some perhaps quite hard. Raeburn climbed something around 1909.

SGORR RUADH, Central Couloir:
Eddie the Eagle 130m V,4. Andy Nisbet, Jonathan Preston. 9 December 2008.
Gains a high hanging gully in the buttress right of *High Gully*. Start 15m right of *High Gully*.
1. 45m Climb a large icy ramp leftwards towards *High Gully* (serious, IV,4 with good ice). Gain a ledge, move right and climb a short blocky ramp leftwards to just below its top.
2. 30m Gain a ledge above and traverse it rightwards until it would become much more difficult to continue.
3. 55m Go up over a bulge, then leftwards on turf to gain the hanging gully. Climb it easily to just below the top (50m), then finish (5m).

Raeburn's Buttress:
Narrow Ridge 160m V,6. Sonya Drummond, Andy Nisbet. 1 December 2008.
The ridge which forms the left side of *Narrow Gully* has one hard tier. The lowest wall was unfrozen so the route started up *Narrow Gully* for 10m, then traversed left on to the crest (20m). Go up to the next steep tier and climb it by a left-slanting grooved ramp, before returning to the crest (50m). Go up the easy crest to the next tier (30m). Climb this near the crest, where slabby ground leads to a steep V-groove topped by a big flake. Move left and climb another steep

groove (15m, crux). Go up to the final tier and climb a groove on the crest. This leads to a small pinnacle on the right, then a larger one at the top. Step down to the easier top of the lower buttress (45m).

Too Late to Tango   105m   IV,5. Mark Walker, James Edwards. 20 January 2009.
1. 70m Start just left of *Raeburn's Superdirect* and climb up near its edge to a large ledge.
2. 35m Climb easily for a few metres to overlook the gully. Go up on turf to easier ground and belay below the steep wall.
3.etc. Traverse leftwards on the line of *Jigsaw*.

Note: The following route should be added to the guide, as the first ascentionists are listed.
Wildcat Gully   140m   I. (1983).
An uncomplicated snow gully to the right of *Riotous Ridge*. It has a detached splintery pinnacle splitting it some way up and the route goes to the right of this.

SGURR A' CHAORACHAIN, No. 3 Buttress:
Kruth   250m   II. Finlay Bennet, Mark Robson. 2 February 2008.
This route follows the right side of No. 3 Buttress. Start near the base of *No. 3 Gully* and trend upwards and leftwards over easy but interesting ground for four pitches to gain a fine position on the crest of the buttress. From here a short but shapely ridge leads with interest to the summit.

SGURR A' CHAORACHAIN, Summit Buttress:
Bantam   65m   VII,7 *. Dave MacLeod, Blair Fyffe. 10 February 2009.
Near the left end of the wall is a prominent icefall on the lower half of the buttress.
1. 30m Start on the left below the hanging fang of ice. Move up and get a low runner on the left. Difficult and bold mixed moves gain a hole behind the icicle where it meets a protrusion of rock (may be easier with ice on this section). Climb the icicle and its continuation to a large ledge below broken ground above.
2. 35m Easy turf climbing leads to the top.

SGURR A' CHAORACHAIN, Upper Cliff, Continuation Buttress:
Inaugural   55m   Hard Severe 4a. Andrew Wardle, Ross Jones. 6 May 2008.
Start at the short open corner just left of the main left corner system left of *Pommel*.
1. 25m Climb the corner and the wall above to the left of the arete to a ledge.
2. 30m Climb the broken corner above and continue to the top.

BEINN BHAN, Coire nan Fhamair:
The God Delusion   240m   IX,9 ****. Guy Robertson, Pete Benson. 10 December 2008.
An outstanding, complex and aggressive voyage up the heart of the mighty *Godfather* wall. The climbing is sustained all the way, and in places bold and strenuous. The lower wall is based on the left-hand of the two right-trending weaknesses. Start about 20m left of *Godfather*, at a prominent chimney-slot.

1. 20m Climb the slot, then go left for a few metres before climbing back up right to a ledge and belay by a short groove and rib.

2. 30m Step right to gain and follow the awkward slim ramps trending right past a wide crack and hard mantelshelf. Continue up the easier fault to gain the snow bay then move up and left to belay left of the corner.

3. 20m Climb the short wall on the left, then traverse hard right below an overhanging fault to a difficult step down across the top of the corner.

4. 40m Steep cracks up the left-hand diagonal weakness are followed with sustained interest to the balcony, then continue direct to belay below huge overhangs.

5. 30m Traverse left to join *Godfather* pitch 3 at the short fierce groove, but above this go hard right to belay below a prominent crack above the overhangs overhead.

6. 40m Go up to below the first groove left of the crack. Pull over the overhang into the groove and follow it to a ledge. Work up first right then back left to another ledge below a more substantial overhanging section. Above is a smooth corner-groove. Right of this, and using a good thin crack to get started, pull desperately up right into a turfy niche. Swing out right onto the edge, then climb steeply up moving back slightly leftwards to a good ledge.

7. 30m Mantel up into the corner above, then go hard left under a nose into a turfy fault which is followed to the upper terrace. Go left along this to an enormous block and cave belay below a wide crack.

8. 30m Climb the blocky overhanging corner-fault on the left to easier ground and the top.

BEN DAMPH, Creagan Dubh Toll nam Biast:

Genghis Khan 350m III,5. Andy Nisbet, Sandy Scott. 4 March 2009.
A shallow gully line left of *Boundary Gully*. Start close to *Boundary Gully* and climb turf leftwards to join the gully. Follow this over a short difficult slot and two more short pitches to a barrier wall. Move right and back left to gain the upper gully which is followed to a steeper finish. With ice or the difficult slot banked out, the route would be Grade II.

Leprechaun 400m III,4. Andy Nisbet. 10 February 2009.
Based on the next gully line between *Genghis Khan* and *Mystic Gully*, but some of the difficulties were avoided by the rib on the right. A direct ascent would need very good ice conditions and perhaps be V,5. Start up turf and ice below the gully line. Climb up into the gully but avoid the first steep section by turfy walls on the right. Gain and climb a left-slanting ramp, then traverse left back into the gully below a deep enclosed section. Steep ice forms down its back left corner but take a hidden right branch to its top. Traverse right on turf above an icy slab to exit on to the rib. Climb a short vertical wall (technical crux) before returning left into the gully. Follow the gully to where it ends in an icefall below an overhang. Move right and climb turf, returning left to the easier upper rib where *Mystic Gully* joins.

Creag an Fhithich:
There is good bouldering on another area of rock down and left of *Maculate*

Slab. A slim right-facing corner in the middle of the lower left-hand wall, finishing direct via a triangular block, is 8m Severe.

Mercury Rising   25m   VS 4c. Jonathan & Diana Preston. 30 May 2009.
The groove and twin cracks between *Crystal Horizon* and *Gem Find*. Start 5m left of the big tree at the base of *Gem Find* at some blocks. Step off the blocks and attain a standing position on a heathery ledge on the right. Step left and make a move up to turf and the base of the groove (this turf could be avoided by stepping right to near the left end of the *Gem Find* ledge, then back left; a bit bold). Climb the groove and move up and slightly right to base of twin cracks. Climb the left-hand finger crack (crux) and finish direct. The right-hand crack is marginally easier.

Holly Tree Groove   25m   Very Difficult. Jonathan & Diana Preston. 30 May 2009.
At the left end of the right section is a holly tree. Bridge up the initial corner on the right behind the holly tree. Move left before a small roof and climb up and left to a corner which is followed to the top.

SEANA MHEALLAN:
Kolus   25m   E8 6c ***. Dave Macleod. 20 June 2009.
The superb overhanging arete left of *The Torridonian*. Climb the arete with increasing difficulty and sparse protection to a culmination just before the slabby upper section. Powerful climbing.

Present Tense   25m   E9 7a ***. Dave MacLeod. 11 July 2009.
A hard and sparsely protected line taking the front face of the buttress left of *The Torridonian*. Climb the lower wall near the right arete to a good break and gear. Pull through the roof and up to an undercut on the hanging rectangular block (marginal micro-wires in thin horizontal). Continue directly with a desperate bouldery sequence through the bulge to gain easy ground on the upper slab. F8b climbing with groundfall potential.

Kelvinator   25m   E8 6c **. Dave MacLeod. 9 July 2009.
A much easier and less death-defying alternative to *Present Tense*, but still technical and excellent moves. Follow *Present Tense* to the micro-wires. Smear and palm leftwards to gain an improving horizontal break. Finish up *Sandstorm*.

Cook the Shooter   30m   E3 5c *. Ed Edwards, Martin Moran. 2 April 2009.
Start up the corner 3m right of *Shoot the Cuckoo* and step left under the first roof to join it. Climb this to level with another roof on the left, step left out of the corner and climb a flake in the wall to a small ledge. Climb the wall above direct to a large break. Mantel onto the break and climb the wall above on the right side of the blunt arete to the top.

Western Sector:
Rare Breed   10m   VS 5a. John Lyall, Jonathan Preston. 14 May 2009.
Just right of *Neville the Hedgehog*. Go straight up the slab to the right-hand crack and at its top follow the steep rippled slab right of the short corner.

LIATHACH CRAGS, Path Crag, Upper Tier:

Two stepped grooves lie 10–15m left of *Pitching* and break through the overhanging walls at half-height. The left groove has loose rock at the overhang.

Debut 20m E1 5a. Andrew Wardle, Ross Jones. 7 May 2008.
Start 6m left of the left-hand groove by a shallow right-facing corner-crack under an overhang. Climb the corner and step left and climb up the side of the overhang to a roof before pulling right onto the overhang. Climb the wall and corner-groove to finish.

Better Higher Up 20m HVS 5a. Ross Jones, Andrew Wardle. 7 May 2008.
Start just right of the arete that splits the two stepped grooves. Climb the wall to a small overhang and pull out left onto the arete. Climb the arete and the centre of the wall left of the groove above on perfect rock.

Lower Tier:

Frogmarch 15m Hard Severe 4b. Jonathan & Diana Preston. 17 May 2009.
The right side of the huge block (*Lower Leftist* takes the left side). Climb the wide right-facing corner-crack to a ledge in a chimney. Shuffle right to the edge and climb to the top of the huge block. Finish up a short steep wall.

Note: *Digitalis* was finished, instead of stepping right, by laybacking up the left edge of a wide crack above to a ledge. Finish up a corner with a chockstone and another natural thread.

Black Wall 15m E1 5b. Jonathan & Diana Preston. 17 May 2009.
The black wall between *Digitalis* and *Foxglove Crack*. Start up a short right-slanting crack. Continue up steeply using horizontal breaks. Make an awkward move left to finish up a layback flake (as for *Digitalis*).

Fence Crag:

(NG 917 558) Alt 90m South-East facing
Close to the road, this little Torridonian sandstone crag is situated by the fence line running near the plantations outside Torridon village (just to the east of the Celtic Boulders). It is an easily accessible alternative for mid-grade climbers with a few hours to spare, and the routes, although short (8–10m), are pleasant with often fine cruxes.
Approach: Park in the same lay-by as for Seana Mheallan, just before the fence and cattle grid. Cross the road and follow the fence north-west to the crag, 10mins. Topos provided.

Jock's Groove Mild VS 4b *. Matthew Thompson, Mark Davies. 10 May 2008.
The obvious left-hand corner on the main buttress is pleasant. Bold in places.

Left Behind E1 5b. Matthew Thompson, Mark Davies. 10 May 2008.
The left edge of the buttress. Climb easily up the arete, then pull directly over the bulge above to distant flakes. Crucial side-runner in *Lucky Strike*.

Lucky Strike E2 5c *. Matthew Thompson. 10 May 2008.
A minor technical test piece. Climb the steady slab to the ledge, then attack the

subtle weakness above by hard pulls on distant holds. Tiny cams essential.

Suspect Cylinder   HVS 5b **. Matthew Thompson, Mark Davies. 10 May 2008.
Safe and stimulating. The central groove is easy to the ledge, then has a great layback move to an easier finish.

Laddow Babster   VS 4b *. Mark Davies, Matthew Thompson. 10 May 2008.
The pleasant slab left of the vegetated corner has sparse protection.

Fiend's Finish   VS 4b ***. Matthew Thompson. 10 May 2008.
A line of most spectacle yet probably least resistance. Climb the tricky groove to the roof, then reach out left and swing merrily upwards on huge holds.

Pylon King's Groove   VS 4c ***. Mark Davies, Matthew Thompson. 10 May 2008.
The excellent grooved arete right of the vegetated corner. Tricky moves into the corner followed by easy bridging up to the roof then a tricky move out right (crux). A delicate slab finishes the route off very nicely.

Fence Crack   Severe. Mark Davies, Matthew Thompson. 10 May 2008.
Twenty metres right of the last route is a slab, the Right Wing; take the crack on the left part of the slab.

Sethbury Slab   E1 5b/c *. Mark Davies, Matthew Thompson. 10 May 2008.
The centre of the slab with a tricky crux move to reach the ledge.

Marmot   Hard Severe 4c. Matthew Thompson. 10 May 2008.
The flake at the end of the slab. Graunch over the ugly bulge, then continue much more easily.

Far Right Wing Direct   Severe 4a. Mark Davies, Matthew Thompson. 10 May 2008.
A right-hand line on a buttress 30m right of the last route.

DIABAIG:
To the left of *Dead Mouse Crack* is a steep gully/bay area, consisting of several broken corners and aretes. The following route climbs the fine corner-crack on the far left.

Dire Leg   20m   VS 4c. Michael Barnard (unseconded). 13 April 2009.
Zigzag up easy slabs to the base of the crack. Climb this to its top (abseil descent).

The following is a variation finish to *Dead Mouse Crack* itself:
Variation: Dire Finish   E1 5c *. Michael Barnard (unseconded). 13 April 2009.
Step left below the top crack and climb the obvious steep shallow groove.

Dead Tree Crag:
(NG 801 580)   South-West facing

This crag has some fine routes and is a good choice in showery weather, its overhangs providing welcome shelter from the rain (though not the midges).

Approach: The right-hand side of the crag, a large overhang and cracked slab, is just visible from the White House on the approach from Alligin Shuas. When approaching from Diabaig, cross the outflow of Loch a' Bhealaich Mhor (passing beneath the crag of the same name) to follow a line leading across the next hill, keeping roughly to the same height. A light sheep path is picked up at this point – this leads around and down past some boulders to the foot of the crag (50mins). Photos provided. The main feature of the crag is a hanging slab sporting a system of cracks and lying above a huge overhang.

Dead Tree Wall   20m   HVS 5b **. Michael Barnard, Ron Dempster. 6 June 2009.
A good route with the crux at the top. Start directly below the middle of the huge overhang. Traverse out right to gain a right-trending crack in the hanging slab above. Step right and move up to a big flake, before stepping back left along a footledge to follow another right-trending crack to the top.

Token V.Diff   15m   Very Difficult. Michael Barnard. 6 June 2009.
To the left of the huge roof is a grassy corner-gully. Climb the crack immediately right of this.

Left again is a shorter wall which is overhung at the base. On the right-hand side of this, and just right of a hard-looking roof crack, is an obvious line of flakes.

Flaking It   10m   HVS 5b *. Michael Barnard, Ron Dempster. 6 June 2009.
Strenuous climbing up the line of flakes.

A short walk up the hill from the top of the main crag leads to some interesting shorter outcrops.

Yosemite Crack   6m   E1 5c *. Michael Barnard (unseconded). 6 June 2009.
The overhanging diagonal crack on the far right wall gives a great wee struggle.

Rolling Wall Note:
The crack of *Brave New World* can be followed throughout at E3 6a (Iain Small).

BEINN ALLIGIN, Horns of Alligin:
Scorpion   260m   V,6. Pete McConnell, Pamela-Jane Monaghan; Anthony Feeney, Mike Hassan. 8 March 2009.
On the NE side of the Horns of Alligin below the First Horn there is a distinct A-shape on the mountain flank. *Deep South Gully* creates the right edge of this while this route goes up the left. The route is Grade II apart from the finish. Ascend a snow gully rightwards to 750m height. Exit the gully onto a shoulder overlooking *Deep South Gully*, head left and directly up for 30m of mixed climbing to a sheltered alcove. Climb up and slightly left for 15m, then traverse left on thin ledges aiming to round the corner. Finally straight up for the last 10m.

LIATHACH, Coire na Caime:
The Dru V,6 ***. Roger Webb, Phil Ashby. 11 December 2008.
Follow the summer line to easier ground. To make it more fun, move left along a ledge on the left side of the arete above and climb the first obvious turfy and well protected chimney-groove.

BEINN EIGHE, Far East Wall:
Note: The peg on *Seeds of Destruction* is no more. No change in grade.

Eastern Ramparts:
Beyond the Pale 110m E2 **. John Lyall, Andy Nisbet, Jonathan Preston. 26 June 2009.
The rib right of Pale Diedre. Start as for *Rampage*.
1. 35m 5b Climb 3m rightwards up *Rampage*, then take a prominent crack leading straight up over a bulge and below a bigger bulge. Walk left along a ledge and climb a shallow corner to a good ledge.
2. 10m 5a Climb a continuation crack-line to the Upper Girdle below *Boggle*.
3. 40m 5c Climb the central of three corners (*Boggle* probably takes the right corner) to below a steep crack-line which continues straight up. Move up and left to gain and climb a corner before returning to the crack and climbing it to an easing. A continuation crack is hard, so move left into a corner. Climb this past a break before making thin moves back right into the crack. Climb this to a ledge which leads into *Pale Diedre*.
4. 25m 4a Climb cracks in the wall above to gain a ledge on the right. Move right along this and climb a short wall close to *Boggle*. Finish up an easy rib.

Gnome Wall Direct Start 45m VII,7. Iain Small, Blair Fyffe, Tony Stone. 7 December 2008.
Start at the same spot.
1. 30m Climb the steep corner-groove that leads to and takes the right side of the large protruding nose. Follow the corner over a roof, then gain a hanging recess on the right before pulling back left onto a ledge.
2. 15m Climb a steep groove at the left end of the ledge to gain the Upper Girdle by the recess belay on *Gnome Wall*.
The route now joins the original winter line, which was thought to be VI,7.

East Buttress:
East Buttress Left-Hand 210m V,5 ***. Ed Edwards, Andy Hyslop, Andy Nisbet. 28 March 2009.
An alternative line up East Buttress, starting up a chimney left of the crest, then following the crest itself (noted in the guide as Very Difficult in summer). Much will have been done before but it makes an excellent route which is completely separate to the line drawn in the diagram in Northern Highlands South. Start up a prominent chimney which is immediately left of the crest and some 15m left of the normal start.
1. 45m Climb the chimney, which may be on ice, to a terrace.
2. 30m Above are two grooves. The left is much steeper and more direct but the right was climbed, followed by a short traverse left into the left one. Continue up to a groove with a deep crack.

3. 40m Climb the groove, then move left below a second groove and climb blocky ground to a ledge. Traverse left to below a chimney.

4. 45m Climb the chimney to below a steep wide crack. Climb clean smooth rock to its right with just enough holds and runners to easy ground.

5. 50m For an independent finish, move left and climb a short bulging corner. Continue left and climb a chimney and blocks above to reach the low-angled upper crest.

Central Buttress Note:

A route was climbed following icy slabs near the summer line of *Slab Route* on the lower sandstone tier. *Desperado Jigsaw* 110m V,6. A. Buchanan, G.W. Hughes. 22 January 2005.

In snowier days it used to cover with snow and ice, and has been climbed as a start to *Central Buttress*.

West Central Wall:

Balla na Gaoithe 100m HVS **. Sonya Drummond, Andy Nisbet. 8 August 2008.

A smaller corner system set between the big corners of *Maelstrom* and *Earth, Wind and Fire*. Start from the Second Terrace at the left end of a long overhanging wall.

1. 30m 5b Climb a wet groove for 5m (this may be the same start as *Maelstrom*), move right round its right arete and return left to a continuation groove. Follow this to the lower Girdle ledge and move right to blocks.

2. 20m 4c Climb the wall just to the left to reach the upper ledge, then traverse right to a break in overhangs. Go through this and up a slabby wall above (bold) to belay on the arete.

3. 50m 5a Continue near the arete to cross an overlap below a corner. Climb the corner bending right until nearly into the easy finish of Earth, Wind and Fire. Traverse left until just above a small rockfall scar, then make a tricky move up into a corner. Follow this corner which finally forms the left side of a large pile of wedged blocks (the initial approach abseil was from the right side of these blocks).

Note: *Earth, Wind and Fire* is worth at least a star also.

Note: The route described as *Maelstrom, Direct Start and Right-Hand Finish* in SMCJ 2008 was in fact a direct line through the start of *Maelstrom* and up via a lower continuation of the parallel corner which *Maelstrom* joins during its third pitch, therefore only joining *Maelstrom* to finish (photodiagram provided). High in the grade at VII,7.

Chop Suey VIII,8 **. Tony Stone, Guy Robertson. 9 February 2009.

By the summer route.

Bruised Violet 90m VIII,8. Ian Parnell, Andy Turner. 10 March 2009.

A phenomenal direct line through the very steep ground *Chop Suey* avoids. Very sustained climbing at the top of the grade.

1. 30m *Chop Suey* pitch 1.

2. 20m Climb cracks up the right wall of the groove (as for *Chop Suey*) to *The Upper Girdle* ledge then pull through the roof and follow the committing groove

for 8m to where the ramp of *Force Ten* heads up leftwards. Arrange gear here (in-situ pecker used as back rope for second) from two good footholds on the left wall before dropping back down into the groove and making an unlikely thin traverse on the lip of the overhangs across the right wall. A good crack in the right arete leads to a small ledge where a complex belay can be made (with enough gear it might be better to continue or alternatively combine pitches 3 and 4).
3. 8m Step up until level with big roofs on the left and swing into a bottomless steep groove which leads to good cracks and possible hanging belay (used since the abseil point was here).
4. 20m Pull up right to a sloping ledge and follow very steep grooves and cracks up slightly leftwards until a final pull round a roof gains a big flake. Pull up left onto ledges atop the prow. Traverse 3m left to a crack which leads to big turfy ledges.
5. 12m Blocky steps via a wide crack to the top.

West Buttress:
Dambusters 60m HVS *. Andy Nisbet, Simon Richardson, Duncan Tunstall. 23 August 2008.
A route up the front face of the final tower of *West Buttress*.
1. 30m 5a Climb a corner which forms the right side of the frontal wall (the bigger corner of Corner Finish is further right), then go up to a roof below the upper face.
2. 15m 5a Move right to where a flake breaks the roof. Layback up this and hand-traverse back left. Climb a crack and good holds above to a ledge with a huge rocking block.
3. 15m Climb a final wall as for the *Direct Finish* (left of the narrow chimney of the normal route).

Grand Slam 80m V,7. John Lyall, Pete Macpherson, Andy Nisbet. 21 January 2009.
Climbs the right side of the frontal wall of the upper tier of *West Buttress*.
1. 35m Start up a flake-line just left of the corner of *Dambusters* and move right after 10m to join the corner. Follow the corner to where a blank section forced a step left on *Dambusters*. Stay in the flake-line on the left and join *Dambusters* at a big ledge above. Move up and traverse right to beneath the flake of *Dambusters*.
2. 20m Traverse right under the roof to reach the right arete of the wall. Climb flakes and cracks immediately right of the arete to where the angle eases.
3. 25m Finish as for *West Buttress*, via the narrow chimney.

Still Game VS *. Andy Nisbet, Simon Richardson, Duncan Tunstall. 23 August 2008.
By the winter line (4c, 4b), good clean rock.

Fuselage Wall:
Pension Plan Hard Severe. Andy Nisbet, Jonathan Preston. 22 May 2008.
A summer ascent of the winter line. Pitch 1 was loose, 4a if you could pull on everything, but actually the crux. Pitches 2 and 3 were run together, 4b and good.

Spitfire 50m HVS *. Jonathan Preston, Andy Nisbet. 22 May 2008.
The pillar right of *Flying Fortress*. Start on its right side.
1. 15m Climb slightly leftwards on to the crest and up this to a big block below the steepest section.
2. 25m 5a The steepest section has a big roof in its centre. Climb a finger-crack leading to the right side of the roof, then either climb a corner on its right and move left or swing left shortly above the roof. Continue up the pillar to a final steep wall.
3. 10m 4c Starting at the right edge, pull on to the wall and climb a wide crack on its right side.

Bandit 65m VII,8 ***. Steve Ashworth, Viv Scott. 29 October 2008.
Quality technical climbing in a stunning position up the pillar containing *Spitfire*. Pitches 2 and 3 are as for *Spitfire* (despite the difference in length).
1. 15m Start as for *Pension Plan* but continue right up easy blocky ground rightwards to a big block on a ledge.
2. 10m Step up right onto a big flake, then up a corner and thin crack above to small ledge under overlaps.
3. 20m Go up and leftwards through overlaps, then up an exposed rib moving left at top to gain ledge under the headwall.
4. 20m From the right of the ledge, go up to beneath the final wall. Pull onto the wall and climb cracks up the centre to a ledge under a capping block. Exit left in a spectacular position.

War Games 55m VI,7 **. John Lyall, Andy Nisbet. 22 November 2008.
An alternative line up the pillar containing *Spitfire*. Start as for the summer line of *Spitfire*.
1. 30m Climb to the big block. Crossing *Bandit*, climb up the steep wall above the left end of the block and move left past a large sharp spike into a groove above an overhung recess. Climb the groove and right-facing corner above.
2. 15m Move right into a small hanging corner between a higher left roof and a lower right roof. Step out right above the right roof on to the crest of the pillar. Climb a crack-line to a ledge, then step left and climb near the right arete of *Flying Fortress* corner to a roof guarding the headwall. Traverse right under the roof to its right edge (*Bandit* also belays here).
3. 10m Step left above the roof on to the headwall and climb a wide crack up the right side of the headwall.

Mosquito 60m Severe *. Andy Nisbet. 26 September 2008.
Start as for *Fight or Flight* (winter). Climb the groove but continue trending left to an overhung recess. Step up right to a ledge, stand on a big flake, then step back left above the overhang. Step right again and go up to the diagonal ledge just right of the pinnacle (30m 4a). Move right into cracks which lead up into a short chimney, then a right-facing corner which forms an opposing pair with *Fight or Flight*'s corner. Climb this fine corner and over its capping roof. Finish direct over a bulge (30m 4b).
Winter: V,7 **. John Lyall, Andy Nisbet, Jonathan Preston. 30 October 2008.
By the summer route, except for the first pitch. From the overhung recess, the

overhang and grooves above were climbed, leading direct to the belay. The second pitch was superb and extremely well protected.

Fight or Flight   Severe. Andy Nisbet, Simon Richardson, Duncan Tunstall. 23 August 2008.
By the winter line, but the first pitch started more direct and continued to above the big flake (4a). The third winter pitch was climbed as a continuation to the second pitch by traversing left into the right-facing corner of *Mosquito* under its capping roof, then pulling through the roof (crux, 4b). Finish on the right.

Ace   60m   VI,7 **. Malcolm Bass, Simon Yearsley. 25 January 2009.
Excellent climbing, taking a direct line up the steep and impressive ground between *Fight or Flight* and *Bombs Away*. Start 2m right of the toe of the buttress.
1. 25m Climb the steep wall then easier ground to a short square-cut chimney leading through a roof. Climb this, then move up and right on blocks and flakes to the ledge below the steep wall at the top of pitch 2 of *Bombs Away*.
2. 25m Climb the compelling steep crack in the wall, moving slightly left at its top (strenuous but well protected). Move up and right to a niche, junction with *Bombs Away*, but then continue immediately straight up to below the impressive capping roofs. Climb directly through these at a surprisingly amenable grade to reach a small alcove just below the skyline. Exit the alcove in a superb position with a steep pull up to easier ground.
3. 10m Easier ground to the top of the buttress.

Sail Mhor:
Cave Gully   100m   V,5 *. Peter Davies, Tim Marsh. 26 Jan 2009.
Climbs a narrow gully cutting into the left wall of *White's Gully*, leading to a large cave. The first steepening in *White's Gully* is level with a prominent overhang on the left; start 10m above this. The route is probably a grade easier with more ice.
1. 30m Follow the gully.
2. 30m Continue past a large chockstone to the base of the large cave.
2. 10m   Traverse a snow ledge past an arete to belay beneath an ice-filled chimney.
3. 30m Climb the chimney to reach easier ground leading to the ridge.

CAIRNGORMS

COIRE AN T-SNEACHDA, Mess of Pottage:
The Truncator   100m   VS *. John Lyall, Andy Nisbet. 24 June 2009.
Good climbing but close to other routes.
1. 45m 4c Follow the first pitch of the winter route, then the second to where it joins *The Melting Pot*.
2. 35m 4b The aim was to climb the pillar above but the start is difficult. On its right is a worn groove, close to *The Message* and sometimes climbed as a more difficult option to that route. From the top of the worn groove, go left up a

roofed groove and make an improbable step left on to the pillar. Climb a corner-crack on the crest of the pillar, then the crest itself (close to *Trunk-Line*) to a ledge near *The Message*.
3. 20m Move right and climb slabs right of *Trunk-Line*/*Truncator* finish).

Droidless (no longer so!) Hard Severe 4b *. Andy Nisbet. 28 July 2008.
The base of the crack-line was gained by pleasant slabs, then climbed direct (the winter route climbs a slanting corner on the left). An awkward bulge was the crux. For the final pitch, the arete right of *Pot of Gold* was climbed (cross *Mariella* to reach it). This is artificial but spectacular and was climbed on the FWA of *Mariella*.

Fishy Business 90m Severe 4a. Andy Nisbet. 28 July 2008.
Based on *Sharks Fin Soup*. Climb this route except that a bulge above the fin required the use of a loose hold, so was passed by a step right into *The Despot* and returning immediately above. Continue up a corner (one of the options for *The Haston Line*) to *The Slant*, then directly up a fault which is the finish of *Yukon Jack* (winter); it starts with a right-curving hollow wedged flake.

The Despot 100m VS. Andy Nisbet. 1 July 2009.
1. 30m 4c Follow the first pitch of the winter route, with difficulty up the left-facing corner.
2. 30m 4a Climb a clean buttress above, starting at its left corner and moving into the centre. For an independent finish, descend rightwards to below *Hidden Chimney*.
3. 40m 4a Follow *Hidden Chimney* for 10m and take a roofed groove on the left (as for *Technicoloured Dream Crack* in winter). Move right below the roof before climbing up. Finish by a short steep buttress on good holds.

Yosemite Jill 50m HVS 5a *. Steve Hammond, John Lyall. 4 June 2008.
A blonde companion for *Yukon Jack*. It is artificial and makes no sense at all, but gives an enjoyable outing that leaves you strangely satisfied. Climbs the pillar between *The Despot* and *Yukon Jack*. Go straight over the initial bulge, then take the next overlap by a slanting crack, followed by steeper moves near the right edge to gain a short right-facing corner. A jam crack leads to a ledge where another crack would lead to easy ground, but this is avoided by traversing right to overlook *Yukon Jack*, where the wall is then climbed on huge holds to easy ground and the abseil point.

Yukon Jack 90m Severe. Andy Nisbet. 15 May 2008.
By the winter line to reach *The Haston Line* (Very Difficult), then scramble up, then left to finish up the winter finish to *Pot Doodles* (4a).

Black Sheep 100m VS. John Lyall, Andy Nisbet. 24 June 2009.
Start about 3m right of *Yukon Jack*.
1. 50m 4c Gain and climb a thin crack which slants left towards *Yukon Jack*. Go through a small overlap and follow a right-slanting corner and continuing fault to cross *The Haston Line* and belay above.
2. 50m Go easily up to and finish up the winter line *Frozen Assets* (Very Difficult).

Technicoloured Dream Crack   50m   Hard Severe 4c *. John Lyall, Steve Hammond. 4 June 2008.

Start about 6m right of *Yukon Jack* and climb up to a thin crack. Follow this through two short corners to cross *The Haston Line* and finish by a steep left-facing corner. Either finish by easy ground to the top or move left to an abseil point.

Winter: 100m VII,7. Ed Edwards, Andy Nisbet. 27 March 2009.

The summer line was followed to belay on *The Haston Line* (25m). This pitch was climbed on very thin ice but could be considerably easier (or harder). The continuation summer line up the left side of blocks led to slabby ground, followed to The Slant (45m). The upper buttress was climbed by going up *Hidden Chimney* for 10m, then taking a groove on its left wall and over a roof at its top (40m).

Potiphar's Wife   50m   VS 5a *. John Lyall, Hamish Burns. 30 July 2008.

Climbs the very thin crack-line just left of *Tasker* (see below). A delicate start is followed by easier climbing until the crack runs out below a nose of rock, where it would be easy to step into the other crack. Instead climb the right edge of the nose and pull left onto a slab and go up to a thin crack. Go direct over blocks on *The Haston Line* and straight up wall behind, crossing a small roof to easy ground.

Tasker   50m   Hard Severe 4b *. Andy Porter, Will Wilkinson. 9 May 2008.

A crack-line some 10m right of *Yukon Jack*; a steeping before breaking onto *The Haston Line* provides the crux. Cross *The Haston Line* via a small tower of blocks (possible belay) and continue up the slabs above to a belay on *The Slant* at a perfect granite bench. Bold on the lower slabs.

Winter: 110m V,6. Ed Edwards, Andy Hyslop, Andy Nisbet. 29 March 2009.

Could be much easier with ice. Follow the summer route in two pitches to *The Slant*. Continue by *Hidden Chimney*, then take the crack come groove on its left wall some 5m right (higher) of the finish to *Potiphar's Wife*. Go up this to where a ramp leads up the right side of the buttress overlooking *Hidden Chimney*.

Hidden Chimney   Difficult. Andy Porter, Will Wilkinson. 9 May 2008.

Messy low down but better in the chimney.

Aladdin's Buttress:

Note: The *True Finish* to *Original Summer Route* was climbed by Michael Barnard on 14 September 2008 at Very Difficult. The crux was the move above the doubtful flake, as in winter. The original summer ascent seems to have climbed grooves just to the right (harder and mossier), but it is likely the *True Finish* up the crest has been climbed before.

COIRE AN LOCHAIN, No. 3 Buttress:

Torque of the Devil 115m VS. John Lyall, Allen Fyffe. 5 July 2008.

Takes the line of the winter route and finishes up *The Crack*. A pleasant start and interesting finish. Start at the toe of No. 2 Buttress at a left-facing corner with a prominent crack in the right wall.

1. 45m 4c Climb the corner and cracks, then move right and follow the obvious

line up right to a ledge. Step right and go up the wall leftwards then up (the winter chimney-line is right of this. Climb the faults in the next wall on great holds.

2. 40m Go up short walls and ledges to below the final headwall.

3. 20m 4c Climb The Crack above with a hard move at the overhang and a big shaky flake higher up.

No. 4 Buttress:
Watergate Scandal   70m   E2 **. John Lyall, Hamish Burns. 23 July 2008.
Climbs the roofed edge right of *Deep Throat*.

1. 30m 5c Follow the edge to a big roof (Friend 0), move right past this and up to a ledge and dirty crack. Move back left to the edge and go up to a small ledge and belay on the right.

2. 20m 5a Climb the left side of the rib to the next roof and follow a crack to a ledge. Move left to regain the edge and follow this to the top of the pillar.

3. 20m An easy gully leads to the top.

STACAN DUBHA:
Havana   150m   III. Andy Nisbet, Jonathan Preston. 25 March 2009.
The rightmost main buttress is an elongated diamond shape and lies right of the large overhung recess. Start easily leftwards up a ramp under a steep base wall (20m). Return right up a turf groove, then zigzag and go further right under slabs (50m). Gain a bay and leave it on the right over a short wall. Go right up a fault to a wall, then back left to a bigger bay (40m). Continue up just right of a prominent rib, then cross over the rib to easy ground (40m). Moderate in summer (Andy Nisbet, September 2008).

SHELTERSTONE CRAG:
Pinpoint   75m   HVS. John Lyall, Jonathan Preston. 1 July 2009.
1. 40m 5a About 25m left of a wet mossy spring at the base of the lower slab, is a short right-facing corner leading onto a big block. Just right of this are two thin cracks running into a shallow corner. Follow this line past awkward overlaps to a ledge.

2. 35m 5a Thin moves up the slab just right of the corner are followed by easier climbing to the Low Ledge.

HELL'S LUM CRAG:
The Grim Whippet   120m   III. Graham Johnston, Kris Wipat. 14 February 2009.
Start some 20m left of *Sic*. Follow the prominent ice ramp up into a steep snow bay. Keeping to the right-hand side of this continue up snow and ice to finish immediately left of the prominent buttress on the skyline.
Note: The route has apparently been climbed before but this is the first recorded ascent.

STAG ROCKS:
Rag the Dog   120m   IV,6. James Edwards, Phil Ashby. 10 December 2008.
An icefall some 30m right of *Cascade Right*. The route can bank out under heavy snow. Intermediate belays can be taken and difficulties can be avoided in many cases on the right.

1. 60m Climb the steep cascade which eases off after 10m to a flat shelf. Climb the next 5m step on vertical ice to another flat shelf. On the left is a corner. Go up this for 8m.

2. 60m Go up a ramp on the left and climb a short steep wall to easier ground.

The Cardinal   120m   IV,4. Donnie Williamson, Hamish Burns, Mark Francis, Dave Bowden. 27 January 2009.

A groove on the right side of *Serrated Rib*. Start in *Diagonal Gully* opposite *Apex Gully*.

1. 40m Climb a turfy groove and go up a wall to a ledge on the left.

2. 30m   Climb directly up a steep wall and surmount a large block to easy ground.

3. 50m Follow an upper turfy ramp below the ridge crest to the top.

Big Alec   85m   IV,6. John Lyall, Pete Macpherson, Andy Nisbet. 20 January 2009.

Start by climbing a short but thin vertical icefall in a corner to the right of the summer line. Move left to join the summer line and follow it to the hidden chimney (20m). Climb this either by a through route or on the outside, then continue up the jam crack (15m). Join *Albino* and traverse right along a fault to easier ground and climb a rib between two grooves (the grooves may be the two options for *Albino*), 50m.

The Tenements, Gorbals Finish   100m   VS 5a. John Lyall, Andy Nisbet, Jonathan Preston. 1 June 2009.

A left-hand finish which maintains good climbing to the cliff-top. Climb the first and best two pitches of *The Tenements*.

3a. 35m 4b Climb up leftwards to below a groove which is immediately left of a sharp arete which forms the left side of the big open groove. Climb this groove to a terrace.

4a. 20m 5a Gain with difficulty and climb a left-slanting bottomless groove above.

5a. 45m 4c Go diagonally left across a long wall to finish by crossing a chimney and finishing up a short rib. This looks artificial but, once on the wall, the easiest line is the one taken.

LURCHER'S CRAG:

Overdraft   230m   V,5. Dave McGimpsey, Andy Nisbet. 25 November 2008.

A devious and quite serious route up some unfriendly ground. Start close to *Credibility Crunch* but take the lower traverse-line diagonally up left to reach a steep wall above. Traverse left along a ledge to its end. Climb the short steep wall (crux) and go up to a big spike (25m). Continue up, then left to a large pinnacle. Traverse its outer wall left to a ledge system (25m). Ignore a tempting line up right and continue traversing for about 12m to a corner. Go up this, make a short hand-traverse right over a slab and go up another groove. Make a more awkward move right over a rib and go up to a bigger groove (35m). Climb this over two steps until a ramp leads up left to easier ground. Go up to join the other routes on the crest (50m). Finish easily up the crest as for the other routes.

St. Bernard's Ridge   150m   IV,6. Kathy Grindrod, Andy Nisbet. 14 January 2009.
The ridge between *Reindeer Ridge* and *Summit Ridge*. The base is blocked by a steep diagonal wall so start just left of the gully between the two ridges. Climb a groove on the right edge of *Reindeer Ridge*, then cross the gully and go easily up to below a left-facing corner which is left of the crest of the main section of ridge (50m). Climb the fine corner, including a difficult overlap (50m). An easier rock section (50m) leads to open slopes and the summit.

Dog Day Afternoon   240m   III,4. John Lyall, Andy Nisbet, Jonathan Preston. 8 January 2009.
The ridge immediately left of the upper section of *Window Gully*. Start close to *Window Gully* and take a fault leading diagonally left. Before its top step, go right into a crevasse on a slab and go beyond this before returning steeply left to the crest. Follow the crest with slight deviations to a break in the ridge. An upper section starts 20m above, and is somewhat artificial. A smooth bulge at 20m was passed on the left and another bulge above also passed on the left. Otherwise the crest was roughly followed, with party members taking slightly different lines.

Sooty   200m   III. Andy Nisbet. 2 February 2009.
A subsidiary ridge left of *Sweep* is rather scrappy. Start 10m right of *Window Gully* (upper) and climb a crack in slabby ground, with some thin moves. Move easily right and follow its vague crest to easy ground. Move right to join *Sweep*. Finish up the left side of its upper tower.

Ten Pins   80m   III. Andy Nisbet. 13 January 2009.
The right of the two shorter ridges. A steep wall at the base was bypassed by going left up a short wall and ramp, then back right up two short shallow chimneys. The crest was followed to the top.

Punchdrunk Direct   120m   III,4. Sean Peatfield, Iain Munro. 23 January 2009.
Start below the obvious right-facing corner and climb a short wall to gain its base. Climb the corner stepping left at the top. Although slightly contrived by the presence of easy ground on the right the corner itself provided an interesting pitch if climbed direct. Finish up the crest as for *Punchdrunk*.

Wolfstone Gully   80m   VI,7. John Lyall, Andy Nisbet. 24 January 2009.
The steep gully at the back of the amphitheatre. Start well to the right and climb turfy ledges up left to the gully below its steepest section (25m). In ideal conditions it should be possible direct on ice but this ascent climbed a crack in a shallow corner on the right to belay under a big chockstone (15m). Climb past its left corner to reach an easier upper gully (10m). Finish up this (30m).

Black Shuck   120m   III. Andy Nisbet. 9 March 2009.
The gully between *Collie's Ridge* and *Hound of the Baskervilles*. The gully base is blocked by a steep wall. Start by climbing up left on turf to a ledge on the right. Step down right, pull up into a recess, then move right again to gain the line of the gully above the steep wall. Finish up the line of the gully.

Bonzo Dog   120m   II. Andy Nisbet. 9 March 2009.
The gully right of *Hound of the Baskervilles*. Start up an icy runnel leading to
snow, then another icy runnel leading to snow. Finish up icy steps. Climbed
when lean but icy.

Desperate Measures   260m   IV,4. Joe Ormond, Will Wilkinson, Andy Porter. 2
Jan 2009.
Takes the obvious depression at the back of a small bay right of *Deerhound
Ridge*. Climb a thin ice pitch for 25m to gain easy-angled ice for a further 75m.
From below a small island of rock, take the increasingly steep right fork (60m)
to a steep step into an obvious and well-defined amphitheatre (30m). Here the
back left corner provides an exit via an obvious and dubious-looking flake (crux,
10m, loose). Continue along easy ground to the plateau (60m).

Canis Minor   40m   IV,5. John Lyall, Andy Nisbet, Jonathan Preston. 8 January
2009.
A steep tower lies at the far south end of the cliff. This route takes a groove on
the left of the crest, with a steep finish.

Canis Major   45m   IV,7. Andy Nisbet, Jonathan Preston. 23 January 2009.
Climbs a groove in the crest of the steep tower. Start up a crack-line which leads
to bulging flakes and into the groove. Climb the groove, then a short chimney on
the right and back into the groove. From the top of the groove, move right and
up to a bay (35m). Finish up a narrow crest to easy ground (10m). There is an
optional tier high up.

SRON NA LÀIRIGE:
Chicane   90m   IV,5. John Lyall, Andy Nisbet. 6 January 2009.
Climbs the left edge of the buttress with *Ghrusome* (SMCJ 2008). Start up
Ghruve and move right to the leftmost of five grooves. Start below this. Climb
the groove, move right to the next groove and continue to below a prominent
arete (40m). This arete is the base of a pinnacle, so pass to its left and gain the
col between it and the buttress. Climb the wall above and into a right-facing
corner which leads to easy ground (50m).

Ghrupie   150m   V,5. John Lyall, Andy Nisbet. 6 December 2008.
Climbs a groove on the left side of the buttress with *Ghrusome*. Climb easily up
left of the lower crest of *Ghrusome* and start below the central of the five
grooves, the one with a dogleg right. These are below and left of the three
grooves mentioned in the description of *Ghrusome*. Climb the groove, which
leads directly to the most prominent groove in the upper buttress (50m). Start up
the upper groove (serious) for about 15m, then break right into ground with
more cracks and follow this up to join the crest of the tower (40m, a good pitch).
Gain the top of the tower and finish up the easy upper crest as for *Ghrusome*.

Count Dracula   150m   V,7. John Lyall, Andy Nisbet. 6 January 2009.
A steep right-curving groove between *Ghrupie* and *Ghrusome* is blocked by a
large block. Start as for *Ghrusome* and gain the rightmost of the five grooves.
Climb this to below the steep groove. Climb the steep groove via an awkward

narrow chimney formed by the block (25m). The groove ends at an overhanging wall, so traverse right to join *Ghrusome*. For a different finish, move left from this route to the crest (40m).

SGÒRAN DUBH MÒR, No.2 Buttress:
Fancy a Rib 150m II. Andy Nisbet. 4 January 2009.
This is the rib leading out of *2/3 Gully* below *Fan Rib*, so arguably is in Fan Corrie. Climb a snaking groove in the lower rib to reach a steep barrier wall. This is not as big as appears from below and is climbed at its right side. Finish up the crest.

SGÒRAN DUBH MÒR, Fan Corrie:
Note: Andy Nisbet climbed *Diamond Buttress* at Grade III on 5 January 2009 by going left up a ramp from the pointed block. At the top of the ramp, traverse left into a shallow gully topped by a chockstone. Crawl under this and gain its top to rejoin the normal route on the crest. The route was thought *** by either line.

SGÒRAN DUBH MÒR, No. 3 Buttress:
Tripoli 150m II. John Lyall, Andy Nisbet. 5 January 2009.
The first big feature left of *2/3 Gully* is a gully blocked by a two-tier chockstone. This route climbs a groove system to its right.

Tristar Groove 160m III. Andy Nisbet. 4 January 2009.
A deep groove in the rib left of the gully blocked by the two-tier chockstone. Start just left of the gully and climb heather slopes which curve left to reach the groove. Climb the groove, ice then turf, to reach its easier upper continuation. From the ridge crest at its finish, a descending traverse leads into *2/3 Gully* and access to routes in Fan Corrie.

Diagonal Rake 400m II. Andy Nisbet. 5 January 2009.
A good mountaineering route. A winter ascent of the diagonal rake may have been made before. It was certainly used to access *Cripple's Cleft* and this is the hardest section, requiring frozen turf. Continue to the top of the rake, then make a small descent into a gully. Follow this over two ice pitches before gaining the crest on the right. Follow this to the plateau, although it becomes scrambling long before this.

SGÒRAN GAOITH, No. 4 Buttress:
Enchanted Ridge 180m V,6. John Lyall, Andy Nisbet, Jonathan Preston. 3 December 2008.
The ridge on the right (facing down) of the descent described in SMCJ 2008. It faces SSE, so needs cold conditions for the turf to be frozen.
1. 30m Climb the lowest part of the ridge on the left of the crest until the ridge is gained just as it steepens.
2. 40m Follow the crest with a short section on the right at a steepening until a smooth rounded section is reached. Pass this awkwardly on the left to regain the ridge below a very steep section.

3. 20m   Descend right to gain a steep turfy corner which is climbed with difficulty to regain the crest.
4. 50m   Follow the crest to another steep section. Pass this by descending leftwards and returning up right on turf strips.
5. 40m   Follow the sharp crest to easy ground.

Note: The map ref for No. 4 Buttress should be NN 907 993 (not 003 as in the new guide).

EINICH CAIRN, Coire nan Clach:
Silver Streak   60m   II. Simon Richardson, Jacques LePesant. 28 February 2008.
The prominent low-angled ice sheet on the left side of the corrie.

Tin Pan Alley   60m   II. Jacques LePesant, Simon Richardson. 28 February 2008.
The icy depression 100m left of *Hey Teacher*.

Copper Barrelled   60m   II. Jacques LePesant, Simon Richardson. 28 February 2008.
Climb the icy buttress left of *Tin Pan Alley* via a broken crack in its centre.

Prospector's Rib   70m   III. Simon Richardson, Roger Webb. 4 October 2008.
There are three well-defined ribs on the right of the corrie containing *Schoolmaster's Gully*. This route takes the leftmost slender rib. Start at the toe of the rib and climb a right-facing corner to reach the narrow buttress crest. Follow this over a series of steps and blocks to easier ground and the plateau.

Alaska Highway   80m   III. Roger Webb, Simon Richardson. 1 February 2009.
The central of the three ribs. Climb a well-defined groove on the left side of the buttress which leads to the left edge. Follow this to the top.

Pure Gold   70m   V,5. Simon Richardson, Roger Webb. 1 February 2009.
The right-hand of the three ribs is an attractive feature comprised of good clean granite. Climb it directly, starting up a slanting crack in the centre of the buttress before moving let to the well-defined left edge.

Luxembourg Rib   80m   II. Simon Richardson, Jacques LePesant. 28 February 2008.
Approximately 100m right of the three ribs is a well-defined broken rib that descends lower into the corrie than the other routes. Climb the rib with a fine snow arete to finish.

BRAERIACH, Coire Bhrochain:
Bhrochain Spectre   160m   IV,3. Andy Nisbet. 13 March 2009.
A line up the open slab left of the corner of *Bhrochain Slabs*. Start at the foot of *North-West Corner*. Climb the first chimney of this to gain snow covered slabs. Head up slightly left to a big icefall in a depression where an upper slab drains on to the lower slab. Climb the icefall to the upper slab. Follow this diagonally left on snow to an arete below a prow at the top left corner of the slab. Pass the

prow on the right and return left to where there is sometimes a break in the cornice at a point where the prow forms a sharp bend in the cliff-top.

Note: The 1960 winter ascent of *Bhrochain Slabs* gave no description of the line, so it is assumed they climbed the summer route. This ascent was always left of it.

High Jinks 180m IV,4. John Lyall, Andy Nisbet. 24 March 2009.
A line based on the edge of the buttress overlooking West Gully. Climbed and graded for good conditions. Start at the foot of *North-West Corner* but climb straight up steep snow to below a very smooth and ice smeared slab (30m). Climb a steep step just to its left, then trend right to gain thicker snow-ice above the slab. Climb grooves to below a bulge (45m). Climb a groove just left of the bulge and continue slightly left to below a steep wall. Trending right would eventually join *Bhrochain Spectre*. For an independent finish up a rather unlikely line, make a traverse left over the top of a gully and across a slab to overlook *West Gully*. Descend a chimney for 6m to where a ledge on the right (facing down) can be gained (45m). The ledge leads into a big slab-ramp which is followed to the plateau (60m).

COIRE SPUTAN DEARG, Snake Ridge Area:
Homecoming Gully 120m II. John Lyall. 27 December 2008.
Go a short way up *Mousehole Gully*, then climb a groove on the right onto a ridge, and follow a wide gully up and left to finish.

Note: John Lyall climbed *Mousehole Gully* direct through the mousehole at Grade II/III on 27 December 2008.

Central Buttresses:
Hate Mail 125m VII,7. John Lyall, Andy Nisbet, Jonathan Preston. 11 December 2008.
A winter route based on *Blackmail* (SMCJ 2008). Pitch 3 is difficult to protect due to its Z-shape.
1. 25m Start up the ramp as for *Blackmail* but continue up to its end.
2. 30m Follow its continuation over a difficult bulge, then make an awkward step left to rejoin *Blackmail* and follow it to its belay.
3. 30m Make a rising traverse right up a shelf and make a step up over an overlap. Gain a ledge at 2m up on the left, then traverse back left to reach the bottom of the ramp on *Blackmail* (delicate). Climb the ramp and direct over the bulge at its top to its ledge.
4. 40m Climb the awkward wall to the arete of *Black Tower*. Follow this and snow slopes to the plateau.

Note: John Lyall climbed *Right-Hand Icefall* at IV,5 on 27 December 2008. This was by a prominent ice pillar. A line at Grade II could not be seen, although the ground just to the right is less steep.

Note: Michael Barnard & Peter Hemmings climbed the start of *Flying Saucers* as a good variation to *The Fly*. They then traversed along a ledge to the S-crack (VS 4c, 31 May 2009).

Terminal Buttress:
Terminal 5   75m   Hard Severe 4b. Paul & Rachel Mather. 24 July 2008.
Start slightly higher up the gully from *Terminal Buttress* beneath some small overhangs.
1. 35m Undercut steeply right to gain a hanging V-groove, then climb up out of its left-hand side via a series of flakes, passing a juggy bulge. This leads to a series of small corners; climb these to a comfortable ledge.
2. 40m   Climb the corner above to join the crest of the buttress, which is followed to the top (junction with Terminal Buttress).

BEINN A' BHUIRD, Coire an Dubh Lochain:
Smooth Buttress   110m   Severe. Simon Richardson, Dan Sutherland, Duncan Tunstall. 27 July 2008.
Climb the crest of the buttress up a vague groove as for the winter line. The upper section was climbed up cleaner rock on the right edge. A fine feature, but very vegetated and best climbed in winter.

Shipton   110m   Severe. Duncan Tunstall, Simon Richardson, Dan Sutherland. 27 July 2008.
The wall and rib left of *Central Rib*. Start just left of *Alpha Gully* and climb turfy cracks up the wall. Continue up the slabby rib to where it eases and finish easily up and left of the final headwall.

Coire nan Clach:
Jack Frost Direct   70m   III,4. Simon Richardson, Duncan Tunstall, 22 October 2008.
A more direct version of *Jack Frost* taking the crest of the buttress.
1. 35m Climb the initial ramp of *Jack Frost* for 10m until a steep break in the left wall leads to easier ground. Move up to the steep wall above and climb this left of centre utilising a large knobbly hold.
2. 35m Continue up the right-facing corner in the upper tower and finish along the final ridge as for *Jack Frost*.

Garbh Choire:
Consolation Gully, Right-Hand Finish   150m   II. Simon Richardson. 5 April 2009.
Consolation Gully splits after 100m. Climb the right branch to reach a broad rib and follow this to exit on to the plateau (no cornice at this point).

Slochd Wall, Direct Finish   60m   HVS. Duncan Tunstall, Simon Richardson. 1 June 2009.
A sustained alternative between the *Left-* and *Right-Hand Finishes*. Probably climbed before.
1. 30m From the stance at the top of the second (main) pitch climb the *Right-Hand Finish* for 15m to where it moves right onto the terrace of *Primate*. Step left and continue up a vertical crack to reach a small ledge.
2. 30m Continue up the wall on the right to join the final arete of *Chindit* and finish more easily up this to the top.

North-West Buttress Arete 65m HVS. Duncan Tunstall, Simon Richardson. 1 June 2009.
The right side of North-West Buttress is defined by two clean aretes separated by a groove.
1. 40m 5a Start below the left-hand arete and climb up 5m to the foot of a short slanting off-width crack. Avoid this by climbing steeply up and right to below a steep triangular wall, then move back down and left (crux) to reach the top of the crack. Continue more easily up the continuation crack, and trend right up easy cracks and slabs to a ledge below the clean-cut upper arete.
2. 5m 4c Climb the arete to the plateau.

Stob an t-Sluichd:
Flight Eight Five November 65m HVS. Simon Richardson, Duncan Tunstall. 1 June 2009.
About 100m left of *Pinnacle Ridge* is an attractive steep buttress under the plateau rim. It receives the sun for most of the day, so is a good option when waiting for the shady West Wall of Mitre Ridge to warm up.
1. 50m Climb a short slab to below a vertical rectangular wall in the centre of the buttress. Surmount the wall via a diagonal break on its right side, then move up and left to a rounded arete that leads up to easy ground.
2. 15m Finish easily up the final ridge to the plateau.

LOCHNAGAR, Southern Sector, The Sentinel:
Paladin 60m Severe. Simon Richardson, Chris Hill. 3 August 2008.
Start 10m left of *Jacob's Slabs* and climb directly up to a steep smooth slabby wall. Climb this on small holds and continue up steep blocky ground to an easy finish.

Sentinel Edge 50m Severe. Simon Richardson, Chris Hill. 3 August 2008.
An excellent little climb taking the hanging right edge of *The Sentinel*. Dries fast after rain. Start as for *Starlight and Storm* and climb through a steep bulge using a good crack. Belay on a good ledge below the upper arete. Climb this on good holds on its right side to a straightforward finish.

Sunset Buttress:
Sunset Buttress Direct 100m VS. Simon Richardson, Chris Hill. 3 August 2008.
Start 10m right of the winter line of *Sunset Buttress* below a smooth slabby wall.
1. 20m 4b Climb the wall on good flat holds to a ledge.
2. 25m 4c Start up the prominent right-facing groove above and step left after 5m into a subsidiary hanging right-facing groove. Climb this and exit left at its top on good holds. Climb the rib above to join the original route at a ledge. Continue up this to the top (55m).

Perseverance Wall:
Forgotten Runnel 80m II. Simon Richardson. 28 November 2008.
The left flank of *Perseverance Rib* is cut by a narrow line of turf. Climb this past a steepening to the easier upper gully.

Never Say Die   80m   III,4. Simon Richardson. 28 November 2008.
Climb the line of grooves up the crest of *Perseverance Rib* to join the final
section of *The Vice* above its chockstone.

The Handrail   80m   III. Simon Richardson. 30 December 2008.
A line up the right flank of *Perseverance Rib* on the left wall of *Remembrance
Gully*. Start on the right side of platform of *Tenacity* and climb a flake and
handrail system on the right flank of the buttress. Continue up to the break that
leads left to the big platform on *Perseverance Rib*. Step right and continue up
the headwall above and left of the finishing grooves to *Remembrance Gully*.

Remembrance Gully   80m   I. Simon Richardson. 30 December 2008.
The prominent snow shoot to the right of *Perseverance Rib*. The easiest line
takes the right-hand groove in the upper section and trends right at the top.
Almost certainly climbed before, but not recorded.
Variation: Groove Finish   50m   II. Simon Richardson. 9 November 2008.
Follow the left-hand groove in the upper section. It is steeper than the easier
right-hand groove, but is furnished with good rock holds and is easier in lean
conditions.

Hanging Groove   80m   III. Simon Richardson. 28 November 2008.
Climb the groove between *Starburst* and *Gale Force Groove* passing a small
rockfall scar (at similar height to square-cut roof on *Gale Force Groove*).

Resolution Gully   80m   II. Simon Richardson. 28 November 2008.
The prominent left-trending gully between *Jason's Groove* and *Lunar Eclipse*.
In early season there is a steep step at one-third height but this banks out with
more snow.

Delilah   80m   III. Simon Richardson. 30 December 2008.
The left side of the buttress taken by *Cumberland* and *Temptress*. Start 5m right
of *The Gift* below twin grooves. Climb the right-hand groove and continue up
the groove-line above past a small snowfield to a junction with *The Gift*. Cross
this and continue up the V-shaped headwall above.

Shadow Buttress A:
The Hooded Groove   60m   VII,8. Simon Richardson, Iain Small. 8 March 2009.
A difficult direct start to *Shadow Buttress A Direct*. Start as for the *Direct* by
climbing the initial gully of *Shadow Buttress A* and belaying in the cave.
1. 30m Move up and right steeply through the roof of the cave to gain a vertical
corner. Climb this and then move up right across awkward mixed ground to
reach the right side of the sloping edge below a steep stepped 'hooded' groove.
2. 30m Climb the groove past two overlaps, exit left at the top and move up to
the terrace and junction with *Shadow Buttress A Direct*. Continue up the *Shadow
Buttress A Direct* to the top. (On this occasion, *The Time Out Finish* was taken as
time was running short).

The Stack:
The following two short routes provide superb sustained climbing on

immaculate rock in a great position. High on the left side of The Stack, overlooking *The Black Spout, Left Branch*, is a grossly overhanging undercut wall. *Ultramontane* takes the left arete, then goes right into the obvious groove. *Heliopolus* takes the obvious groove and wall left again. The routes were gained via a single 60m abseil from an obvious block anchor immediately above the routes.

Ultramontane 50m E4 **. Adrian Crofton, Guy Robertson. June 2009.
Start at the base of the arete. Move up to below a crack then swing right to gain and stand on the obvious flat hold with some difficulty. Climb the cracks above to the overhang then pull back left round the edge to a rest. Climb the wall above, then mantel onto a sloping ledge. Balance right along this and climb the fine groove then slabs to belay well back (35m, 6a). Go left and climb the obvious groove to the top (15m, 4c).

Heliopolis 50m E3 **. Adrian Crofton, Guy Robertson. June 2009.
Start just left of *Ultramontane*. Climb the groove to an overlap then pull right and follow the right side of the big flake to its top. Swing up left to a footledge then gain and follow the superb quartz dyke in the wall above until precarious moves lead right to a groove and easier ground (35m, 5c). Go left and finish up the groove, as for *Ultramontane* (15m, 4c).

Hittin' the Wall 25m E2 5c *. Michael Barnard, James Duthie. 31 July 2009.
The obvious thin hanging crack on the left wall overlooking the top of the main branch of *The Black Spout*, gained by a quick scramble down the gully from the plateau. Start directly below the crack. Climb easily up a blocky wall on the left, before moving right to ascend a crack and corner to below a large overlap. Step out onto the slab on the right, move up using the edge (crux) and follow the thin crack to the top.

THE STUIC:
A Wall Too Far 70m VII,8. Iain Small, Simon Richardson. 1 November 2008.
The vertical wall bounding the left edge of *The Stooee Chimney*.
1. 10m Climb the initial groove of *The Stooee Chimney* to a good platform.
2. 20m Start 2m left of the right edge of the wall, climb straight up to a turf boss (bold), move left through the overlap and continue up the cracks above to a second overlap. Pull over this to a small niche. A steep and sustained pitch.
3. 15m Move right from the niche and climb discontinuous cracks up the wall above until it is possible to move left using turf to exit directly above the niche.
4. 25m Continue up the crest of the buttress above.

Bilberry Edge 70m II. Simon Richardson. 22 February 2009.
The broad buttress on the left side of the North-East Face of The Stuic to the left of the fault taken by *Bathtime Buttress*. Start below the left edge and take a zigzag line up short walls to finish up the easier angled upper buttress. Moderate in summer (S.M. Richardson, 29 September 2008).

Water Whirl 70m III. Simon Richardson. 22 February 2009.
Between *Bathtime Buttress* and *Plug Groove* is a steep wall cut by two left-

slanting grooves. Climb the left-hand groove (defined by a rock pillar on its left side) to easier ground and the top.

Coriolis Effect 70m III,4. Simon Richardson. 22 February 2009.
The right-hand of the twin grooves is steep in its lower section, but has good ledges between the moves. Easy ground then leads to the top.

Coire Lochan na Feadaige:
Dotterel 110m II. Simon Richardson. 22 February 2009.
A right to left diagonal line. Start near the right end of the buttress and climb mixed ground up to the central snow field. Move up this and trend diagonally left to gain the left side of the upper headwall. Move left around this and climb a broken gully cutting through its left side to the top.

Cnapan Nathraichean:
Left Flank 100m III. Simon Richardson, Duncan Tunstall. 6 February 2009.
Start 40m left of *The Sentry Box* below the next break in the smooth lower wall. Climb a shallow, right-facing slot, move right into a vague corner and follow this to the top.

GLEN CALLATER, Creag an Fhleisdeir:
Farewell to Tajikistan 160m IV,5. Rick Allen, Simon Richardson. 10 February 2009.
A varied mixed route running the full height of the cliff.
1. 60m Start 5m left of *Central Slabs Cleft* and climb the shallow S-shaped gully over several moderate ice steps, to a steepening below an icy wall.
2. 40m Move up to the wall, pull through an overhanging step and pass behind a block. Climb the short icefall behind the block to reach the midway terrace above. (*Central Slabs Cleft* and *Bonspiel* finish here.) Move up to the foot of the rock crest forming the right side of the upper tier.
3. 30m Start to the right of the crest, and climb the first tier via two consecutive corners.
4. 30m Move up the broad crest above and climb the headwall trending diagonally left to where the angle eases.

GLEN CLOVA, Winter Corrie:
Wild Cat Wall, The Tiger Finish VI,7 *. Brian Duthie, Sandy Simpson. 8 February 2009.
1. and 2. 100m Climb the first two pitches of *Wild Cat Wall* but belay on the far right end of the inverted triangle.
3. 50m Move up steeply at first trending leftward and belay at the left end of the final vertical wall.
4. 30m Step left and head up to a short vertical corner. Climb the corner then move up rightwards until beneath a large sloping roof. Move steeply up leftwards to a good ledge-cum-semi-cave under a steep right-slanting groove.
5. 25m Strenuously surmount the groove above (crux) and climb this to finish on the left end of the horizontal ledge. A serious pitch.
6. 25m Finish as per the original route.

Dun Mingulay (Central Section), Mingulay, Hebrides.
Topo: Steve Crowe.

Central Section

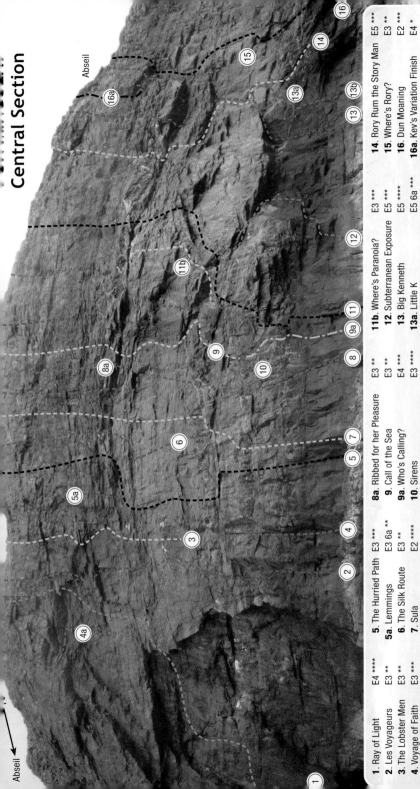

Abseil

1. Ray of Light E4 ****
2. Les Voyageurs E3 **
3. The Lobster Men E3 **
4. Voyage of Faith E3 ***
4a. Ocean of Air Finish E4 ****

5. The Hurried Path E3 ***
5a. Lemmings E3 6a **
6. The Silk Route E3 **
7. Sula E2 ****
8. The Silkie E3 ***

8a. Ribbed for her Pleasure E3 **
9. Call of the Sea E3 **
9a. Who's Calling? E4 ***
10. Sirens E3 ****
11. Perfectly Normal Paranoia E6 ***

11b. Where's Paranoia? E3 ***
12. Subterranean Exposure E5 ***
13. Big Kenneth E5 ****
13a. Little K E5 6a ***
13b. Wee Craig E5 6a

14. Rory Rum the Story Man E5 ***
15. Where's Rory? E3 **
16. Dun Moaning E2 ***
16a. Kev's Variation Finish E4 *

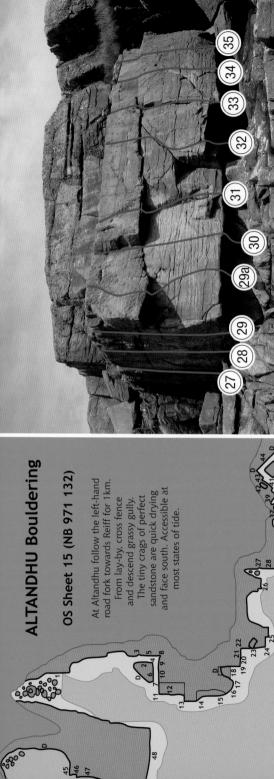

ALTANDHU Bouldering

OS Sheet 15 (NB 971 132)

At Altandhu follow the left-hand road fork towards Reiff for 1km. From lay-by, cross fence and descend grassy gully. The tiny crags of perfect sandstone are quick drying and face south. Accessible at most states of tide.

Sketch map not to scale.

1. 3a isolated wall
2. 3b east wall of Pinnacle
3. 3b broken corner
4. 5a direct up arete*
5. HVS 5b 6m black wall with two breaks*
6. 4a south wall of Pinnacle*
7. 3c flakes to left of 6
8. 4b inset corner*
9. 5b shallow pod
10. 6a/b smooth wall not using right edge*
11. 5c edge using outer crack, bold at top

14. 5a left end of ledge, good mantle*
15. 4c right end of ledge
16. 4b prow from the left*
17. 5b prow direct
18. 4a cracks and flakes
19. 5c undercut arete from right, bad landing, bold at bottom*
19a. 6a wall between 19 & 20*
20. 5c layaway flakes direct*
21. 5b shallow corner
22. 4b inset corner

25. 3a little corner
26. 5c small wall
27. 3b black cracks, often wet
28. 4c broken cracks
29. 4c cracks near prow*
29a. 5c right side of hanging prow, bold*
30. 5a first hanging corner*
31. 4c second shallow corner to right*
32. 4b slanting crack and wall*
33. 3b crack and descent
34. 4b wall to right of crack

36a. 5c overhanging north side of boulder
37. 4a wet black wall
38. 4b arete direct
39. 4c inset wall to right
40. 3c undercut flake then step left
41. 4c slanting crack, often wet*
42. 4c crack to and over boulder*
43. 4c flake crack not using block at back
44. 3a slab wall
45. 4a black wall
46. 3a shallow corner

Corrie Fee:
Note: Dave Adam notes that *The Comb* was climbed by John Thomson & I. Robb in 1975, predating the 1986 ascent by A. Thomson and S. Cameron in 1986 (SMCJ 2008).

The Pyramid Continuation 120m Severe. Gwilym Lynn, Rachel Gill. 21 February 2009.
A continuation of *The Pyramid*, following the obvious line upwards. Climb a short chimney to a heathery ledge. Follow the line up the next buttress to below the final steepening. Climb up the arete and cracks to the right to reach the top of the buttress.

GLEN ESK, Bruntwood Craig:
Rock and Two Veg 200m HVS. Duncan Tunstall, Andy Nisbet. 10 June 2008.
An old-fashioned route on the steep cliff which holds *Eagles Fall* on its left side. Start below a quartz dyke which lead up towards a large triangular roof high up (biggest roof on the cliff).
1. 25m Climb just right of the dyke line, then go diagonally left well beyond it to a grassy area below a gully.
2. 45m Go right to near the dyke line, then back left, mostly on rock. Go up a vague gully, then make a long traverse right in jungle, until a tricky move up gains a fine perch on a block.
3. 30m Move up right, then traverse back left into a gully (above the dyke line) and climb to a large vegetated area below the triangular roof. Move left to belay.
4. 45m 4c Gain and climb a hanging slab which leads above the roof to a platform. A spectacular pitch on good rock.
5. 45m 4c An awkward short wall gains a ramp of steep heather which leads to a final wall.
6. 10m Finish up left.

GLEN ESK, Craig Maskeldie:
Bouncing Balls 230m V,5. Simon Richardson, Duncan Tunstall. 15 February 2009.
The leftmost gully-depression on the cliff north of Carlochy (approx. NO 394 793). Avoid the first short steep icefall on the left and then continue by the easiest line up the second icefall (70m). Continue for 50m up easy snow to reach the headwall where it is cut by a steep gully. Climb the gully for 20m, continue up a steep corner and exit right on to easy ground (35m). Continue more easily to the top (75m).

Craig Maskeldie, North Face (NO 388 798):
Unich Gully 200m 1. Dave Adam 24 January 2009.
An obvious wide gully, situated to the left of the main buttress that extends towards the Falls of Unich.

Dochty Gully 200m II. Dave Adam. 10 February 2009.
A narrow gully to the left of the pyramid shaped buttress bordering *Unich Gully*. Contains two small ice pitches.

Bouldering at Altandhu near Reiff.
Topo and photo: John Mackenzie.

GLEN ESK, Couternach (NO 413 837):

This sunny south-east facing crag can be seen from Queen's Well in Glen Mark. It cuts across the hillside of the south-east spur of Knowe of Crippley just left of the track leading up to Mount Keen. The climbing is on good blocky schist in an idyllic situation. The routes were climbed on sight, so a little vegetation remains.

Boom and Bust   30m   HVS 5b. Simon Richardson, Duncan Tunstall. 15 June 2008.
The leftmost buttress is split into three tiers, and best climbed in three short pitches. Climb the initial wall (4b), and then surmount the prominent roof via a crack (5b). Finish up the left edge of the headwall via a hanging scoop. (5a).

Spiky Arete   30m   Very Difficult. Duncan Tunstall, Simon Richardson. 15 June 2008.
The prominent arete of stacked blocks, situated left of centre, provides a good fun climb.

Black Monday   40m   Very Difficult. Duncan Tunstall, Simon Richardson. 21 September 2008.
The next feature right is a smooth slab split by a terrace at one-quarter height. Climb an awkward crack on the left side of the lower wall and continue up the left arete in a fine position to the top.

Singing in the Rain   30m   VS 4b. Simon Richardson, Duncan Tunstall. 15 June 2008.
The central buttress is the most prominent feature on the cliff. Start on the left side of a prow on the front face of the buttress just right of a vegetated corner. Climb a blunt rib to a ledge, and continue up the wide crack above to the capping roof. Traverse left along a ramp and finish up a short diagonal crack.

Speculation   30m   HVS 5a. Duncan Tunstall, Simon Richardson. 21 September 2008.
A prominent crack-line splits the right side of Central Buttress. Start by climbing twin cracks (awkward – rest taken) to gain an easy ramp. Step right into the main crack-line and climb this over a bulge and finish up the steep continuation crack and off-width.

Tulips from Amsterdam   35m   VS 4c. Simon Richardson, Duncan Tunstall. 21 September 2008.
The corner right of Central Buttress is a prominent feature, but very vegetated at its base. Start 10m right of the corner below a series of cracked blocks in the steep wall. Climb through the blocks, climb a short left-facing corner to a large vegetated ledge. Continue up the right side of the slab above and finish up an easy flake-crack.

New Deal   35m   VS 4c. Simon Richardson, Duncan Tunstall. 21 September 2008.
The wall right of *Tulips from Amsterdam* is defined by a striking arete in its upper half. This route climbs the corner to the right of the arete. Start 5m right of *Tulips from Amsterdam* and climb a left-facing fault bounding the left edge of

the imposing lower wall. Move right at its top on good holds to gain the corner, which leads steeply to the top.

Market Crash 20m Very Difficult. Duncan Tunstall, Simon Richardson. 21 September 2008.
The furthest right buttress on the cliff (overlooking the Mount Keen path). Climb a short slab and pull over the overlap above to reach easy ground. A fun-looking line, but spoilt by easy ground to the left.

NORTH EAST OUTCROPS

SOUTH COVE, The Priest:
The Worm 15m E5 6a *. Tim Rankin, Piotr Wisthal. June 2008.
The thin crack up the wall on the left side of the *The Spinechiller* arete gives a serious pitch. Belay at the base of *The Mitre* and hand-traverse the shelf of *Invertebrates Wall* right. Pull over the roof and up to a hand ledge below the crack and dubious protection (RPs in opposition and skyhook in a quartz pocket above). Now either climb the wall on tiny crimps or palm up the arete to a break and the first real protection. Continue more easily up the left side of the arete to a left-slanting groove and finish up this. Inspected on abseil.

The In-betweeners 15m E1 5a. Tim Rankin, Piotr Wisthal (on-sight). June 2008.
A worthwhile route up the left wall of *The Mitre* belay below the line. Climb a left-slanting crack through a niche and continue boldly to below the upper arete. Climb this direct or on the left to a ledge, finish up the short crack above.

SOUTH COVE, The Kettle Walls:
Fearless 25m E5 6a *. Poitr Wisthal, Tim Rankin. May 2008.
On the left side of *The Spigolo* is an obvious crack up the south-facing black overhanging wall. This impressive and often-spied line climbs a thin crack to finish up the well-defined left-hand upper crack. Approach the base of the route by abseil from stakes either right of the line and take a poor hanging belay at a flake or better abseil left of the line to a sloping platform and belay from the rope. The route is on generally excellent quartzite but let down by a friable section at the start and middle but will be worth 2 stars when properly clean. Previously top-roped.

SOUTH COVE, Red Hole South (Optimist's Walls):
Weak Ender 15m VS. Martin Holland, Pamela Millar. 2 July 2009.
A hanging V-groove left of *Day Tripper*. The climbing and pro were good up to the final grassy V-groove, which was fairly unpleasant.

BERRYMUIR HEAD:
The Vanishing Pool 25m E7/8 6c *. Tim Rankin, Dan Richardson. 16 April 2008.
A fine but unbalanced pitch featuring an unprotected short intense crux up the

wall left of *Recess Route*. Boldly climb the overhanging wall on tiny holds to
where it joins the arete. Now traverse left and rock up on to the slab and the first
protection (2 micro-cams in a tiny break down left). Step back right and climb
the fine slab to twin faults. Move left to a large niche and junction with *Toxic
Terrestrials*. Continue up this to the top. Head pointed but graded for an on-sight
ascent assuming the rock pool hasn't dried out or been emptied!

BERRYMUIR HEAD, Gully Wall:
The Septic Spaceman   20m   E3 5c **. Russell Birkett. Dan Richardson. 8 May
2008.
A direct line crossing *The Flatulent Alien*, giving a good sustained pitch. Climb
The Flatulent Alien to below the steep bulge where that route moves right. Pull
through the bulge following the faint curving crack to gain the twin breaks
above. Continue direct up the bold yellow wall and shallow corner above, with a
short wall to finish.

CRAIG STIRLING, West Buttress:
Escape the Grind   25m   E3 6a. Tim Rankin, Gordon Lennox. June 2008.
A worthwhile route if only to avoid the start of *Green Vomit*! Start from the tidal
ledge right of *Bone Machine*. Climb a thin crack up the right side of the black
wall to a slab. Step left, then climb the crack through the roof until forced to rock
right on to the slab by the second roof. Trend right across the slab in to *Green
Vomit* and finish up this (reasonable but HVS 4c). Inspected on abseil.

The following two routes are approached by abseil direct over the edge from the
two stakes. The rope should be left in place to aid topping out and will run to the
right of the lines.

Prayers for Rain   20m   E2 5c*. Tim Rankin, Mark Scott (on-sight). July 2008.
A fine pitch up the diagonal crack in the wall right of *Green Vomit*. Start 3m
right of *Green Vomit*. Climb to a ledge and follow the crack until just below and
right of a hanging corner. Step left and climb the corner on to a slab. The
slanting corner above is loose so instead swing right around the arete and climb
the cleaned slab up right to its highest point and the abseil rope. Belay or pull up
the last 5m of near vertical grass using the rope to the top.

Disintegration   20m   E5 6b *. Tim Rankin, Dave Cowan. July 2008.
The wall and thin crack right again before the obvious crack of *The North Wind
Blows*. Trend right up excellent black rock to a ledge below the thin crack
(micro-wire on the right in a pocket); make a bold step up to jugs and arrange
protection. Stand on the jugs and rock up to a quartz hold above the break
(crux); span left to an obvious block and protection. Follow the crack right over
the bulge to good holds, step back left and climb to a break. Pull right, then left
over a bulge and continue direct up the fine overlapping slab to the abseil rope
and belay or pull up the last 5m of near vertical grass using the rope to the top.
Cleaned and inspected on abseil.

Rotter's Rock:
Powerpole   10m   E4 6a *. Tim Rankin, Piotr Wisthal. August 2008.

A good steep route up the overhanging wall left of *Powerfinger*. Start 2m down left from *Powerfinger* and climb a slanting crack to a break. Continue up pockets to the next break and use a pocket up right below the curving overlap to gain the next break (crux). Finish straight up. A good sustained route well cleaned from the first ascent. High in the grade. Previously top-roped.

NEWTONHILL, Harbour Wall:
Back in the Saddle   15m   E5 6a ***. Tim Rankin, Piotr Wisthal. June 2008
A stunning route climbing the grossly overhanging black groove and roof right of *Desederio*. Climb the groove to the obvious split block and good resting saddle on the edge. Move up left to below the roof and use a side pull to gain the lip and Friend placement. Power over the roof and climb the wall and blunt arete above to finish. Very well protected yet committing! Top wall inspected on abseil.

War of the Winds   15m   E6 6b **. Tim Rankin (unsec, head pointed). July 2008.
Left of *Ripper Roo* is a fine wall leading to a layback flake through the very lip of the cave. Start below a small niche at 2m; climb through the niche to a break. Move left and up to an obvious pinch and slot; gain a good hold up and left almost on the edge of the wall (crucial 000 cam in break on right). Pull back right, then up to jugs and a perfect no-hands rest in the slot on the left. Step back right and power over the bulge and up the layback crack through the lip (crux). Swing right to jugs and triumphantly pull over the final bulge and belay on the ledge (large cam). Traverse grass ledges off right with care. A superb and well-protected route, outrageously steep on excellent rock.

DYKES CLIFF:
Sills Route   15m   Hard Severe 4b. Gwilym Lynn. 27 August 2008.
Continue to traverse north from the main part of Dykes Cliff following the easiest line above the high tide mark until it is possible to scramble up to the cliff-top, near where a concrete wall protrudes.

COLLIESTON, The Graip:
Dinnae Faa   E3 5b *. Tristram Fox, Michael McGhie. 17 May 2009.
Surprisingly independent climbing up the thin cracks in the blank-looking slab, to the left of *Elbow Groove*, and the right of *The Keyway*. Finish direct from the small ledge. Quite bold.

Note: George Allan notes that *The Vineyard* (SMCJ 2004) shares the same top section on the arete with *Never Mix Graip and Grain* (SMCJ 2007).

MEIKLE PARTANS:
Sonar   10m   E7 6c **. Tim Rankin (head pointed). 9 April 2008.
The logical direct finish to *Blind Optimism* continuing up the grossly overhanging arete and upper crack. Climb *Blind Optimism* to the good hold and a fight to place a crucial small cam (first crux!). Gain a good flat hold on the right arete then use the crack to make desperate moves up the left side of the arete to better holds. Swing left and pull over using the crack; continue triumphantly up the easier crack and arete to finish.

THE RED WALL:

Rifle   25m   E3 6a. Tim Rankin, Piotr Wisthal. 6 May 2008.
A worthwhile eliminate up the fine wall between *The Arrow* and *Tomahawk*.
Pull over the overhang just right of *The Arrow* at good flakes to gain a good rest
at an obvious thin flake (good small nuts). Now either climb straight up with
great difficulty to gain a break (6b very eliminate) or use an obvious slot up right
on the edge of the *Tomahawk* crack to move back up left to the break. Step left
and climb straight up to the edge of the wall. Continue up the edge and easy
ground above to the top.
Note: A doubled 50m rope only just reached the top on both this and *Tomahawk*;
therefore both *Tomahawk* and *The Bow* are 25m long.

THE SEA-QUARRIES:

To the south of the stone ruin above South Buttress is a small hanging grass
bowl easily seen from the top of the Red Tower to the right and above
Bananaman. Below this bowl is a fine slab of excellent rock seemed with
cracks. A good choice when the wind is from the south and west when it
provides an excellent and easily accessible sun trap. Descend into the bowl
from either the south or the north down steep grass and rock steps. At the back
south corner is a short steep slab, just left of this is a good thread belay. A 20m
abseil from here leads to good belays at the base of the slab.

Piotr's Groove   18m   Hard Severe *. Piotr Wisthal, Tim Rankin. 24 January
2008.
The most obvious feature is a shallow but well-defined left-facing corner at the
right end of the slab. Start from the gap and climb a shallow groove to enter the
corner from the left. Follow the pleasant corner then easier ground up left to the
abseil point.

Pole Full of Passion   18m   E2 5c *. Tim Rankin, Piotr Wisthal. 24 January
2008.
An innocuous-looking route, climb the shallow groove as *Piotr's Groove* but
continue to the small roof. Use flakes on the left to move up then make a
difficult rock up right to gain the crack again, climb this to a ledge and finish
straight up.

North East Pole   20m   VS 4c *. Tim Rankin, Poitr Wisthal. 24 January 2008.
The next crack left again started from a ledge at the base of the gap. Climb the
crack easily at first until a difficult layback up flakes leads to a ledge. Climb the
slab groove above which leads to the abseil point.

LOGIE HEAD:

Note: The cracks forming the finish of *The Central Belt* are HVS 5b climbed
from the bottom. There is another crack-line to its right which is also HVS 5b.
Though looking trivial, the climbing is surprisingly intricate.

REDHYTHE POINT, West Wall:

What Swimming Pool!   12m   E1 5b *. John Lyall. 1 July 2008.

Climb a thin overhanging crack and pillar between *Slingsby's Last Stand* and *Stiral Sparecase*.

Overhanging Wall:
The best starting point for the next three routes is from a non-tidal small ledge and good belays at the base of the Y-groove of *Rachel's Rescue*.

Sir Galahad 10m Very Difficult *. Pete Hill, Ian Broadley. 29 July 2009.
Step up from the ledge and when possible move onto the black slab to the left of Rachel's Rescue. Follow this keeping left, exiting via a small broken slot at the top.

Sir Launcelot 8m Difficult. Pete Hill, Ian Broadley. 29 July 2009.
Climb directly upwards, taking the right branch of the Y.

Castle Anthrax 10m Severe **. Pete Hill, Ian Broadley. 29 July 2009.
Step right from the belay ledge and follow the obvious hand-traverse rising rightwards.

Python Wall:
This is an area of short routes, excellent for beginners and those learning to lead. Towards the end of the promontory, approximately 25m beyond the top of *Sir Launcelot*, a large slab drops down to the right (east) which allows either an easy scramble or a short abseil to a ledge that is only affected at very high tides. Climbs are described from right to left.

Midget 8m Very Difficult *. Pete Hill, Ian Broadley. 29 July 2009.
From the base of the descent, follow the slab staying just right of Piglet.

Piglet 8m Very Difficult *. Pete Hill, Ian Broadley. 29 July 2009.
Two metres left of the descent, a blocky crack leads to a small niche and a right-trending crack. Climb up to the niche and then the crack on the right, following its continuation to the top.

Winston 8m Difficult. Pete Hill, Ian Broadley. 29 July 2009.
Starting at the same point, take the left-trending fault-line.

Dingo 8m Very Difficult. Pete Hill, Ian Broadley. 29 July 2009.
Two metres left of the previous route, take the left-trending fault-line that is only obvious in its upper section.

Zoot 10m Moderate. Pete Hill, Ian Broadley. 29 July 2009.
At the left end of the ledge, take the obvious slanting fault-line.

Note: The routes *Wobble* and *Cardinal Biggles* (SMCJ 2008) had been previously climbed by Pete Hill & Paula Griffin on 30 September 2005, named *Dennis's Mother* and *Lovely Filth*.

Camelot Slabs (NJ 576 669):
This slab offers a number of routes in the lower grades. The climbing is far

better than it looks, the rock solid and the protection generally very good. Care should be taken of a few small fragile flakes in the upper reaches. The rock architecture around is impressive and it is an excellent place for swimming in calm seas.

Approach: The slabs are reached by taking the normal approach to Redhythe Pont until just before the ruin. Take a sharp right and follow a rib of grass downwards, just east of a hummock, to the top of the slab which is seen from some way off. Descent to the ledge, which is only covered at high tide, is either by an easy abseil on the left (looking out), or by down-climbing the obvious wide chimney.

The first two routes take a little while to dry out.

King Arthur   18m   Severe 4b. Pete Hill, Ian Broadley. 31 July 2009.
Around the corner on the left of the slab, this is the far left line. Start above a small boulder beach at an alcove and go straight up, trending left towards the top to avoid the grass. Take care with the rock in the upper reaches.

The Black Knight   18m   VS. Pete Hill, Ian Broadley. 31 July 2009.
A metre to the left around the corner of the main slab is an obvious rising crack. Follow this, starting at some white boulders, to a ledge, then more easily over the bulging slab above.

The next five routes are on the main face of the slab.

Sir Robin   23m   Severe 4a *. Pete Hill, Ian Broadley. 31 July 2009.
At the left edge of the slab, take the crack to the ledge and then continue straight up to the top.

Roger the Shrubber   20m   Mild Severe. Pete Hill, Ian Broadley. 31 July 2009.
Near the centre of the slab at head-height is a quartz pocket. Start just left of this up a leftwards slanting crack, then head straight to the top.

Bridgekeeper   20m   Very Difficult. Pete Hill, Ian Broadley. 31 July 2009.
Start at the quartz pocket and head directly upwards.

Brother Maynard   20m   Difficult *. Pete Hill, Ian Broadley. 31 July 2009.
Two metres right of the quartz pocket is a shattered crack-line, which is followed direct, keeping left towards the top to avoid a grass-filled gully. Much better than it looks.

Prince Herbert   15m   Moderate. Pete Hill, Ian Broadley. 31 July 2009.
Two metres right again is a blocky crack, which is followed to a grassy ledge.

Right of *Prince Herbert* is an obvious chimney. Right again is the north-facing wall of an easy-angled slab. The next climb starts at a small ledge only accessible at low tide.

Tim the Enchanter   10m   VS 4c *. Pete Hill, Ian Broadley. 31 July 2009.
From the ledge, step onto the wall and follow the centre of it in a rising traverse leftwards, topping out at the extreme left end.

ROSEHEARTY:

Stone Country   15m   E6 **. Guy Robertson, Trevor Wood (both led). May 2009.

An exciting and sustained route starting up the crack just left of *Heart of Stone* before crimping left to the big flake then continuing direct. Climb the thin crack immediately left of *Heart of Stone* to place a high runner where obvious edges lead left. Follow these out to the flake (Friends) where more hard moves gain an obvious line of pockets and, hopefully, the top.

Note: Heavily cleaned on a top-rope prior to the first ascent, the section by the flake is now solid. The remainder of the rock is good.

Rosy Futures   20m   E3 *. Guy Robertson, Trevor Wood. May 2009.

Eliminate but with good rock and fine climbing. Start below the short wall right of *Raining Roses*. Climb a thin crack then trend up left to the large boss on *Raining Roses*. Continue up left into a short groove and exit this to a junction with *Cocaine*. Finish straight up through the notch.

DEESIDE, VAT BURN:

A number of climbs have been done near NO 420 998. Details later.

GLEN CLOVA, Central Crag:

Bark at the Moon   15m   E8 6c ***. Tim Rankin, Guy Robertson (head pointed). May 2008.

The stunning overhanging prow and crack up the left edge of the wall. Start from a good pedestal belay as for *West Side Story*, the best approach to which is either a rising traverse from the below *Empire of the Sun* or from directly below up the ridge and groove (Difficult). Climb juggy hollow flakes just right of the arete to a good flat hold at a break from where protection can be arranged. Gain a sloper on the lip above and make a sequence of desperate slap up side-pulls to a good hidden hold at the base of the hanging groove. A further hard move up the groove leads to good holds; swing right then up to jugs and a rest. Move out left, then up to pull over at the crack. Excellent powerful climbing, well protected after a bold crux.

Sunset Song Direct   30m   E6 6b. Iain Small. 24 May 2009.

Follow *Sunset Song* to where the hanging corner can be gained from the left. Instead make a long undercut move to gain spaced holds leading up left to better holds.

HIGHLAND OUTCROPS

POLLDUBH, Dundee Buttress:

The Howff   20m   E2 5c. Jonnie Williams, Anna Trenaman. 5 October 2008.

Initially takes the same line as *Heading for the Howff*, but takes the direct finish up the left corner with good micro-wires for protection.

Styx Buttress:

Inimitable   20m   E8 6c *. Dave Macleod. 9 June 2009.
The flake and blank scoop in the left wall below *Resurrection*. Start at the foot of
the wide fault and layback up the flake to its termination (low wires). Continue
up and move leftwards with difficulty to eventually gain a jug in the scoop by a
sustained sequence. Finish easily into *Resurrection*.

That Hollow Feeling   20m   E1 5b **. Bob Hamilton, Steve Kennedy. 19 April
2009
Climbs the steep wall overlooking the initial slab of *Fidelity* leading onto the
slab of *Right Wall*. Make a few moves up the slab then pull steeply out right into
a V-shaped recess.   Undercling a hollow-sounding block in the headwall and
make an awkward rock over move onto the slab on the right. Climb the slab
directly above to the tree and finish up *Right Wall*.

Black's Buttress:
Avalon   30m   HVS 4c *. Steve Kennedy, Bob Hamilton. 10 June 2009.
The slab immediately left of *Shergar*. Slightly eliminate but nice climbing.
Quite bold. Start at the lowest point of the buttress just left of the birch tree
(close to the second pitch of *Zelos*). Climb up and rightwards to a quartz seam
(crossing *Knuckleduster*). Climb the seam then directly up the slab to the right
of a small overhang. Finish by some thin moves just right of the edge.

DUNTELCHAIG, Dracula Buttress:
Transvision Clamp   15m   E6 6b. Rich Betts, Nick Carter. 7 May 2008.
The arete left of *Cyclops* climbed on its right-hand side. Hard climbing with just
enough protection. An in-situ thread was used on the first ascent. Head pointed.

Monsters Edge   15m   E4 6b. Rich Betts, Nick Carter. April 2008.
The overhanging arete left of *Frankenstein*. Climb through the roof as for
Frankenstein, then break left to climb the hanging arete on its right-hand side
with a long reach between the obvious breaks. Finish up the slab. Head pointed.

Note: *BFG* (SMCJ 2007) should be HVS.

The Main Crag:
Dark Vision   30m   E2 6a. Andy Tibbs, Davy Moy. 27 May 2008.
Start right of the monolith where the crag base turns and starts to go uphill.
1. 15m 6a Pull steeply into an overhung crack. Climb out leftwards onto the
arete and climb this and easier ground to huge flakes.
2. 15m 5b Climb cracks in the wall above which lead to a small pine tree (on
Druim).

The Latch Key Kid   27m   E2 5c. Andy Tibbs, Davy Moy. 30 May 2008.
Start 3m left of *Misty Crack* where the ledge narrows. Climb a steep narrow
corner and pull out left at its top. Continue up and climb the right of two cracks
which leads directly to the small pine tree.

Too Strong for Scotland   8m   E4 6a. Andy Tibbs. 10 June 2008.
On the steep wall above *Excavator* is a right-slanting wide crack. It can be

approached by descending from the abseil trees at the top of *Misty Crack* or *Dragonfly*. Climb the crack which is steep, sustained and well protected.

Mojo Slab   15m   E3 5b. Davy Moy, Will Wilkinson. 30 June 2008.
On the steepest cleanest part of the slab, 3m right of *Excavator*. Start at a flake feature beneath a wee tree at mid height. Go up the flake to the tree (runner), then straight up to finish on a grassy/mossy slope (wire for the final move). Sustained climbing with hardest move onto the grass (not much pro).

BINNEIN SHUAS, West Section:
Medusa   30m   HVS 5a. Andy Nisbet, Jonathan Preston. 20 May 2008.
A crack-line between *Blaeberry Grooves* and *Gorgon*. Start immediately right of *Blaeberry Grooves*. Move right, up and back left to gain and climb the crack-line which is about 2m right of Blaeberry's crack-line.
Note: *Blaeberry Grooves* is very good and worth a star or two. It and nearby routes can be climbed as a single pitch to a ledge (as the above route did), omitting the easier upper pitch. An abseil means several routes can be climbed. *Gorgon* is HVS 5b, maybe E1. The descriptions of the lines left of *Blaeberry Grooves* make little sense. *Comraich* and *Bearberry Groove might* even be the same and a good quality direct line was climbed by the above party at E1 5b which could fit either description. *Cowberry Groove* certainly is misplaced at the grade.
Note: *Gorgon* was first climbed by J.R. Mackenzie (unseconded) in 1971.

CRAIG A' BARNS, Polney Crag:
Aretenophobia   15m   E2 5b. Michael Barnard, Georgianna Watson. 11 October 2008.
Climb the right side of the arete between *Poison Ivy* and *Consolation Corner*. Follow the latter route through its initial bulge before stepping left to follow the arete. A bit eliminate, but not overly so and gives some good bold moves.

BEN NEVIS, AONACHS, CREAG MEAGAIDH

BEN NEVIS, Observatory Buttress:
Point Blank   350m   HVS. John Lyall, Andy Nisbet. 29 June 2009.
A summer ascent based on the winter line, but picking cleaner dry rock over wet grooves.
1. 45m Climb the rib, as for pitch 1 of *Left Edge Route*.
2. 45m 4c Go diagonally right into a corner and back diagonally left into the groove of Left Edge Route. The chimney-crack above (*Point Blank* winter) was wet, so move right as for *Left Edge Route* and belay some 10m up its slab-ramp.
3. 25m 5a Make a rising traverse left across a clean slab to step into the chimney-crack. After a couple of moves up, climb its right arete until forced to step back into the chimney-crack. Make a thin move to gain a hanging belay.
4. 25m 4c Go left across a thin slab to overlook *Point Five Gully* (as for the winter route, but 10m not 5m). Climb the steep ramp to a terrace above.
5. 35m 4b Climb the slanting groove to another terrace.

6. 45m 4c The winter route seems to gain the crest more easily but a complex line was necessary, slanting left up sloping shelves until a long step right gained it. Trend right up steep ground to where the angle eased.
7. 8. and 9. 130m Follow the easing crest to the top.

Echo Wall:
Echo Wall 100m Ungraded ****. Dave MacLeod. 28 July 28th.
A spectacular route taking the huge sharp arete of Echo Wall, well seen from Tower Ridge or when ascending Observatory Gully. Poorly protected in general with groundfall potential at 20m near the end of the crux section.
1. 30m Climb easy slabs to a belay at the foot of the grossly overhanging arete of the buttress.
2. 70m Pull into an overhung groove and exit this with immediate difficulty. A hard and poorly protected boulder problem leads to the roof and an upside down rest (wires, poor Camalot 6). Pull leftwards over the roof with desperate climbing up the wall just right of the arete to a shakeout (RP & skyhook in suspect rock). Move left to the arete and make very serious moves up this to a good spike and reasonable gear. Continue with more ease up the arete (runout) to a small ledge (drop your left-hand rope to relieve drag). Continue up steep flakes in a great position to gain easy ground and a short solo to reach *Tower Ridge*.

The Brass Monkey 135m VII,8. Tim Marsh, Pete Davies. 5 December 2008.
A superb mixed climb following the summer line throughout. Large hexes and Friend 4 useful.
1. 40m Climb the slab in a direct line towards the corner. Belay beneath a short wall level with the Echo Wall arete.
2. 20m Overcome the short wall on the left on thin ice and follow the icy upper slab to base of the corner.
3. 10m Climb the cracks in the corner for 3m, then make strenuous moves right (crux) to reach more cracks leading to a belay.
4. 40m Climb the sustained off-width crack, exiting right to a good ledge.
5. 25m Continue up the corner-crack, steeply at first to where it becomes a chimney. From the top of the chimney, back and foot outwards in a superb position to top out on the chimney's right wall.

Goodeve's Buttress:
Tales of the Unexpected 200m IV,4. Robin Clothier, Simon Richardson, Andy Forsyth. 11 April 2009.
The buttress between *The Gutter* and *The White Line*. The first pitch has probably been climbed before. Start by climbing *Glover's Chimney* for 100m and belay below the prominent icy groove cutting the right wall.
1. 60m Climb the V-groove, exiting steeply left at its top. Move up snow and belay just right of the icefall of *The Gutter*.
2. 50m Climb a line of ice on the left flank of the buttress for 20m, then pull right onto the buttress itself. Move up, step right and pull over a steep step to a good ledge.
3. 30m Step rightwards across a gully cutting into the right flank of the buttress,

move up a steep slabby corner, then trend right up an icy groove to reach the top of the buttress.

4. 60m Continue up easy ground to the top.

Close Encounters   140m   III,5. Simon Richardson. 13 April 2009.
A counter-diagonal to *Tales of the Unexpected*. Start just left of the upper section of *The White Line* (most easily reached by climbing *Glover's Chimney* for 150m and traversing right across the snow terrace). Climb a snow ramp leading right, and then cut back left up the gully that cuts into the right flank of the buttress. Continue up the gully to the buttress crest then move up to a steep chimney blocked by an overhang. Pull steeply out right (crux) and continue up the easy ground above to the plateau.

The Alpine Princess   140m   IV,4. Simon Richardson, Zoe Hart. 24 February 2009.
A natural line of weakness up the left side of the buttress. The left side of the buttress (delineated by the ice gully of *Hale Bopp Groove* to its left) is cut by two diverging snow ramps.
1. 40m Start at the foot of *Hale Bopp Groove* and take the upper wider ramp to the foot of a steep icy gully with a flat chockstone wedged across its top. Climb the gully, squeeze under the chockstone, and exit right onto a good ledge.
2. 40m Step left around the buttress to enter the slanting groove of *Hale Bopp Groove* and climb this to the top of the buttress. Alternatively and better, climb the rib between *The White Line* and *Hale Bopp Groove* by climbing thinly iced grooves past a steepening to an impasse. Step left, and continue on ice to finish just right of the final gully of *The White Line*. (Simon Richardson, 14 April 2009.)
3. 60m Continue up easy ground to the top.

Three Men on a Rope   160m   III. Andy Forsyth, Simon Richardson, Robin Clothier. 12 April 2009.
A natural line of weakness cutting right across the front face of Goodeve's Buttress. Start by climbing the lower of the two diverging ramps and continue up easy mixed ground to belay beside a large tower-shaped block. (50m – junction with *Goodytwoshoes*.) Continue up and right in the same line below the smooth wall cut by the faults of *Techno Wall* and *The Borg Collective* to join the ramp section of *Beam Me Up Scotty*. Follow this to the steep icy bulge (50m) and continue more easily to the top (60m).

Big Wednesday   140m   VI,6. Maxime Turgeon, Simon Richardson, Ian Parnell, Zoe Hart. 25 February 2009.
A good mixed route based on the well-defined left-facing groove in the upper part of the buttress.
1. 25m Start 10m right of the lower ramp of *Three Men on a Rope* below a steep wall cut by a fault. Climb the fault and exit through a bulge onto easier ground. Move up to the foot of a short steep groove defined by a flake on its left side.
2. 15m Climb the groove (often icy) to a good ledge that leads right to the foot of the well-defined left-facing groove.

3. 40m Climb the groove moving left through a bulge at its top. An excellent and well-protected mixed pitch.

4. 60m Continue up easy ground to the top. (Note that the second pitch was interchanged with *The Alpine Princess* on the first ascent.)

Creag Coire na Ciste:
Note: Rich Cross and Nick Williams made the second ascent of *Cold Play* (VIII,8) up the steep pillar right of *Archangel*. They found an alternative crux pitch, which they named the *Snow Patrol Variant* (VIII,8).

South Trident Buttress:
The Minge   VII,8. Ed Edwards, Pete Macpherson. 6 February 2009.
Start just below the obvious black wide crack at the foot of a right-trending icy ramp.

1. 15m Climb the icy ramp on thin ice and turf and belay below the crack-cum-groove of *The Minge* summer line. About 6–8m further up the ramp there is a large block which is used to belay, but it is worth extending so the belayer is below the next pitch.

2. 20m Climb the crack-cum-groove on poor tool placements (bold) until it becomes a shallow left-facing corner below a bulging crack. Climb the bulging crack with poor sloping footholds onto the slab above. Belay halfway up the slab.

3. 40m Traverse right across the slab on invisible footholds and tiny tool placements to the crack on the right. Climb the crack (strenuous but good gear) to an easing in angle and follow the groove/chimney system above to turfy ramps.

4. and 5. 70m Follow a choice of lines up turfy grooves to the right of the ridge to reach the crest.

Central Trident Buttress:
Metamorphosis   105m   VIII,9. Iain Small, Gareth Hughes. 23 March 2009.
A winter line taking the *Cranium Start*, then gaining the corner.

1. 25m Follow the deep crack of *Cranium Start* to belay in the cave.

2. 25m Take the ramp/fault line out right and tenuously cross the wall by twin diagonal seams. Gain the corner and follow it to a long ledge on the right wall.

3. 30m Make bold thin moves up and right to gain the flake-line. Struggle to the top of the huge flake, then launch up the blank-looking wall above, leading to easier ground.

4. 15m Climb to easier ground.

Note: A winter ascent of *Heidbanger* (with a direct start) by Rich Cross & Andy Benson on 23 November 2008. No details.

Note from Colin Moody:
Centurion pitch 4 should read, 'Move back into the corner and climb it to an overhanging crack. Traverse left across the wall and climb the arete on the left to a stance.'

Carn Dearg Buttress:
Sassenach IX,9. Andy Turner, Tony Stone. 9 March 2009.
The summer route was followed throughout with the crux being the overhanging groove and flake of the second pitch. In-situ gear from a previous attempt made the crux easier. The squeeze chimney higher up was tech 8.
Note: This route has been considered for many years. A potential attempt (which probably would have failed) by Brian Sprunt & Andy Nisbet in 1979 was thwarted by lack of snow. Snowy and stormy conditions allowed it to be snowy and iced in the crux groove, and judging from the pictures, no complaints about full winter condition.

North Wall Carn Dearg:
The Cone Collectors 310m VIII,7. Iain Small, Simon Richardson, 14 December 2008.
A good varied mixed route up the wall left of *Macphee's Route*. Pitch 3 is very serious and merits the overall grade in its own right.
1. 70m Start by following the ramp of *Easy Way* that cuts up the buttress. At its top move right past a tiny pine tree (the origin of the route name) to a join a second ramp (taken by *Macphee's Route*) trending back right. Belay below a steep crack cutting through the wall above.
2. 30m Climb the crack to the terrace above. An excellent pitch.
3. 30m The next tier is comprised of blank and unhelpful rock. The only line of weakness is a diagonal right-to-left break that leads into a hanging V-groove. Cross the fault (steep and barely protected) to enter the V-groove. Climb this (strenuous) to the top of the wall. A daunting and very serious pitch.
4. 60m Move easily up and right up the mixed ground above to belay below the impending deep chimney cutting the left side of the triangular wall right of Waterfall Gully.
5. 40m Climb the chimney (reminiscent of a mini *Gully of the Gods*) over a couple of overhanging chockstones. Another sustained pitch.
6. to 7. 80m Continue up the upper section of *Waterfall Gully* for two pitches to join the ridge section of *Ledge Route*.

Cousins' Buttress note:
Cousins' Buttress is named after the two cousins C.W. Walker and H. Walker who made the first ascent. Accordingly it should be *Cousins' Buttress* not *Cousin's Buttress*.

MAMORES, Mullach nan Coirean:
Yo Bro 70m VIII,9. Dave MacLeod, Malcolm Kent. 14 December 2008.
The overhanging groove right of *Himalayan Shuffle*. The first 20m are very sustained and, in the first half, serious.
1. 35m Climb the overhanging groove with little respite to the angle change; continue on easier ground to large ledges.
2. 35m Continue easily on the same line to the ridge.

AONACH MOR, Coire an Lochain, North-East Face:
Note: Peter Duggan notes that at the bottom of p227 in the Ben Nevis Guide it

should say: 'The apex of the corrie rim is cut by a broad snow gully which lies almost due **west** of the lochan.'

Downstairs 100m III. Sonya Drummond, Andy Nisbet. 22 February 2009.
The next icy groove right of *Ribbing Corner* (SMCJ 2007). Climb the groove and icy turfy ground to below a steeper buttress (45m). Moving right would be easier but instead climb the icy buttress to below a final wall (35m). Pass this on the right and continue to the cornice (20m).

Lord's Groove 120m IV,4. Sonya Drummond, Andy Nisbet. 22 February 2009.
The next icy line left of *Two Queens* (SMCJ 2007), but a lower tier was also climbed. Start at a prominent rib in the lower tier. Climb an icy groove immediately on its right and continue slightly leftwards to an icy right-facing corner in the steep wall above the terrace from which the routes to the right start (50m). Climb the steep corner and trend slightly left to an upper buttress (40m). Climb this to the cornice which was breached after a 10m traverse right across a scoop to the next ridge right (30m).

Web Buttress:
Off the Cuffs 100m III. Richard Gilbert, Richard Watson. 19 February 2009.
Heading south from Web Buttress, the cliff base descends below a triangular buttress. This is about halfway between *The Web* and *Piranha*. Left of this buttress is a right-slanting gully (diagram provided). Climb the gully in two pitches to finish up steep snow leading to the cornice.

Ribbed Walls:
Man Friday (SMCJ 2007) was climbed by Bob Hamilton & Steve Kennedy in February 2004. No change of name or grade sought!

Monkey Buttress:
This is the proposed name for the buttress on the left side of the south defining ridge of Coire an Lochain. See SMCJ 2008 for more routes.

Chimpanzee 60m III. Simon Richardson. 1 January 2009.
The prominent central line of ice to the left of *Monkey Business*. Climb up a wide gully, step right at a bulge and continue up the continuation gully to the top.

Muggle-Wump 70m II. Simon Richardson. 1 January 2009.
The gully defining the right edge of the buttress containing *Monkey Puzzle*. Climb over a short bulge to reach a snow slope and follow this to the top.

AONACH MOR, WEST FACE:
Note: Andrew Moore & partner climbed the prominent dog-leg gully right of *Daim Buttress* at II/III in February 2009. Start up the left side of the gully and climb a short ice pitch up the rocky narrows. Head up right towards the snowfield just below a subsidiary buttress at half-height. Slant right up the snowfield, then trend up and left over some steepish turf steps to join the upper gully and thence to the easy upper ridge of *Daim Buttress* which leads directly to the summit cairn.

Gordon Macnair climbing Bloodlust (E1 5b) at Sheigra, on the SMC Easter Meet.
Photo: Noel Williams.

AONACH BEAG, North Face:
Through the Looking Glass   300m   II. Simon Richardson. 1 January 2009.
The left-trending line of weakness defining the left edge of the easier-angled central section of cliff. Start left of *The Black Prince* and climb easy-angled ice to join the shallow line that leads up and left to join the *North-East Ridge*.

Graduate Gully   200m   III. Simon Richardson, Roger Webb. 3 January 2009.
Left of *Mayfly* is a well-defined square-cut gully that cuts through the upper rocks on the face. Start as for *Mayfly* and climb snow up to the foot of the icefall. Trend left below the steep section of the icefall and follow a sort of icy gully/depression to reach a snow slope. Move left across this for 20m to enter the gully and climb this for 60m over a chockstone top join the *North-East Ridge* just above the Pinnacles.

AONACH BEAG, West Buttress:
Jurassic Shrimp   100m   III,4. John Higham, John Hutchinson. 30 March 2008.
The line lies on the steep buttress that lies to the immediate right of *Blind Faith*. Take a descending traverse to the foot of the ridge from the Aonach Mor–Aonach Beag col. Follow the crest of the ridge on moderate ground and where the ridge becomes overhanging move right to find an ice gully that leads up to an ice pillar (40m). Follow the gully via the steep ice pillar back onto the crest of the ridge to belay on a small col (30m). Ascend the ridge behind the col for one pitch (30m), then easy ground leads to the plateau. Diagram provided.

AONACH BEAG, Stob Coire Bhealaich:
Ledgemaster   180m   IV,3 **. Bob Hamilton, Steve Kennedy, Mark Shaw. 1 November 2008.
Follows the prominent ledge system running rightwards across the upper part of the main face. The route finishes near the top of the upper ridge of *The Ramp*. Spectacularly exposed in places and quite serious for the grade. Start just right of the icefall at the foot of *Next Janeration*. A short step leads to the wide ledge which is traversed rightwards to a belay in the lower groove of *The Clare Effect* at the end of the initial ledge system (50m). Climb up and move right to surmount a steep icy corner, then climb directly up to the left end of the upper ledge system (25m). Pull steeply onto the ledge which is traversed horizontally right in an exposed position to a thread close to where the ledge eventually peters out (45m). From the end of the ledge climb steep mixed ground (left of the finish of *Helter Skelter*), then move up rightwards to finish on the ridge (60m). Easy ground leads to the summit.

AONACH BEAG, An Aghaidh Garbh, Summit Buttress (SMCJ 2007):
Le Passage   70m   IV,5 *. Bob Hamilton, Steve Kennedy. 29 December 2008.
Left of *Close Encounters* are two short gullies divided by a narrow buttress. This route takes the left-hand gully. Best done early in the season. Climb the easy snow slope left of the start of *Close Encounters* then easy ice steps to a belay at a small rocky alcove. This is directly below the right-hand gully. Step left and climb a short icy rib then move leftwards up easier ground to a short, steep icefall. Climb the icefall to reach the narrow gully above and a flake belay. Steep slopes led to a snow arete on the right and a vague break in the cornice.

Top: Star Jelly found lying on the highest of the three 'Parallel Roads' in Glen Roy (350m).
Note the clumps of small black spheres near the upper edge. Photo taken 30 October 2004.
Bottom: The Wishing Stone near Lochaline, opposite Mull. Photo taken 28 November 2004.

Much can bank out later in the season but the cornice is usually huge and likely to be extremely problematic.

GREY CORRIES, COIRE NA CEANNAN:
Happy Bunny! 30m II/III. D. Strachan, S. Lawrence, R.S.D. Smith. 13 January 2009.
Climb the obvious icefall in the outflow burn 250m NE of the small lochan at NN 264 751.

STOB COIRE AN LAOIGH:
Full Frontal 60m VII,7 *. Tony Stone, Viv Scott. 22 November 2008.
Takes the arete between *Pentagon* and *Taliballan*, finishing up the obvious overhanging off-width at the top. Steep, exposed and technical climbing but helpful where most needed.
1. 25m Start up a short corner halfway along the wall left of *Taliballan* to a ledge. Climb another short corner above, then move left climbing a cracked wall to gain a block on the arete. Go up from this moving left round the arete, then back right to beneath a left-facing groove.
2. 45m Pull into and climb the left-facing groove. Traverse the wall beneath the roof with interest (small cams useful) to gain a second left-facing groove. Go up this slightly rightwards to a turf ledge. Move right and climb a bulging groove and steep wall, then a slab (bold) and blocks above with sustained interest to a large ledge (possible belay). Climb a steep corner to the overhanging off-width at the top of the buttress. Tackle the off-width breaking out rightwards to gain the top.
Note: Viv Scott thought VII,8.

BEN ALDER, Garbh Coire Beag:
Kryptonite 195m IV,4. Sonya Drummond, Andy Nisbet. 30 December 2008.
Climbs the centre of the face between *Smallville* and *Bheoil Pfeiler*. Reach the start by following the initial gully of *Left Gully* to snow slopes, then moving slightly left to below a prominent wide groove.
1. 50m Follow the groove to the snow terrace which crosses the whole face.
2. 50m Follow its continuation, then go slightly left by snow patches until near the slight rib right of *Smallville*.
3. 50m Go diagonally right, then traverse right on a narrow turf ledge to easier turf. Go up to steep walls until forced left up ramps (crux) into the turfy groove which *Smallville* climbs lower down. Go up this almost to the crest.
4. 45m Go left up a narrow turf ramp to join *Smallville*, then back right up its groove (steep ice) to the final crest.

Ben Alder Cottage Crag:
Described in the Ben Nevis guide as an amphitheatre, it is more of an inverted L shape with a vertical west-facing wall running for 100m south to north up the right side of the crag. At the top of this is an easy grassy gully, below which is an outcrop of three pinnacles. West of the grassy gully the crag swings round 90 degrees and runs west to another slightly steeper grassy gully. Both gullies can be used for descent. West of this second gully the crag continues for another

150m in a series of ribs, walls and buttresses before petering out into the hillside. Routes described from right to left (as this is the easiest way of locating them in relation to features already mentioned).

Adam's Apple   35m   HVS 5b. James Woodhouse, Jonathan Preston. 30 June 2009.
Below and left of the first (right-hand) grassy gully is a slab split by a crack. Climb the crack with one awkward move at half-height. Continue right of a heathery ledge and climb flakes. Step back left at the earliest opportunity and climb slabs to easier ground.

The right side of the second (left-hand) grassy gully is formed by a distinct arete.

Remote Control   25m   HVS 5a. Jonathan Preston, James Woodhouse. 30 June 2009.
Start just left of the base of the arete. Climb steeply up and rightwards onto a slab (bold). Move up the slab and left to the sharp arete. Make a series of steep moves up just right of the crest of the arete before making an airy traverse left onto a ramp leading to a niche. Finish up cracks in the wall above.

Well left of the second grassy gully is a blocky buttress. The left side of this is formed by a fine west-facing russet-coloured slab.

Hotter than July   25m   HVS 5a *. Jonathan Preston, James Woodhouse. 30 June 2009.
Start on steep grass below the centre of the slab. Move steeply up right to reach flakes. Climb these to gain a good crack and then climb directly to a large rectangular ledge. A short corner leads to the top.

CENTRAL HIGHLANDS, GEAL CHARN, Creag Dhubh:
Wee Softie   45m   II/III. Martin Holland, Pamela Millar. 2 December 2008.
This route is on a crag high on left of the crag shown NE of the main crag. It is on the left/upper tier of this crag at approx. NN 596799. The lower level of this crag may be the one where the routes *Flight of the Navigator* and *Map and Compass* are described in SMCJ 2004. Although the map ref is wrong (it's in the loch).
1. 18m Start 5m right of the cave and climb turf and ice steps to the higher of two bent-over trees.
2. 25m Continue up turf and ice to two saplings at the base of an iced slab. Climb the slab leftwards to pass a triangular overhanging nose on its left.

GLEN COE

BUACHAILLE ETIVE MOR, Great Gully Upper Buttress:
Jamay   30m   E3 5c ***. Michael Barnard (unsec). 10 July 2009.
The obvious direct finish to *Yamay* gives a tremendous pitch, steep and sustained but well protected throughout. Start as for that route but instead of traversing right continue straight up (thin) to gain a small finger-edge just below

an obvious slot in the overlap (good Friend 0 in this). Reach up for better holds above and pull over strenuously (crux) to gain the crack above, which is followed with continued interest to the top. Two rest points used.

GEARR AONACH, Yosemite Wall:
Sublime 35m E8 6c *. Dave MacLeod. 8 May 2008.
Climbs the 45 degree roof and impending wall right of *Sweet Disregard for the Truth*. Arrange an assortment of runners below the roof and climb it directly (bouldery crux) to a resting place on the headwall. Difficult climbing up the wall above (small cams) leads to a finish through the top bulge of *Glorious Youth*.

CHURCH DOOR BUTTRESS:
Critical Mass 130m VII,7. Iain Small,Tony Stone, Gareth Hughes. 11 December 2008.
A direct line up the steep front of the buttress, then finishing straight up the headwall where *Dark Mass* traverses off right. Start at the right side of the frontal face, left of the recess where *West Chimney* begins.
1. 60m Take a line of steep right-facing corners to easier ground and a block belay where *West Chimney* through route emerges.
2. 30m Climb the rib above to belay on the large block at the start of West Chimney's traverse.
3. 40m Follow *Dark Mass* until above the shallow chimney-groove, then move left into a groove leading to a ledge below a steep wall. Pull steeply leftwards over this into a niche and take grooves to finish up an off-width crack.
Note: *Templer Nights* (SMCJ 2007) Should be *Nights Templar*.

STOB COIRE NAM BEITH, North Face (The Pyramid):
Vertex 130m IV,5 **. Bob Hamilton, Steve Kennedy. 6 December 2008.
Climbs a line close to the right (west) edge of No. 6 Buttress overlooking the initial gully of *The Causeway*. A reasonable choice if doubtful conditions prevail higher up. The existing route, *Pyramid*, takes the left edge of the buttress. Quite technical in places and climbed in deep powder conditions. Start behind a huge detached block directly beneath the right edge.
1. 45m From a chockstone belay move up and traverse left into an obvious groove line just left of the edge. Climb the groove to a large flake below steep wall. Climb the slabby wall on the left, then move back right and continue up a groove to a detached flake and thread on the edge overlooking the gully.
2. 45m Awkward moves lead steeply up a wall on the left into a groove which leads to a slabby corner. Climb the steep wall just right of the corner and continue up short steps to easier ground.
3. 40m Further short walls lead to the final steepening which is avoided by a short traverse left to the edge. A narrow snow arete leads to the top of the buttress.
   Either finish by *Cleftweave* or *The Causeway*. Alternatively, if a shorter day is required, abseil off a block on the narrow ridge at the top of the buttress leftwards into the initial gully of *Cleftweave* on the left which leads fairly easily back into the corrie.

AONACH DUBH, West Face:
Bungee 100m E4 ***. Blair Fyffe, Guy Robertson (on-sight). June 2009.
A superb exposed route, starting up *Yo-Yo* then breaking out round the right arete onto the wall to its right. A prominent feature is the striking crack high on the headwall
1. 30m 5b *Yo-Yo* pitch 1.
2. 30m 6a Step delicately down right and traverse under an obvious overlap to a precarious perch near the edge. Move up into a hanging groove and climb this then a crack on the left with difficulty to a sloping ledge. Traverse right along this to climb the first obvious groove with an awkward exit onto a ledge.
3. 25m 6a Above is a clean-cut triangular niche with a finger-crack above its right end. Climb steeply up to gain and follow this crack, then pull left into another crack which is followed with increasing interest to another good ledge.
4. 15m 5b Climb the steep wall above to the terrace.

GLEN ETIVE, STOB COIR' AN ALBANNAICH, North Corrie:
Right of the corner of *Plumbline* is a broad buttress containing a shallow gully line above a large snow bay. Right again is a triangular-shaped buttress with a prominent right-slanting ramp in the lower part.

Hors d'Oeuvres 70m III *. Alan MacDonald, Bob Hamilton, Steve Kennedy. 1 February 2009.
Climbs the shallow gully line mentioned above. A short icefall leads into a large snow bay. Continue to the foot of a steep icefall, then move rightwards and climb an icy corner to easier ground. Steep snow leads to the top.

Air of Detachment 80m IV,6 *. Steve Kennedy, Bob Hamilton, Alan MacDonald. 1 February 2009.
The prominent ramp in the centre of the triangular buttress to the right of the above route. The corner forming the left wall of the ramp was climbed for about 10m before thin ice forced a traverse out right to the edge of the buttress. Sustained climbing leads up the buttress edge. Near the top of the buttress edge a left-slanting crack leads back to the top of the ramp. Follow a ledge out right, then zigzag up the broad buttress above following a system of ledges (55m). Easier mixed ground leads directly to the top (25m).

BEINN SGULAIRD (GLEN CRERAN):
Back to Work 100m III,4. Ian Stennett. 5 January 2009.
The route takes an obvious icefall (visible from Elleric) which forms after a prolonged cold spell, starting at an altitude of 700m. The water source comes from the corrie north of the main summit. Start at the base of a frozen waterfall with pool beneath, NN 050 465, north-west aspect. Climb the waterfall steeply for about 30m then follow a series of less steep height gains. The line eventually meets an awkward chockstone in an enclosed part of the gully at alt 745m. After this it becomes less steep and ends in walking.

GARBH BHEINN (ARDGOUR), South Wall:
Sgian Dubh 60m V,6 **. Neil Adams, Alasdair Fulton. 25 January 2009.

Follow the summer line with varied and interesting climbing, well protected and technical, high in the grade.

1. 20m Back-and-foot, torque, thrutch, jam and sketch up the initial chimney (crux), then move leftwards along the ledge to a good stance.

2. 40m Move steeply up and left via cracks, flakes and a small roof to a right-trending ramp. Follow this ramp to its right end, then up flakes to easier ground. The first ascent was climbed in icy conditions and the route may be significantly harder without a thick coating of rime ice.

Note: Colin Moody notes that *The Pincer* starts independently up the rib right of *Chela*, and was written correctly in older guides.

Garbh Choire Buttress:
Drum Beat 60m HVS. Andy Hyslop, John Lyall, Andy Nisbet. 25 July 2009.
This buttress didn't look as clean as the stars would suggest, but the left end had the cleanest rock. Start at slabs right of the corner of *Percussion*.
1. 25m 4c Climb the slabs and join *Percussion* briefly to share its belay below its groove.
2. 35m 5a Step left and climb the right-hand of two steep grooves, with a step left into the left groove near the top. Continue more easily, largely on rock .

ARDNAMURCHAN, Creag an Fhir-eoin:
Lust 15m E1 5b *. Steve Kennedy, Bob Hamilton. 18 May 2008.
An eliminate but good route which follows the left-facing corner immediately left of *Greta Gabbro* throughout. The upper part of the route is climbed by *Lava Lout* which traverses in rightwards from the next corner to the left. Start up the slab directly below the corner to reach a small overlap at the foot of the corner. Climb the corner direct.

Meall Meadhoin, Apron Slabs:
Gall Variation Andy Hunter (unsec). 10 May 2009.
The crack of *Gall* being wet, climb the slab some 2m left of it (unprotected but one runner in the crack), and joining it just below the belay ledge. This was thought to be right of *Solas*.

SOUTHERN HIGHLANDS

BEINN ACHALADAIR:
Manifestation, Variation 40m III. Matt Griffin, Adrian Dye. 21 March 2008.
A good-quality variation to the second pitch. Instead of climbing the groove directly above the belay, traverse 8m left and climb a different groove over a couple of steepenings on good turf to a ledge (40m). Follow the easy buttress to the top as per the original route.

BEINN UDLAIDH:
Sugarmouse 90m III. Jim Graham, Iain MacCallum. 6 February 2009.
The route takes a chimney-line to the right of *Quintet* and goes up below the right wall of the big gully containing *Organ Pipe Wall*.

1. 50m   Go up a chimney and underneath a chockstone. Traverse left into another chimney and continue up to a corner on the left.
2. 40m Follow the chimney to the top.

BEINN CHUIRN, Coire na Saobhaidhe:
Under the summit is this turfy crag. The biggest gully has been climbed at Grade I and a steeper narrower one to its right 'slightly harder' – see older district guides. The buttresses are short, steep but very turfy.

Bullion Buttress   70m   III. Dave McGimpsey, Andy Nisbet. 24 November 2008.
The buttress between the two gullies. A central line was taken, moving right and back left towards the top.

Goldilocks 60m   III,4. Dave McGimpsey, Andy Nisbet. 24 November 2008.
The buttress right of the right gully. Start 10m right of the gully and climb the front face, including a short thin section low down.

Silver Star 60m   II. Dave McGimpsey, Andy Nisbet. 24 November 2008.
The next gully to the right leads to a big overhanging wall with icicles. This route takes the easiest line up the buttress to the right. Even easier would be to start up the overhung gully and move right on to this line.

Krugerrand 60m   III. Dave McGimpsey, Andy Nisbet. 24 November 2008.
The next buttress is beyond a groove and features smooth steep walls with large lumps of turf. Climb up the centre to reach the steep walls. Move left and gain a narrow turf ledge. Traverse right along this to gain and climb a turfy groove which leads to a headwall. This was climbed direct (optional).

BEINN IME:
The Double Flash   190m   IV,4. Ron Dempster, Emily Ward, Sarah-Beth McClelland. 7 February 2009.
Halfway along the snowy terrace above the left buttress there is an icy chimney. Squeeze up the icy chimney below the icefall (20m). Continue up easier ground to the top.

THE COBBLER:
Sweetshop 10m E4 5c. Kev Shields. 14 May 2008.
The crag sits on the left side of the tourist path 5–10mins beyond the Narnain boulders. Climb the obvious line to the left of a ramp in the centre of the crag starting at a large obvious pocket.

BEN DONICH, Number 4 Buttress:
Fourth Dimension 55m IV 5 *. Andrew Fraser, Ian Magill. 1 February 2009.
The buttress has a stepped shelf running diagonally up the buttress, from bottom left to top right. Follow this shelf via two difficult steps to its end at a good flake 3m from the right edge of the buttress (30m). Climb a difficult rock slab just right of the belay, then continue up and left to climb the final icefall (25m).

BEINN AN LOCHAIN, North Face:
Footsteps of Giants 180m IV,4 *. Andrew Fraser, Ian Magill. 30 March 2008.
This is the large rambling buttress below and right of the *Monolith Grooves*
buttress, topped by a crazy-angled pinnacle. It was first climbed in November
1902 in summer conditions by Harold Raeburn and the Inglis Clarks by two
indeterminate lines. This route starts just left of the bottom left toe of the lowest
buttress, and after an initial bulge follows a shallow gully to belay in the second
cave (60m). Move up to the next cave which is exited by a traverse left to easier
ground below a steep face. A steep traverse left above a gully outflanks this
(25m). Continue up over a bulge to easier ground and a belay beneath a steep
chimney immediately below the left side of the crazy-angled pinnacle (45m).
Climb into and up the chimney which turns into a through route which exits onto
the col behind the pinnacle (25m). Above and left is an easy left-trending and
wide ramp. Climb up to this, then tackle the steep headwall above (approx 7m
left of its right corner, 25m). The omission of the last pitch would permit a
traverse across to the routes on the monolith, giving an excellent long climb

BEN LOMOND:
Shooglenifty 100m III,4. Sonya Drummond, Andy Nisbet. 30 November 2008.
The rib between the left and central of the three gullies which separate B and C
Buttresses. Start up a groove about 5m from the right end of the rib. Climb this
leftwards, then traverse right into another left-slanting groove which leads to the
crest. Follow the crest over a thin step to an easier section (60m). Climb a short
steep wall, then easier again to a steeper finish.

BEN CRUACHAN, Coire Chat, Noe Buttress:
Noe Gully Right-Hand 50m III. Jamie Bankhead, Guy Steven. 2 November
2008.
From a pitch up *Noe Gully* (before the upper slot), traverse right under
Thunderbolt Chimney onto turfy steps and grooves leading to the top of *Noe
Buttress* (the route).

BEN CRUACHAN, Meall nan Each, East Face:
The east face is characterised by a band of overlaps at two-thirds height situated
left of *Epona Gully*. The following three good routes are situated left of these
overlaps and are easily approached via a short descent to the north from the col
separating Meall nan Each and Stob Dearg.

East Chimney 150m IV,5. David Ritchie, Neil McGougan. 12 January 2008.
Climbs the obvious shallow chimney running the full height of the crag in three
50m pitches. Each pitch contained a short steep section of interest.

Obelix 170m IV,5. David Ritchie, Neil McGougan. 5 December 2008.
Climbs the fault-line running up the buttress immediately right of *East Chimney*.
Start at the foot of *East Chimney*.
1. 65m Move right into a shallow groove and follow this to below a steep wall.
2. 50m Climb the steep wall via cracks (crux), then slabs above to belay left of
a prominent perched block.
3. 55m Follow easier ground directly to the top.

Blue Hex Buttress 170m IV,5. David Ritchie, Neil McGougan. 6 December 2008.
Climbs the right side of the buttress lying to the left of *East Chimney*. Start 15m left of *East Chimney*.
1. 55m Climb the turfy fault surmounting one or two steep steps to a wide ledge below some large blocks just left of *East Chimney*.
2. 45m Climb past the blocks, then up steeper ground trending right overlooking *East Chimney* before moving back left to directly below the centre of a band of overlaps.
3. 50m Climb through the overhangs via the obvious left-slanting open corner to reach easier ground above. Move right, then up past an off-width crack and open fault above to gain a slab. Traverse right across the slab then up to below a short tower.
4. 20m Climb the right side of the tower to finish.

GLEN LONAN:
Wee Steal 100m II. Andy Spink. 9 February 2009.
A frozen north-facing burn at NM 943 269.

KNAPDALE, Kilberry, The Coves (NR 717 612) Non-tidal:
This small headland is found at the minor B8024 road, approx. 14 miles west of Tarbert and 2 miles south of Kilberry. The Coves are signposted at a bend where there is parking for a few cars near the sign. There is also a small lay-by a further 100m along the road to the north.
Approach: Follow the path passing a waterfall and after about 100m look back and you will see a small pinnacle with the gap between offering a steep bouldering wall (Slingsby's Wall) approximately 10m high on the landward side of the gap. A post at the bottom of the wall had Slingsby and Co. written on it, hence the name. The grooves at the left and right ends of the wall have been climbed and a route to the left of the central overhang (Brian Davison, 31 October 2008).
    Continuing south along the beach from here one passes a natural archway and then behind a pinnacle where an old fence is stepped over. A steep south-facing wall is visible above on the left, pass this and go into a rocky narrows where it is necessary to scramble up a slabby wall and traverse inland at the other side of this. Above is a second steep wall of very weathered rock.
    This overhanging wall has a rib or buttress running down from its highest point with sculptured rock on either side. The routes are described from right to left, starting to the right of the central rib. An abseil rope is worth taking to save a long walk round or an awkward down-climb. All routes were cleaned on abseil and some loose and friable rock removed. The cliff is obviously used by shags for nesting and should be avoided during the nesting season.
    The first four routes start from the top of a 5m high pinnacle next to the base of the cliff.

Scooped Up 18m VS 4b. Brian Davison. 31 October 2008.
Climb the weathered scoops to the right of the rib to end up right of a large block at the top. From the top of the pinnacle step across to the worn scoop and follow

to a tricky long reach to the next worn scoop above. Move up friable horizontal rocks to the top. Solo after abseil inspection.

Scoop Arete   18m   E1 5a. Brian Davison. 31 October 2008.
Climb the front of the rib at its steepest on good but worrying holds. Step from the pinnacle to the overhanging rock of the rib and climb up overhangs to easier ground and a sit down near the top. Finish near previous route. Rope solo after abseil inspection.

Guano Groove   18m   VS 4b. Brian Davison. 31 October 2008.
Climbs the deep groove to the left of the rib. Step from the pinnacle to the left of the rib and climb steeply to a ledge at the start of the guano covered groove. Follow the groove easily past a nest to a steep exit onto jugs on the headwall and finish next to the large block.
Variation: HVS 5a. Brian Davison. 31 October 2008.
Follow *Guano Groove* to the nest then make moves left over steep ground on good holds to finish to the right of the block at the top. Solo after abseil inspection.

To the left of *Guano Groove* a compact wall restricts easy access to the steep headwall. A right-to-left diagonal line runs from *Guano Groove* under this compact section of wall to end above a second rib or buttress not as impressive as the right-hand one.

Rib Corner Right-Hand   15m   Severe 4a. Brian Davison. 31 October 2008.
From below the left-hand overhanging rib climb a short easy wall to the corner to the right of the rib, follow the corner to a ledge. Step up and right on big holds to a steep finish.

Spare Rib   15m   HVS 4c. Brian Davison. 31 October 2008.
Climb the front of the rib on several steep weathered holds. Rope solo after abseil inspection.

Rib Corner Left-Hand   15m   Hard Severe 4b. Brian Davison. 31 October 2008.
Start left of the rib and climb up the corner on its left-hand side.

Cove Rib   25m   Moderate. Brian Davison. 29 October 2008.
The left arete of the wall offers an enjoyable climb to a grassy finish. A useful descent in dry conditions.

BEN LAWERS, Bealach Crag (SMCJ 1999):
Chockstone Gully   70m   III. Douglas Stewart, Alastair Brightman. 26 March 2008.
A shallow gully to the right of a more obvious gully which is on the left of the crag (picture provided).
1. 25m   Enter the gully and belay on the left. The obvious overhanging chockstone was turned on the right to gain a turfy rib. The rib delineates the two possible starts to the route. Belay at the top of the rib.
2. 45m   Re-enter the gully and climb to a constriction where bridging moves gain a snow bay. From the bay a turfy groove leads to the top.

Note: *Raven's Gully* is not on Creag an Fhithich but on a scrappy buttress below Bealach Dubh and above the west end of Lochan nan Cat (NN 639 425) i.e. as marked on the OS map.

MEALL NAN TARMACHAN, Cam Chreag:

Rhombus Buttress 100m II. Martin Holland, Davy Virdee. 15 December 2008. The route is on a buttress approx. 150m east of the easy gully descending from the Meall Garbh/Meall nan Tarmachan col. The buttress is bounded on both sides by obvious gullies, has a 4m rock wall on the left at its base and finishes some 50m east of the col. Follow the easiest line up the buttress on easy turf steps and snow. Protection and belays are sparse.

Cauldron Gully 100m I. Martin Holland, Pamela Millar. 17 December 2008. The gully bounding the left edge of *Rhombus Buttress*. Finish by a narrow gully left of the small central buttress at the top.

The Siren 40m II/III. Martin Holland. 18 February 2001. An obvious shallow chimney-gully which leads left across *Carlin's Buttress*. This icy line starts from about a third of the way up the easy descent gully described for *Carlin's Buttress*.

Hicky 30m III,5. Simon Tait, Andrew Innes. 4 January 2009. An icefall located at NN 585 386, just above the 'g' of Cam Chreag on the OS 1:50,000 map. Consists of slabby ice with the last 6m a curtain of water ice.

BEINN HEASGARNICH, Coire Heasgarnich:
NN 413 388   Alt 850m   North facing
The cliffs on the right of the corrie provide some easy climbs in a fine setting with a remote feel.

The Wanderer 150m I/II. George Allan, Billy Hood. 7 April 2008. The broken buttress on the left margin provides go-as-you-please climbing.

Cub Gully 150m II *. George Allan. 25 March 2008. The obvious gully to the right of *The Wanderer* gives a good climb with an ice pitch in its lower reaches.

Leo 125m III *. George Allan, Billy Hood. 7 April 2008. Narrow icefalls can form on the lower section of cliff right of *Cub Gully*. The first of these forms on a small buttress adjacent to *Cub Gully*.
1. 40m Climb the groove to the right of this small buttress to easier ground.
2. 35m Move up left to near *Cub Gully*, then right to the foot of a chimney with a chockstone.
3. and 4. 50m Climb the chimney, exiting left, then climb up and slightly rightwards via short corners and walls.

The Rambler 140m II. George Allan, John Thomas. 6 March 2009. Start where the lower cliff becomes less steep.
1. 60m Climb a depression into a bay (sometimes icy) and exit easily from the top right corner.

2. 45m   Traverse horizontally left above the bay to belay at an obvious overhanging slot.
3. 35m Climb the ramp on the left.

To the right of the largest section of cliff is a big snow basin from which there are a number of easy exits. On the approach, two short gullies, which form a V, can be seen cutting into the steeper rocks starting from the top left corner of the basin.

Gateway Gully   100m   II. George Allan, John Thomas. 28 February 2008.
The right arm of the V.

The Gatepost   100m   II/III. George Allan, Billy Hood. 8 April 2008.
The small buttress right of *Gateway Gully*. Start just up *Gateway Gully*, traverse right onto the buttress and ascend short walls and grooves. A better start further right may await.

Prayer Flag   90m   II. George Allan. 25 March 2008.
There is a small buttress in the centre of the basin dividing the easy exits. Start at its base and follow a ramp rightwards. Where this reaches steeper rocks, traverse left, then work rightwards and climb the crest.

ARRAN

BEINN TARSUINN, Full Meed Tower:
Sunshine Edge   60m   Severe. Billy Hood, Brian Williamson. Easter 2007.
Climb the left edge of *Full Meed Chimney* till forced out left by a rib. Continue up to broken ground.

BEINN TARSUINN, Meadow Face:
Note: A likely FFA of *Brachistochrone* was made by M. Lynch, E. Cleasby on 26 May 1974.

LOWLAND OUTCROPS

THE TROSSACHS, BEN A'AN:
Note: Douglas Stewart notes that *Coriander* is described in Tom Weir's book Highland Days as having been climbed by him, predating the 1970 ascent in Lowland Outcrops.

AYRSHIRE, The Quadrocks:
The Whispering Eye   10m   E3 6a. Kev Shields. 24 May 2009.
Climb the blank overhanging face to the right of *Green Corner*.

ROSNEATH QUARRY:
Lyndsay Mackintosh notes that it is very overgrown and no longer worth a visit.

AUCHINSTARRY QUARRY, Amphitheatre Area:
Scream 2 12m E1 5b. George Duncan, Julie Mesarowicz. June 2008.
At the rear of the brick building, an obvious groove can be seen (west wall) leading to below a large tree at the top of the wall. Gain the obvious groove from the right. At half-height achieve a good hold and gear. Balance past the blank wall above (weighted sling runner) to a pre-arranged lower-off.
Note: Old routes in this area, like *Black Death* (HVS 5a) and *Valentine* (E1 5a) could not be found. The area has changed, although *Flake Wall* (Hard Severe 4a) was found but changed. *Sooty* and *Keystone* (Very Difficult) were cleaned.

Car Park Area:
Vertical Limit 14m Severe 4a. George Duncan, Julie Mesarowicz. 23 August 2008.
On the opposite side of the rock from main car park climbs, beside water in an overgrown path and past old building is an east-facing buttress (Scream 2's crack is visible from here). Start 10m to the right of this. A broken face with an arete and spike make the climb. Gain a good ledge 2m up. Balance up to the spike and stand on it to finish up to the top.

Neilston Quarry:
Note: Andrew Hunter climbed an 8m route of about Very Difficult, starting at the front of the right wall of *Strawberry Crack*. Move up and right at the front of that nose to a bulge, then pull up over it, finishing up beside the tower. It's not the indefinite crack that goes up the right wall of *Strawberry Crack*.

CAMBUSBARRON, Fourth Quarry:
Note: David Shortt and Allan Wallace note that a pillar near *Toddle* has fallen down, so that route has an unjustifiably dangerous finish. *The Doobie Brothers* has been affected near its top, but probably is unspoilt and the same grade. The area of rock right of *Another One Bites the Dust* has had a lot of rockfall and may be dangerous.

GALLOWAY HILLS, The Merrick, Black Garries:
The Mosses, Slaps and Styles 130m III. Andrew Fraser, Iain Magill. 2 January 2009.
This is the shallow gully 30m right of the icefall of *Interstellar Overdraft*. Easy and possibly banked out ice leads to a belay 6m below a long steep wall which guards entry to the gully. Climb this and start up the gully above (30m). Climb the remainder of the gully (35m). Easier climbing to the top following the line of most ice (70m).

Craignaw, Snibe Hill, Grit Buttress:
This tiny buttress lies on the very far right of the crag.
Almscliffe 8m HVS 5b. Stephen Reid, Andrew Fraser. 30 August 2007.
Start 2m right of the mossy central corner and climb the wall easily enough until an exit leftwards onto a sloping slab.

Wisdom Wall:

This short wall lies on the far right of the crag, just right of *The Seven Pillars*.
Hooves of Fire   20m   E1 5a *. Andrew Fraser, Stephen Reid. 10 June 2007.
Climb undercut flakes rightwards up the lower wall and then boldly into a scoop above. Exit up leftwards.

Long Tall Sally   20m   HVS 5b. Stephen Reid, Andrew Fraser. 10 June 2007.
The obvious thin crack on the right of the wall has a hard move to get off the ledge.

Cornarroch Walls:
Eau de Goat   38m   VS. Andrew Fraser, Stephen Reid. 30 August 2007.
Start at a clean cracked rib just left of a large heather shelf at head-height.
1. 25m 4c Climb cracks in the rib to heather, surmount a short wall and then twin cracks to a ledge.
2. 8m 4c Climb the right-hand groove to runners, then traverse left, across the left-hand groove and stride left before mantelling up. A large block belay lies just above.

Craignaw Slabs (See SMCJ 2007), Newfoundland:
The rightmost slab gives ungradeable routes. Maybe they are just boulder problems with long walk-offs! Descents are possible either side.

Going for a Gander   100m+   Easy.
Crosses the slab at two-thirds height in either direction; the crux is stepping over the wet streak – a useful descent.

Nova Scotia   60m   Difficult 4b *. John Biggar, Ian Brown. 3 June 2009.
Climbs the left side of the slab, the best start being 3m left of an obvious vertical crack in the lowest overlap, with a St. Andrew's Cross etched in veined relief on the slab above and left. Make a tricky mantelshelf or rock over move leftwards onto the slab, or climb the crack. Continue easily up the middle slab to an overlap and runners at 40m, then finish up the slightly steeper top slab on nice pockets.

Icebergs   50m   Difficult 4b *. Ian Brown, John Biggar. 3 June 2009.
Climbs the right side of the slabs about 5m left of *Titanic*. Start at a flake with a finger-crack behind it. From the top of this flake make an awkward mantelshelf onto the slab above. Climb the fine second tier to reach the main slab. Walk up this crossing two crevasses, then continue climbing upwards and leftwards to a hidden belay.

Titanic   50m   Severe 4c **. John Biggar, Ian Brown. 3 June 2009.
At the right end of the crag is an obvious arete. This route climbs the steep wall about 1m left to a huge jug, then onto the slab. Cross the two crevasses above and step onto the fine 4m wall above the second one. Continue up the right edge of the slab above before trending left.

Atlantic Slab:
The middle slab is unfortunately too low an angle to give any proper climbing, but can be climbed anywhere at Easy or Moderate.

Scotland Slab:
On the right is a slab bearing some resemblance to a map of Scotland (see SMCJ 2007).

North Sea Slab:
The foot of this slab is about 30 or 40m right of the mid-height on Scotland Slab.

Flounder 45m VS 4a. John Biggar, Ian Brown. 3 June 2009.
Start at the very toe of the slab and climb the pleasant and easy but unprotected lower slabs to runners at 20m. Continue up towards the obvious triangular niche and enter it from the left. Flounder awkwardly up and leftwards (currently very mossy) to eventually reach a large grass terrace.

The Knee of Cairnsmore:
This small crag is the first encountered when following the approach detailed above, about 30mins walk from the end of the forestry road, across generally benign Galloway moor. The crag is easily seen and approached and is at NX 514 657. The crag is more easily angled than it first appears and there are three pleasant easy routes, all about 20m long. Descend either side. This crag is nice as a warm-up venue if you are heading for the Slab of the Spout or the Spout of the Clints. Protection can be sparse; the belay is another 10m back from the top of the crag.

Left Cheek 20m Very Difficult *. David McNicol, John Biggar. 20 April 2009.
Climb up and left from the lowest rocks and follow cracks to the top.

Wounded Knee 20m Very Difficult *. John Biggar, David McNicol. 20 April 2009.
Climb the groove in the arete and continue to the top.

Right Rib 20m Difficult. David McNicol, John Biggar. 20 April 2009.
Climb the ribbing on the right of the crag and continue to the top.

The Slab of the Spout:
A grand piece of Galloway granite, fairly clean and smooth and uninterrupted for 25m. Spout Slab is located about 100m south of the Spout of the Clints and about half-height on the cliff. There is a pleasant flat grassy base and a very pleasant outlook to the east. Loses the sun typically at 2–3pm. Protection is tricky to arrange and requires many small to medium cams and faith in small flaring cracks, luckily the cruxes of both routes are relatively low down. A 50 or 60m rope is needed to reach belays which are well back (and slightly right) from the top of the crag. Approach the Slab of the Spout as for the Knee above but continue onwards for about 20 minutes. The crag is clearly seen if following this approach.

Faith in Flares 25m HVS 4c/5a **. John Biggar, David McNicol. 20 April 2009.
Climb the vertical crack on the left of the slab with an awkward crux at 5m near the little overlap, protected by poor cam placements in flaring cracks! Continue more easily to the top.

Pao de Spout   25m   VS 4c *. David McNicol, John Biggar. 20 April 2009.
The main central crack which trends slightly leftwards, quite bold, possibly only
Hard Severe when cleaner.

Craigdews:
No Goat's Toe   50m   VS 4c. Iain Magill, Andrew Fraser. 22 July 2008.
Ten metres right of the start of the *Dark Side* is a steep, pale and relatively clean
prow, with a recess to its right. Climb the prow, continue up mossy rock, past a
vegetatious bulge then up further walls to belay at the top of a heather slope.

GALLOWAY SEA-CLIFFS, The Thirlstane, Right Wall:
Into the wind   E2 5b. David Wands. 3 May 2008.
Start up *The Rib*. Climb to reach the cut-back on to *Catechumen Groove*, but
instead hand-traverse left underneath the overhang and climb it at its widest part
with a big reach for the top hold.

Crammag Head:
The Black Slab   30m   Hard Severe 4b *. Andrew Fraser, Iain Magill. 28 June
2008.
An adventurous half-day trip, only accessible at low- to mid-tide. Further south
than the existing routes and just before the start of the hill of Dunman is a small
island, joined to but separated from the mainland. The landward side of this is a
large black slab, up which the route lies.

Access is by walking 200m uphill to the top of the prominent descent gully
just south of the Black Slab. Descend this, scramble over the col between the
Black Slab and the mainland then descend to the base of the Black Slab.

The climb traverses right onto the slab to avoid the initial overhanging bay,
then continues directly to the top of the slab. Descend over the top of the island
to descend the vegetatious line above the aforementioned col (VDiff).

To regain the top of the mainland opposite either retrace steps up the descent
gully or climb the innocuous shallow gully just left of the col (loose, vegetatious
and no protection and a rope placed down this in advance is recommended).

Many of the following routes have probably climbed before but not recorded.
All about 8–10m long.

Little Wall:
The small wall on the north side of the gully, immediately north of the main
Lighthouse Wall. The main feature is a huge hanging flake in the centre of the
crag. Great rock and steep, but the lines are not obvious.

Crackin' Corner   Severe **. John Biggar, Linda Biggar. 2 April 2009.
Climbs the crack and awkward left-sloping corner above.

Fly by Wire   Moderate *. John Biggar, Linda Biggar. 2 April 2009.
From the bottom of the descent gully climb diagonally leftwards passing behind
the giant flake. On the supposed first ascent of this steep Moderate the crux was
found to be protected by an in-situ wire!

Unnamed   Severe. Linda Biggar, John Biggar. 2 April 2009.
The wall just right of the big flake.

Slingsby's Slab   Difficult **. John Biggar, Linda Biggar. 2 April 2009.
Extremely steep for the grade but covered in jugs! The steep left-sloping slab at the right end of the wall.

Lighthouse Walls:
Unnamed   12m   Very Difficult *. Linda Biggar, John Biggar. 2 April 2009.
Step across the gully from *Marine Boy/Little Flasher* and climb the arete, avoiding the easier ground further left.

RATHO QUARRY:
Between Contracts   25m   HVS 5a. Andy Main, Tim Cross. 13 May 2008.
Start just right of *Shoskred*. Layback the flake, then surmount two giant blocks. Follow the chimney and crack straight up, then swing right onto the arete resisting the temptation to use the main crack of *Cracking-Up*. Swing back left to a ledge and exit straight up.

Baby Face   6m   4c. Fran Sheridan. 28 July 2008.
Climb the small face to the left of the entrance to the EICA, Ratho. Start at the right edge on good ledges, and continue to a hold on the right. Break round the roof to higher ledges to finish. No pro!

Onion Face   20m   Hard Severe 4b *. John Proctor, Joe Larner. 22 March 2009.
Between *Jungle Rock* and the *Grapes of Ratho*. Climb luxuriant and steepening vegetation direct to a ledge with a tree. Climb straight up to ledge at two-thirds height. Traverse right and climb a shallow groove to top.

EAST LOTHIAN, Yellow Craigs:
Who Forgot the Picnic   10m   Very Difficult *. Stephen Breuer, Martin Gillie, Stuart Campbell. 4 July 2008.
From the centre of the gorse-free bay, climb the stepped right-facing corner until it fades. Take the arete on the left to finish.
Note: *Introductory Slapping* is probably Difficult (or even Moderate).

Kae Heughs Fort (NT 763 518):
Squiggly Wiggly   20m   Severe. Terry Lansdown, Roy Harrison, Dave Frankland. 25 May 2009.
The route is on the first east-facing buttress, on the east end of the crag. Follow the obvious snaking fault with crack-line.

Squiggy Splosh   20m   Hard Severe. Terry Lansdown, Roy Harrison. 24 June 2009.
The route is in the middle of the crag, going up the face immediately to the left of *Splish Wiggly*, finishing on that route to avoid steep grass at the top.

Splish Wiggly   20m   Severe. Terry Lansdown, Roy Harrison, Dave Frankland. 15 June 2009.
This follows a line in the middle of the crag between two deep cracks facing each other NE and NW respectively.

Splish Splosh   20m   Severe. Roy Harrison, Terry Lansdown. 8 June 2009.
Follow the obvious deep crack 5m to right of *Splish Wiggly* to a ledge, then trend right up grassy steps.
Direct Finish   VS. Terry Lansdown, Roy Harrison, Dave Frankland. 8 June 2009.
From the grassy ledge, finish direct.

Note: See: <http://www.quicksnapper.com/ThinGrip/image/key-heughs-fort>

Traprain Law, Overhang Wall:
Piglet's Not Gay   20m   E1 5b *. Pete Reynolds, Jonnie Williams. 20 September 2008.
A straight variation of *Piglet*. Continue the line of the groove over the overhang and up the slab and corner above.

BERWICKSHIRE, Souter Area:
Usaidtheredbefish   10m   Hard Severe 4a. Michael Barnard. 2 April 2009.
On the south-east face of the Second Sight Fin and lying between *Gull Talk* and *The Fish Business* are three short corners (p416 in Lowland Outcrops, mentioned in the description for the latter route). Climb a line up the short corners to finish up the slab above (bold).

ST ABB'S HEAD:
There are number of felsite sea stacks in the NTS Nature Reserve. The rock is loose and climbing is not recommended. The route below is listed for historical purposes. Permission was sought and given by the Warden, climbed out of season and all equipment removed. Access to the Downies Goats stacks (NT 911 684) requires a steep scramble down the cliff which has no solid anchors.

Downies Goats West Stack   60m   Mild Severely Loose 4a. Ross Jones, John Sanders. 18 October 2008.
Scramble up on to an outcrop of rock to the south-west of the 40m west stack and belay. Descent is by simultaneous abseil or down-climbing the route.
1. 20m 3c Step across a gap onto the stack and climb a broken corner to a large stance on easy ground.
2. 40m 4a Climb easy ground to a headwall. Climb a ramp line forming a break on the right and follow loose ground along the ramp before climbing direct to the top.

BURNMOUTH AREA:
The following routes are on a small fin a few minutes walk south from Burnmouth harbour, walking towards the Maiden's Stone sea-stack.

Thinking of Bagels   10m   Severe. Robert Askew, John Proctor. 1 March 2009.
Climb the obvious crack towards the seaward end of the north face of the fin. Continue up the ridge to the top.

Extreme Gardening   10m   Severe. John Proctor, Robert Askew. 1 March 2009.
On the south face of the fin (landward side), climb the leftmost crack. The crack opens out, then blocky and vegetated ground leads to the top.

MISCELLANEOUS NOTES

The W.H. Murray Literary Prize

As a tribute to the late Bill Murray, whose mountain and environment writings have been an inspiration to many a budding mountaineer, the SMC have set up a modest writing prize, to be run through the pages of the Journal. The basic rules are set out below, and will be reprinted each year. The prize is run with a deadline of the end of April each year. So, assuming you are reading this in October, you have six months before next year's deadline in which to set pencil, pen or word processor on fire.

The Rules:

1. There shall be a competition for the best entry on Scottish Mountaineering published in the *Scottish Mountaineering Club Journal*. The competition shall be called the 'W.H. Murray Literary Prize', hereafter called the 'Prize'.

2. The judging panel shall consist of, in the first instance, the following: The current Editor of the *SMC Journal*; The current President of the SMC; and two or three lay members, who may be drawn from the membership of the SMC. The lay members of the panel will sit for three years after which they will be replaced.

3. If, in the view of the panel, there is in any year no entry suitable for the Prize, then there shall be no award that year.

4. Entries shall be writing on the general theme of 'Scottish Mountaineering', and may be prose articles of up to approximately 5000 words in length, or shorter verse. Entries may be fictional.

5. Panel members may not enter for the competition during the period of their membership.

6. Entries must be of original, previously unpublished material. Entries should be submitted to the Editor of the *SMC Journal* before the end of April for consideration that year. Contributions should preferably be word-processed and submitted via e-mail, although double-spaced typewritten hard copies will also be accepted. (See Office Bearers page at end of this Journal for address etc.) Any contributor to the SMC Journal is entitled to exclude their material from consideration for the Prize and should so notify the Editor of this wish in advance.

7. The prize will be a cheque for the amount £250.

8. Contributors may make different submissions in different years.

9. The decision of the panel is final.

10. Any winning entry will be announced in the *SMC Journal,* and will be published in the *SMC Journal* and on the SMC Web Site. Thereafter, authors retain copyright.

THE W.H. MURRAY LITERARY PRIZE 2009

THE WINNER of this year's W.H. Murray Prize for his article *Sgurr Thuilm* is club member Hamish Brown.

This year the editor was pleased to receive a healthy number of submissions and space considerations meant that he had the difficult task of having to omit some worthy articles. He is pleased to keep these on file for consideration in leaner years.

This year saw the 80th anniversary of the opening of the CIC Hut, the 70th Anniversary of the first Greater Traverse of the Cuillin, as well as the 50th Anniversary of the opening of the Coruisk Hut (Glasgow JMCS). The editor used this as an excuse, perhaps unfairly, to favour articles on the two themes of Ben Nevis and the Cuillin of Skye.

Some of the submissions this year were exceptionally long and the fact that the winner's piece was of more modest length will perhaps encourage restraint in future. However the three longest pieces were all well written and drew favourable comments.

Not perhaps a vintage year, but the winning article was a unaminous choice which leapt out at the judges. 'So did the author really meet Bonnie Prince Charlie on top of Sgurr Thuilm? Who knows? But this clever, charming and punchy treatment of an apparent blend of fact, faction and fiction is simply quite unlike anything else and had this reader quite beguiled. Not just with the concept, but the nifty execution that brings it to life and somehow renders it plausible. And all in remarkably few words.'

The profile of *Graham Macphee* by Ken Smith is a good read and gives a fine flavour of this forceful character and also the very different climbing scene on Ben Nevis more than 50 years ago. (It complements an excellent profile of Brian Kellett which Ken wrote for Climber & Rambler almost thirty years ago.) With *A Scotman's Duty* Gordon Smith has again written a very entertaining account of his youthful adventures on Ben Nevis and in the Alps. Although it doesn't have the impact of his winning piece last year, it still paints a fine picture of his younger days as a peniless but very talented climber.

Also overly long but extremely well written was *The Case of the Clandestine Case* by M.J. Conrad-Doyle. This has a very authentic Conan Doyle ring to it and races along at a compelling pace. *Buried Treasure* by former prizewinner Peter Biggar was also regarded as: 'Well written and interesting, some nice touches (the recurring dragon reference, Skye family background, hints of what Roger and the author learned about each other on the descent)...'

Snakes and Ladders by Ian Sykes was an amusing read. Also enjoyable was *Last on the List* by Phil Gribbon: 'Touching tale with some universal themes (things done, maybe not done and needing doing to be sure) with some nice variations of rhythm ("Oh! The top, at last. Stop. Sink. Soporific sun.") and effective use of slightly unexpected wording ("The long solstice days of summer arrived."). Perhaps occasionally confusing in swinging back and forward through time, but overall very likeable and easy to identify with.'

A poignant piece by new club member Helen Forde about her father and his 'immortality' was also admired. At last an article from the ladies.

Congratulations to Hamish Brown, and many thanks to all contributors. As usual a copy of the winning article can be downloaded from the SMC website.

SCOTTISH WINTER NOTES 2008–9

By Simon Richardson

WINTER CAME early to the Scottish mountains. The first blizzards hit the hills at the beginning of October, but it was a sustained period of northerly winds and heavy snowfalls at the end of the month that had many winter climbers enthusiastically searching out their axes and crampons.

The early snows led to a flurry of routes in the North-West and in the Cairngorms, and sustained cool weather through November and December resulted in a superb series of hard new mixed routes on Ben Nevis. After the customary Christmas thaw, heavy snowfalls in January and February raised everyone's hopes for a classic ice season. Alas, it was not to be, and despite cold forecasts, February fizzled out in warm drizzly rain and a deep thaw. More cold weather in early March provided another spate of hard routes, before temperatures warmed up again leaving Ben Nevis the late season venue of choice.

NORTHERN HIGHLANDS

Without doubt the most significant ascent in the Northern Highlands, and one of the most important Scottish winter routes for several years, was the first ascent of *The God Delusion* (IX,9) on the Giant's Wall on Beinn Bhan. This 200m-high vertical cliff in Coire nan Fhamair between *Gully of the Gods* and *Great Overhanging Gully* has an aura of impregnability that is truly jaw-dropping. The sandstone face is close to vertical, bristles with overhangs and has no continuous lines of weakness. Its defining gullies are sought after winter prizes in their own right, and when Martin Moran and Paul Tattersall climbed the line of *The Godfather* (VIII,8) up the left side of the wall in 2002 it was seen as a significant step forward in North-West climbing. The Godfather finishes up a vertical corner, the only significant feature on the upper wall, so when news of a new route to its right appeared on the Internet, it created real excitement.

The God Delusion (IX,9) was the work of Pete Benson and Guy Robertson, one of the most successful Scottish winter partnerships of recent years. They are no strangers to the cliff and made a spirited second ascent attempt on The Godfather with Es Tresidder a couple of seasons ago. Unfortunately Benson fell within a few metres of easy ground at the top of the route and broke his ankle. The ensuing retreat down seven pitches of vertical to overhanging terrain in the dark, followed by a long walk out was a sobering experience, but both Benson and Robertson were struck by the possibility of adding another line to the wall.

They first attempted The God Delusion in December, but Robertson took a big fall when he pulled off a TV-sized block on the sixth pitch. They returned a few days later, climbed the first two pitches in the dark and by early afternoon they had reached pitch 6. It was very steep and there was no obvious way to go. 'You look up and all you see are roofs,' Robertson recounted. 'But incredibly each roof was fringed by a turf moustache! I tried to probe a way through the steepest section to the left, but on the second try I looked across and saw a more promising line. For about 15 metres the climbing was pretty futuristic, but when mantelling onto an undercut ledge I realised that I was absolutely spent. I said to

Pete that I'd lost it and just let go. One of my tools pulled, but the second tool stayed in and I was left hanging from my spring leash. Fortunately I was able to prusik back up the leash and continue the pitch.'

December days are short, and they completed the last couple of pitches in the dark to emerge on the summit plateau under a brilliant starlit sky. The pair thought the crux pitch was technical 9, but every other pitch was 7 or 8 making it the most difficult winter climb yet achieved in the Northern Highlands. But it was not just the sustained difficulty of the route that caught everyone's imagination, but the style the route was climbed. 'If you stick to traditional ethics' Robertson explained, 'there's no avoiding the total commitment required to climb hard mixed routes in Scotland, especially new ones. No summer knowledge, no pre-inspection, no fixed gear. Just rock up and go for it, bottom to top. That's the gauntlet; anything else is heresy.'

A series of cold snaps in the early and middle part of the winter brought the North-West into good condition. One of the highlights was the first winter ascent of the very technical *Hung, Drawn and Quartered* (VIII,8) on Sgurr nan Gillean on Skye by Martin Moran and Nick Dixon. Graded E4 in summer and overhanging for much of its height, this is said to be the most difficult summer gully climb on the island. Back on the mainland, Ian Small and I made the first winter ascent of *Castro* (VII,8), the prominent line of weakness on the 300m-high Magic Bow wall on Sgurr an Fhidhleir, and nearby on the West Face of Quinag, Andy Nisbet, John Lyall and Mark 'Ed' Edwards made the first ascent of the spectacular overhanging chimney of *Assynt of Man* (VI,6).

Beinn Eighe was another scene of intense activity and the Fuselage Wall area saw a number of new additions including *Spitfire* (VII,8 – Viv Scott and Steve Ashworth), *Mosquito* (V,7 – Andy Nisbet, John Lyall and Jonathan Preston), *War Games* (VI,7 – Nisbet and Lyall), *Grand Slam* (V,7 – Nisbet, Lyall and Pete MacPherson) and *Ace* (VI,7 – Malcolm Bass and Simon Yearsley). On West Central Wall, the showpiece crag on the mountain, Guy Robertson and Tony Stone pulled off a notable coup with the first winter ascent of *Chop Suey* (VIII,8). This summer E1, which was described as 'dangerously loose' by the first ascensionists, resulted in a superb winter route.

The big event on Beinn Eighe was the first ascent of *Bruised Violet* (VIII,9), to the right of Chop Suey, by Ian Parnell and Andy Turner. After a couple of failures and a nasty avalanche incident earlier in the season, Parnell was in a determined mood when he returned in early March. His first attempt to climb the initial overhang on the second pitch was thwarted when the ice clipper krab on his harness became wedged into a crack. Higher up he went the wrong way, down climbed, and then had his arms lock up due to cramp and he dropped a tool. The pair eventually finished the five-pitch route in darkness. For Parnell, a new route on West Central Wall was the realisation of a long held dream, and he explained afterwards that the route 'doesn't really follow the slabbier summer lines of the two E2s here, but searches out steeper ground with deeper better hooking cracks.... The hardest thing on this wall is finding the line and convincing yourself that the route will go through such hostile looking territory.'

CAIRNGORMS

The Nisbet–Lyall team added a number of good routes in the Cairngorms. On their familiar haunt of Sron na Lairige above the Lairig Ghru they found

Ghrupie (V,5), which takes a groove on the left side of the buttress containing *Ghrusome*. On the more remote Coire Sputan Dearg they were joined by Jonathan Preston for *Hate Mail* (VII,7), a winter version of the summer route *Blackmail* that follows a series of ramp lines on the right side of The Black Tower. The same team also continued exploring Lurcher's Crag and added a number of good new middle grade routes, including the fine *Wolfstone Gully* (VI,7). Lyall first attempted this prominent feature at the back of the amphitheatre in the centre of the crag in 1997 and he had been waiting ever since for enough ice in the main groove to form. 'Sure enough there wasn't enough ice,' Nisbet explained, 'so we climbed a crack-line on the right. If the ice was ever to form, it would be a great pitch.'

The early February snowfalls blocked many roads and made access to the high crags difficult and time consuming in the deep powder. Brain Duthie and Sandy Simpson took good advantage of the cold conditions with a repeat of *Wild Cat Wall* in Winter Corrie in Glen Clova. As they approached the headwall, they noticed an independent line of grooves to the left, which they followed to give the two pitch *Tiger Finish* (VI,7) a fine addition, and now the hardest pitches on the cliff.

Over on Lochnagar, Iain Small and I climbed a difficult direct start to *Shadow Buttress A Direct*. *The Hooded Groove* (VII,8) takes the prominent double-overhang corner in the centre of the face, and judging by the rotting retreat pegs it had been first attempted over 20 years ago. On the west side of the mountain on The Stuic, we put a long-term objective to rest with the first ascent of *A Wall Too Far* (VII,8), the impressively steep feature to the left of *The Stooee Chimney*.

Andy Nisbet made a couple of visits to Coire Bhrochain on Braeriach. His objective was a line based on the edge of the buttress containing *Brochain Slabs* overlooking West Gully. Climbing solo on his first visit he was diverted by a line of ice up the centre of the slabs to the right. *Bhrochain Spectre* (IV,3) turned out to be an exciting outing with the sun breaking through the clouds and softening the snow on the south-facing crag. 'Conditions were strange on the crux,' he told me. 'Both axes and feet seemed to hold well even though the snow seemed a bit soft. It continued spooky up the top snow covered slab to a spectacular finish up a snow arête where there was a lucky break in the cornice.' Nisbet returned a week later with John Lyall, and climbed *High Jinx* (IV,4), his original objective.

At the end of a rather warm and unsettled March, a cold northerly blast of snow brought the higher cliffs into condition. Andy Nisbet and Ed Edwards made a couple of good additions to the Mess of Pottage in Coire and t-Sneachda in the Northern Corries. *Technicoloured Dream Crack* (VII,7) was based on a recent summer line and relied on some very thin ice, and *Tasker* (V,6) takes the crack-line some ten metres right of *Yukon Jack*.

CENTRAL HIGHLANDS

Tony Stone and Viv Scott visited Stob Coire an Laoigh in the Grey Corries and climbed *Full Frontal* (VII,8), the arête between *Taliballan* and *Pentagon*. The route is based on two hanging grooves, linked by a horizontal crack, and features some superb and bold wall climbing with an overhanging off-width to finish. 'Tony made a superb lead of the main difficulties, and made it all look depressingly easy,' Scott told me afterwards. Also of note, was the first winter ascent of *Sgian Dubh* (V,6) on Garbh Bheinn by Alasdair Fulton and Neil Adams. Further west, Andy Nisbet and Sonya Drummond made the long approach into Ben Alder and climbed *Kryptonite* (IV,4) up the centre of the triangular face between *Smallville* and *Bheoil Pfeiler* on the Alderwand face of Garbh Coire Beag.

Across in the Mamores, Dave MacLeod and Malcolm Kent added the fierce sounding *Yo Bro* (VIII,9) to the granite crag on Mullach nan Coirean. The route took the prominent central groove on the cliff with an undercut start. It took MacLeod over an hour to climb the first few metres, and he thought the moves were harder than the indoor mixed climbing competition at the Ice Factor the night before. Kent, who has extensive dry tool experience, thought the difficulties warranted M8+, but it was the on-sight nature of the ascent that made the experience really memorable. 'After nearly three hours, my arms were almost spent,' MacLeod explained on his blog. 'I found myself wobbling into undercut torques on a block (that moved!), and staring out a big turf ledge right above. It was nice to be back in fully committed land again.'

BEN NEVIS

Ben Nevis is fast becoming the venue of choice for early season mixed climbing. Big news in October was the third ascent of *The Secret* (VIII,9) by Blair Fyffe and Tony Stone, with Stone making an impressively smooth lead of the awe-inspiring second pitch. Strong northerly winds and heavy snowfall at the end of November brought the high mixed routes rapidly into condition and Rich Cross and Andy Benson were quick off the mark with an early repeat of the modern classic *Sioux Wall* (VIII,8) on Number Three Gully Buttress.

Two days later they returned to the mountain in a raging blizzard. Conditions were awful high up so the pair decided to attempt the first winter ascent of *Heidbanger*, a three pitch E1 on Central Trident Buttress to the right of the classic ice line of *Mega Route X*. Benson led the first pitch up the summer *Cranium Start*, an awkward overhanging crack leading to an off-width slot perched in the lip of an overhang. Above, a steep exit from the belay cave led to an intimidating blank wall. 'Veins of snow promised hooks and gear, but delivered only blank rounded seams,' Cross recounted afterwards. 'It was all slightly disappointing. Thirty feet of teetering, thin hooks, long reaches, and spaced pro finally brought a blob of turf into reach – phew!' Benson completed the final pitch in the dark, a time consuming combination of powder covered slabs, unhelpful blind grooves and hard won gear.

Although the route was given a similar grade to Sioux Wall at VIII,8, it is clearly a more demanding proposition. 'Heidbanger had spaced gear on the second pitch,' Cross told me. 'I climbed it on tenuous hooks, so it felt bold. The first pitch was very strenuous, and the top very insecure on slabs or blind grooves with hard won protection. By comparison, Sioux Wall felt well protected and very positive.' With many climbers reluctant to overgrade their routes, the Grade VIII level now covers a wide spectrum of difficulty, and more ascents of these climbs will be required to achieve a consensus.

Andy Benson returned to Ben Nevis a few days later with Ian Parnell to make the first winter ascent of *Devastation*, another summer E1 on South Trident Buttress. Parnell had set his sights on this objective for a couple of seasons and the pair was rewarded with a sustained and absorbing climb. The route had two technically difficult pitches, but the protection was generally good, and they graded their ascent a surprisingly reasonable VII,8. Choosing a steep rocky mixed climb was a good choice, because those that ventured onto more easily angled mixed climbs that day such as Castle Ridge, struggled with unconsolidated snow and unfrozen turf and had to retreat. The modern mixed climbs on the Trident Buttresses do not rely on frozen turf so are excellent objectives early in the season before the mountain is properly frozen.

In December, Pete Davies and Tim Marsh pulled off a big tick with the first winter ascent of *The Brass Monkey* (VII,8) on the east side of Tower Ridge. This imposing corner which bounds the right side of Echo Wall is a rarely climbed summer HVS, but was an obvious winter target, which had repelled at least one previous attempt. Late in the season the foot of route builds up into an impressive snow cone but early in the season it was bare rock. 'We expected the first two pitches to be straightforward,' Davies explained, 'but they proved quite tricky, with powder covered rock and some committing moves on thin ice. These probably bank out later in the season, which would make the overall route less sustained. The three pitches up the main corner gave some of the best mixed climbing I've done, on a par with things like *Neanderthal* and *Central Grooves*. Conditions were good – lightly rimed, well frozen turf, powder on anything that would hold it and the cracks not too icy.' All pitches were led on sight, although Davies fell off seconding after dropping his headtorch. Marsh heroically prusiked the last pitch in total darkness dragging both rucksacks behind him, and the descent of Tower Ridge under heavy powder with only one torch took a while. They eventually reached the car park at 12.30am after a 19 hour round trip.

Iain Small and I made the other significant addition to Ben Nevis in December when we climbed *The Cone Gatherers* (VIII,7) on the North Wall of Carn Dearg. The route takes a line left of the *Kellett's North Wall Route* before finishing up the unclimbed triangular headwall, to the right of *Waterfall Gully*. The final overhanging gully was reminiscent of a mini *Gully of the Gods* on Beinn Bhan. The route has all the hallmarks of an Iain Small Nevis route, with sustained climbing on the lower wall including a bold rising traverse across a vertical wall that was protected by a single hand-placed ice hook. High up in Coire na Ciste, Rich Cross and Nick Williams made the second ascent of *Cold Play* (VIII,8), last season's addition up the steep pillar right of *Archangel*. They found an alternative crux pitch, which they named the *Snow Patrol Variant* (VIII,8).

In early February, Pete MacPherson and Ed Edwards continued the trend of hard new mixed routes on the Ben with the first winter ascent of *The Minge* (VII,8) on South Trident Buttress. This rarely climbed VS (it may not have seen a second summer ascent) takes a wet crack line on the right side of South Trident Buttress, and as one of the last summer climbs in the corrie not to have been climbed in winter, it was an obvious target. MacPherson first tried the line last year with Graham Briffett, but his tool ripped on the second pitch and he fell onto a hex that was his only runner. They felt the route was a little too bold for their liking and retreated. On 4 February this year, a determined MacPherson returned with Ed Edwards, and spent three hours leading the second pitch. It was difficult to find protection and he had to chip away at concrete hard dirt in the few cracks to find gear placements. Edwards continued up onto the third pitch but the weather turned bad as it was getting dark so they abseiled off in a blizzard.

They returned two days later with slightly better weather and climbed up to their high point. 'Ed cruised the third pitch,' MacPherson told me. 'He crossed a scary slab with virtually nothing for his feet and little for his tools to a crack which was steep but had good placements. From there we headed up *Pinnacle Arête* for a couple of pitches to the top. I'm so glad to have finally got it done!'

In early March, one of the most glittering prizes in Scottish climbing fell to Andy Turner and Tony Stone when they made the first winter ascent of *Sassenach*. This provocatively named climb was first climbed by Joe Brown and Don Whillans in April 1954 and was the first route to breach the impressive front face of Carn Dearg Buttress. Sassenach takes the prominent chimney in the steep central section, and is defended at its base by a severely overhanging corner. Brown and Whillans aided through this and then continued up the chimneys and grooves above. The route was graded Very Severe (the highest grade at the time) and was climbed free 15 years later by Steve Wilson at E3 6a, although the chimneys themselves are thought to be worth E1 5b in their own right.

A winter ascent of this great line had been considered for nearly 30 years and Al Rouse talked about it in the early 1980s. The route is rarely in condition, so ever the innovator, Rouse had a plan to divert a stream at the top of the cliff so it ran down the line and would ice up the following winter. Rouse never did attempt the route, but during the cold snowy winters of the 1980s the lower section did indeed ice up. Snow melt from the ledge above formed an icefall that led past the aid section, but the upper chimneys remained typically bare and nobody took up the challenge.

The explosion of mixed climbing standards over the last few years has transformed Sassenach from an unlikely ice climb to a demanding technical mixed challenge. Carn Dearg Buttress is not often in mixed condition, but it does hold hoar frost and powder snow most winters. Turner attempted the line with Steve Ashworth in February 2008, and succeeded in climbing the lower part of the route through the aid section using two rest points, but the pair ran out of steam and abseiled off. They left a few pieces of gear in place in the overhanging corner that they were unable to retrieve because the route was too steep.

Early in March 2009, Turner returned with Tony Stone to attempt Sassenach once again. The pair was full of confidence having made the third winter ascent of *Centurion* (VIII,8) with Iain Small three days before in a very swift eight hours. More importantly Carn Dearg Buttress was white with powder snow. 'This is a route that needs specific conditions,' Turner explained on his blog. 'The whole of the Ben can be plastered white after a storm but that part of Carn Dearg always stays black. What it needs is the "Perfect Storm" – north-west gale force winds and loads of snow.'

Stone led the first pitch and soon Turner was facing the crux. 'When Don Whillans first led this pitch he used several pieces of aid,' Turner continued. 'There are no useful footholds anywhere. On the left wall everything slopes the wrong way. Clipping the frozen Friend and Bulldog I placed the previous winter, it never crossed my mind that the Friend wouldn't hold a fall. Trying to remember any useful holds was useless, as ice had changed the whole appearance of the pitch. At one point my feet ripped and I was left hanging with my feet dangling in space. I've never understood the use of "power screaming" but I found myself screaming my lungs out just to force myself on. Several sketchy balancy moves later saw me standing relieved at the base of the chimney.'

Stone immediately went to work on the next pitch. 'He set off slowly, getting higher and higher, and further and further into the mountain. The chimney was drawing him in. At one point he had to take his helmet off just to turn his head to see where he was going. I think a good old gritstone apprenticeship was the order of the day. Eventually the thrutching ended and a belay was found.' The rest of the chimney passed relatively uneventfully and the pair finished up some beautiful icy grooves. They reached the summit of the buttress, just as darkness fell, with the historic first winter ascent of Sassenach (IX,9) in the bag.

The winter ascent of Sassenach was very impressive and deserved to hit the headlines, but incredibly, it was equalled at the end of March with the first winter ascent of *Metamorphosis* by Iain Small and Gareth Hughes. This sustained three-pitch route on Central Trident Buttress has a reputation for being a stiff summer E2. The pair started up The Cranium Start to Heidbanger, that was climbed by Rich Cross and Andy Benson earlier in the season, before moving right. Iced up cracks on the first pitch made it difficult to protect, but the ice was essential on the crucial third pitch. 'Leaving the belay there were no cracks, but fortunately the flat holds were covered with a thin layer of ice,' Small told me. 'It felt very bold, but once I reached the big flake above I knew I was going to do it. The upper wall was very tenuous too, with no gear in sight, but I knew if I fell off it would be into space, so I just focused on the climbing.' Metamorphosis was graded VIII,9 and rates as one of the most difficult winter routes on Ben Nevis. It was a fitting finale to an outstanding season where standards have been continuously pushed and the pace has been truly breathtaking. One can only dream of what next winter will bring!

MOUNTAIN RESCUE COMMITTEE OF SCOTLAND INCIDENT REPORT 2008

Mountaineering Incidents 2008

1. There was a 16% rise in the number of incidents compared to 2007. This may be due to better reporting by teams or the effect of the credit crunch giving people more time off! Mountain Rescue Teams now report standbys/alerts and incidents where casualties are talked off the hill.

2. Hillwalking in summer (47% of incidents), hillwalking in winter (28%), and winter climbing (12%) are the three most common categories of incident reported by teams.

3. The number of fatalities is the same as reported in 2007.

4. Technology: The first documented rescue in Europe initiated by a SPOT Satellite GPS Messenger took place on 12 May 2008 when a walker set off his device in Glen Etive. Mobile phones, text messages and even e-mails to team websites have been used by walkers and climbers in need of assistance to alert Mountain Rescue Teams and the Police. One wonders what further developments the future will bring.

5. A number of mountaineering accidents have been reported on the UKClimbing.com Forums by members of the public. This has generated varying responses from the users of this website. For example, there was a thought-provoking article by the partner of a mountaineer involved in a fatal accident on Fuar Tholl. I received permission to use this article in my report on the accident. Any lessons learned from such incidents are passed on to the Scottish Mountain Safety Forum. I am now a member of the Scottish Mountain Safety Forum and will be able to provide up-to-date information to members. I have also liaised with the Scottish Avalanche Information Service and the Mountain Weather Information Service. Mountaineers use both these services on a frequent basis for guidance and advice.

6. Helicopters from the Royal Air Force, Royal Navy, Maritime and Coastguard Agency, Police and Ambulance Services continue to provide outstanding assistance to Mountain Rescue Teams. Unfortunately there are some casualties who think that if they need assistance for very minor ailments they will be 'plucked off the hill' in any weather. Fortunately the Police, Mountain Rescue Team Leaders and the ARCC (Aeronautical Rescue Co-ordination Centre) monitor this problem and manage to filter such requests!

7. 'Border Reivers' Scottish Mountain Rescue Teams and SARDA Southern have assisted the Rescue Services in England on at least eight occasions and these incidents are not included in the Scottish figures.

8. The Police, Mountain Rescue Teams, MCA, RAF and RN Helicopters and the ARCC are thanked for all their input and for assisting in completing incident reports. In addition thanks to Mike Walker for his IT Support and Bob Sharp for all his historical and analytical advice. Scottish Mountain Rescue Teams spent just under 28,000 man-hours assisting the public in 2008.

Table 1: Mountain incidents

Year	Incidents	Fatalities	Injured	No Trace	Persons Assisted
2008	387	20	198	3	518
2007	333	20	154	2	522
2006	315	30	156	1	469
2005	321	27	173	4	447
2004	308	18	159	1	419
2003	289	19	151	3	393

Non-Mountaineering Incidents 2008

These are on the increase (12% up on the figure for 2007). This seems to be mainly due to an increase in the number of searches for suicidal/depressed persons and the elderly. Clearly, the use of some MRTs by the Police is changing.

Table 2: Non-mountain incidents

Year	Incidents	Fatalities	Injured	No Trace	Persons Assisted
2008	140	37	25	11	133
2007	125	28	29	12	131
2006	117	19	32	3	117
2005	114	16	28	9	120
2004	86	17	15	3	81
2003	99	15	24	14	101

Incidents by Mountain Areas

Next year it should be possible to return to giving details of individual incidents by mountain areas. Information last appeared in the Journal in this format in 2002.

Please note

The MRC of S Statistics are copyright the MRC of S. The information may be reproduced free of charge, in any format or medium, for research, private study, or for internal circulation within an organisation. This is subject to it being reproduced accurately, and not used in a misleading manner. The material must be acknowledged as Mountain Rescue Committee of Scotland copyright, and the title of the publication specified.

D. 'Heavy' Whalley
MRC of S Statistician

100 YEARS AGO: THE CLUB IN 1909

THE 20TH ANNUAL Meeting and Dinner took place on Friday 4 December 1908 in the North British Station Hotel, Edinburgh, with Gilbert Thomson presiding. Treasurer Nelson announced a balance of £222 6s 2d, which together with the Life Membership Fund brought the Club's total funds to £527 14s, of which all but a few pounds were invested in 4% South Australian Government Stock. Secretary Clark announced 16 new members, bringing the total to 182, and Librarian Goggs reported that 40 new volumes and 60 new slides had been added to the collections. At the Reception preceding the meeting, Secretary Clark showed several slides demonstrating colour photography. Some of these appeared in the Journal for September 1909, illustrating a 12-page paper outlining the tedious procedures necessary to produce such images – a heroic process to daunt all but the most zealous photographer. Indeed, the Journal in question was daunting throughout, offering beside Clark's piece only a rambling sermon on 'Courage in Climbing' by Naismith – devoid of Scottish reference, a repulsive essay about the new craze of 'ski-running' by Allan Arthur, and a 27-page botanical paper about the 'Berries of Scotland' by John Macmillan worthy only of the dreary volumes of the Royal Society. One can well imagine Joe Stott hurling it across the room in disgust. Certainly it was a strange conclusion for Douglas's 18 years as Editor: perhaps the effort of producing his magnificent guide to Skye for Volume IX, and finishing the eight-year-long Guide Book project, had exhausted him.

The New Year Meet was held at the Killin Hotel, and attended by 23 members and 5 guests. Preceding blizzards persuaded many to travel encumbered by ski, but Hogmanay brought a prodigious thaw; the snow was soon gone, and little was achieved. On the 2nd, William Boyd, Ling and Raeburn drove to Luib in a wagonette to keep a tryst with seven members of the LSCC below the north face of Stobinian, where they cavorted in a short icy gully (the male element serving as porters rather than guides), before joining the Ladies Meet for tea at Crianlarich and returning to Killin by train. On the 3rd, Boyd, MacRobert, Raeburn and Austen Thomson (guest) managed an ascent of the *Great Gully* of Creag na Caillich. This gully was first climbed in 1902 by Gillon, Mackay and Geoffrey Young, and had previously defied Lawson and Raeburn in 1898. An overflow Meet of eight members and three guests was held at Inveroran. Again, frothing at the mouth for ski-running, they found a flood on the ground floor on Hogmanay morning. Only sodden hill-walks were managed, some by ingenious use of the hotel boat, but the evenings were enlivened by debates and games of Piladex (indoor volleyball with a balloon).

The early months of the year saw several members running about on their new ski. Even Naismith succumbed, plunging down from Carn Sguliard over heather and grass in happy abandon – 'the pace was tremendous, and many unrehearsed pirouettes and somersaults were indulged in'.[1] Henry Alexander reported better results from the Cairngorms, with the Aberdeen members running hither and thither from late February through March. He proudly trumpeted, 'This winter the Post Office supplied the postman at Braemar with ski, and during the

---

[1] *SMCJ* 1909, X, 270

snowstorm he used them regularly between Braemar and Inverey. In view of the success of the experiment, the Post Office authorities plan to equip other postmen in rural areas with ski. This is the first official recognition of ski-running in this country'.[2] Dr and Mrs Inglis Clark again preferred the Alps. Arriving in February, they skied some small peaks around the Arlberg and Davos.

On the way to the Easter Meet at Fort William (8–12 April), six members combined with seven LSCC members in a stunning assault on Beinn an Dòthaidh, making two difficult new climbs. This forms the subject of a separate note below. Dr Clark also dallied on the way to the Meet, taking advantage of his 15 hp Humber motor to climb the *Great Ridge* of Garbh Bheinn with son Charles and the Walker cousins.[3] Fort William's Alexandra, Caledonian and Imperial Hotels accommodated 45 members and eight guests, breaking last year's record turnout. On Friday Raeburn, Ling, Gibbs and Mounsey climbed *Tower Ridge* in six hours, including the Boulder by the *West Ridge* and finishing by the *Recess Route*, while Goodeve, Workman and Young, just arrived from Glasgow, were repelled from *The Castle* by a series of ice avalanches. On Saturday, Raeburn, Goggs, Thomson and Unna climbed the *North-East Buttress*, beginning with an ascent of the slabs to the right of *Slingsby's Chimney*; Workman, Young, Goodeve, Macalister, and MacRobert climbed *Tower Ridge*, again including the Boulder; Euan Robertson, White, Edwards, and Menzies climbed *Castle Ridge*; and Garden, Gibbs, Miller, Mackay, Mounsey, and Russell climbed the *Great Ridge* of Garbh Bheinn. On Sunday, Goodeve, Glover, Ling, the Walkers, and Worsdell drove to the head of Glen Nevis and set off from there at 8 a.m. on the route march to the *North-East Ridge* of Aonach Beag, roping up in two groups at 1.15 p.m. Below the final gendarme, Ling, Glover and Harry Walker decided to try a new variation to the right, while the others followed the normal route. Failing on their variation, Ling's party made the strange decision to descend the whole ridge and retrace the route back to Glen Nevis. Fortunately a trap was waiting, but even so they didn't sit down to their dinner until 10.50 p.m.[4] Monday was a poor day, but Collins, Ling and Naismith struggled up *North Castle Gully* through the blizzard. Meanwhile, having cycled to Kingshouse Inn on the previous day, Raeburn surprised two visiting English climbers, W.A. Brigg and C.C. Tucker, expecting some rock climbing, by taking them up *Crowberry Gully* in full icy condition complemented by snowstorms throughout, and including an avalanche.[5]

Edred Corner and his medical friends, Drs Johns and Pinches, continued their Munro-ological investigations at Easter, assisted by Mrs Corner and by Howie and Meares, who joined up with them after the Meet. As in 1908, several aneroids were carried, the Quoich Hills, the Grey Corries and the Mamores were surveyed, and Corner delivered a detailed report.[6] Perhaps the most remarkable height reported was 3055ft for Am-Bàthaich (Quoich). Although this height was given in the 1921 revision of the Tables, and Corner noted a drop of 440 feet,

[2] *SMCJ* 1909, X, 346

[3] *SMCJ* 1910, XI, 61–9, 'A Roundabout Journey to the Fort William Meet, 1909'

[4] Ling's Diary, Book 8, p4 (Alpine Club Library)

[5] *SMCJ* 1911, XI, 255–62, 'The Crowberry North Gully, Buchaille Etive'

[6] *SMCJ* 1909, X, 348–57

Am-Bàthaich was not promoted to separate mountain status. [It's now given as only 892m. Ed]

In May, Ling and Glover made their first foray into the Fionn Loch area, exploring and describing Beinn Lair and Martha's Peak, but little else of note was recorded until the summer exodus abroad. Solly and Rohde attended the newly-formed Alpine Club of Canada's Summer Camp at Banff, climbing several 10,000ft peaks. The entire Clark family drove to the Dolomites and back in the Humber, climbing peaks in the Brenta, Marmolada, Sassolungo and Sella groups. Most members enjoyed very poor weather in the Alps. Ling and Raeburn managed the Aiguille du Midi, were guided up the Aiguille de l'M and Petit Charmoz by a Miss C.M. Campbell, and failed high on the Moine Ridge of the Verte because of a troublesome German climber whom they had picked up along the route. After this setback, they were pleased to get up the Grépon in difficult icy condition. Bad weather drove them from Montenvers to Macugnaga whence they climbed the *East Face* of Monte Rosa and crossed to Switzerland. They then portered for Ruth Raeburn, Miss E. Gray and Miss N. Yovitchitch on the Rimpfischhorn, before finishing their holiday with a traverse of the Wellenkuppe and Ober Gabelhorn. The Walker cousins from Dundee made an enterprising visit to the Lofotens in August, finding 'the worst summer for forty years'. Despite this, three unnamed peaks to the south of Rulten (two of them new) were climbed, then the awkward Rulten itself, and finally eight unnamed peaks (six new) around the head of Meraftasdalen. They were able to reach these remote regions by means of a primitive motorboat hired from Svolvaer, and elaborate camping arrangements.

As in the spring/early summer, very little activity was recorded in the autumn. The weather may have been unusually bad. It was certainly bad in Wales, where the British monthly record for rainfall of 56 inches was achieved in October!

                                                                Robin N. Campbell

TWO OLD NEW ROUTES ON BEINN AN DÒTHAIDH

BOOK 7, page 80, of William Ling's Diary, held in the Alpine Club Archives, records an ascent of Beinn an Dòthaidh on 8 April 1909 by a large party, consisting of George Lissant Collins, William Douglas, William Garden, William N. Ling, Alexander M. Mackay, and Harold Raeburn (SMC); and Miss M. Inglis Clark, Miss D. Gillies, Misses A. & Pauline Ranken, Miss Ruth Raeburn, and Misses J.F. & Lucy Smith (LSCC).

The occasion was created by a coincidence of the LSCC Easter Meet at Inveroran and the SMC Easter Meet in Fort William. The party gathered at Bridge of Orchy around 9 o'clock, climbed in the North-East Corrie of Beinn an Dòthaidh, and thereafter proceeded to Inveroran by brake and to Fort William by train. Ling records that the party split into three mixed ropes below the North-East Face, having tossed coins to choose routes. From the photographs included in his Diary, together with his text, it is obvious that these arrangements were made at the back of the corrie at the bottom of the run-out of *West Gully*. According to the report in our Journal, 'One group [took] the main gully [*West Gully*, first climbed in 1894], another the subsidiary gully to the left, whilst the

SMC Easter Meet 2009 – Inchnadamph

back row l. to r. - G. Cohen, J. Hay, G. MacNair, I. Smart, M. Smart (guest), P. Gribbon, P. Biggar, D. Lang, C. Stead, C. Forrest, P. Brian, R. Campbell, R. Allen

front row l. to r. - Rona (guest), W. McKerrow, D. Rubens (President), C. Anton (guest), H. Forde, P. MacDonald, D. Broadhead, J. Fowler third ascended the well-defined arête on the buttress running up the right side of the main gully.'[1]

The route followed by the second group – described by Ling as 'a long, narrow, icy gully' must be the line of *Taxus*, mistakenly given in the current guidebook to Arthur Ewing and Sandy Trees in 1969. Twenty years later, Mabel Inglis Clark described this ascent in some detail. 'All went well with my party until we were faced with a very steep rock face, entirely plastered with ice, and slightly overhanging at the top. Here my leadership skills broke down entirely, and Mr Collins had to take the lead. He cut handholds and footholds on the icy face, and as if by magic he was soon over what appeared to me to be an insurmountable difficulty. After bringing me up, he left me to reassume the responsibilities of leadership, while he unroped and traversed to the right across a narrow sloping ledge of snow, and so gained the summit of the mountain.'[2] It is clear from Miss Clark's account that they finished the route by traversing off to the right at the bifurcation of the gully above its principal difficulties, whereas Ewing and Trees forked to the left at this point. Unfortunately, she doesn't identify the other two climbers on her rope.

Ling was in the third group, together with Ruth Raeburn, Lucy Smith and Sandy Mackay. Their route on the arête of the buttress, which started with 'a very steep and awkward corner' must be the line of *Stairway to Heaven*, mistakenly given in the current guidebook to D. Evans & A. Kay in 1982. The lead was shared by Lucy Smith (bottom half) and Ruth Raeburn (top half, above 'a snowy platform'). The composition of the *West Gully* party is not recorded in any of the three accounts of the day, but Miss Clark noted that there were two SMC members in each party. Raeburn might have been the unidentified male member of Miss Clark's party, but this is unlikely, since Collins was allowed to grapple with the crux. So it may be that Raeburn opted for the easy and previously-ascended *West Gully*. He may just have lost the toss, or – perhaps more likely, since he was roped to three of the less experienced ladies – he may have chosen it as a suitable place to train these novice members in mountain craft, a role he fulfilled frequently in the early days of the LSCC. I had hoped that the LSCC Annual Record for 1909 might resolve some of these uncertainties about the composition of the groups, but it contains no information about the Meet beyond a list of participants, and hills climbed.

The omission of these interesting early climbs from current records is easily explained. The original Guide Book article to Beinn an Dòthaidh appeared in Volume 7 of the Journal – seven years beforehand, and the Club didn't get around to publishing a district guidebook until John Wilson's guide of 1949, by which time these enterprising efforts had been forgotten. While *Taxus* is a worthy name, and might perhaps be kept, *Stairway to Heaven* is somewhat ridiculous. I suggest that whoever edits the next Southern Highlands climbers' guide should rename it *Ladies' Arête*.

Robin N. Campbell

---

[1] *SMCJ* 1909, X, 336, Easter Meet Report by J.R. Levack
[2] *LSCCJ* 1929, 29, 'Reminiscences of Snow Climbs in the Highlands'

The SMC 'Easter' Meet 2009 - Inchnadamph.
Photo: David Stone.

MY RECOLLECTION OF THE FIRST ASCENT OF THE DIRECT NOSE ROUTE ON SGURR AN FHIDHLEIR

By Neville Drasdo

IN THE SPRING of 1962 Mike Dixon* and I had been enjoying a tour of some of the relatively unexplored crags of the Northern Highlands. We had scrambled and climbed on Ben Loyal, Ben Hope and Foinaven and were making our way south down the west coast. From the summit of Stac Pollaidh we observed the striking prow-like profile of Sgurr an Fhidhleir with its shadowy north face. This was quite spectacular and was to leave a lasting impression.

The following day we chanced to meet Tom Patey who was on his daily rounds near Ullapool where he was the doctor. He invited us to stay in a small bunkhouse attached to the Doctor's House and we met in a hotel in the evening where we exchanged yarns of our climbing adventures over a bottle of whisky. The conversation turned to Sgurr an Fhidhleir and it was then that Tom suggested we should take a look at the possible line up the nose of the buttress which we were surprised to learn had still not been climbed.

The following day we left our car at a convenient point on the road. It was about 2.30 p.m. and we had little expectation of completing the climb that day but wished at least to investigate its feasibility. It was a dry if slightly windy day, but as we approached the crag we were surprised to be showered with water which was occasionally being picked up from the lochan by gusts of wind and hurled high into the air. At the foot of the buttress, on its right-hand or northerly face, it was sheltered from the wind and after consulting our old SMC guide which gave details of Ling and Sang's early visit we commenced our climb. The rock was initially rather vegetated but not without interest eventually giving enjoyable slab climbing. After about six hundred feet we arrived at a belay on the arête where the rock was steeper and the difficulty increased dramatically.

I remember that at this stage the air was still for periods of a minute or so, interspersed with violent gusts lasting perhaps twenty seconds. During these gusts the quivering loop of spare rope was extended about sixty feet easterly out into space, virtually horizontally from the stance on the ridge, emphasising the exposure and the perilous isolation of our position. However, stepping slightly rightwards into a right-angle corner, the wind was less noticeable and here, after ascending a few steps, I came to a difficult move. At first I felt that it was probably impossible and I pondered on the seriousness of a fall in such an isolated position but, as often happens, eventually I adapted to the situation and in one of the calm periods, after breathing out to get my centre of gravity as close as possible to the rock, I placed my foot experimentally on an improbably steep surface and found myself moving delicately upwards. The difficulties gradually eased from Hard VS, down to Severe after a few feet, and soon I was ascending more easily to a belay.

After Mike joined me we continued up the ridge, but we were confronted with

---

* Christopher Michael Dixon (1931–2004) my companion had pioneered about a dozen routes in the Cuillin 1950–55 (e.g. *Fluted Buttress, Crack of Dawn, Black Cleft* etc.) with Bill Brooker, Tom Patey and other climbers from Aberdeen.

a problem because although the line of the route was clear, up a crack of perhaps Hard Severe grade, which was a pleasure to climb, I repeatedly reached a certain point and then sensing the next gust of wind approaching had to descend very rapidly to avoid being blown off. This happened countless times and as the afternoon wore on we were by no means certain of completing the route before dark. We did not at that time use chock runners, so after many attempts I took a piton up and managed to insert it just as the next gust was beginning. I stayed clipped on until the gust had passed and then quickly climbed the upper section of the crack. After this we encountered no significant difficulty climbing up the ridge to the summit. Here we saw that the weather was deteriorating as great squalls of rain were sweeping towards us from the Atlantic.

In dense mist and rain we found ourselves making an uncertain line across the three or four miles of swampy land towards our car. Although there was at that time no recognisable path, by an amazing coincidence, a figure loomed out of the mist and we came face to face with Tom Patey who, fearing the worst, had set off to search for us. At our car he had left a note written on the back of a prescription form: 'I have gone to look for your bloody bodies. Back shortly. Tom.' It had been written in fountain pen ink and the rain had washed the ink in a downward direction, giving it a curiously artistic 'Sherlock Holmesian' appearance. I kept it for many years as a memento but eventually, to my great regret, it was lost.

It had clearly been a remarkable day, leaving us with abiding memories of the aesthetic quality of our situation on the arête and the difficulty, tension and satisfaction of the successful climb. The periodic wind which I never again experienced is a rare phenomenon which has apparently been studied mathematically. It was probably the reason for the statement in the SMC Northern Highlands Guide (1970) by Thomas Strang, where in the description of the *Direct Nose Route* on p130 it states: 'a cross wind on the exposed upper section could be intimidating'. The only regret we felt after this experience was that Tom could not have been with us on the climb. As always, despite his great ambition for pioneering such routes, he was generous in his congratulations. A legendary figure.

CATCH A FALLING STAR

A STRANGE jelly-like material has been found lying on the ground in the outdoors going back at least several centuries. It is commonly known as *star jelly* because of the rather fanciful extraterrestrial explanations for its origin. Somehow it became widely linked with stars or meteor showers, and so it is also called *pwdre sêr* (rot of the stars) in Welsh, and *sternenrotz* (star snot) in German.

Over the last year or so the BBC Radio Scotland *Out of Doors* programme has been largely responsible for publicising recent sightings of this material and for stimulating a slightly more scientific discussion on its origin. This has not stopped some listeners from asserting that this material is stag semen, and others that it is the silica gel derived from disposable nappies ejected from high-flying passenger aircraft!

It would seem that there are several similar types of gelatinous material found in the outdoors – these include slime molds (Mycetozoa), cyanobacteria (Nostoc) and jelly fungus (Tremella concrescens). However, star jelly is distinguished by being clear and colourless. A sample of such jelly recently tested at the Macaulay Institute proved to be mainly water.

The most popular theory for the origin of this clear jelly is that it is the contents of frog or toad oviducts regurgitated by a bird or mammal. Amphibian eggs are encased in a material which is highly hygroscopic and swells up significantly when it absorbs water. Herons, birds of prey, otters and polecats have all been suggested as animals that might be responsible for bringing up this swollen mass. Sightings of star jelly seem to be more common in the autumn even though frogs don't normally lay their eggs until March.

Before this latest flurry of interest in star jelly developed I happened to come across two separate samples when out taking photographs of geological features. The first sample I encountered was lying on grass growing on the highest of the three Parallel Roads in Glen Roy (350m). This sample had small clumps of black, spherical bodies in it which look to me very much like amphibian eggs. The second sample I came across was lying on the very top of a rather unusual natural rock feature called the 'Wishing Stone' (a fine example of a igneous dyke) which is situated close to sea level near Lochaline. It was a little older than the previous sample and had started to flatten out and evaporate, but its location would suggest that it had probably been regurgitated by a bird rather than a mammal. See the two photographs opposite page 459.

If you are out and about in the outdoors and come across such jelly then consider taking a photograph of it. Better still, see if you can spot the creature actually producing it. It would help solve a long-standing mystery.

D.N. Williams

IF YOU GO DOWN IN THE WOODS TODAY – AND OTHER TALES ABOUT LYME DISEASE

By Alan R. Walker

IT WAS SAD to read in the 2008 journal about troubles with Lyme disease, but this alerted and explained to Club members a problem about which there is increasing concern amongst the general public and official agencies. An example is the recent series of meetings about this convened at the Scottish Parliament by Michael Russell, Minister for Environment. I have been invited to these as a member of staff at the Royal (Dick) School of Veterinary Studies, having researched and taught these types of diseases since the 1960s. I recently completed a five-year field study, mainly in Galloway, on the beastie involved (*Ixodes ricinus*, the deer or sheep tick) and its relation to the transmission of another disease agent that some people have regarded as a threat to humans. Information was published on the risk of exposure to these agents of disease.

Lyme disease is classed by the NHS in Scotland as a Notifiable Disease, thus the statistics on its occurrence are detailed. It is increasing, but the numbers of new cases per year in Scotland remain in the low hundreds, as do rubella and meningococcal infections. If diagnosed and treated early using antibiotics it is readily cured, but its symptoms are variable and confusing. A small minority of infections progress to where the bacterium responsible is able to hide from the body's immune system in joint capsules (e.g. the knee) and nerve sheaths (e.g. a particular facial nerve). There it is much more troublesome and only prolonged heavy doses of antibiotic will cure it. Other microbes are transmitted by these ticks in other regions. Tick borne encephalitis, for example, is a problem in eastern Europe, so a visit to the Tatra Mountains justifies getting vaccinated – available on private prescription through the NHS, but start early as a course of three inoculations is needed. There was a vaccine against Lyme disease developed in the USA but it has not been a success.

As with all microbes transmitted by insects or ticks the most important defence is avoidance of the transmitter. How to avoid our local tick? Firstly, although the brains of these creatures are small they are not so daft as to go climbing mountains. There are not enough animals to feed on up there, and unlike midges which have larvae living and feeding in peat bogs, all ticks feed exclusively on blood. Where our tick likes to be is in woodland; conifer or deciduous. There the adults can feed on those other woodland animals, roe and red deer, and some of the immature ticks can also feed on mice and voles. Sadly our ancestors cut down most of the woods, so now the red deer roam disconsolately on the moors, spreading ticks there, as will sheep and cattle. But our tick is sometimes called the wood tick, because they occur there in numbers at least 10 times greater than on moorland. **Advice 1**: if you go down in the woods today – protect yourself!

This bacterium, *Borrelia burgdorferi* mainly, is a parasite of rodents, highly adapted to live in their blood. So when a larval tick feeds on an infected wood mouse the bacterium will survive in the overwintering tick which moults to a nymph which may feed on an uninfected vole. The infected vole then . . . you get the picture. So, fewer rodents mean less Lyme disease because it is not generally transmitted between the larger animals, and certainly not from human to human. These rodents thrive in woodlands. **Advice 2**: if you go down in the woods – protect yourself **carefully**!

Our small-brained bloodsucker knows it needs to stay damp and keep out of the cold, otherwise it desiccates or freezes. Two more reasons why they like to live in woods, but they are not fussy about what type of vegetation is around as long as there is plenty of it. They are not vegetarians, so have no special preference for bracken, as is often claimed. On moorland the main rodent is the short-tailed field vole but these are less favourable to both the bacterium and ticks. So ticks on moorland are far less likely to be infected with *Borrelia* than those in woods. **Advice 3**: the thicker the woodland undergrowth, of any kind, the more ticky it will be so avoid it; keep to constructed paths. These ticks are a cold-blooded lot, so they don't like the snow. But they do need to get feeding as soon as possible, so expect them in much greater numbers starting March through to September. **Advice 4**: stick to skiing; failing that winter climbing will do.

Unlike midges – hit and run rogues – these ticks develop an intimate relationship with their hosts. They crawl across fur or clothes till they find bare skin; anywhere on humans will do. There they drill in and fasten with barbs. Saliva is secreted containing some chemical that stops the pain receptors, and others that dissolve deeper tissues and keep the blood flowing. By the next day the inflammatory defence against this assault begins to itch and the little blighters are noticed and scratched off. Too late to stop most of any microbes getting into you, but don't panic – only a minor percentage of ticks are likely to be infected with anything. Even if the tick is infected the *Borrelia* are most likely to be killed off very soon by simple immune mechanisms. After all, you are probably not the rodent they need to be in. **Advice 5**: if you have ignored all the above advice then sometime between finishing your tea and opening the whisky, de-tick yourself. Commercial tick-hooks made of plastic are best for pulling them straight, and fine tweezers are effective. Vaseline, nail varnish, paint stripper – forget it! But a fingernail will suffice because you do not need to worry about leaving those barbed mouthparts in, that is no more serious than a tiny skelf. Some people advise that twisting them anti-clockwise is necessary, but if you are doing this in Australia you need to twist them clockwise. Similarly, some people give dire warnings about squeezing the ticks when what they really mean is: grip them close to skin before removing them. Wear your reading glasses: the larvae and nymphs that will feed on you appear as dark spots no bigger than a pin-head (adult ticks very rarely try to feed on humans).

I nearly forgot: about that protection. **Advice 6**: never wear shorts. If you insist then wear them in winter, or climb in the Sahara. Instead wear long trousers, with gaiters, or failing that tucked into long socks. If you do go down into the woods, then extra protection in the form of strong midge repellent, at least 50% DEET, liberally applied to those socks is good. [Though DEET can dissolve some synthetic fabrics. Ed.] Even light-coloured trousers are useful, then you can see the bleeders as they crawl after your blood. Of course this is all easy to write, but so easy to fail to observe. The last time I was badly ticked was at the Glen Marksie crags by Contin, where I got lost in woodland and undergrowth ideal for deer and ticks. Long trousers yes, socks no, because my rock boots are too tight for long socks. Silly me. But roaming across the open moorland and hills, properly kitted, I don't come across a tick more than once a year. **Advice 7**: worry about lightning strike instead.

For more medical information go to a sensible website. Concerning human health that last phrase may be an oxymoron. However, start with the very sensible Health Protection Scotland <www.hps.nhs.uk>, Health Protection Agency of UK Government <www.hpa.org.uk> and Centers for Disease Control of US government <www.cdc.gov>. A few private sites are fine, but beware. If you trawl just a little deeper you will dredge up all sorts of weirdness: quack remedies, people who call themselves 'Lymies'; you might find Morgellons, or even 'Cryptostrongylus' worms there although you won't find them in the real world. And finally, if you want to know precisely where these ticks are, take your dog with you, but please de-tick it afterwards.

(AN ATTEMPT AT) **A BIBLIOGRAPHIC STUDY OF THE SCOTTISH MOUNTAINEERING CLUB'S GUIDE BOOKS**

IT APPEARS that today's varied and colourful guide-books were born out of a Special General Meeting of the Club, held on 7 December 1894, when not only were seven gentlemen, including no lesser a personage than Mr E. Aleister Crowley, elected to membership, but the following motion, proposed by Mr William Brown, and seconded by Mr A.E. Maylard, was passed:

That this meeting

1) approves of the Committee's recommendation that a Climber's Guide to Scotland should be published under the auspices of the Club;

2) pledges itself to co-operate heartily in the work of production;

3) appoints an editor to take such steps as may be required to collect the necessary materials, with power to nominate a small committee to assist in the work; and

4) votes £10 out of the Club funds to cover initial outlays.

The debate on this motion is recorded as follows:

In speaking to his motion, Mr Brown explained that there was an opening at present for a work which would combine the accurate and precise information of a guidebook, written from the climber's standpoint, with general articles descriptive of Scottish Mountaineering from the pens of competent and well-informed writers. Such a work might be divided into two parts, viz.:- 1st, Introductory, containing perhaps articles on Scottish Mountaineering, past and present, Snowcraft, Rockwork, Equipment, Mountain Photography; and 2nd, a more technical portion, containing brief accounts of all the Scottish Mountains of a certain class or height to be afterwards fixed, with information as to their physical features, where to climb them from, lines of ascent, &c. &c.

The book ought to be well illustrated, and should also in its introductory portion be as attractive and interesting as possible. In this way a sale would or might be insured among the general public. The time might not be fully ripe for such a work, but competition was threatened which might encroach upon the information in possession of the Club; and at any rate, it was certain that the starting of such a work would, by stimulating members to greater activity and directing their efforts into the proper channels, tend to create means by which it could be expeditiously carried out.

After some discussion, in which Professor Smith, Messrs James Maclay, R.A. Robertson, and H.T. Munro took part, the motion was unanimously carried, on the footing that the committee to be appointed should be left to decide upon the details of the scheme. Mr W. Douglas was unanimously appointed Editor.

At the seventh AGM of the Club, held on 13 December 1895, the hon. Editor reported, with, it seems a certain degree of wild optimism, 'that the Guide Book was making fast progress, and that the Committee appointed to assist him were, Messrs Brown, Hinxman, Jackson, Munro, Phillip, Naismith, Rennie, and Thomson.'

By January 1901, however, at SMCJ vi 112, we read, alas, that:

THE Editor of the S.M.C. Guide Book has met with insuperable difficulties in completing the work in the form originally contemplated, and to enable some progress to be made, he proposes, when space permits, to run portions of it through the pages of the Journal. Members will thus have the use of what has already been written, and allow the Editor to have the benefit of any corrections or suggestions that may occur to them.

The nature of these difficulties is not further described. The intended structure of the work, however, was set out:

The arrangement of the book falls naturally into six divisions, and it is proposed to name them as follows:
1. SOUTHERN HIGHLANDS. – Includes all south of Fort William, Glen Spean, and Loch Laggan, west of Highland Railway, and all north of the Forth and Clyde Canal.
2. EASTERN DIVISION. – Includes all south of Inverness, east of Lochs Ness and Lochy, and north-east of Glen Spean, Loch Laggan, and the line of the Highland Railway from Dalwhinnie to Perth.
3. WESTERN DIVISION. – Includes all west and north of the Caledonian Canal, and south of the Dingwall and Skye Railway.
4. NORTHERN HIGHLANDS. – Includes all north of the Dingwall and Skye Railway.
5. SOUTHERN UPLANDS. – Includes all south of the Forth and Clyde Canal.
6. THE ISLANDS OF SCOTLAND.

The next couple of issues of the SMCJ each contain several descriptions of 'groups' of mountains, some detailed, and some exceedingly brief, accompanied by pleas from the Editor for more information. After September 1901, with Vol vi, No 6 the path becomes faint, as the Glasgow Digital Library's run of SMCJ ends <http://gdl.cdlr.strath.ac.uk/smcj/journals.html>.

The Journal for June 1913 (SMCJ was then issued three times a year) has no reference to the Guide Book, but at the twenty eighth General Meeting held on 1 December 1916, the hon. Secretary, George Sang reported that the Special Committee had recommended that publication of the Guide Book be delayed 'till times of peace'.

With the Great War finally over, the April 1920 issue (now reduced to twice a year) not only carries a photograph of the War Memorial Tablet, to defray the cost of which a levy of 10/- was collected from each member, which is now to be seen in the Club's Raeburn Hut, but more importantly, an update on the Guide Book.

As with so much else the events of the recent years have played havoc with the progress of this scheme of the Club. But now that we are shaking off the foul miasmas of war, it is surely the moment for the Editor to hail the members to the hills that they may bring the work to a successful issue.

The Editor then asserts, encouragingly, that, 'Ere 1914, much work had been done and well done.' He goes on, however, to add that:

Much still remains to be done. A neglected breach has to be filled, and it now behoves those who can, to give the most loyal support to the future sub-editor of Division III, by acquiring information and preparing articles ahead of his appointment. It is a far cry to the lands of Knoydart and Glen Shiel, and the forests of Glen Affric and Strath Conon. Let those who may go, have pen and camera with them and mind alert, and let those who have been, render their account.

He goes on to shine a little light on the cost of living: 'What would have cost us, when the idea was first mooted, some £300, will now cost £1,000, or perhaps £1,200.' For financial reasons, therefore the Guide would not be published in one complete volume, but section by section.

To 'meet the needs of the large majority of our younger members at the forthcoming Meet at Forth William, the first section to be published will be Section E, of Volume I, that for Ben Nevis...' The Editor's hopes were justified, for on the back cover is an advertisement for the Ben Nevis section at 5/3d, post paid! This was a paper-back, in the same format as the Journal, but with a cover of a bilious yellow! The same advertisement expresses the hope that Section A, containing the 'general articles' would be published in June of 1920.

The divisions of the Guide, although slightly differently described, are the same as those set out in 1895.

By April 1922, the hon. Secretary was able to report that the 'Ben Nevis Guide Book' was (just) in profit, but that the unexplained 'exceptional cost' of the production of the General Section was such that even at the high price of 7/6d, it would never go into profit. The Committee, he reported, had sanctioned the production of the Guides dealing with the Islands, including Skye, but that they would not be able to send this to the printers, until some settlement had been made to bail out the General Section!

This settlement would appear to have been made, for, on the cover of the October 1923 issue is an advertisement for the Club's Guide to the Isle of Skye, at 10/-d, plus 4d for postage. An interesting feature is 'a special contour map of the Black Cuillin contained in a pocket on the cover.' This had been produced specially for the Club from photographic triangulation by Howard Priestman, Esq. Extra copies of this map could be had for 2/-d, together with copies of a Sron na Ciche Panorama for the same price.

This volume, and the General Section appear to have been the first definitive issues in the original series of the Club's Guides. These are produced in red cloth covered boards, with rounded corners, gold blocking on front and spine, and with a cream coloured dust wrapper, with a single black and white photograph on the front cover.

The gloomy prognostications anent the General Section do not seem to have been wholly borne out – in the Forward to the 1933 'New Edition' the proto-Munroist, the Rev A.E. Robertson, who was known to the children about the McCook's house in Benalder Bay as 'Archie E', writes that the 1921 Edition was sold out in 1929, when a photographic reprint was made. It would appear that this General volume had stopped being the General Section of Division I, the Southern Highlands, and had become the General Volume of the whole work. It carried chapters on Photography, Geology, Meteorology, Botany, Bird Life, Equipment, Rock Climbing, Snow Conditions, (only recently re-issued as *Hostile Habitats*?), Rock and Snow Climbing Centres, Photography and 'Notes on Maps, Compasses and Aneroid Barometers' as well as Munro's (but not Corbett's!) Tables, all in one neat volume. The articles on Photography, in the first edition, by W. Inglis Clark, and in 1933 by Percy Donald are resources in their own right for the photographic historian. It is interesting to read that by 1921 there were already several single exposure colour processes available, of which Lumière & Co's fast 'autochrome' reversal plates then held the palm. In bright summer sunshine these required an exposure of only 20 seconds at f:16!

By 1924, however, momentum might be thought to be being lost – at the AGM in that year, cursed by a slide projector hired for the meeting, which would not focus sharply, and a hall with bad acoustics, the hon. Secretary felt that unless advertised in some form, the then current stock of Guide Books would stagnate. Sub-Editors were, with great courtesy, invited to get their acts together and prepare their manuscripts for the printer, and then 'come forward to the Club for a subsidy and orders'.

A year later the Meeting considered a suggestion that a fore-runner of *A Century of Scottish Mountaineering* might be assembled out of the first hundred issues of the Journal (plus ça change, plus c'est la même chose!) for the Christmas market, but this was turned down as a distraction to the Guide Books' market, which was worrying the Committee.

At the 38th AGM, in 1926, intriguingly it fell to the President, James A. Parker, who would edit the Western Highlands volume, published first in 1931, and who after the next war sent the finished manuscript of the third edition off two days before his death, to make 'an interesting statement' about the Cairngorm volume, which he hoped would be ready for the press early in the following spring – this only slipped a little, the first edition being published in 1928 at 10/-d bound, and 7/6d 'uniform'(?).

The following year the new President called upon J.H.B. Bell to propose a motion to appoint 'A special Assistant Guide-Book Committee' but since Mr Bell was, for unknown reasons, absent, the motion fell. The next year this motion was proposed again, and caused 'very considerable discussion'! The purpose of the special committee was to investigate and report to section editors on already published climbs in their respective districts. The members of the committee were to be selected by the office-bearers!

By November 1931, the General Editor of the 'Guide Book' was able to give a fairly upbeat report in the Journal, rather than at the AGM, summarised in the minutes.

The 'Guide Book' ('Book' clearly still in the singular) was divided into three volumes, each further sub divided into sections.

Volume I:
  A. General
  B. The Lowlands
  C. Southern Highlands
  D. Central Highlands
  E. Ben Nevis (described as 'an island in I.D.')
  F. Ben Nevis Panorama

Volume II
  A. The Cairngorms
  B. Western Highlands
  C. Northern Highlands

Volume III
  A. Island of Skye
  B. The Islands, and Index (an Index to the whole 'book'?)

What actually saw the light of day was as follows:

Volume I
  A. *General*: J.R.Young, published 1921, reprinted 1929; 3rd edition 1933.
  B. *The Lowlands*: does not appear to have ever been issued in the original series – *The Southern Uplands* was published 1972, reprinted 1976, in the second series.
  C. *Southern Highlands*: J.D.B. Wilson, first Edition 1949.
  D. *Central Highlands*: Harry MacRobert, Published 1934.
  E. *Ben Nevis*: Published in card covers 1920, Harry MacRobert's revision of Dr W. Inglis Clark's Guide Book article in the Journal; revised edition, in red cloth boards, Dr G. Graham Macphee, 1936.
  F. There is no evidence of the publication, separately, of the *Ben Nevis Panorama* – it is to be assumed that this/these were the four panoramic views from the summit of the Ben, drawn by Mr James E. Shearer, SSA, during a week of perfect weather in June 1895. They were published by him subsequently, but James A. Parker, when President bought the originals and presented them to the Club. They were reproduced in the 1936, revised edition of the Ben Nevis guide, revised and touched up by the artist for reproduction.

Volume II
  A. *The Cairngorms*: Henry Alexander, 1928, reprinted 1931; 2nd ed 1938; 3rd Ed (revised by William A. Ewen) 1950; 4th Ed (Adam Watson, J.C. Donaldson, G. Scott Johnstone & I.H.M. Smart) 1968 (? second series).
  B. *Western Highlands*: James A. Parker, 1931, reprinted 1932; 3rd, revised 1947; 4th Ed 1964.
  C. *Northern Highlands*: W.N. Ling, 1932; 2nd revised Ed (W.N. Ling & John Rooke Corbett) 1936; 3rd Ed (E.W. Hodge) 1953.

Volume III
  A. *Island of Skye*: E.W. Steeple, G. Barlow, H. Macrobert & J.H.B. Bell, 1923, reprinted 1931, 1935; 2nd revised edition, 1948; 3rd Ed 1954.
  B. *The Islands of Scotland (excluding Skye)*: W.W. Naismith, 1934; 2nd Ed (revised by E.W. Hodge) 1952.

There followed a **second series**, with sharp corners, and glossy dust wrappers, with flashy coloured stripes, then a **third series**, without dust wrapper, but with a uniform blue livery, and now a **fourth series** has started, with each volume colour coded for instant recognition.

Richard Spencer

THE SCOTTISH MOUNTAINEERING TRUST – 2008
Scottish Charity SCO09117

THE TRUSTEES met on 11 April, 4 July and 31 October 2008.

During the course of these meetings support was given to the National Trust for Scotland (Mountains for People Project), the Mountain Rescue Committee for Scotland (Rescue Conference), the Dundee Mountain Film Festival, the SMC (CIC Hut), the Ethnobotany Nepal Himalaya Project 2008, the Mountaineering Council of Scotland (Visually Impaired Course 2008), the Jonathon Conville Memorial Trust, the Mountaineering Council of Scotland (Access and Conservation), the John Muir Trust (Quinag Path Repair Project), Mapland Scotland (Schools Programme), Heather Morning (MSc, second year) and Clachnaben Path Repair Works.

The present Trustees are P.V. Brian (Chairman), R. Aitken, R. Anderson, J.T.H. Allen, B.S. Findlay, A. Macdonald, C.R. Ravey, R.J.C. Robb, D. Rubens and D.N. Williams. J. Morton Shaw is the Trust Treasurer.

The present Directors of the Publications Company are R.K. Bott (Chairman), K.V. Crocket, C.M. Huntley, W.C. Runciman, M.G.D. Shaw and T. Prentice (Publications Manager). R. Anderson is the Convener of the Publications Sub-Committee and attends Company Board meetings. He provides a valuable liaison between the Company and the Trust.

The Trust wishes to record its appreciation for the contribution and services to the Trust given by A.C. Stead in his capacity as a Trustee for the last four years and Chairman of the Trustees for the last two years. The Trust also wishes to record its appreciation for the contribution and services to the Trust given by C. Huntley who has retired as Trustee by rotation.

The following grants have been committed by the Trustees during 2008:

National Trust for Scotland, Mountains for People Project	£30,000
	(over a period of 5 years
	i.e. £6,000 per annum)
Mountain Rescue Committee for Scotland, Rescue Conference	£4,000
Dundee Mountain Film Festival	£1,500
SMC, CIC Hut up to a maximum of one-half of the total cost	
or the sum of £100,000, which ever is the lesser	
(of which 50% a grant and 50% a loan)	
Ethnobotany Nepal Himalaya Project 2008	£500
Mountaineering Council of Scotland, Visually Impaired Course 2008	£2,400
Jonathon Conville Memorial Trust	£1,352
Mountaineering Council of Scotland, Access and Conservation	£30,000
(payable £10,000 per annum for 3 years)	
John Muir Trust, Quinag Path Repair Project	£12,050
Mapland Scotland, Schools Programme	£5,000
Heather Morning, MSc (second year)	£552
Clachnaben Path Repair Works	£5,500

The Trustees are grateful for a donation received from Richard Cooke CBE.

The Trustees wish to record and acknowledge with appreciation and respect that a bequest was received (to the SANG Award) from the estate of the late Malcolm Slesser.

J.D. Hotchkis
Secretary

MUNRO MATTERS 2009

By Dave Broadhead (Clerk of the List)

With climbing Munros well established as a national pastime, the seasonal flow of fascinating letters continues despite the credit crunch and ensuing recession, and the List keeps growing. Many thanks to everyone who has written to me. The following report gives a flavour of the correspondence which makes my job so interesting and enjoyable.

As before, the five columns give number, name, and year of Compleation of Munros, Tops and Furths as appropriate. * SMC member, ** LSCC member.

4028	John Dinning	2008		
4029	Sean Turner	2008	1997	
4030	Wallace B. Nicoll	2008		
4031	Jacque Whyte	2007		
4032	Thomas R. Buchan	2008		
4033	Donald F. Irvine	2002 2002 2008		
4034	Robert Parkin	2008		
4035	Stuart McKeggie	2008		
4036	Jennifer Shaw	2008		
4037	Sue Lyth	2008		
4038	Humphrey NdeV Mather	2008		
4039	Howard O. Smith	2008		
4040	Jacqueline Powell	2008		
4041	Alan Wiggins	2005		
4042	Janine Roper	2008		
4043	Duncan Henderson	2008		
4044	Howard Smith	1999		
4045	Anthony Maries	2008		
4046	Chris Maries	2008		
4047	David J. Robertson	2007		
4048	Billy Sands	2003		
4049	Andrew Porter	2005		
4050	M. A. Lowther	2008		
4051	Vivian Wright	2008		
4052	*Andrew G. Fraser	2001		
4053	Fiona I. Marshall	2008		
4054	Kenneth C. Ballantyne	2008		
4055	Jonathan Dennett	2008		
4056	Douglas A. K. Law	2008		
4057	Derek J. Pratt	2008		
4058	Peter Dalrymple Hay	2008		
4059	Thomas Benton	2008		
4060	Jake Manson	2008		
4061	Oonagh McElligott	2008		
4062	Michael G. Barnard	2008 2008		
4063	Jolyon Medlock	2008		
4064	Margaret Stewart Mimer	2008		
4065	Clive Griffiths	2008		
4066	Robert Mott	2008		
4067	Pete Jones	2008		
4068	Mark Helie	2008		
4069	Donald J. Smith	2008		
4070	Christopher Redmond	2008		
4071	Des Oakes	2008		
4072	Mark Andrew Cassinelli	2006		
4073	Philip Nalpanis	2008		
4073	David le Fleming	2008		
4075	Cathy Whitfield	2008		
4076	Will Whitfield	2008		
4077	Celia Blanche Barker	2008		
4078	Michael Ivan Barker	2008		
4079	Mary-Anne Buntin	2008		
4080	Andy Buntin	2008		
4081	Fiona Reid	2008		
4082	Michael Watson	2008		
4083	Ian Cowan	2008		
4084	Tom Lawfield	2008		
4085	Vanessa Jackson	2008		
4086	Raymond Addlet	2008		
4087	Duncan McPherson Smith			
		2008 2008 2005		
4088	David McSporran	2008		
4089	Iain C. Russell	2008		
4090	Iain M. Craig	2008		
4091	Peter Davis	2008		
4092	* David G. Todd	2008		
4093	Andrew Tait	2008		
4094	Ralph S. Whiting	2008		
4095	Steve Girt	2008		
4096	David Parkinson	2008		
4097	A. Martin McNicol	2008		
4098	Kate Thomson	2008		
4099	Angus Speirs	2008		
4100	Colin MacLennan	2008		
4101	Sandy Sharp	2008		
4102	Jo Cooke	2008		
4103	Richard Cooke	2008		
4104	M. J. Smith	2008		
4105	Clair Hutchings	2008	2004
4106	Maida C. Gibson	2008		
4107	James N. Gibson	2008		
4108	Charles Kilner	2008		
4109	S. Barry Clayton	2008		
4110	Julian Stark	2008		

4111	Christine George	2008	
4112	Ben Brown	1992 2007	
4113	Barbara Campbell	2008	
4114	Iain Campbell	2008	
4115	Douglas Crabbe	2008	
4116	Gordon Old	2008	
4117	David Bibby	2008	
4119	David Nelson	2008	
4119	Raymond Mackeddie	2008	
4120	Frank Johnstone	2003	
4121	Michael Stevenson	2008	
4122	Kennedy Hamilton	2008	
4123	John L. Steel	2008	
4124	Wilma Kelt	2008	
4125	Mike Holmes	2008	
4126	Andrew Gillespie	2008	
4127	Douglas Wilson	2008	
4128	Robert Kyle	2008	
4129	William G. Williamson	2008	
4130	Chris Mennim	2008	
4131	Paul Goodman	2008	
4132	Alan J. Thomson	2008	
4133	Alexander D. Macmillan	2008 2008	
4134	Marl Allwood	2008	
4135	Barbara L. H. Mackinnon	2008	
4136	Jack Higham	2008	
4137	George Allan	2008	
4138	A. Meeson	2008	
4139	Angus Swanson	2008	
4140	Grace E. Pippard	2008	
4141	Catherine Gemmell	2008	
4142	Morris Rodham	2008	
4143	Joan Martin	2007	
4144	A. R. Auld	2008	
4145	Jenny Spinks	2008	
4146	Neil Spinks	2008	
4147	Michael John McLaren	2008	
4148	George T. Robertson	2008	
4149	Jane Bache	2008	
4150	David Bache	2008	
4151	Norman Wares	2008	
4152	Trish Schooling	2008	
4153	Gordon Ingall	2008	
4154	David A. Duncan	2008	
4155	Tom McGregor	2008	
4156	John A. Gosling	2008	
4157	Alastair Boyd	2004	
4158	John R. Taylor	2008	
4159	David Childs	2008	
4160	Roderick Chalmers	2008	
4161	Bev Edenden	2008	
4162	Peter Charles Clark	2008	
4163	Yvonne Warren	2008	
4164	Thomas Warren	2008	
4165	John A. E. Macdonald	2008	
4166	David Baird	2008 2008	
4167	Andrew W. Armstrong	2008	
4168	Mike Reynolds	2008	
4169	Victoria Fuller	2008	
4170	David McSporran	2005 2008	
4171	Robin McBride	2008	
4172	George West	2008	
4173	Grant Macdonald	2008	
4174	Mark S. Crawford	2008	
4175	Brian Johnston	2008	
4176	Richard Laing	2008	
4177	Colin Spence	2008	
4178	Helen Proud	2008	
4179	Craig Thomas Dunderdale	2008	
4180	Richard King	2008	
4181	John W. Christie	2001	2008
4182	John B. Donald	2008	
4183	Brian Johnston	2008	
4184	John Milner	2008	
4185	Adrian Snowdon	2008	
4186	Fred Findlay	2008	
4187	Peter Robinson	2008	
4188	Jim Presly	2008	
4189	Sandy Muirhead	2008	
4190	Niall Paterson	2008	
4191	Elizabeth Muncie	2008	
4192	William Muncie	2008	
4193	Ron Brown	2008	
4194	Chris Rogers	2008	
4195	Andrew Botterill	2008	
4196	Denny Robinson	2008	
4197	Malcolm Robinson	2008	
4198	Irene Morris	2008	
4199	David Morris	2008	
4200	Richard John Cooke	2008	
4201	Christine Russell	2008	
4202	Paul Harte	2008	
4203	Ralph Godsall	2008	
4204	Susan Bremner	2008	
4205	Michael McGavigan	2007	
4206	Scott Girvan	2008	
4207	Bob Copeland	2008	
4208	Brian A. Trickett	2008	
4209	Grant Robertson	2008	
4210	Sandra Taylor	2008	
4211	Rodney Royles	2008	
4212	Martin Ross	2008	
4213	Trevor Carter	2008	
4214	Derek Williamson	2008	
4215	Eleanor Gledhill	2008	
4216	Martin Gledhill	2008	
4217	John O'Gara	2008	
4218	Gordon Nicoll	2008	
4219	Ian Turner	2008	
4220	Campbell Gunn	2008	
4221	John D. G. Perks	2008	
4222	Allan Martin	2008	
4223	Alan Thomas	2008	

4224	Roger Mitchell	2008
4225	Caroline P. Swain	2005
4226	Vivienne Rule	2008
4227	Graham Gammie	2008
4228	Sheryl Harvey	2008
4229	Mark Denham-Smith	2008
4230	Ian Martin	2008
4231	James Riches	2008
4232	David Andrews	2008
4233	Joyce Stewart	2008
4234	Elizabeth Stewart	2008
4235	Eric Roycroft	2008
4236	Norman Waugh	1990
4237	**Jacqueline Turner	2008
4238	Catherine Walton	2008
4239	Muriel Cochran	2008

4240	Rose M. Hancock	2007 2007 2008
4241	Robert J. Hancock	2007 2007 2008
4242	Hector Mackenzie	2008
4243	Colin R. Black	2008
4244	Jasmin Cameron	2008
4245	Doug Millington	2008
4246	Stuart Bradley	2008
4247	Simon Winton	2008
4248	Sheila Ritchie	2008
4249	James Gardiner Marshall	2008
4250	Christopher John Chapman	2008
4251	John Field	2006
4252	Paul Sammonds	2008
4253	Alex Taylor	2008
4254	Victor Barber	2008

STATISTICS

Comparing the year 2008-2009 with the previous year (in brackets) shows some interesting variations. The total number of 227 Compleations was a drop from last years record figure (257). Of these 21% (19%) were women and 12% (18%) couples. 55% (64%) were resident in Scotland, average age 54 (54), taking an average of 21 (23) years and celebrating their Compleation with an average party of 14 (16).

STARTS

Martin McNicol (4097) was born into an SMC/LSCC family and introduced to the hills by a galaxy of stars of the era. He remembers as a young boy celebrating the late George Roger's (109) last Munro, the only SMC President to Compleat while in office. In a similar vein, Gordon Ingall (4153) 'was fortunate to grow up in a keen outdoor family, my father being a rock climber with the Fell & Rock...with a home library including a set of SMC District Guides and an old buff SMC journal listing Munro's Tables.' Charles Kilner (4108) climbed his first Munro 'aged 5 with my parents – a wet day, wore small wellies.' Scott Girvan (4206) 'started my Munros while still at school climbing Ben More (Crianlarich). This was almost my last as I found the hill to be an unremitting trudge.' Sandra Taylor (4210) started on Beinn Dorain which 'nearly killed me.' Jim Presly(4188) vaguely remembers 'my very first Munro was as a young Boy Scout away back at the end of the 1950s, Mount Keen.' Alex Taylor's (4253) first Munro 'was done with Dingwall Academy's hillwalking club, in a time when interest was expressed by raising your hand and turning up the next day – no need for parental consent, health & safety seemed to be organised through common sense (well we had no accidents).' Barbara (4113) and Iain Campbell (4114) 'were inspired by Muriel Gray's *First Fifty* and thought it would be fun to do 50 before 50.' On Compleation their combined age was 126. Douglas Crabbe (4115) was 'inspired by *Scottish Mountaineer* magazine to do something positive when a close friend was diagnosed with terminal cancer.' By Compleation 18 months later he had raised £8,500 for Maggie's Centres. David Bibby (4117) 'had my first Munro trip over the Queen's Jubilee celebrations in June 1977, traversing the Carn Mor Dearg arête to climb Ben Nevis to see the bonfire.' Angus Swanson (4139) 'was looking for something to do on a summer

Geoff Cohen leads the President up a new route on the SMC Easter Meet 2009.
Photo: Noel Williams.

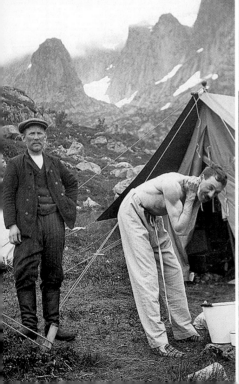

uachaille Etive Mor fully equipped with some

:d on the first *Boots Across Scotland* charity
arted 'in the Cairngorm Mountains…following
a trip, where we had crash landed the previous
hills but having walked out in one piece, I was
about them.' Sheryl Harvey (4228) started by
est day' on a cycle trip from Glasgow to John o'
Robinson (4196 & 4197) 'didn't mean to climb
ow they were there. What we really intended to do
was to continue our long continuous walk northwards after the Pennine Way.'
Thirty years later their Munro Log 'runs into 3 volumes in Lever Arch files of
handwritten diaries and photos.' The five closely typed pages of 'Preface and
Summary' they sent me make a fascinating read. Having achieved his target of
Compleating in his 64th year (remembering the Beatles song *When I'm 64*)
Andrew Botterill (4195) gives the following 'three recommendations to any
young person contemplating 'doing the Munros': live in Scotland not the south
of England, start in your twenties (and keep going) and retire early from the day
job.'

SCARES

Richard Laing (4176) had to be 'helicoptered off Creag Mhor in April 2003
having collapsed with heart problems. Two of my sons ran 10km to raise the
alarm and the Royal Navy from HMS Gannet were superb.' Peter Robinson
(4187) 'had just got back into serious hillwalking by 2004 when I was diagnosed
with prostate cancer. After surgery I was determined to regain my fitness and set
about the Munros with a real enthusiasm.' Under the heading of 'My Assent of
The Munros' John Milner (4184) starts his story by explaining 'In 2001 there
was foot and mouth disease in England and we were not able to go walking for
4 months. Then we heard that we could walk in Scotland.' This cloud had a
silver lining, not like the one covering Cairn Gorm. 'I went to take out my
compass again to check my direction only to find it was gone. After searching
for 45 minutes…I decided to call the mountain rescue…I did eventually find my
way down with instructions from the leader of the rescue team, John Allen, over
the mobile phone.' John now plans to visit all the Tarns in the Lake District, well
below cloud level. Joyce J.K.Stewart (4233) and Elizabeth Stewart (4234)
introduced themselves as sisters-in-law, married to brothers. Their Compleation
was blighted by bad weather and worse, on Stob Ghabhar 'on probably the worst
day for rain this year. At least we got a view from the top and some sun to go
with the champagne and whisky. Unfortunately a friend fell on the descent and
broke her ankle. We had to call the Mountain Rescue helicopter.' Golden
Munroist Christine Russell (4201) was sometimes 'curtailed by serious
orthopaedic problems. After each operation (shoulder reconstruction, disc
removal, spinal fusion etc) a few tears were shed when I got to the next top.'
James Gardiner Marshall (4249) 'started doing the Munros after recovering
from a bad ski injury on left leg…not bad going as I was told by a surgeon I
might not walk without a limp'.

SUCCESS

On Ben More (Mull) Paul Goodman (4131) 'took the last step' companion, too ill to join us in person, 'walking' with us on the phone.'

On the same hill, Andrew Gillespie (4126) 'celebrated with a wee Highland Park from my hip flask, using silver quaichs to hold the precious liquid.' Over on Skye, Derek Grieve (4025) 'even managed to play the bagpipes on the summit and one of my mates and I both wore our kilts' on Blaven, while on Schiehallion Bev Edenden (4161) 'was piped on the summit (using a mini music system).' Tom Lawfield (4084) 'did most of the round solo in two trips, for environmental reasons by public transport and not having a tent, used my bivi bag instead. I am 22 years of age does this make me the youngest solo?' Ralph Whiting (4094) belongs to a group called the *Pill Ptarmigans* and informs me that 'there has been a Pill Ptarmigan expedition to the Scottish Highlands in the last week of May every year since 1989.' Morris Rodham (4142) a clergyman from Leamington Spa, was accompanied by his wife on Ben More (Mull) where 'we celebrated with a small bottle of champagne and a dance move called 'Supergirl' which involves me throwing her up onto my shoulders while she adopts a 'supergirl' pose.' Having 'started by doing Lochnagar on my own in 1960 at the age of 16 in welly boots and a raincoat' John B Donald (4182) 'thoroughly enjoyed every one. They have been walked, run, summer and winter climbed, cycled, boated, skied, snowboarded and the last one (Sgorr Dhonuill) by pushing a pram with my 8 week granddaughter, half way up.' With so many outdoor interests it is not surprising that John was able to persuade 84 people to join him! Rose and Robert Hancock (4240 & 4241) reported that 'as a link to our other passion in life, that of campanology, we celebrated our Compleation in the ringing, with eight others, of a peal on the ten bells of All Saints Belltower, Inverary, comprising 5,284 changes in 3 hours and 41 minutes...the tower top giving clear views that day of Ben Ime and Beinn Bhuidhe'.

Simon Winton (4247) dashed a Round in 18 months, raising £33,000 for the National Association for Colitis and Crohn's Disease. He was joined on his final summit, Glas Tulaichan, by 79 others, an impressive sight in distinctive red NACC T-shirts. This Compleation was also unique in that Simon's parents own the mountain and the surrounding estate.

SLOWLY, SLOWLY

Ben Brown (4112) Compleated way back in 1992, but waited until he had finished the Tops and Corbetts before owning up. Vivian Wright (4051) explained that her round had taken 32 years because 'I don't have a car, the majority of the 284 being reached by public transport; as I usually walk alone and rarely enter cloud I have often had to make repeat visits to some areas.' Occasional enquiries into obscure Munrological facts and records, often via the Webmaster, have prompted me to attempt to get this unexpected aspect of my job into better order, and I hope to have some FAQs on the website soon. I have always admired those who have been patient enough to stretch their Munro round and prolong the pleasure over almost a lifetime. To celebrate such achievement I propose to designate as Munrosis longius aureus individuals who have taken more than 50 years to Compleat. This year's *Golden Munroists* are

Howard O. Smith (4039) 51 years, Peter Dalrymple Hay (4058) 55 years, Gordon Ingall (4153) 51 years and Christine Russell (4201) 56 years.

SPECIALS

With the exception of the first two Compleaters, the List has always been strictly egalitarian, with no titles or qualifications recorded, encompassing people from all walks of life. This year our clerical pioneers, the Reverends Robertson(1) and Burn(2) were joined on the List by Jack Higham (4136) retired Canon Chancellor of Peterborough Cathedral; Ralph Godsall (4203) Canon Emeritus of Rochester, Priest Vicar of Westminster Abbey and Rev. Morris Rodham (4142). Richard Cooke (4103), Commander of the Order of the British Empire was another distinguished Compleater, while Alan (Lord) Haworth (2625) finished his Furths. Clair Hutchings (4105) was accompanied on her round by Crowdie, a border terrier, who has also Compleated the Furths, with only a few remaining Tops to scamper up. 'We have had a fantastic time together. Sometimes she had to be carried, sometimes she rode in a basket on a bike and other times she had to wear boots to protect her paws.' Wilma (2162) and Ron (2318) Forsyth were a rare Corbett Compleating couple.

STRIDE ON

One of my predecessors asked, out of curiosity, for Compleaters to indicate what they planned to do 'post-Munros'. This continues to elicit a wide variety of responses. Vivienne Rule (4226) wrote 'I'm getting myself a Labrador pup which I hope will accompany me on the hills, however I have no intention of ticking off any more Munros. Once was hard enough.' Craig Thomas Dunderdale (4179) had punctuated his round with ascents of Kilimanjaro and Mont Blanc, and was 'going to the Himalayas and hopefully climbing Mera Peak in 3 days time.' Kenneth Christie (1964) went on to do the Furths, in the course of which 'I had become addicted to winter outings, first climbing Raeburn's Gully in Creag Meagaidh...culminating with Point Five Gully, my first Grad V. My biggest regret now is not having started this winter climbing thing 30 years earlier!' He also managed to fit in an ascent of Elbrus, one of the Seven Summits.

SUNDRIES

In the course of his round of Munros, Tops and Furths, Duncan McPherson Smith (4087) has 'come up with my own system of classifying hills, based on geographical, topographical and subjective factors...a total in Scotland of 325 hills with 463 subsidiary peaks (of all heights).' He also enclosed a substantial paper defining 'the Duncans'. Eleanor Gledhill (4215) gave the secret of her success as 'over the years I've learned the most essential things to take are my cigarettes, ashtray and my i-pod. When I get fed up trudging up a hill, I have a wee break, have a ciggie and then put on my tunes.' Richard John Cooke (4200) did some analysis of weather for his Round and reported 'of all ascents 83% were in conditions where visibility was either okay, good or excellent. 36% were completed in what I might describe as perfect conditions....It was not luck; more good planning. Once I retired I had the opportunity to go for the hills whenever I spied high pressure coming in.' Unbeknown to Catherine Gemmell (4141) her Compleation was reported in the *Helensburgh Advertiser*, under the catchy headline 'The height of achievement'. Presumably with the help of a high altitude mole, reporter Leslie Maxwell gave a remarkably accurate and succinct history and summary of the whole sport, complete with a colour picture of Catherine approaching the cairn through the now traditional triumphal arch of walking-poles. Michael B. Slater (358) reported an eighth round, commenting 'about 12 years ago I had a target of completing my seventh round by my 65th birthday; I've managed to slip another one in with two and a half weeks to go.' Robert H. Macdonald (375) finally added the Tops to his seven round tally, as did Steve Mann (1612) despite 'having taken up employment in Moscow in 2002 and living in the Russian Federation.' Ken Falconer (408) reported a second round 'as a non-driver, my first round was done almost entirely using public transport and a bicycle, which in those days one could put in the guards vans on the Highland trains without the need to make reservations in advance. This is less easy now, and I reached rather more of the hills in friends cars.' Reporting Compleation of his Corbetts, Tony Weetman (2342) calculated 'I took 135 days over 8 years, compared to 109 days over 5 years for the Munros.' Rob Woodall (816) is attempting to become the first person to visit all 6,100 surviving OS triangulation pillars in Britain, which makes Munro bagging seem a doddle.

SADLY

John R. Taylor (4158) wrote 'to request the inclusion of my brother in law, Alastair Boyd (4157) and myself onto the Compleaters List. Alastair sadly passed away aged 50 (only a month after Compleation) whilst ascending Meall a Choire Leith, leaving a wife and three young children.' David Gemmell (1645) also passed away last year, one of the five members of the largest simultaneous Compleation in 1996. A Catholic priest, he was probably the only Monsignor to have done the Munros. I have also been asked to note the passing of David Unsworth (1192) in tragic circumstances at the early age of 32, and well on his way to finishing a third round.

SORRY

To Steve Perry (3114) whose continuous winter round between December 2005 and March 2006 was omitted from *Munro Matters*. Steve thus became the first person to accomplish two continuous Munro rounds, both in aid of *Cancer Research UK*. Jeffery Quinn (3393) also reported a continuous round 'starting on 1 April 2008 on Ben Hope and finishing 22 June on Ben Lomond (83 days) aided with my campervan as refuge every night. I hope to raise over £3,000 for *Childrens Hospice Association Scotland*'. Belated apologies too, to readers of SMCJ 198 (2007) whose table of Amendments at the end of *Munro Matters* has the dates of multiple rounds printed upside down! Adrian Snowdon (4185) enclosed a copy of the email he had sent to all his hill-going friends because 'I decided it would be better to climb my final Munro alone.'

SIGHTS

Fiona Reid (4081) and Michael Watson (4082) concluded 'We've seen some amazing sights over the years, some of the highlights include:
- Traversing the Lawers Ridge in winter above a perfect temperature inversion.
- Being joined on the summit of the Devils Point by a Golden Eagle.
- Perfect weather and no midges on the Fisherfield six.

• Witnessing a fogbow on Beinn Liath Mhor.'
Julian Stark (4110) 'could have sworn I met Jude Law on Sgurr nan Ceathremhnan.'

SITES
As well as the ever popular photo gallery which accompanies the List online at **www.smc.org.uk** a number of Compleaters have sent details of their own sites as follows:

www.hill-bagging.co.uk
www.prog99.com
www.munrodoug.pwp.blueyonder.co.uk/index/html
www.mennim.com/munroindex.html
www.scottishhills.com
www.pipedtothetop.com
http://website.lineone.net/~munrover/index.html
http://mountains.dontexist.com
http://paul.sammonds.com
http://www.ancientbrit-adventures.com

SUMMARY
My favourite for this year comes from David Childs (4159) who wrote: 'It has been interesting to note the changes in the hills over the time I have been walking them (started 1982), footpaths and trods were few and far between in the first ten years or so and now one seems to automatically look for a route along the ridge or to the top without thinking. I must of course accept some responsibility for the erosion of the hillsides in my outings and have been conscious of the effect of human impact on the mountains. In the overwhelming sense of enjoyment and wonder they have given me I hope that I have treated them with respect and reverence.'

AMENDMENTS
For many dedicated hill-goers, registering their first Munro Compleation is just the start of a never ending journey taking in more rounds, the Tops, Furths, Corbetts etc. Part of the Clerk of the List's duties includes updating entries to cover new achievements, as follows. Each Munroist's record is shown in full. The six columns give number, name, and year of Compleation of Munros, Tops, Furths and Corbetts.

2161	Donald Brown	1999			
		2003			
660	Paul Gillies	1989	2005	2006	
2774	Howard Jones	2002			2008
3438	Hazel Holmes	2005			
		2008			
959	Mike Dixon	1991	2008	2000	1996
1279	Nigel P. Morters	1994			1999
		2008			
2871	Peter Hamilton	1992		2002	1997
		2002			

		2008			
1801	Lindsay Boyd	1997	2002		2004
		2000			
		2002			
		2008			
3173	Julian Kirk	2004	2008		
2625	Alan Haworth	2001		2008	
3850	Maggie Carr	2007		2007	
3851	Mike O'Donohoe	2007		2007	
1473	L. Liney	1995			
		2008			
2125	James Henderson	1999			2008
1256	Keith Yates	1993	1997		
		1998			
		2004			
		2008			
3158	David A. Bunting	2004	2008	2007	
3393	Jeffrey Quinn	2005			
		2008			
486	Peter Bellarby	1987	1987	1987	2000
		2008			
3195	Richard Tait	2004	2008	2005	
358	Michael B. Slater	1984	1987	1987	
		1988			
		1990			
		1993			
		1996			
		1999			
		2003			
		2008			
380	Tom Stewart	1984			
		1994			
375	Robert H. Macdonald	1984	2008	1989	
		1987			
		1990			
		1992			
		1995			
		2002			
		2007			
1612	Steve Mann	1996	2008	1998	
2342	Anthony P. Weetman	2000		2004	2008
408	Ken Falconer	1985		1985	2001
		2008			
1964	Kenneth Christie	1998		2008	
754	Charles R. Haigh	1988	2003	1982	1999
		2008			
3296	Colin Lesenger	2004	2008		
3596	John M. Tweddle	2006	2006	2008	

2390	Colin Scott	2000			
		2008			
3196	Jim Wallace	2004			2008
2346	David Allison	2000	2003	2002	2008
2162	Wilma Forsyth	1999			2008
2318	Ron Forsyth	2000			2008
621	Alistair Milner	1988			2008
4062	Michael G. Barnard	2008	2008		
596	Brian R. Johnson	1988	1991		
		2007	2007		
258	Iain R.W. Park	1981			
		1997			
		2007			
808	John Barnard	1990	1990	1990	
		2001	2001		

This information is of course also available at **www.smc.org.uk** along with the increasingly popular Munroists Photo Gallery. To register a Compleation or amendment, please write to Dave Broadhead, Cul Mor, Drynie Park North, Muir of Ord, IV6 7RP. If you would like to receive a certificate for either Munro or Corbett Compleation, please enclose an A4 sae (with the correct postage please). Once you have received a number, a Compleation photo can be posted or emailed to the Webmaster.

Enjoy your hills.

Dave Broadhead,
Clerk of the List.

IN MEMORIAM

SCOTT JOHNSTONE j. 1953

IN HIS EULOGY at Bill Wallace's funeral in 2006, Malcolm Slesser made the telling observation that for many Club members, life falls into three discrete parts – climbing, work, and family. It was a measure of Scott Johnstone's passion for Scotland's hills, and of his good fortune, that in the days before professional climbing offered a livelihood, he was pre-eminently successful in weaving those three life strands into a happy, mutually reinforcing, and profoundly satisfying combination.

Born in Glasgow in 1922 and educated at the High School, Scott came to the hills through the Scouts, with Arran as his early playground. His training in Geology at Glasgow University – where he helped establish the GUM Club, finally constituted in the dark days of 1941 – was interrupted by war service, which led him to Kent and work as an electronics engineer. But in 1945 he emerged from Gilmorehill with a first-class degree and a life partner in Molly, newly qualified in medicine and equally enthusiastic for the hills. They celebrated their marriage with the first ascent of *Haakon's Highway* on Beinn a' Chliabhain in September 1945.

Joining the Geological Survey in Edinburgh, Scott soon found his metier, in mapping and unravelling the immensely complex Moine structures of the Highlands. Through the 1950s and '60s this work was of fundamental practical relevance to the surge of hydro-electric development, especially in the western Highlands. Between his decades of fieldwork in geological survey, which led him into many unfrequented corners, and his weekends of climbing with Molly, Scott acquired an exceptional knowledge of the Highlands and islands. In that sense he was in direct line of succession to the early SMC geologist members Peach and Geikie, Hinxman and Harker. Those heroes of the revolutionary era of Scottish geological exploration in the late nineteenth century, and their botanist counterparts, had a grasp of Scottish mountain geography which the pioneer climbers could scarcely match.

Scott put this knowledge at the service of the Club through work as Guide Books General Editor from 1958–64, as Editor of District Guides 1964–66, and in his revision of the Club's Western Highlands guide in 1966. After he retired, Scott undertook as senior editor the considerable task of compiling the first edition of the Corbetts guide in 1993. As well as writing entries for a good number of tops, especially in the Western Highlands, he contributed a number of his own fine photographs; but he also, with characteristic conscientiousness, undertook lengthy sorties in pursuit of better pictures of various frankly uninspiring bumps. At the same period he represented the Mountaineering Council of Scotland on the Council of the National Trust for Scotland, where he brought his specialist knowledge and careful judgement to the Trust's Countryside and Nature Conservation Committee.

A rummage through old Journals and District Guides illustrates the range of Scott's avid exploratory stravaigings across the Highlands, usually with a rope and always with an eye for a promising line on ridge or crag. Particularly in the 1950s, nearly always with Molly, he found new routes – mountain routes rather than hard climbs – on hills from Arran to Ben Hope, taking in Aonach Beag, Kintail, Liathach, Stac Polly, and Cona Mheall, with diversions to Harris. They continued climbing in Scotland and abroad with undiminished enthusiasm into the new millennium.

The climbing couple has, of course, been an established feature of the Scottish mountain scene since the days of Willie and Jane Inglis Clark. There have been at least a dozen notable SMC-LSCC couples where one or both became Presidents of their respective clubs. But those partnerships, with their lifelong bonds of shared commitment to Scotland's mountains, were inevitably understated – indeed rarely recognised – in the annals of the SMC during its long era of gender apartheid. It is a mild irony that Molly, one of those LSCC Presidents, has probably featured second only to Anne Bennet in frequency of appearance as the artfully positioned foreground figure in illustrations to SMC guide books.

Scott was a genial but reserved and unassertive man, most at ease among close friends and professional colleagues, where he revealed a pithy humour and wide-ranging erudition. A distinctive figure, lean and rangy, alert, engaged. Quintessentially a man of the Scottish mountains.

Robert Aitken

EDWARD (EDI) THOMPSON j. 1965

WITH THE DEMISE of Edi, who died on 14 July 2008, the club has lost one of its most colourful characters.

Edi's inspiration came from his music, from the mountains of Scotland and other lands and latterly from his work as a potter in Rodel, Harris.

He was brought up in Dunoon, where scarlet fever in early childhood destroyed his hearing. This handicap did not prevent Edi from acquiring an MA (Music) and a BMus at Glasgow University. He also became a Fellow of the Royal College of Organists.

For many years Edi taught up at the Royal Scottish Academy of Music and Drama where he also held the post of librarian. Former pupils have affectionate and appreciative memories of his reign there. He was noted as a sharp dresser and would deliver lectures dressed in either an immaculate business suit or tight-fitting black motorcycle leathers.

Edi was a generous host and many will remember outstanding dinner parties at his flat in Doune Quadrant. He was a superb cook and did his own wonderful variation on Cullen Skink.

It was not in Edi's nature to criticise other people but he would comment with subtlety, humour, and precision on any circumstance or event of which he disapproved. On the other hand, he told many stories against himself...he recounted how, one Sabbath when he was the organist at Dunfermline Abbey, the alarm clock in his briefcase beside him went off during the sermon and Edi, with his hearing aids switched off at this point, was the only person in the entire congregation who was unaware of this intrusion.

Many will remember that climbing with Edi was seldom without incident. The impossibility of communication between one end of the rope and the other made for interesting and occasionally precarious climbing. With his deafness he did not receive the warning whiz and whang of falling stones and in the days before hard hats his polished head had a permanently battle-scarred appearance. He was of course oblivious to the missiles he dislodged onto his forebearing seconders below but any attempted 'reprimand' would be cut short by a beaming observation from the belay above 'rock's jolly loose chaps!'

Edi's commentary on events or situations was always succinct and one remembers an ascent of *Bastinado* on Sron na Ciche. Both climbers were wearing exceedingly bendy Timpson's hiking boots and Edi, leading the crux, called down very primly and politely, 'it's getting rather steep up here!'.

Although not known for his technical climbing prowess, throughout his life Edi made the most of his freedom to explore and enjoy the mountains throughout Scotland, in winter and summer. Abroad, he climbed in the BC Coast Range, Norway, Turkey and the Alps. On one visit to Arolla, success on many of the classics was followed by a very swift ascent of the Dent Blanche. The descent to the hut was made down the South Ridge, in the most ferocious blizzard, when verbal communication would have been impossible anyway, even without Edi's handicap.

Edi was a member of the colourful Hillman Imp 'Mountain Imp' team which drove to the Taurus mountains in Turkey. Edi survived being chased by one of the infamous Anatolian sheep dogs and succeeded in an ascent of Demir Kazik.

In the Coast Range of British Columbia Edi took part in a number of climbs including first ascents of Mount Burkett by the South-East Ridge[1], and of Mount Gilroy.

In the Lofoten Islands, Edi made a number of ascents including Higraftiende by the East Ridge, Geitgaljartinde, Rorhoptiende, and Langstrendtiende.

Edi often used his musical knowledge with great humour – there is a memory of sailing into a Norwegian harbour in poor visibility. Having explained that the tone of the ship's foghorn was a perfect fifth, he assembled the group near the bow, gave each one a note to sing and on his cue they performed. The resulting composite tone emulated the ship's horn precisely.

In mid life Edi made a bold career change. He exchanged his academic appointment and Glasgow West End flat for a potter's wheel and a beautifully refurbished tiny house in Rodel. Edi the potter took great delight in using the minerals he found in Harris to produce glazes of exquisite colour. He held yearly exhibitions of his work in Edinburgh or Glasgow which were invariably sold out. He was not a natural salesperson when at work in his pottery and was well known for his tendency to rush off up the hillside at the first awareness of an approaching tourist customer.

He loved the rugged mountains of Harris and clambered regularly over all the hills there. He surely knew every boulder on Roneval above his cottage. However, Edi developed Parkinson's disease which he endured over an exceptionally long time span of more than twenty years. He referred to his illness as 'Parky' and regarded it as a visitor who called at first infrequently but then with increasing regularity. He bore this affliction with extraordinary courage and humour. He gradually lost his physical freedom, his fingers could

---

[1] Eddie Thompson, *The Ascent of Mount Burkett in 500 Words,* SMCJ 1966, XXVIII, 189–90.

no longer work his clay and eventually he became deprived of the ability to play his piano, particularly the music of his favourite composer Mozart. He was largely paralysed for the last eight years or so but remained extremely alert of mind, with the very sharpest of memories and could recall past adventures in the mountains in the greatest detail. It was stunningly sad for Edi's friends, off on privileged travels around the world, to think of Edi entrapped in his chair in the Gatehouse, Rodel, looking out over Roneval.

In a Cairngorm blizzard or on a cloudless day on the hills of Harris, Edi was the best of companions. Edi will be hugely missed by his fellow mountaineers and by numerous other friends across a very wide range of interests.

Robin Chalmers

QUINTIN CRICHTON j. 1959

QUINTIN WAS educated at Morgan Academy, Dundee before commencing his apprenticeship as a Chartered Accountant. At school he was a House Captain and was a member of most of the school sports teams including rugby, swimming, athletics and golf where he was awarded a 'cap'.

Introduction to 'the hills' came by chance via one of the teachers who led a group of boys to an overnight stay in Clova. The walk in was in darkness and next day a round of sodden tracks in mizzle and mist should have made that the first and last outing but inexplicably Quintin was fascinated by everything.

At that time, the cost of a trip was difficult for a schoolboy and therefore membership of the Grampian Club, Carn Dearg MC and Perth JMCS was a boon for the regular bus outings. Cycling was always an option and when the SYHA took over Glendoll Lodge it made all the Clova hills so much more accessible. The equipment was basic to say the least; the first rope was 80ft hemp with ex-WD axes in winter. (Anyone who can recall these will remember the rope when damp and frozen became akin to a steel hawser and just as intractable.) However, like many beginners they were naive and full of misplaced confidence, but picked up techniques and experience along the way.

All this came to a sudden end in 1953 when the mass radiography unit picked up a chest infection and within a few weeks he found himself in hospital, in of all places, one of the Angus glens – where he remained for the next 18 months.

On resuming his career the medics advised against strenuous sports so out went rugby with the F.P.s, and golf, fishing, modest hill-walking, cycling and road biking took up his spare time.

After qualifying as a Chartered Accountant he moved to a firm in Glasgow who had clients in the Borders and Northern Ireland before returning to Dundee to join a well established professional firm, ending up as senior partner before retiring in 1999. In earlier years he lectured at both Glasgow and Dundee in various accounting subjects, updating the ongoing changes in the syllabus. The firm became involved in a national consortium which entailed more travelling and less spare time through Dundee Football Club's development funding affairs, which ran for 20 years.

A man of many interests, he played squash and tennis into his mid sixties. He was an enthusiastic sub-aqua diver with his own boat which he used to dive widely round the west and east coasts. He was also a black belt at Judo. After retiring be did a lot of mountain biking and used his bike to access the more distant Cairngorm corries including Ben a' Bhuird where he did a 50th anniversary ascent of his *Quartzvein Route* in Coire na Ciche in 2003. He was a keen angler and enjoyed walking into hill lochs to fish. Through his whole life the one constant was his love of the hills and climbing. He was a natural rock climber and made it look very easy. Because of his natural ability he thought everyone else found it easy and wouldn't need a belay. It took us years to get him to take a proper belay, though in his later years he was much more protection aware. As the years went by he curtailed to some extent his climbing although he and I did a climb the winter before he died.

He had a very enquiring mind and retentive memory which made him a very informative and interesting companion on the hills. His dry sense of humour and sharp wit will be missed by all who knew him. When he knew he was dying he had a look round and decided he wanted to be buried in the small churchyard in Glen Clova opposite the hotel where he now lies at peace among his beloved hills.

Our sympathies go out to his wife Pamela and their three daughters.

N.Q.

DOUGLAS SCOTT j. 1944

DOUGLAS, WHO died last year at the age of 97, was one of the grand old masters of the pre-industrial age of mountaineering. In the pre-war years he was part of the Murray-MacKenzie-MacAlpine-MacKinnon galaxy (immortalized in Tom Patey's *Ballad of Bill Murray*), climbing major routes mostly on the Ben and the Buachaille in summer and winter. Much of this activity is recorded in Murray's Mountaineering in Scotland. In the pre-war years he also climbed with Tom Weir and Rob Anderson. (Rob is still with us and approaching his century.) In August 1935 he led Alastair Borthwick of *Always a Little Further* fame up a number of routes on the Buachaille.

Before that (seventy-seven years ago in fact, in 1932) he spent a summer in Iceland on a Geographic Society project investigating 'ice damming of Hogavatn in the Langjokul district' with Dr Todd Wright and no less a luminary than Ben Humble.

In the war he was in the Royal Corps of Signals, ending the war in India in 1945. Before returning home he got local leave and made a solo trip into the Garwhal Himalaya.

This was the seed of the 1950 Scottish Himalayan Expedition of which Douglas was the originator. Although Bill Murray became the acknowledged leader, overall organizer and writer of the classic book on the expedition, it was Douglas who initially recruited the others, did the basic organization and booked the passages on the boat to India. Once the show was on the road Douglas remained a source of strength but, as was his habit, merged into the scenery. He was biologist enough to appreciate the importance of protective colouration. Dougie was the last surviving hero of that Expedition. The others – Tom

McKinnon, Bill Murray and Tom Weir preceded him in that order on the voyage to the happy isles of Tir nan Og, or wherever it is that such stout souls end up. To recapture the spirit of the pre-industrial period it is worth looking at the photograph of this historic quartet in Murray's book.

After the Himalayan trip he was in the Lofotens in 1951 with Adam Watson and Tom Weir. (See Tom's *Camps and Climbs in Arctic Norway.*) They made the first post-war ascent of the Horns and as they jumped between the topmost pinnacles the ships in the harbour sounded their sirens. In 1952 he, the two Toms, and that other stolid pillar of the Club, George Roger, were back in the Himalaya, this time in the Rowaling region. (See Tom Weir's *East of Katmandu.*) In 1955 he was in the Moroccan High Atlas with Tom Weir and in the next year in Kurdistan, again with Tom. The latter was one of his favourite trips. He and Tom appeared to have got on well with the heavily-armed Kurds who were intrigued by this strange, friendly, unpretentious couple of outsiders who did not conform to any known pattern except their liking for mountains. Things are different today.

In 1958 he was in Greenland as a member of the Scottish East Greenland Expedition. Although sociable, he required periods of solitude and would generally contrive to be alone for a period on any expedition and managed this inoffensively. During the 1958 trip he hitched a lift on a light plane into the remote Schuichert Dal and continued on to the Inuit settlement at Syd Kap, returning solo through the wilderness to the airstrip at Mestersvig.

In 1966 he was on Mount Kenya. In 1970, again in East Greenland, he and Audrey made an unsupported canoe trip round Ella Island. In 1987 with C.N. Eccles, his son Christopher and myself he made a trip to the Bear Islands in Scoresby Sound. This was a slow voyage as our outboard engine performed sub-optimally as it was slightly bent following failure of a parachute during an airdrop. Douglas led the ascent of the highest peak of the Bear Islands which had a final pitch of Mild Severe standard.

For the first fifty years of his life Douglas was Scotland's most successful bachelor, the focus of much admiration. For the next forty-seven years he was Scotland's most successful husband. When he and Audrey got married Dougie's life expanded. Audrey was adventurous in her own right and she and Douglas led a life of physical, intellectual and cultural endeavour. Their home near Spean Bridge was a hospitable and civilised refuge for friends passing to and from the north. They were both bold ski mountaineers in Scotland and the Alps. They canoed extensively in the Western Isles and explored the world furth of Scotland from Poland to Africa.

I am conscious that very little of Dougie's 'persona' has emerged from this account of some of the main events in his life. This is because Douglas, in spite of, or perhaps because of, his learning, artistic abilities and social graces, liked to merge with the scenery.

My happiest memories of Douglas stem from 'The Ancient Mariners Canoe Meets'. For a number of years on the first weekend of November Douglas, the learned Rob Anderson, a deep well of ancient lore, and two junior ancient mariners (Malcolm and me) would meet with our canoes somewhere on the west coast and explore the bays and islands in sunlight and storm. One occasion I remember in particular. We were camped in a gale by the waters of the Dorus

Mor. While the wind, rain and sea raged in the darkness around our tent we discussed the relation of the psyche to the land – the genius loci, specifically the genius Scotiae – this bond we have with our native land. I now realize this was an important historical link between two generations; our elders passed on to Malcolm and me so much arcane lore that strengthened the links we have with this curious and demanding country of Scotland. Printed records are all very well but ideas lose their immediacy when trapped on a page and, most importantly, they lack the intonations and presence of the human voice passing on the oral tradition from generation to generation. It doesn't take much effort for me to hear Douglas's soft voice and quiet chuckle as we shared a dram of the water of life in the eye of the storm so many short years ago.

Iain Smart

DOUGLAS SCOTT was renowned as an explorer and mountaineer, and his achievements in these domains are recognized elsewhere. However, he was also a prodigiously talented photographer. Members will be familiar with his excellent photographs illustrating accounts of his expeditions with Tom Weir, and used extensively by Tom and by Bill Murray in their well-known books. Before the 1950 Garhwal Expedition, Douglas was already contemplating a photographic career. In a letter to Weir dated 7 August (probably 1949) he mentions an offer to work with W.S. Thomson at Fort William. The same letter provides evidence of a deliberate and contemplative approach to mountain photography: after a visit to Handa, he 'dawdled south concentrating on photography, difficult work for the weather broke and much waiting and luck was needed.' However, after the expedition, Tom and Douglas maintained a busy studio in Douglas's house at 7 Orleans Avenue. According to Tom in *Weir's World* (p. 69), they spent 'a disciplined twelve months of darkroom and writing to fill the coffers.' They made enough money from the combination of Tom's writing and their joint photography – particularly from helpful contracts with the National Geographic Magazine – to finance further expeditions.

Murray had suggested to Tom that he and Douglas should take premises in central Glasgow if they wished to expand their business. This did not happen, although they shared a darkroom for a while with the well-known Glasgow portrait photographer J. Stephens Orr, a charismatic figure described by Douglas as 'always wearing a kilt and driving a battered old Bentley about town.' Neither man would countenance the obvious source of additional income – wedding photography – and in the end they went in different directions; Tom to the Scots Magazine and other magazine photo-journalism; Douglas to freelance commercial photography for a wide range of businesses, including the Templeton carpet factory where he had originally been an employee.

Of course, Douglas continued with nature and mountain photography at every opportunity, and took on work of this sort occasionally, for example postcard photography for J. Arthur Dixon and a partnership with A.D.S. Macpherson, a mountaineer and photographer from Stirling whose patient work was also used by Bill Murray: Macpherson would apparently wait on the same spot all day if necessary for the best conditions for a particular landscape shot. However, it was the commercial work which provided his principal income. Recently, I had the pleasure of sorting through Tom Weir's black and white print collection. Because of the close connection between the two men, there were many of Douglas's prints mixed in amongst Tom's, which I extracted and returned. Besides the helpful backstamp, there were other attributes that distinguished Douglas's work from Tom's – better resolution, finer grain, lower range and contrast, and always printed with scrupulous precision. Eventually I could pick them out without needing to examine the backstamp. This is not to say that his work was better than Tom's, but it had a real distinctive quality of deliberation and care.

Douglas exhibited his nature and mountain work occasionally. I know of one exhibition at the Arlington Baths in the 1970s, and in his last years he had an exhibition at the Discovery Centre in Dundee – a sequel to his being honoured, on the occasion of their Centenary, by the Scottish Photographic Federation in 2003 at the suggestion of our member James Renny. This exhibition was supported by our Trust, and after some months at Dundee it moved to Fort William for a second run. It was a sorrow to me that these exhibitions were dominated by his colour work, and showed very few of the monochrome prints which had so beguiled me in the trawl through Tom's collection. Perhaps this omission may be rectified in the future.

Douglas was also honoured by the Institute of British Photographers for his work in Greenland. And although he was not much given to writing, besides his address to the Federation in 2003, he gave talks on many occasions and to photographers as well as to mountaineers. The Edinburgh Photographic Society, a careful recorder of its history, notes talks given by Douglas on 12 Oct 1949 – *A colour show by a mountaineer*; 6 Nov 1957 – *Mountain Adventure*; 30 Oct 1963 – *Wild Country of Scotland*; and 23 Jan 1961 – *The Scottish East Greenland Expedition, 1958*. In speaking regularly at the Edinburgh society, Douglas followed in the footsteps of earlier members William Inglis Clark and Reverend Robertson, and alongside those of his contemporary Douglas J. Fraser.

Robin N. Campbell

BLYTH WRIGHT j. 1972

I THINK this is how it started.

There was Jock Mackay, Neil MacNiven, Jim Gibson, Wull Thompson; our mentor was Jock Mackinnon, who was older than us but had the experience of the hills. We all started climbing at Kirkcaldy High School in the sixties. Jock was head boy; Neil was Dux; they were all a couple of years older than me, and I was a newcomer in from Fourth form. None of us belonged to the rugby crowd; Wednesday PT could see us in the reject pile cross country team, vanishing off toward Thornton for a good run in the woods or a smoke.

We were at the tail end of those days where your mountaineering club would hire a bus and go off for the weekend; before someone got a car; before we went to University. Off we would go to the Trossachs, Glen Coe or Crianlarich. We had our first sight of Buachaille Etive; our first touch of rock; our first nights in the pub; our first rain-drumming nights under Blacks of Greenock cotton. Or more simply, the peace of the Lomond Hills, watching over the Lang Toon.

Those tiny, broken crags had the same allure as a new Alp or Himalaya; everything was new. Carlin Maggie; Ravenscraig; Aberdour; those little vertical bits of the earth so close to home where no-one had set foot. It was a revelation. We shared that gift of the outdoors, a gift which is still magically available to us despite all we do to the earth.

We fell a lot. Sometimes all together in a pile. On Bishop Hill there is a scruffy crag, and we had two pegs, mail ordered from Blacks; we would be like the Dolomite Immortals in the climbing books we avidly devoured. So I led up and hung from a peg; then, Blyth and Jock hauled up the rope and up I went to put in the second one; then down to knock out the first one, then back up to knock it in a little higher; each time, Blyth and Jock hauling down the escarpment in a tug of war; until finally, a peg came out and we all rolled down erse fir elbie down the hill till we landed in a wifey's back garden in Scotlandwell and I broke my wrist and I am looking at it now and it is still gibbled, and I have a tear in my eye.

Or at Dunkeld...where Blyth expressed mild astonishment in his sardonic way as another peg came out and I hurtled past to stop just above the ground, thanks to his belaying skills. I think you broke your glasses. That was a climb called *Mouse Trap* and it probably has another name now and is probably solo climbed by 12 year olds.

So perhaps from these incidents we learned how to belay properly.

Or in the Fannichs, where in the depths of winter, on a slow approach climb up a slope in the fog we saw the nearby cliffs moving upward; however, it was the snow moving downward.

So perhaps this was the start of Blyth's distinguished avalanche career as we toppled over, no damage done.

University days seem now so long though they were so short. Although brilliant, Blyth did not get on too well with the dominies at St. Andrews; I was at Edinburgh, scraping through. Blyth introduced me to the Corriemulzie Club, a group dedicated to exploring the North West Highlands. Philip Tranter was the driver, and his energy led to a unique approach; we each would pack a piece of a large tent which would be assembled as a base camp; it was called 'The Nalley'. It was a long A frame and a cross between a refugee camp and a crematorium; it could sleep ten, twenty at push...it burned down twice. It would disappear into the Highlands for weeks on end, and folks would gravitate towards it. Blyth and Philip and the others made many of these trips, and many new routes were done. These trips and their legacy of exploration are very well regarded today; tragically Philip was killed in a car crash in Turkey. One of their achievements was a continuous circuit of Glen Nevis over a 24 hour period; a bold concept of many Munros, involving all of the Mamores and the Nevis group.

Aye weel...farewell old friend, you've gone too soon. We will miss your unfettered judgment, always well argued and weel kent; your sardonic wit; your existential lunges into experience, and most of all, your uncompromised search for your own truth.

Ian Rowe

I FIRST MET BLYTH WRIGHT at the Aberdeen University Mountaineering Club dinner where he was attending as the representative of the St. Andrews University club. At our first meeting Blyth displayed the characteristics that those who knew him would recognise – he was very sociable and gave an entertaining speech and then demonstrated that he enjoyed a good time and a drink, loved to talk about mountaineering and Scotland and liked to sing – usually badly but with enthusiasm. As I got to know him better he revealed he could be determined, stubborn, entertaining, annoying, awkward and opinionated but he was always interesting company. During his life, Blyth's career and mine intertwined and we eventually ended up in adjoining offices at Glenmore Lodge where he was the head of the Scottish Avalanche Information Service. Like everyone who knew Blyth, I will sorely miss his company both at work and play.

Blyth started climbing while at school in Kirkcaldy and throughout his life engaged in almost every aspect of mountaineering. As a member of the Corriemulzie Club he climbed in the far North West of Scotland when it was more remote and serious than today and retained a great fondness for this part of the country. After university and teacher training college Blyth spent some time as a youth worker in Edinburgh before turning to hills for a career. After early climbing visits to the Alps he worked at ISM in Switzerland along side Dougal Haston in the 1960s and was a well known figure in Club Vagabond in Leysin. Blyth then spent time at the Loch Eil Centre where he helped develop the Polldubh Crags and, along with Klaus Swartz, co-authored the first real climbing guide to this area. Blyth then moved on to Glenmore Lodge where he worked for some 20 years. Besides instructing in all aspects of mountaineering he also taught sailing and skiing. He also developed an interest in mountain rescue and trained a rescue dog named Einich, remembered by all that met it as the nearest thing to a psychopathic Alsatian ever to be let loose on a mountaineering casualty. At this time Blyth was also one of the team that did the first coast to coast crossing of Scotland on skis – a feat unlikely to be repeated in these days of climate change. Outside of work Blyth continued to climb and explore and helped develop many crags, particularly in the North West.

It was during this time that Blyth developed an interest in avalanches and avalanche forecasting and with Bob Barton wrote *A Chance in a Million?* which has remained in print ever since and is essential reading for anyone interested in going to the hills in the winter. Blyth was then the obvious person to head the Scottish Avalanche Information Service when it was started and remained at its head until his death. It is in this role that many will remember him. Blyth was passionate about this service and educating the mountaineering world about the dangers of avalanches. His drive and determination greatly contributed to the expansion and success of the service. It would not be the service it is now without Blyth.

Blyth however, had wider interests than mountaineering and avalanches. For a while he raced motor bikes – something of a family tradition for his brother Charlie was a former Scottish motor bike champion. He had a flair for languages, particularly French, and translated several books into English. He was also very knowledgeable about mountaineering literature and built up an impressive collection of early and rare mountaineering books, often signed first

Top Left: Douglas Scott.
Top Right: Douglas performing tree surgery aged 93. Both photos: Audrey Scott.
Bottom: Blyth Wright. Photo: Charlie Wright.

editions. He mentored a number of talented young Scottish climbers on their first visits to the Alps and later he visited the Himalaya where he climbed Ama Dablam. Blyth was a staunch Scottish Nationalist and an active party worker. He was the election agent for Fergus Ewing in the 1992 Westminster election and then again in 1999 when the SNP won the seat at the first Holyrood election. A tribute to Blyth from Alex Salmond, the Scottish First Minister, was read at Blyth's funeral and the depth and breadth of the many friendships Blyth formed during his lifetime were shown by the mourners there.

Allen Fyffe

PROCEEDING OF THE CLUB

The following new members were admitted and welcomed to the club in 2008–9:

TIM BLAKEMORE, (37), Mountain Guide, Haddington, East Lothian.
IAIN FORREST, (31), IT Manager, Bannockburn, Stirlingshire.
DIAHANNE GILBERT, (35), Mountaineering Instructor, Grantown on Spey.
ROBERT HAMILTON, (59), Fisherman, Duror of Appin.
BARRY G. HARD, (50), Site Manager, North Kessock, Inverness.
PETER T. MACPHERSON, (31), Shop manager, Inverness.
MATTHEW J. MUNRO, (33), Software Engineer, Glasgow.
COLIN A. SIMPSON, (42), Tourism Co-ordinator, Munlochy, Inverness-shire.
CHRISTOPHER THORNE, (31), Mountaineering Instructor, Pwllheli, Gwynedd.
GRAEME S. TOUGH, (49), Materials Scientist, Edinburgh.
GRAHAM J. TYLDESLEY, (29), Student, Aberdeen.
LEE WALES, (28), RAF Engineer, Elgin.

The One-Hundred-and-Twentieth AGM and Dinner

BRIGHT SUNSHINE and snow down to sea level greeted members as we assembled for the 120th AGM and Dinner which was held again in Fort William.

For those not out on the hill, Brian Shackleton talked us through the Club expedition to East Greenland which took place in May 2007. The team visited the Stauning Alps, well known to a number of Club members. By the use of a flight onto the glacier and then skis to travel on the ice fields they claimed numerous first ascents from two separate glaciers. It was good to see Donald Bennet was able to join us for that part of the day.

Then on with the AGM. A major talking point was the CIC renovation and expansion work undertaken in the 'summer' months of 2008. The committee reported that despite dreadful weather the work was largely completed, was within the expected budget and the building was almost ready to take bookings for 2009. A second financial concern was that the Treasurer had requested an increase in membership subscriptions. The over sixty-fives had also noticed that their proposed percentage increase was far higher than that for the ordinary members. A discussion ensued, but the younger majority supported this injustice and the Treasurer's proposal was carried!

The evening concluded with the Club Dinner. We welcomed 135 diners including guests from our Kindred Clubs and the Principal Guest, Simon Yates. In his speech our Club President, Paul Brian, spoke of his pleasure in attending some of the Kindred Club Dinners during the year, and noted that the LSCC had celebrated their centenary. He also spoke of the recent death of Douglas Scott at the grand age of 97.

There have been rumblings in recent years about the after-dinner formalities being unduly long. However they were sufficiently streamlined this year for Curly Ross to slip in an unplanned rendition of Dark Lochnagar. Des Rubens stepped up to accept the trappings of office as our new President before the evening finished with the traditional retirement to the bar – for more catching up, and laying of plans for future days in the hills.

Chris M. Huntley

CIC Hut Meets 2009

The CIC Hut meet on 30 January/1 February saw the first use of the new extension. A gale force wind and a rapid thaw created a challenge in even reaching the hut on Friday night. Eventually there were 6 members including the custodian Robin and the President Des Rubens. Robin had 2 guests which he used as pack horses, and we also gave accommodation (which was charged) to 3 Londoners who had intended to camp. The violent wind blew all night and was still gale force when the President attempted a walk to Coire Leis, which resulted in him being blown off his feet and catapulted onto a boulder injuring his left arm.

The hut itself was still in an unfinished state; no electric lighting, no toilets or drying room were operational. Initial impression was that the drying room was totally unfit for purpose compared to what we previously enjoyed. Many hours of discussion ensued as how best the new areas could be utilised. There was also a great deal of clearing up work done while the storm raged outside.

Sunday's weather was a great improvement so much so that we actually got climbing! Messrs Clothier and Forsyth climbed Garadh Gully, Glover's Chimney and then Smith's on Gardyloo Buttress. Messrs Rubens and Broadhead climbed Green Gully while Stead & Lang made an ascent of No2 Gully Buttress. Robin's guests abandoned an attempt of Zero Gully.

The February meet was attended by 6 members plus a guest. They endured horizontal rain on the Saturday which turned to horizontal snow on Sunday. The only activity was a 14 pitch ascent of Castle Ridge by Messrs Findlay & Higham.

Initially 12 members and 2 guests attended the April meet. Again the weather was abysmal, rain with snow higher up but the freezing level was above the summit as the only pair to venture forth reported having soloed up Tower Gully via Tower Scoop area. The Huts Convener James and past President Brian braved the rain to attend an afternoon meeting with the current President Rubens and the hut custodian Clothier. This meeting went on for over 2 hours, hopefully the discussions would result in actions to be taken regarding the finalisation of the extension work.

Half the attendees went down on Saturday night, there was no improvement of the conditions by Sunday morning and all but 2 headed down hill. Messrs Suess and J.T.H.Allen managed an ascent of Tower Scoop as J.T had just passed his three score years and ten anniversary.

D.F.L.

Ski Mountaineering Meet 2009

Ladies Scottish Climbing Club hut, Milehouse, Glenfeshie, 7–8 March 2009.
Members present: Richard Bott, Ewan Clark, David Eaton, Colwyn Jones, Ann MacDonald, Peter McDonald, Heike Puchan, Bob Reid, Brian Shackleton, Graham Tough, Brian Whitworth. Guest: Dave Coustick.

The excellent Ladies Scottish Climbing Club hut called Milehouse in Glenfeshie was the latest venue for the annual Scottish Mountaineering Club ski touring meet. Members and one guest arrived steadily throughout Friday evening despite the frequent showers and mild westerly winds which had been forecast and, as predicted, duly materialised. As numbers increased in front of the roaring stove, whisky was sipped and the conversation slipped between skiing plans for the weekend, climbing and touring trips over the not so recent past and expedition plans for the coming year.

As consistently happens after every Friday, Saturday dawned, albeit reluctantly on this occasion, calm and mild in the wooded glen. Brian Whitworth and Heike rose early in an effort to beat the worsening forecast weather and headed to Coire an t-Sneachda for a quick approach, a quick route and a quick exit. They climbed The Seamstress (IV,6 **) on Fiacaill Buttress, which was *'in very good nick'*, before retreating to Aviemore for cappucino and cake; caffeine and chocolate the legal drugs of choice of the masses!

Ewan, Bob and Dave Coustick had an abortive look at the hills east of Glen Feshie then also made for the Cairngorm ski carpark and skinned up to the summit of Cairn Gorm (4084ft/1245m). Due to a strong south-west wind the route down was via Cnap Coire na Spreidhe (3772ft/1151m) into a gully leading into the Ciste, skiing to the limit of the snow before traversing back to the car.

Ann, Colwyn and Dave Eaton cut straight to the chase and headed up to the Cairngorm ski carpark. From here they skinned up to the top of Lurcher's Gully where the wind was very perceptible and the final pull to the summit of Cairn Lochan (3983ft/1215m) was in somewhat low visibility. Owing to the close proximity of unseen cliffs dropping into Coire an Lochain the GPS was switched on and this led to a merry circular tour of the summit plateau with the GPS directly contradicting the traditional compass. Despite the gale, recalibration of the GPS was ultimately achieved and it finally pointed to the top of the Shelter Stone Crag where the gully between it and Carn Etchachan was sought (GPS height 1045m). Castlegates gully is described in the current SMC Cairngorms guidebook as, *'A long well defined gully which is quite low angled for the grade. ...a useful descent as well as a scenic ascent (200m, Grade I).'* The first ascent of the gully was in July 1904 by Hugh Stewart and A.B. Duncan and was recorded in the Cairngorm Club Journal (CCJ No. 24, January 1905). Stewart gave no detailed explanation for the title *Castle Gates Gully*, but mentioned that *'the rock scenery is extremely fine'*, a sentiment I am happy to echo. Interestingly, in a recently published book entitled *A Cairngorm Chronicle* by A.F. Whyte, the author describes a descent of the 'Slithering Gully' prior to the July ascent. Whyte wrote:

> I believe that a month later another party of climbers called it the Castle Gates Gully. Doubtless they noted some feature which prompted this title and, moreover, we were using it as a toboggan slide from above, whereas they would see it in more dignified guise from below as a stiffish climb, with the walls of the gully at the top looking like the gates of a castle.

The first ascent of the gully under snow was reported to be in Easter 1914 just a few short months before the assassination of Crown Prince Franz Ferdinand in Sarajevo, which precipitated the First World War.

By the outbreak of war one of the first summer ascentionists Hugh Stewart had been appointed Professor of Classics at Canterbury College, Christchurch. He was described in his obituary as a born soldier and leader of men and endured a life of personal tragedy. However, rather more tragic were the dangers for both mother and baby during childbirth at that time (from the Dictionary of New Zealand Biography)! Despite being wounded in June 1915 during hand-to-hand fighting, Stewart survived the First World War, rising to become commander of the 2nd Battalion of the Canterbury Infantry in 1916, after being awarded the Military Cross and French Croix de Guerre for his courageous leadership at Gallipoli. The overall Gallipoli or Dardanelles campaign, essentially a diversion, was a tactical disaster with over 200,000 Allied dead; many deaths resulting from disease. Those serving in the ANZAC forces were also slaughtered. The number of Turkish deaths is not clear but it is generally accepted that they were also over 200,000. The eight month campaign therefore cost 400,000 lives – 1500 individual deaths for each day of the campaign.

The first winter ascent of Castle Gates Gully was made by J. McCoss, W.B. Meff, R. Clarke and W. Shepherd; the first two were members of the Cairngorm Club, the second two were listed as guests.

One Cairngorm Club member of this young ultramontane group survived the slaughter of The Great War. James McCoss saw service in the North Scottish Royal Garrison Artillery (coastal defences) and after the war recorded new routes in the 1930s. He died in 1951 and his obituary in the Cairngorm Club Journal (Vol XVI, No. 88, 1951–2) showed he was an all round climber, including an ascent of the Matterhorn described as, *'no more difficult technically than some climbs on Lochnagar, though of course a good deal more physical effort was required.'*

The second Cairngorm Club member, William Meff, died a day after receiving shrapnel wounds while serving with the 7th Battalion Gordon Highlanders, in France on 14 November 1916. If conscious after being struck by fragments of red hot metal, he would have endured 24 endless hours of pain beyond belief, just twenty months after the first winter ascent of Castle Gates Gully. In his obituary it stated Meff *'...was a pleasure to those who climbed with him to see his...smiling face and to hear his humorous remarks. These were never lacking even in the foulest weather, and often, after a strenuous day, they enlivened the homeward journey along the mountain paths he loved so well.'* (CCJ Vol VIII, No. 48, 1917). Sending young men and women to be slaughtered and maimed in wars is a recurrent human failing, an idiocy which continues today.

Aside from the 1904 summer and 1914 winter ascent date, this history was unknown to me at the time and the ski descent of Castlegates Gully was variable, dignified, but successfully achieved. At the foot of the gully as I looked back up at the Castle Gates I felt elated and relieved, and I concur with the guidebook writer that it is *'A useful descent as well as a scenic ascent.'* Even the discontinuous sculpted cornice allowed me a safe entry to the gully, which in the 1914 CCJ (Notes on the Easter meet to Braemar, Vol VIII, No. 43) was described as: *'a peculiar twin buttressed cornice formed by the wind.'*

The traverse across the spectacular head of the Loch A'an basin was in soft, wet snow and skis may have been the only sensible tactic to get around that afternoon. Skinning back up Coire Domhain and round the top of Sneachda (1176m) allowed a swift descent of the Fiacaill a' Choire Chais onto the scarred north face of Cairngorm with the pisted runs back to the car park café. I well remember our eloquent past Vice-President Colin Grant describing the

Cairngorms with their rounded tops and long dreary glens. This was more in keeping with the Professor's after-dinner speech.

Brian Shackleton, Richard and Graeme thought better of visiting the poorly snow-covered hills of Glen Feshie and headed up to the ski area arriving just in time to reach the main carpark packed with enthusiastic piste bashers. A direct skin up the Fiacaill a' Choire Chais soon left all the downhill impedimenta behind and with the help of harscheisen, the icy upper section of the ridge gave way to the easier slopes of upper Coire Raibeirt. A pleasant traverse round into Coire Domhain, past the vacant line of snow holes, led onto Cairn Lochan. Poor visibility required some careful navigation and gave continuous snow with finally clear visibility down to the head of Lurcher's Gully. Disappointingly, the snow was soft and wet with the increasingly heavy rain so the anticipated reward of a fantastic downhill run at the end of the afternoon was not to be realised. All that remained was to retire to Milehouse to dry out over steaming mugs of tea and a somewhat belated lunch.

Sunday dawned windy with a fresh but light fall of snow around the hut. Very pleasant on the eye! The Whitworths headed back to Cairngorm and fought their way into the Northern Corries, climbed Wavelength (III,4 *), then fought their way out again. They had to downclimb the Goat Track roped up to prevent Heike and BJ being blown away. BJ short for 'Brian junior' was the provisional name for their new baby who was still some months from appearing. However, BJ was already ascending Grade IV winter climbs while still in utero. The wind was gusting to 80mph according to the Cairngorm weather station.

Ewan, Bob and Dave Coustick looked at some options around Drumochter but howling winds in the valley floor and limited snow in the gullies meant, wisely, nothing was attempted that day.

In contrast Ann, Peter, Graeme, Brian Shackleton and Colwyn made a swift ski ascent of Geal-charn (3005ft/917m); the one above Balsporran Cottages at the Pass of Drumochter. As Butterfield writes in his book The High Mountains. *'Of the drab heathery mounds bordering the Drumochter Pass, A'Mharconaich with its snout and Geal-charn with its distinctive cairns, are the most readily identified.'* Precision navigation meant that the summit was reached directly despite the fierce blizzard, but this had the consolation of a generous following wind and some new snow on the ski back to the railway crossing at Balsporran. The Inverness to Perth railway was approved by Act of Parliament in 1861 and the single track line opened just two years later. When the railway opened in 1863 there was a signal box at Balsporran, hence the presence of the adjacent cottages. The Inverness to Perth railway passed south through Forres via Grantown, Kingussie and Drumochter summit to Dunkeld where it met with the Perth and Dunkeld Railway which had opened in 1856. Nearly 150 years later we still benefit from that single track line. Perhaps it is time to consider investing in a double rail line up the backbone of Scotland as sadly a multiple car crash that day had closed the A9 highway, and resulted in a prolonged detour via Fort William to drive back to the central belt.

Colwyn Jones

(With grateful thanks to Robin Campbell and Greg Strange for furnishing the article with much essential historical information)

Easter Meet 2009 – Inchnadamph

The 'Easter' meet was held at Inchnadamph Hotel on the weekend after Easter, Thursday 16–Monday 20 April. Those who arrived on the Thursday travelled through poor conditions to better weather in the west. In spite of the cool east wind members climbed on lower crags and walked the hills in fair conditions.

On the Friday night Noel Williams gave an illustrated talk on the fascinating geology of Ben Nevis and the surrounding hills. Over the next few days numerous members were seen to be gazing at rock formations trying to improve their understanding of the local geology. The weather improved as the days progressed and the Saturday evening meal was enjoyable. The group photograph taken on the Sunday morning is a fine record of the party, including Quinag and the manholes of Inchnadamph.

Members climbed Foinaven, Beinn Leoid Glas Bheinn, Arkle, Quinag, Ben More Assynt, Conival, Ben Mor Coigach and Ben Hope, and visits were made to Smoo Cave, Handa Island and Eas a' Chual Aluinn. In the cool mornings and sunny afternoons a variety of crags were climbed on, including Ridgeway View Crag, Sheigra, Rhiconich Crag, Laxford Bay Slabs, Reiff, Glaciated Slab and Red Slab. A couple of new routes were also put up on a quartzite crag overlooking Loch Glendhu.

Members attending were President Des Rubens, Paul Brian, Robin Campbell, Douglas Lang, Peter MacDonald and guest Calum Anton, Iain Smart and guest Margaret Smart, Colin Stead, Dick Allen, Peter Biggar, David Broadhead, Geoff Cohen, Helen Forde, Campbell Forrest, John Fowler, Phil Gribbon, John Hay, Bill McKerrow, Gordon Macnair, David Stone and Noel Williams.

Dick Allen

Skye Spring Meet 2009

Allt Dearg Cottage near Sligachan was again booked for a whole week, this year over 16–23 May. The weather was mixed, but better than average. Various outings were made in the Cuillin, Red Hills and elsewhere. The author of Skye Scrambles was somewhat crocked, but dispatched parties to do further checking for the new guide. A recent Iain Thow discovery was repeated on the South Face of Sgurr nan Gillean and a fun rib found on Preshal More. In the evening the comfy sitting room again encouraged convivial banter. We still live in hope of our visit one year coinciding with a heatwave.

Members present: Paul Brian, Robin Campbell, Peter MacDonald, John Mitchell, Raymond Simpson, David Stone, Noel Williams.

Guests: Linda Simpson, Andrew Wielochowski, Fay Wielochowski.

D.N.W.

JMCS REPORTS

Edinburgh section: JMCS members have had another active year in the mountains. The core activities are of course rock and winter climbing, but many members also reach their mountains using skis, kayaks, sailing boats, snow shoes, mountain bikes and even fell running attire.

Regular midweek meets are held every Wednesday. This year we added some variety to our winter wall meets by going to Ratho once a month. Summer midweek meets have been well attended – the usual favourites of the Hawkcraig and Traprain are always popular but good trips were also had further afield including Northumberland. Monday meets at Alien Rock, or sometimes outside, remain popular too.

Winter meets had the usual mixed bag of weather, but enthusiastic members persevered and some good climbing was had in amongst the rain and sleet. Summer meets had a good run of weather luck and were very popular, with extra places in the huts having to be booked on occasion! A number of keen new members have joined the club during the year and have boosted attendance on meets. We are always keen to attract new members and at our last AGM a change to the club constitution to make it easier to join the club was unanimously approved.

After a great deal of work, our new hut 'The Cabin' in Balgowan, near Newtonmore, is nearing completion. The official opening will be in November and we are already taking bookings for winter 2009–10. Interested clubs should contact the custodian (details below).

Officials elected: *Honorary President*, John Fowler; *Honorary Vice-President*, Euan Scott; *President*, Patrick Winter; *Vice President and Smiddy Custodian*, Helen Forde (30 Reid Terrace, EDINBURGH, EH3 5JH, 0131 332 0071); *Secretary*, Robert Fox (10/3 South Gyle Loan, EDINBURGH, EH12 9EN, 0131 334 5582, secretary@edinburghjmcs.org.uk); *Treasurer*, Bryan Rynne; *Meets Secretary*, Sue Marvell; *The Cabin Custodian*, Ali Borthwick (01383 732 232, before 9pm please).

Robert Fox

Glasgow Section 2008: The Glasgow JMCS continues to prove very popular and has a good mix of both young blood and more mature members. The winter meets were well attended and started with the popular Burn's supper meet at the Raeburn Hut. A number of ice aficionados also supplemented the normal Scottish winter weekends with a trip of ice cragging in Cogne, Italy. The winter continued well until Easter and the annual club trip to Elphin coincided with an arctic blast which saw snow down to the road for four days. This allowed for a unique alpine traverse of Stac Pollaidh in knee-deep powder under blue skies and a winter route on the hill for another team.

The start of summer was very promising with almost a month of dry weather in April and May allowing many members to enjoy Scotland at its best. The North-West of Scotland proved particularly popular and allowed for an exceptional few days at Coruisk, Skye at the club hut, with wall to wall sunshine and a breeze to keep off the midge why go anywhere else?

The club mid-week meets on the Glasgow outcrops also started up in May, continuing right through the summer, with the Whangie BBQ attaining classic status. The legendary Midsummer meet on the Cobbler did go ahead but with a much depleted team but Frosty Jack kept the inclement weather at bay.

As usual summer is the time for many to travel overseas to climb, cycle or trek. Several teams travelled to Africa and succeeded in climbing Kilimanjaro and Mount Kenya. Europe also proved popular with climbs in the Dolomites, French Alps and Gran Paradiso.

As the nights drew in the club calendar became even more hectic. It started with the outgoing President's 'Mystery Meet', this year at a bothy in the Borders near Innerleithen, and then moved quickly on to the annual club dinner. Held at the Kingshouse Hotel it was enjoyed by over 50 members – old and new – and proved to be the most popular in years. As always the year ended well with the annual Christmas meet at Lagangarbh famous for the mince pies and a chance to show-off one's achievements in the slide show. Fortunately the meet coincided with a winter snap which resulted in some early season routes being climbed.

Officers for 2009: *President & Secretary*, Paul Hammond, 162 Springfield Road, Linlithgow, 01506 844795; *Treasurer*, Richard Jewell, 33 Holyknowe Road, Lennoxtown, 01360 310314. For others and for further information on meets and other events see the club website: www.glasgowjmcs.org.uk

Paul Hammond

London Section 2008: The year began in the customary manner with the President's meet hosted at Glanafon, our cottage in Bethesda with typical wet and windy North Wales weather constraining the activity on the hill but not the evening pleasantries. The now traditional Scottish winter meet held this year at the Elphin hut was anything but wintry thanks to the lack of snow but the sunshine was enjoyed – congratulations to Robin Watts for ascending Suilvan at the grand age of 76. At Easter we were based at the Clogwyn hut near Tremadoc and in May returned to Scotland to Glencoe with long days out in superb weather. It was the Peak District in July with a mix of climbing, walking and mountain biking but the highlight of the year was probably the trip to Lundy in September, with everyone active on the rock with scores of routes done from V diff to E2 in between stormy days. Foz is thanked for organising this week. Club members were also active abroad in August.

The use of Glanafon increased, where improvements have been made including new windows, new gas cookers, new kitchen units, new plumbing and wiring. Thanks to Foz, Ted Wilkins, Mark Anderson and David Mitchell for their work on the cottage and to our long serving hut custodian Rod Kleckham.

The year culminated in another enjoyable club dinner in Coniston after a day spent mountain biking or walking. Congratulations to David Hughes, who in recognition of his outstanding service to the club has been granted life membership. Overall membership in 2008 varied between 35 and 38 excluding life members.

Officers elected for 2009: *President*, Steve Gladstone; *Treasurer*, David Hughes; *Secretary*, John Firmin (0208 291 2141); *Hut Custodian*, Rod Kleckham (01252 721049).

John Firmin

Perth Mountaineering Club (JMCS Perth Section): The Perth MC have enjoyed a busy and successful year. The annual club dinner was held at the Kingshouse on a glorious late November weekend with snow and ice down well below the hotel itself so all the attendees enjoyed a wonderful weekend on the hills as well as an excellent dinner. The Club has benefited over the year with a steady stream of new (and generally younger!) members and nearly all the meets have been well attended and, more often than not, fully subscribed.

The highlight was another weekend of brilliant weather in Knoydart, members descending on Barrisdale from a variety of different directions and by a variety of different forms of transport – canoeing, on foot and by boat from Arnisdale. The weekend highlighted one of the strengths of the Club when members team up or go their separate ways, meeting again in the evening to share experiences.

There is a good mix of rock climbers and general mountaineers; up to half a dozen or so have 'compleated' or are within a hair's breadth of 'compleating' the list of the Munros although a recent change in the list might have caused a few hiccoughs! With a total of about 100 members and a nucleus of up to 50 active ones the club looks forward to continued good health in 2010. Contact details can be found on the club website: www.perthmountaineering-club.co.uk

Des Bassett

SMC AND JMCS ABROAD

South America

JOHN STELLE REPORTS: The JMCS London Section moved from Nepal to Peru this year for their third consecutive expedition. The plan was, as before, to combine a long trek with one or two peaks. The area chosen was the popular Cordillera Blanca in northern Peru, although in fact it turned out to be modestly quiet.

The main base was a town called Huaraz at 3000m, a sort of Namche Bazar of Peru. So having come straight from sea level in Lima most of the first week was used in day trips to acclimatise.The second week saw us trekking up the Santa Cruz valley and over the Punta Union Pass, with several side trips, including Alpamayo base camp. The third week, we chose Yanapaccha, a somewhat secluded snow peak for our training climb, topping out on pte 5100m. Several days later we ascended to high camp to attempt Pisco (5752m) and after a very early start reached the summit in mist around 8 in the morning, descending in a snow storm.

A very enjoyable trip amongst some of the most attractive ice peaks in the world and thanks to John Biggar in UK and Damain Vargas in Peru.

Team Members: John Steele (leader), Barbara Gibbons, Trevor Burrows, Andy Hughes.

Arctic Norway

DAVID RITCHIE REPORTS: In the spring of 2005 Neil McGougan and I visited the Lofoten islands for two weeks basing ourselves close to Henningsvaer on Austagoya. We climbed some shorter rock climbs but unfortunately at some point during every day it rained. Our choice of time of year also meant that several of the recommended higher crags were still wet from snow melt. The weather worsened during our last week so we resorted to hiring a car and exploring the islands and taking in two or three fine, if damp, hill walks. Passing many impressive crags, some holding onto the remnants of the previous winters ice, we quickly became aware of the huge winter climbing potential these islands have to offer.

We returned for two week trips in the winters of 2006, 2008 and 2009, basing ourselves close to Leknes on Vestvagoya. We found generally settled weather, ice forming down to sea level and some superb winter climbing venues amidst spectacular scenery. We encountered no one else climbing on any of the crags we visited and nearly every summit climbed was deserted. From single pitch icefalls to 3000ft mixed faces rising from sea level the islands have a wide variety of routes waiting to be climbed, not to mention some fine peaks suitable for winter hill walking or ski touring.

With no winter guidebook available most of the climbing has an exploratory feel and for those seeking solitude and fine Scottish style winter climbing within the arctic circle these islands are highly recommended.

Siberia

SANDY REID REPORTS: Siberia has many assets, including beautiful scenery, mountains, forests, rivers, lakes and cities. Until recent years, however, it was difficult for foreigners to explore the country, because of the political situation. I have experience of ski touring in Norway and, in addition, speak Russian and, in early 2009, considered combining the skills. So I searched the Internet and came up with many varied trips to that region, organised through the Russian company, K2 Adventures. These included a ski tour:

http://www.adventuretravel.ru/travels/eng/trekking/shumak.htm

I was invited to join a group of Russians on a trip from the city of Omsk to the Eastern Sayan Mountains, near Lake Baikal. I obtained a visa, booked flights to Moscow and Omsk, and in early March 2009, set off with skis, a heavy rucksack and some trepidation.

The temperature of -21 degrees Celsius on landing at Omsk airport was a foretaste of things to come. I had time to wander round the city, which seemed interesting and pretty, before I was introduced to my six companions. We left Omsk railway station on 9 March and travelled for two days by the Trans-Siberian Railway. This was itself a great adventure. On the journey we became acquainted, both among ourselves and with others in the carriage, shared the bottle of malt whisky I had taken and sampled numerous local beers from stations on the way. We reached Irkutsk and then Sludyanka, on Lake Baikal. This is five hours east of Moscow, from which it is much further than Moscow is from the UK (three hours). We were then transported by van to the Sayan Mountains in an area near the village of Nilova Pustyn. The van deposited us in a forest and sped off, leaving us to find a campsite and spend the night out.

We carried axes and saws and chopped down a couple of dead trees, which we cut up for firewood. Food was cooked over a fire in two large pots, suspended by chains from a wire slung between two trees. Washing dishes was easy: I just put my plate on the ground for 10 seconds and it froze. The first night was spent in tents at -27 degrees Celsius.

Next morning we set off on foot, carrying full rucksacks and skis, through forest, with the snow-clad mountains of Mongolia glistening against blue sky to the south. I had taken narrow waxable Norwegian Asane Telemark skis, but rapidly found I could not get the waxes to grip. No doubt this reflected some lack of skill, but snow conditions in Scotland make this difficult to acquire. My companions had wider, wooden skis with cable bindings. Through a hole in the skitips they passed a cord, by which they attached them to their rucksacks and were thus able to drag them behind. I carried mine strapped vertically to the sides of my rucksack, but found they kept catching on tree branches. On the third day we reached the first of many frozen rivers and were able to walk up the ice on crampons. We soon reached snow on which we could ski uphill, by which time I had abandoned waxes and resorted thereafter to skins. We skied and walked up to a high camp below the Shumak pass at 3000m. Next day we walked up to the pass itself, from which we had spectacular views of the mountain range. The Sayan mountains are volcanic and somewhat like the Cuillin of Skye on a grand scale, with jagged snowy peaks. For the descent of the top vertical section on the other side of the pass a rope proved useful. The ski descent of a long valley led to Shumak, a collection of wooden huts, where health-giving water bubbles from the ground in numerous hot springs. Here, we spent one night in a heated cabin. The warden thought I might be the first Scotsman to visit the place and we shook hands on it, but a claim for the Guinness book of records would be premature. Next day we set off up a gorge on another frozen river. This led in due course to the Obzorny pass, from which we had more fine views. I was told there were no glaciers and indeed I saw no sign of past glaciation in the mountains. We then made our way down the river Kitoi. After a night in tents, we reached the Ara-Oshey river, which was spectacularly beautiful, and made our way up its tributaries on crampons and skis and crossed the Khubiti pass. A long descent of the big frozen River Khubiti, circumventing several large frozen waterfalls, finally led back to the early part of our ascent route and next day we finished the tour. The van came to collect us and transport us to Sludyanka, from which we went by train to Irkutsk, arriving on 22 March. Here we parted company, as the others travelled on by train to Omsk, while I spent a couple of nights in Irkutsk. I found it to be an interesting and beautiful city and was sorry to have to leave. I flew home from Irkutsk to Moscow to London.

The Siberian rivers were fantastic, with great tributaries and huge waterfalls, all frozen. The ice was particularly beautiful. We agreed that they were the highlight of the trip and kept us interested and delighted, despite the intense cold. The mountain range is vast and no doubt has great climbing possibilities. There would, for example, be endless scope for ice-climbing on the waterfalls and rivers. The local culture is Buddhist, with much of interest to see.

My Telemark skis were possibly a mistake. They were too light and slippery and I found them difficult to control. I kept skins on for one of the downhill sections to slow me and one of my companions suggested frivolously that if had put them on back to front I might have been even slower. Alpine type skis with bindings that lock at the back might have been better, but would, of course, have been heavier on the long sections of rough terrain when we had to carry them. I noticed that my companions' wooden skis with cable bindings gripped well on the uphill sections and seemed easier to control on the downhill sections. Although for such a trip one needs to be a competent skier, great technical skill is not necessary, as it is difficult to perform fancy stunts when carrying a 20kg rucksack. It is more important to have general mountaineering experience and to have the equipment and skills to survive in hostile conditions.

I had expected it to be cold and it was around -20 to -25 degrees Celsius most nights. My Russian companions looked after me extremely well and were great fun, always good-naturedly tolerant of my language mistakes. They were always keen to discuss world affairs and ask me about Scotland. I felt it said much for their sense of values in life that, despite our heavy packs, they were also prepared to carry a guitar over the mountains in order to make music round the campfire at night.

It would have been difficult to undertake this trip without a reasonable knowledge of the Russian language. Perhaps a group could request a guide who spoke English. Personally, however, I thought it was a great adventure and would not have missed it for the world.

Details of the full itinerary, together with pictures of our trip, are now on the

website listed above. Anyone wishing to have further details is welcome to get
in touch: sandy.reid@ed.ac.uk

New Zealand

MARK LITTERICK REPORTS: Milford Sound is a must for visitors to New
Zealand's South Island. It is a place of epic beauty where massive waterfalls
tumble into a deep fiord and spectacular mountains rise straight out of the water
to untouchable heights. No visitor to the area could fail to be impressed with the
centrepiece – Mitre Peak. I had seen the mountain many times during my travels
through the Island – in every other postcard it seemed. Despite this when I
finally arrived at Milford I was overwhelmed with the sheer splendour of the
peak and as a mountaineer I was drawn to the summit. Back at the hostel I soon
found out that an ascent was a feasible proposition and made arrangements for
travel across the water the following morning.

Hunter carefully nudged his boat against the rocks near the mouth of the
Sinbad River. With a few words of advice and a few more words of warning (he
seemed somewhat concerned at my solo status) we said our goodbyes and
agreed on a rendezvous time of 7 p.m. It was already after 10.

The annual rainfall of over 200in, combined with moderate temperatures,
produces a perfect barrier to pedestrians – the temperate rainforest. Progressing
through the undergrowth involves twisting, turning, shoving, pulling and
vaulting – all of which add up to very hard work. Within minutes I was soaked
in sweat, this was going to be a hard day. Gradually the bush relented a little
with occasional evidence of past traffic. Sticking to the broad crest of the ridge
was easy enough on the way up and after negotiating a house-sized boulder a
distinct trail appeared. Occasional threads of blue wool dangled from the
branches to remind me that this was not completely virginal bush – it just felt
like it. After a few hours I took a breather on top of The Footstool, a 2700ft
subsidiary summit, still below the bush line.

The first surprise of the day was a steep 500ft descent to a col that was not
obvious from the postcards or my rough map. Fortunately there was a good track
down and even at the col I was still feeling privileged to have experienced the
wild rainforest unadulterated by the Department of Conservation tourist paths.
At this stage I hit the most ridiculous bush yet; the trail vanished as a Medusa of
strong, woody vines interleaved their way down a very steep slope. Progress
was only possible by pulling hard with arms, shoulders and back, feet flailing
uselessly behind. Eventually the angle eased and the forest gave way to
outrageous tussocks hiding spiky cactus-like plants drawing blood and curses. It
was a tired climber that eventually sat down on a bare patch above the bush line
at 3000ft. For the first time I was able to admire the spectacular view over the
top of the Footstool to Milford with its improbable airstrip, busy cruise-boat
terminal and, well nothing else really. Beyond Milford the Darren Mountains
beckoned – spectacular granite peaks apparently surrounded on all sides by
skirts of vertical rock.

After some food and water I started out on the top part of the mountain. The
sun was beating down as I climbed first up some improbably steep tussocky
grass then along a superbly exposed ridge of jaggy rocks like the back of some

huge Stegosaurus. The going was straightforward but the exposure immense – the left side dropping vertically down and away to the Sinbad gully, the right side steeply down to the fiord. Suddenly the second shock of the day appeared in the form of a deep notch in the ridge. The way into the notch looked feasible but steep; the other side looked completely outrageous. Exposure was wild; now the vertical drop on the Sinbad side looked timid compared to the vast sweeps of rock that stretched all the way from the summit to the fiord on the right. Careful scrambling into the notch revealed that the 100ft wall opposite was not vertical and was well provided with excellent holds. This wall turned out to be an immaculate scramble up perfect rock in the most fantastic situation.

Broken rock and careful walking brought me to a huge expanse of slabs stretching into the distance. They were loose and horrible but with appropriate care and attention, and a lot of wandering around, I soon scrambled past them to confront the next obstacle, a vertical buttress that was clearly not going to go. Closer inspection resulted in me turning the cliffs on the left by stepping across a yawning gap onto a dubious jammed block and gingerly reaching some broken ground. That move was probably the scariest on the mountain – far too much fresh air between your legs and an awful lot of loose rock about.

Scurrying away from danger I was soon scrambling up perfect rock and suddenly popped out on the compact summit. At 5556ft the panoramic view was awesome. The Tasman Sea out to the west sparkled in the afternoon sun, spectacular mountains were all around and the deep, dark waters of Milford sound stretched out below me. It was not however a comfortable place to relax since the thought of reversing the route weighed heavily on my mind. I was pretty tired and thirsty, realizing only then that two litres of water just wasn't enough to keep hydrated in the heat and effort of the climb. After a few summit photos I was soon carefully picking my way back down the ridge trying to control my anxiety.

In the event the descent of the top part of the mountain went without incident. The upper rocks and chock-stone were easier in descent. The slabs were awkward and dangerous but were dispatched with considerable care, and the notch was just as enjoyable on descent as it had been hours previously. Now that I knew the route, the fear of the unknown had been overcome and cautious travel took me down to the bush line. It was only 5pm and I was on schedule to make the rendezvous with Hunter – I'd cracked it.

The descent of the temperate jungle on the other hand turned-out to be a disaster. This side of the hill was in shadow now and it was very difficult to keep orientated in the dense bush. Descending the Medusa I was only marginally in control and found myself below the col on the fiord side. Below stretched thousands of feet of bare rock where a recent landslide had stripped the hill bare. The effort to climb up the steep slope and traverse over to the col had me completely exhausted. This section took over an hour and I knew I was now running late. By the time I'd crested the Footstool I was running out of steam, cramps were coming thick and fast and I was feeling nauseous. I forced myself to stop, lie down and stretch frequently – by this time I knew I'd missed the boat. Even below the Footstool I could not keep track of the path that had seemed so easy to follow on the way up. The vegetation obscured the ground from above, whereas I could see underneath it on the way up. I repeatedly wandered off the

Winter climbing in the Lofoten Islands, Norway.
Photo: Dave Ritchie.

crest of the ridge and ran into more steep ground and landslide scars. Regaining the ridge would always take an incredible amount of effort that I no longer had in me. By this stage I was getting cramp in my calves, thighs, shins, hands and chest, breathing was laboured and I was overheating badly as my sweat dried up.

At one point I thought I heard a boat but when I tried to shout I nearly gagged. I was close to the bottom by now and changed course for the river that I could hear nearby. Within a few moments I had wandered into a minefield of rotten fallen trees – a veritable crevasse field in a timber glacier. My feet shot through and I came down hard on my outstretched arms with feet dangling in the air gap beneath the man-trap; the sudden fright provoking a dry retch. I knew I was pushing it, but I had to keep going. My mind was wandering and concentration was difficult but I could not allow myself to pass-out in the depths of the forest. After stabilizing my breathing I got to my feet and carefully made my way to the river, stumbling gladly onto the polished rocks. The twilight was fading fast as I splashed down to the sea, not daring to go back into the dark forest. On the edge of the fiord I could hear a boat; I quickly emptied the contents of my sack all over the ground and grabbing the torch signalled out to the vessel. I was almost overcome with relief when the fishermen pulled into the shallows – I was in no fit state to bivouac that night. Wading out to meet them I was pulled aboard and ferried across the fiord to Milford.

After a shivering walk back to the hostel I searched without success for Hunter. I tried to take a shower but the cramps made it impossible. Following a short lie down I went back to look for Hunter. The girl at the hostel counter sat with me a while on the porch and presented me with some water and a beer. I knew I shouldn't drink alcohol, but it did me no harm at all – it tasted great on the way down, but as soon as I stood up I projected it across the car park. Hunter arrived soon and it was with great relief that he phoned the rescue services with the good news. A sleepless night of continuous cramps and persistent sipping of water was followed by a major day of rest with lots of fluids and increasing amounts of food.

The following day I went kayaking with the dolphins and looked up at Mitre Peak with a considerable amount of respect and more than a modicum of contentment.

Views of Mitre Peak, Milford Sound, New Zealand.
All photos: Mark Litterick.

REVIEWS

The Mountains Look on Marrakech: Hamish Brown, (Whittles Publishing, Caithness, 2007, hardback, 304pp, ISBN 978-1870325-29-5, £25)

Hamish Brown's first substantial book on Morocco is long overdue. Published in 'well got up' hardback it recounts his 1995 marathon walk along the length of the Atlas Mountains in Morocco – the GTAM (*La grande traversee de l'Atlas Marocain*) – 900 miles in 96 days. Accompanied by Charles Knowles, and his 'man Friday', local guide Ali, and Hosain the muleteer, the trek begins at the north-east end of the Atlas with the necessary purchase of two mules. The route, which travels south-west across the Middle and High Atlas, had never been completed in one attempt, though Peyron's two volume paperbacks (1990 West Col) describes the route in reverse, calling for some dimensional thinking, compounded by the Frenchman's travelling time, which seemed unduly brisk to our team.

Route finding problems were encountered almost daily as maps and terrain did not match, place names were duplicated or interchangeable and some peaks had different names depending on from which angle they were viewed! Hamish confesses to his continuing frustration, though he is delighted on one occasion that the map, Peyron, the locals and his team are all in agreement.

The team was joined intermittently by some of the author's regular Morocco fans – the Flowers Group and later the Phud's, but the final challenge west of Tichka – the Ridge of 100 Peaks – was above and beyond the capabilities of mule kind and was completed by Hamish, Charles, Ali and two fit companions. Scorpions, snakes and flash floods were real, if rare, hazards but the enthusiasm of the local Berbers to support, guide and feed the party were biblical in their generosity.

The Author's 40-year love affair with Morocco has been bulletined in his annual reports from Morocco in this and other journals, where he has oft likened the Berbers in the remote Atlas with our hardy stock in the more rural crofting communities of Scotland – where folk pulled and pooled together for their common good and survival. He reflects on change – gone are the brass water carriers and the brown cloaks – but delight and laughter abound – more grins, fewer gripes, much more laughter and less lament than our well trodden hill tops. *'Laughter is the yardstick for judging the ripeness of civilisation.'* Where else, says Hamish, would you see graffiti which reads 'I am very happy!' My own memories of storks and swifts and of the rag taggle of chasing children were stirred.

As ever, Hamish's narrative is informative, reflective, sometimes grumbling, but always entertaining. Homilies like *'You never visit Morocco once'* and *'Experience is the sum of near misses'* abound. There are amusing tales of a charismatic holy man communicating vocally with the recently buried dead and an explanation from Ali of the major disparity between the male organ of the donkey and the camel.

An essential glossary of Moroccan terms beyond cuscus is very useful, together with an extensive bibliography and a brief history of exploration in the Atlas. An index is absent – but with the anarchy of place names, a grid reference to a map would be necessary – perhaps for the next book? Photographs are evocative though many are small and rather dark. The outline maps are adequate but not always helpful to check the detailed progress of the walk. Minor gripes aside, this book is a fine testimony to Hamish's enthusiasm for Morocco and his love for the High Atlas and its peoples shines out from every page.

...And so the Marathon reached to the Sea...Hamish admits that the GTAM revealed much potential for further exploration – some of which he has since realised. So there is more to tell – can we look forward to his 'Definitive Atlas Guide'?

For those thinking (even with armchair aspirations) of a visit to Marrakesh and Morocco – the magic is still there – and this book offers a real taste of that very special magic – that of the Atlas Mountains.

Chris Robinson

A Camera in the Hills: The life and works of W.A. Poucher: Roly Smith, (Francis Lincoln, 2008, hardback, 192pp, ISBN 978-0-7112-2898-6, £20).

This is a book of two halves. The first half follows the career of the young Walter through college and his apprenticeship as a pharmacist. It seems that his flair for elegant clothes and gentlemanly bearing came from his employer in that company.

It was here that he had his first taste of photography as in those days pharmacists were where you took your films to be processed. Around this time he became a very accomplished pianist and could well have made a career in this field.

It then takes you through his experiences in the First World War as an officer in the RAMC and his wedding to a lady whose family were in the soap business. The first mention of mountaineering is with his 10-year-old son on Snowdon. His son would later be handed on his father's Leica camera when Walter received the latest model from the factory – lucky lad. There follows much detail of his rise to fame in the world of cosmetics in which he was regarded very much as a genius. He was already a prolific writer and one of his books on that field is still in use today.

The second half finally gets to the mountaineering aspect of this man's life although it was his standing in the scent business that made him wealthy enough to be able to spend six months a year wandering the hills and taking photographs for his famed series of guide books. A meticulous recorder it was his boast that he could find any negative within 30 seconds. With forty books to his credit that would be some feat.

I only met the man once when he came into Nevisport to check on sales of his guide books and he was quite impressive in an immaculate suit, subtle makeup and white gloves. He stood out amongst the other clientele that day. I recently photographed a pair of his well polished and heavily nailed walking boots and these are now in the safe keeping of the Scottish Mountain Heritage collection at Glen Roy.

I still treasure the signed copy of his Scottish Peaks but must say that I much preferred his colour photography when he moved to that medium although black and white was much more adaptable to drawing on the white lines of his routes.

This is a fascinating insight into a remarkable man who leaves a vast collection of pictorial mountaineering literature.

This is not a book you would return to in the same way we once did, and still do, with the books by the man himself, but one that must be read to appreciate W.A. Poucher.

Alex. Gillespie

Himalayan Playground: Trevor Braham, (Neil Wilson Publishing, 2008, paperback, 128pp, ISBN 978-1-906476-00-7, £9.99).

Exploration of peripheral ranges and lesser peaks in the Himalaya has, if anything, waned over the last 30 years. Today's generation appears addicted to the standard itineraries offered up by commercial expedition companies. Mera Peak, Island Peak, Ama Dablam, Cho Oyu, Everest….these few iconic peaks see thousands of visitors every year, while the other 99% of Himalayan and Karakorum mountains remain untravelled. Yet with modern means of travel many fabulous and remote ranges can be penetrated within the timeframe of an annual holiday.

In this short but engaging book Trevor Braham reminds all those who flock to the honeypots of the Khumbu that there is a world of endless fascination beyond. Braham recounts his post-war journeys in Garhwal, Sikkim, Karakorum and the North-West Frontier, spanning the period 1947 to 1972. None of these trips achieves spectacular results. Indeed Braham's wanderings are notable for their lack of success! And herein lies the charm of the book. The spirit of mountain travel is what really counts to Braham. He grasps every brief period of leave from his job in the sub-Continent to visit new valleys and obscure peaks, sometimes with a team, but often with just a single companion.

The accounts convey the flavour of Himalayan travel after partition and independence. The protagonists had to accept lengthy delays in getting permits. A week spent idling at the doors of bureaucracy in Islamabad was not unusual. By contrast, a great deal of privilege and courtesy awaited the traveller once the gates were opened, not just loyal porters but also armed escorts in volatile regions.

Many of the places visited in Pakistan, such as Swat valley and Waziristan are now hotbeds of Islamic fundamentalism and terrorism, and have been off-limit to Westerners in the last decade. Braham gives us a glimpse of their culture in a less frenetic and happier time.

The narrative switches pleasingly between the human, geographical and cultural themes. There are excellent line maps and original photographs. Braham's style is perhaps a little short of vivid personal anecdote. A retrospect from a vantage of 30 years inevitably loses the sparkle of immediate experience. Nevertheless, those who aspire to a genuine mountain ethos, released from the bondage of commercial pressure and personal ego, will find these recollections highly enjoyable, and will regret only their brevity.

Martin Moran

Staying Alive in Avalanche Terrain: Bruce Tremper, (Bâton Wicks, 2008, paperback, 320pp, 118 photos, 150 diag, ISBN 978-1-898573-75-3, £14.99).

This is a very good guide to defensive behaviour, pertinent knowledge and appropriate attitudes in avalanche terrain. The author, Bruce Tremper, is Director of the US Forest Service Avalanche Center in Utah and is well established as a prominent, entertaining and expert communicator in the avalanche field. Like many avalanche specialists he combines a lifetime passion for skiing with a scientific approach to snow and its many manifestations.

Tremper has an effective command of the striking phrase. 'A wet avalanche resembles 10,000 concrete trucks dumping their loads all at once' may be all you need to remember on a warm, wet day in Observatory Gully. However, his efforts to avoid a dry, academic style sometimes take him into the irritatingly folksy. 'Mechanically, depth hoar is one nasty dude' is not likely to be mistaken as coming from the pen of Winthrop Young.

The book is illustrated by a combination of extremely well chosen photographs and copious diagrams. The cover shot, showing a skier at the moment of release and fracture of a slab at the top of a steep slope in the Canadian Coast Range, grips the attention and much of what follows is similarly effective. The captions throughout are most informative. The cover picture is identified as a slab releasing on the skier's second turn 'after the snow profile had been carefully assessed and considered safe.' A clear lesson there about mixing the best of your predictive efforts with a large measure of caution

A number of panoramic photographs indicating safe and hazardous terrain and route choices are of enormous value, especially to anyone heading for the greater ranges. It is a rare opportunity to have an expert interpreting terrain in this detailed way. The chapters on Terrain Management, Safe Travel and Routefinding, and the Human Factor are strong and of great relevance to Scottish climbers, but other sections can be patchier.

Hazard evaluation is ultimately about refining a great deal of disparate data, into a form that will generate a sensible practical plan for action. Tremper has spent a lifetime doing this but his guidance to others seems to get distracted by a need to explain a number of different checklist systems, each aiming to do the same thing in subtly different ways. Brilliant stuff for an advanced seminar but inclined to confuse the neophyte.

He succeeds in explaining the important relationship between snowpack temperature gradient and the development of facets but the reference image given is of an advanced facetted form. These are much less common in Alpine and Scottish snowpacks than are the less spectacular, but equally important, early forms so an image of these would have been welcome.

The book's greatest strength comes from the author's ability to give a realistic and convincing estimation of the value of some particular technique or observation and what it can or cannot tell us. Too many avalanche teachers trot out Rutschblocks or shovel shear tests as though they were so many magic wands. Tremper's pragmatic, level gaze and his willingness to admit to large gaps in our knowledge give much more confidence and, ultimately, better decisions too.

The book is unashamedly North American in its origins, sources and idioms with only the most cursory attention given to Europe and elsewhere. Also, the cover indicates the book's target audience as skiers, snowboarders and snowmobilers with climbers only getting a brief mention on a single page of the main text (on which Tremper advocates the wearing of transceivers). However there is much else of interest to mountaineers and they are likely to read with amazement the techniques of sluff management that the late great Doug Coombs developed for skiing on some inspiringly steep Alaskan faces.

The limited attention given to climbers and to Europe is not necessarily a fundamental flaw since a great deal of good practice in avalanche avoidance is generic. A skier skilled in assessing avalanche hazard in the North Cascades would have much to contribute to making the right choice on a nasty day in Crowberry Gully and a climber schooled in the Cairngorms could be expected to make a decent stab at picking a sensible campsite on an Alaskan glacier, yet each would also, to a degree, be limited, not least by dramatic differences of scale.

The comprehensive nature of this book could be rather intimidating to the novice but it is an excellent and stimulating source for further study by anyone who has progressed beyond a basic understanding of snow and avalanche. Nobody could read this book with attention and fail to become both more expert and more measured in their judgment so I was pleased to see that, like so many avalanche writers before, Bruce Tremper quotes the salutary advice of the great André Roch 'Remember, the avalanche does not know you are an expert'.

Bob Barton

Scottish Rock, Volume 1 (South) & Volume 2 (North): Gary Latter, (Pesda, Vol 1 2008, 480pp, ISBN 978-1-906095-06-2, £23 / Vol 2 2009, 480pp, ISBN 978-1-906095-07-9, £23).

After many years in the making Gary Latter's guide has been published. It has changed radically from the earlier drafts and now looks thoroughly modern, similar to the North Wales selective guide. It is strange to see Erraid on the cover; there was a time when these routes were too short to record!

I can find selective guides irritating as I always want to know what climbs are on the other features around the selected climb. In that respect Scottish Rock is much better than other selective guides. It is crag selective and misses out whole cliffs but seems to include most routes on many of the cliffs covered. When the guide gets more selective it has led to problems; for example the first pitch of Apparition (Glencoe) is 'as for Guerdon Grooves', but Guerdon Grooves is not described.

A lot of text is lifted directly from the SMC guides. To quote from the scottishclimbs website: 'you should not copy any information that is the work of the guidebook authors.... You can use the guidebook to check facts'. Either Gary was not aware of this or has decided to ignore it.

But, he has done a lot of research so routes such as Pagoda Ridge (Arran) get technical grades for the first time.

Some sections of the guide are thoroughly up to date and many crags, especially in the Outer Hebrides, are in a guidebook for the first time so there is tons to go at. Seeing topos for these islands at last is amazing and makes me wish I had more time off, photos of crags taken on sunny days make me want to get out climbing.

Other sections appear to be trapped in the past; Quality Street (Glen Nevis) was missed out of *Scottish Rock Climbs* (SMC) because it was so vegetated (maybe someone will clean it again). Staffin Slip Buttresses (Skye) still have their original star ratings even though some of the routes are now very vegetated. It's hard to imagine anyone re-cleaning Staffin, so climbers visiting will be very disappointed with many of the routes.

There are numerous interesting historic photos throughout the guide and some stunning shots such as King Kong, but why do tiny photos get published in guidebooks? The FRCC Lake District selective guide excelled in this field of ridiculously small photos. Scottish Rock has many crackers such as Sugar Cane Country which should have been enlarged, or removed from the guide altogether.

A number of routes are given 'on sight' or 'on sight solo' details for the first ascent. I have my doubts about this information as it would be impossible to complete and therefore gives a false impression of past activities; Gary has even made a guess at the style in which I climbed some routes!

The quality rating has been used with enthusiasm, but if *The Torridonian* is one of the 'best climbs on the planet' the author clearly needs to get out more (but perhaps that was a joke that I missed).

The topos look very professional but it is easy to find clangers. The line marked as Piety (VS, Skye) is actually the approximate line of Left Edge (Very Difficult). Many lines at Staffin Slip are in the wrong place, but the photo is small so it possibly will not cause route-finding problems.

There are other faults, which could have disastrous consequences for blinkered climbers. The line marked as Clingfilm (Very Difficult in Torridon) is actually Heather Said Sunshine (HVS). Similarly I'm told that the line marked as Mandolin Rain (HVS, Ardmair) is unclimbed and it will probably be E3 6b when it gets a first ascent. Some routes marked on Sub Station Crag (Arrochar) are also unclimbed and will result in very poorly protected (and pointless) eliminates.

The description of The Pincer (Ardgour) is wrong in recent SMC guide books – the route is independent of Chela. Scottish Rock gets the routes correct; Chela starts up the corner groove, The Pincer starts up the arête. There is even a photo of a climber on The Pincer in the guide and Chela is clearly off to the left. But they are wrong on the topo, so I assume the lines on the topo were simply copied from *Scottish Rock Climbs* (SMC).

After 'facts' appear in print they are often accepted so here are a few corrections: Dougie Mullin (not Murray Hamilton) tipped off Pete Whillance about Edge of Extinction. The Harp was climbed the day after The Lost Ark; that was a productive raid. Rob MacDonald was on the first ascent of Mother's Pride, he came up with the route name. Morris MacLeod seconded Disturbing the Wildlife not Neil Horn.

These two volumes are inspiring and they fill some gaps in Scottish Climbing guides. They must be selling well as I've never seen so many climbers on Mull.

Climbers now know where to go as long as they don't put their faith in the topos!

Colin Moody

Deep Powder and Steep Rock – The Life of Mountain Guide Hans Gmoser: Chic Scott. (Assiniboine Publishing, 2009, hardback with CD, 386pp, ISBN 978-0-9811059-0-1, $50.00).

Chic Scott will be known to many mountaineers and skiers in Scotland through his appearances at the Dundee Mountain Film Festival, and at climbing clubs and on the Royal Scottish Geographical Society lecturing circuit. Through his talks, Chic has brought the world of Canada and its fabulous mountains to a wider audience, and his history of Canadian mountaineering, Pushing the Limits, (2000) ranks as one of the best accounts of any country's mountaineering traditions in print.

Deep Powder and Steep Rock is a biography of one of the greats of twentieth century Canadian mountaineering, Hans Gmoser. The book is thoroughly researched from diaries, letters and interviews, and is composed in Chic Scott's lucid, readable style – this is 'prose like a window pane.' The book is also one of the most beautifully produced I have read, with the design and illustrations being of the highest quality. For added measure the book is accompanied by a DVD, running time just under an hour, of some of Gmoser's mountain films, based on his adventures.

Gmoser was born in Braunau, Austria (the same village as Hitler) in 1932 into a working-class background. He underwent the hardships of the 1930s and the years of Nazi occupation of Austria before starting work in the VOEST steelworks after the conflict ended. But he had discovered the mountains and as a youth, largely self taught, he began exploring the Austrian Alps and was soon climbing to a high standard. Enticed by the prospect of a new life and by the Canadian mountains, Gmoser emigrated on his own to Canada at the tender age of 19.

His impact on the rather staid world of Canadian mountaineering at that time was phenomenal. After less than a year in the country, with fellow Austrian expatriate Leo Grillmair, he put up Grillmair's Chimneys, the first route on the fabulous Yamnuska face. Scott comments, 'This ascent is now considered one of the most important events in Canadian mountaineering history.' (p.74). Before that time people in Canada did not tend to climb direct routes on rock faces, and many European Alpine routes were designated as 'suicide climbs.' More from Gmoser was to follow and in 1957, again with Grillmair, he climbed Diretissima on 'The Yam', and Scott comments, 'Sixth grade climbing, as originated by the great European masters of the 1920s and '30s, had come to Canada.' (p.131). By the mid 1950s Gmoser was guiding full time and was the leading mountain guide in Canada, and one of the founders of the Association of Canadian Mountain Guides. But as Chic Scott points out, Gmoser's 'last cutting edge rock climb' was the Gmoser Route on Mount Louis – in 1961, before he was even 30 years old. What happened?

It was not that Gmoser retired from the mountains. He continued to ski at a high level, attempting the first traverse of the Canadian Icefields in 1960 and to organise successful expeditions to Alaska and elsewhere. The last of these was to culminate in the successful first ascent of Wickersham Wall on Mount McKinley in 1963, 'the most demanding climb of Hans' career' (p. 204) according to the author of this book. This experience appears to have been a shadow line that Gmoser crossed, as the expedition to Wickersham Wall was hit by a storm and the party survived, according to Gmoser himself, largely by luck, and he talks of waking up at night on the Wall when 'our situation would almost drive me out of my mind with fear.' (p.217). But there were other opportunities beckoning in the Canadian mountains in the early 1960s, and soon Hans was on a completely new path.

Always a charismatic communicator and great organiser, Hans exchanged his mountain guiding activities for heli-skiing, and in the mid 1960s started the company that would become Canadian Mountain Holidays. This would lead to the establishment of a large number of back country resorts, and to Hans becoming a multi-millionaire. From being a romantic, vagabond protector of the wilderness, Hans became one of the prime agents for opening it up, and his activities attracted criticism from those who saw him as having sold his soul, and having made accessible to the rich and famous he now schmoozed with, previous wilderness areas reserved for real mountaineers. Gmoser defended himself vigorously whilst running Canadian Mountain holidays, but later on in retirement commented that: 'If I had known when it all started, what it would turn into, and had the perspective I have today, I probably would not have done it.' (p.311) – observing that many of his well-heeled clients had little real love for the mountains they experienced.

Chic Scott does not himself pass an opinion on the nature of Gmoser's Faustian deal with the Devil (or Mammon), but he provides the reader with the necessary information upon which to base a judgement. The Jekyll and Hyde nature of Hans Gmoser, top mountaineer and mountain guide for about 15 years but heli-ski operator for twice that long, is fascinating. I was left wondering; why did he change roles? Was it facing death on Mount McKinley, that made him feel he had reached his limits as a mountaineer? Was it the lure of money to a man (a North American mountaineering idol by 30, but still impecunious) brought up in harsh poverty who once commented that 'There is nothing like a little hunger and despair to clear your vision.'? Whatever the reason, Chic Scott tells well the engrossing story of how the mountaineering world lost a cutting edge climber and gained a cutting edge entrepreneur.

Ian R. Mitchell

OFFICE BEARERS 2008–09

Honorary President: W.D. Brooker
Honorary Vice-Presidents: G.S. Peet
President: Desmond W. Rubens
Vice-Presidents: Charles J. Orr and William H. Duncan

Honorary Secretary: John R.R. Fowler, 4 Doune Terrace, Edinburgh, EH3 6DY.
Honorary Treasurer: John A. Wood, Spout Close, Millbeck, Keswick, CA12
4PS. **Membership Secretary:** Campbell Forrest, Strathview, Fintry Road,
Kippen, Stirling, FK8 3HL. **Honorary Meets Secretary:** E.R.(Dick) Allen,
Croft Head, Kentmere, Kendal, LA8 9JH. **Honorary Editor of Journal:** D.
Noel Williams, Solus Na Beinne, Happy Valley, Torlundy, Fort William, PH33
6SN. **Honorary Librarian:** John Hunter, 2 Lorraine Road, Glasgow, G12 9NZ.
Honorary Archivist: Robin N. Campbell, Glynside, Kippen Road, Fintry,
Glasgow, G63 0LW. **Honorary Custodian of Slides:** David Stone, 30
Summerside Street, Edinburgh, EH6 4NU. **SMC Webmaster:** Kenneth V.
Crocket, Glenisla, Long Row, Menstrie, FK11 7EA. **Convener of Publications
Sub-Committee:** Rab Anderson, 24 Paties Road, Edinburgh, EH14 1EE.
Convener of Huts Sub-Committee: Andrew M. James, 41 Urquhart Road,
Dingwall, IV15 9PE. **Committee:** John T.H. Allen, James Beaton, Peter J.
Biggar, Andrew M. James, Ross I. Jones, Colin A. Moody, Alan R. Walker, and
David Whalley.

Journal Information

Editor:	Noel Williams, Solus Na Beinne, Happy Valley, Torlundy, Fort William, PH33 6SN. **e-mail** <noel@beinne.plus.com>
New Routes Editor:	Andy Nisbet, 20 Craigie Avenue, Boat of Garten, PH24 3BL. **e-mail** <anisbe@globalnet.co.uk>
Photos Editor:	Andy Tibbs, Crown Cottage, 4 Crown Circus, Inverness, IV2 3NQ. **e-mail** <teamtibbs@hotmail.com>
Distribution:	Dougie Lang, Hillfoot Hey, 580 Perth Road, Dundee, DD2 1PZ. **e-mail** <douglas.lang@btinternet.com>

INSTRUCTIONS TO CONTRIBUTORS

The Editor welcomes contributions from members and non-members alike.
Priority will be given to articles relating to Scottish mountaineering. Articles
should be submitted before the end of March if they are to be considered for
inclusion in the Journal of the same year. Material is preferred in electronic form
and should be sent by e-mail direct to the Editor.

Acceptable file formats in order of preference are (best) Open Document
Format (odt), Rich Text Format (rtf), Plain Text (txt) or MS Word (doc/docx).
Open Office is an open-source, multi-platform productivity suite which is free
for individuals to download from http://www.openoffice.org/

Those without access to e-mail can send hard copy (typewritten and double-
spaced) by post to the Editor's home address.

SCOTTISH MOUNTAINEERING CLUB JOURNAL
BACK NUMBERS

	Year
£5.00	1972
	1977
	1978
	1979
	1980
	1983
£5.50	1985
£5.70	1986
	1987
	1989
	1990
	1991
	1992
£6.95	1993
	1994
	1995
£8.95	1996
	1997
	1998
£11.95	1999
£12.95	2000
	2001
	2002
	2003
	2004
£13.95	2005
	2006
	2007

Post & Packaging is extra.

Please contact: David 'Heavy' Whalley
Fuar Tholl
47 Grant St
Burghead
IV30 5UE

e-mail: <heavy_whalley@hotmail.com>
tel: 01343-835 338   mob: 07754 595 740

i

SCOTTISH MOUNTAINEERING CLUB HUTS

CHARLES INGLIS CLARK MEMORIAL HUT, BEN NEVIS
Location: (NN 167 722) On the north side of Ben Nevis by the
Allt a' Mhuilinn. This hut was erected by Dr and Mrs Inglis
Clark in memory of their son Charles who was killed in action
in the 1914–18 War.
Custodian: Robin Clothier, 35 Broompark Drive, Newton
Mearns, Glasgow, G77 5DZ.
tel (work) Mon to Fri only 0800–1800hrs 01560-600 811;
mob (0800–2200hrs) 07836 637 842;
e-mail <cichutbennevis@hotmail.co.uk>

LAGANGARBH HUT, GLEN COE
Location: (NN 221 559) North of Buachaille Etive Mor near
the River Coupall.
Custodian: Bernard Swan, 16 Knowes View, Faifley,
Clydebank, G81 5AT.
tel 01389-875 505; answering service 01389-800 478;
mob 07710 785 227; e-mail <bswan99686@aol.com>.

LING HUT, GLEN TORRIDON
Location: (NG 958 562) On the south side of Glen Torridon.
Custodian: John T Orr, 8 Fleurs Place, Elgin, Morayshire,
IV30 1ST.
tel 01343-545 248; mob 07881 621 864;
e-mail <john@orr388.fsnet.co.uk>.

NAISMITH HUT, ELPHIN
Location: (NC 216 118) In the community of Elphin on the
east side of the A835.
Custodian: Andrew Tibbs, Crown Cottage, 4 Crown Circus,
Inverness, IV2 3NQ.
tel 01463-240 297;
e-mail <teamtibbs@hotmail.com>.

RAEBURN HUT, LAGGAN
Location: (NN 636 909) On the north side of the A889
between Dalwhinnie and Laggan.
Custodian: Check the SMC website. A new custodian is due
to be appointed from 1 January 2010.

SMC Web Site

For a wealth of information about
mountaineering in Scotland
including the latest news about
SMC guidebooks, huts and
Munro compleaters
visit the SMC Web Site

www.smc.org.uk

SCOTTISH MOUNTAINEERING CLUB GUIDEBOOKS
Published by
THE SCOTTISH MOUNTAINEERING TRUST

HILLWALKERS' GUIDES
The Munros
Munros GPS data sets – from SMC website
The Corbetts and other Scottish hills
The Cairngorms
The Central Highlands
The Islands of Scotland including Skye
The North-West Highlands
The Southern Highlands
The Southern Uplands

SCRAMBERS' GUIDES
Highland Scrambles North
Skye Scrambles

CLIMBERS' GUIDES
Scottish Rock Climbs
Scottish Winter Climbs
Arran, Arrochar and the Southern Highlands
Ben Nevis
The Cairngorms
Glen Coe
Highland Outcrops
Lowland Outcrops
North-East Outcrops
Northern Highlands North
Northern Highlands Central
Northern Highlands South
Skye
The Islands

OTHER PUBLICATIONS
Ben Nevis - Britain's Highest Mountain
A Chance in a Million? - Scottish Avalanches
Hostile Habitats
The Munroist's Companion
Scottish Hill Tracks
Ski Mountaineering in Scotland

e-BOOKS
Cairngorms Scene and Unseen
A Century of Scottish Mountaineering
A History of Glenmore Lodge

Full details of these publications can be found on the Scottish Mountaineering Club Web Site (www.smc.org.uk) where they can also be purchased online direct from the suppliers. If you have any queries please complete the 'feedback form' available on the *Contacts* page.

Distributed by: Cordee Ltd, 11 Jacknell Road, Dodwells Bridge Industrial Estate, Hinckley, Leicestershire, LE10 3BS.
Tel: Leicester 01455 611185 Fax: 01455 635687
www.cordee.co.uk

These publications are also available from bookshops and mountain equipment suppliers.

All profit from the sale of SMC climbing and hillwalking guides goes to the **Scottish Mountaineering Trust** and provides much of the Trust's revenue. The Trust is a grant awarding Charity, which for more than 40 years has been helping people enjoy and appreciate mountains and mountain environments, both in Scotland and throughout the world.

In the past 10 years grants totalling over £600,000 have been made. Some of the major areas which have benefited are; footpath repair and maintenance, land purchase, wildlife studies, and mountaineering education and training.

For further information about the Scottish Mountaineering Trust see the *Trust* section on the SMC Web Site.

Highland Conglomerate
Graeme Ettle on The Dark Side (F6c), Moy Rock.
Photo: Andy Tibbs